"A nationally recognized expert on childhood sexual abuse with particular expertise in the treatment of men who were abused as boys, Richard Gartner graces us with his fifth book on this worldwide epidemic. Gartner, a clear and thoughtful writer, has been published widely in psychoanalytic journals, national newspapers, magazines, and has testified at the Markey hearing, where he made a reasoned and impassioned plea for changes in the New York State statute of limitations for reporting childhood sexual abuse. In *Healing Sexually Betrayed Men and Boys: Treatment for Sexual Abuse, Assault, and Trauma* Gartner brings together experts in the field to address a variety of crucial issues such as: Can sexually abused men find compassion and understanding for the shame and anger they live with? What are the long-term, potentially dire consequences for sexually abused boys as they move through adolescence into manhood? How do therapists and society cope with the male sexual perpetrator whose violence has its roots in unprocessed, dissociated sexual trauma? This volume is a must read for anyone who works in the field of trauma!" – **Sheldon Itzkowitz**, Ph.D., ABPP, co-editor, *The Dissociative Mind in Psychoanalysis: Understanding and Working with Trauma*

"*Healing Sexually Betrayed Men and Boys: Treatment for Sexual Abuse, Assault, and Trauma* is a welcome addition to the literature on the victimization of males because the scope of the book is wide and the chapters have depth. The contributors are knowledgeable and well-respected practitioners who see first-hand the damage caused by sexual abuse, but also know that healing is possible. It ought to be a part of every training program's library." – **Mic Hunter**, Psy.D., author, *Abused Boys: The Neglected Victims of Sexual Abuse* and *Honor Betrayed: Sexual Abuse In America's Military*

"For too long, boys and men who have been sexual abused or assaulted have been overlooked, neglected or minimized by society and the health care community. This extremely powerful book is a must read for all mental health professionals who want to right that wrong and deliver trauma-respectful and empowering care to their male patients. In this volume, recognized experts intersperse descriptions of various treatment approaches with clinical cases sharing inspiring stories of healing from the complicated aftermath of sexual betrayal and violation of trust. These males' strengths, courage to confront fears, and reclaim of lost experiences are unforgettably illustrated." – **Joan Cook**, Ph.D., Yale School of Medicine; 2016 President, Division of Trauma Psychology (Division 56), American Psychological Association

"A comprehensive, exhaustive and invaluable resource for understanding the suffering of victimized boys and men… enthusiastically recommended." – **Gary Brooks**, Ph.D., Co-Founder, APA Division of Men & Masculinity; author, *Beyond the Crisis of Masculinity*

"Richard Gartner is a pioneer in studying the impact of trauma, especially sexual trauma, on men. His first book, *Betrayed as Boys,* broke new ground twenty years ago. Now, with the release of two new volumes he has broadened the field by including the work of other clinicians struggling with the same challenges, dilemmas, and achievements in working with male survivors of sexual abuse. Grappling with issues of violence and the damage done to boys and men (as well as to girls and women) and the world we live in takes courage and fortitude, but understanding and altering post-traumatic pathways in male development is critical to our shared future." – **Sandra L. Bloom**, M.D., author, *Creating Sanctuary: Toward the Evolution of Sane Societies*; co-author, *Restoring Sanctuary: A New Operating System for Trauma-Informed Systems of Care*

Healing Sexually Betrayed Men and Boys

Healing Sexually Betrayed Men and Boys: Treatment for Sexual Abuse, Assault, and Trauma is the new authoritative source for treatment of men and boys with histories of sexual victimization. Male victims and survivors of sexual trauma lived in shadow until the turn of the 21st century, when scandal after scandal about the sexual abuse of boys and men shed light on their suffering. These men and boys require different treatment roadmaps than their female counterparts. Yet there is little in the professional literature to help a clinician work with sexually traumatized boys and men.

Richard B. Gartner is a seasoned psychologist/psychoanalyst who has worked therapeutically with sexually abused men for over three decades. He is a clinician, advocate, teacher, lecturer, and nationally and internationally recognized expert on the subject. Dr. Gartner's classic book, *Betrayed as Boys: Psychodynamic Treatment of Sexually Abused Men*, is one of the few written to guide clinicians. Now, nearly two decades after writing that groundbreaking volume, he follows up on his earlier work. *Healing Sexually Abused Men and Boys*, together with its companion volume, *Understanding the Sexual Betrayal of Boys and Men*, is a thorough, comprehensive guide to learning about and healing male victims and survivors.

Dr. Gartner has invited a group of experts to write about specific problems faced by these boys and men. Specialists from the psychoanalytic, psychodynamic, trauma, and legal worlds fill in the details about a wide range of interconnected subjects related to the complex reverberations of male sexual trauma. *Healing Sexually Betrayed Men and Boys* covers such diverse topics as:

- therapy with young sexually traumatized boys;
- the aftermath for men who were raped as adults;

- covert seduction of boys and its aftereffects;
- treatment for substance addictions and sexual compulsions;
- couples work with male survivors and their partners or spouses;
- bodywork with male survivors;
- treatment for male veterans who suffered sexual trauma in the military;
- profiling sexual predators and working with survivors who have also been sexual predators.

This book is a valuable resource for clinicians at every level of training. With strategies for how survivors can build support networks and descriptions of clinical, familial, and community-based treatments, *Healing Sexually Betrayed Men and Boys* is essential reading for clinicians of all theoretical persuasions who work with male sexual abuse survivors. Filling in gaps in the relatively scant literature on the subject, it will also help sexually abused or assaulted men themselves understand what is available to them.

Richard B. Gartner is Training and Supervising Analyst, Faculty, and Founding Director of the Sexual Abuse Service at the William Alanson White Psychoanalytic Institute in New York City; author of *Betrayed as Boys: Psychodynamic Treatment of Sexually Abused Men* (1999) and *Beyond Betrayal: Taking Charge of Your Life after Boyhood Sexual Abuse* (2005); and editor of *Trauma and Countertrauma, Resilience and Counterresilience: Insights from Psychoanalysts and Trauma Experts* (2017) and *Memories of Sexual Betrayal: Truth, Fantasy, Repression, and Dissociation* (1997) as well as the companion volume to this one, *Understanding the Sexual Betrayal of Boys and Men: The Trauma of Sexual Abuse.* Co-Founder and Past President of MaleSurvivor.org, he is a pioneer in treating sexually abused men and is quoted widely in the media on the subject.

PSYCHOANALYSIS IN A NEW KEY BOOK SERIES

DONNEL STERN
Series Editor

When music is played in a new key, the melody does not change, but the notes that make up the composition do: change in the context of continuity, continuity that perseveres through change. Psychoanalysis in a New Key publishes books that share the aims psychoanalysts have always had, but that approach them differently. The books in the series are not expected to advance any particular theoretical agenda, although to this date most have been written by analysts from the Interpersonal and Relational orientations.

The most important contribution of a psychoanalytic book is the communication of something that nudges the reader's grasp of clinical theory and practice in an unexpected direction. Psychoanalysis in a New Key creates a deliberate focus on innovative and unsettling clinical thinking. Because that kind of thinking is encouraged by exploration of the sometimes surprising contributions to psychoanalysis of ideas and findings from other fields, Psychoanalysis in a New Key particularly encourages interdisciplinary studies. Books in the series have married psychoanalysis with dissociation, trauma theory, sociology, and criminology. The series is open to the consideration of studies examining the relationship between psychoanalysis and any other field—for instance, biology, literary and art criticism, philosophy, systems theory, anthropology, and political theory.

But innovation also takes place within the boundaries of psychoanalysis, and Psychoanalysis in a New Key therefore also presents work that reformulates thought and practice without leaving the precincts of the field. Books in the series focus, for example, on the significance of personal values in psychoanalytic practice, on the complex interrelationship between the analyst's clinical work and personal life, on the consequences for the clinical situation when patient and analyst are from different cultures, and on the need for psychoanalysts to accept the degree to which they knowingly satisfy their own wishes during treatment hours, often to the patient's detriment. A full list of all titles in this series is available at: https://www.routledge.com/series/LEAPNKBS

RECENT TITLES IN THIS SERIES:

Vol. 41 *Understanding the Sexual Betrayal of Boys and Men: The Trauma of Sexual Abuse* Edited by Richard B. Gartner

Vol. 40 *Healing Sexually Betrayed Men and Boys: Treatment for Sexual Abuse, Assault, and Trauma* Edited by Richard B. Gartner

Healing Sexually Betrayed Men and Boys

Treatment for Sexual Abuse, Assault, and Trauma

Edited by Richard B. Gartner

Routledge
Taylor & Francis Group
LONDON AND NEW YORK

First published 2018
by Routledge
2 Park Square, Milton Park, Abingdon, Oxon OX14 4RN

and by Routledge
711 Third Avenue, New York, NY 10017

Routledge is an imprint of the Taylor & Francis Group, an informa business

British Library Cataloguing in Publication Data
A catalogue record for this book is available from the British Library

Library of Congress Cataloging in Publication Data
Names: Gartner, Richard B., editor.
Title: Healing sexually betrayed men and boys : treatment for sexual abuse, assault, and trauma / edited by Richard B. Gartner.
Description: Abingdon, Oxon ; New York, NY : Routledge, 2018. | Series: Psychoanalysis in a new key book series ; 40 | Includes bibliographical references and index.
Identifiers: LCCN 2017009522 (print) | LCCN 2017010199 (ebook) | ISBN 9781138942240 (hbk : alk. paper) | ISBN 9781138942257 (pbk : alk. paper) | ISBN 9781315673226 (ebk) | ISBN 9781317375524 (Web PDF)| ISBN 9781317375517 (ePub) | ISBN 9781317375500 (Mobipocket/Kindle)
Subjects: LCSH: Adult child sexual abuse victims—Treatment. | Male sexual abuse victims—Treatment.
Classification: LCC RC569.5.A28 H43 2018 (print) | LCC RC569.5.A28 (ebook) | DDC 616.85/8369—dc23
LC record available at https://lccn.loc.gov/2017009522

ISBN: 978-1-138-94224-0 (hbk)
ISBN: 978-1-138-94225-7 (pbk)
ISBN: 978-1-315-67322-6 (ebk)

Typeset in Times New Roman
by Swales & Willis Ltd, Exeter, Devon, UK

For Jane

Contents

Acknowledgments

I am grateful to many colleagues, friends, and family who offered help, support, and encouragement as I prepared the manuscripts for this book and its companion volume, *Understanding the Sexual Betrayal of Boys and Men: The Trauma of Sexual Abuse*. I am especially appreciative of my colleagues at MaleSurvivor: National Organization against Male Sexual Victimization and the William Alanson White Psychoanalytic Institute's Sexual Abuse Service; my personal cohort of peer supervisors with whom I have met weekly for over 30 years; my publisher and editors; the contributors to this volume; and my closest family and friends. You all know who you are. Thank you.

But I want most to acknowledge the candor, courage, and generosity of the men I have met over the years who taught me what it means for a man to be sexually abused. My patients, numerous members of MaleSurvivor, colleagues who are openly both survivors and professionals, and prominent men who bravely revealed their histories to the world, thus encouraging others to seek help: You are the people I acknowledge as being central to the success of this book. You deserve compassion, admiration, and a welcome place at life's table.

Contributors

Kenneth M. Adams, Ph.D., CSAT-S, is a licensed psychologist, faculty member with the International Institute of Trauma and Addiction Professionals (IITAP) and the clinical director and founder of Kenneth M. Adams and Associates in suburban Detroit, Michigan. In addition to maintaining an active clinical practice, Dr. Adams is a national lecturer, workshop leader, and consultant in the areas of child abuse, dysfunctional family systems, and sex addiction. He is the author of numerous peer-reviewed publications and *Silently Seduced* and *When He's Married to Mom* as well as co-editor of *Clinical Management of Sex Addiction-Revised*. He was the co-recipient of the 2001 "Readers Choice Award" for his paper on shame reduction and affect regulation. In 2011, Dr Adams received the "Carnes Award" for "outstanding work in the field of sexual addiction and compulsivity and in 2016 received the "Lifetime Achievement Award" from IITAP for his work with trauma and addiction. He is a certified Sex Addiction Therapist (CSAT), a CSAT supervisor, and CSAT training facilitator as well as an Eye Movement Desensitization and Reprocessing (EMDR) practitioner. For more on Dr Adams visit www.drkenadams.com

Linda S. Barnard, Ph.D., is a licensed Marriage Family Therapist in private practice in Sacramento since 1981. In addition to a very active practice, Dr. Barnard has also served as a consultant and trainer for various organizations and programs in northern California. She holds credentials as a Board Certified Expert in Traumatic Stress from the prestigious American Academy of Experts in Traumatic Stress. She is also Board Certified in Domestic Violence from that same organization. Dr. Barnard frequently testifies in court as an expert witness in cases related to domestic violence, sexual assault and traumatic stress. She is regularly a speaker at seminars and conferences around the state.

Craig Bolton has been working in the social work field since 1998. He has extensive experience working with marginalized people and those experiencing homelessness. In his current role, Craig is a mental health practitioner with a community health agency, working with individuals who experience severe and persistent mental health challenges. For the past five years, Craig has been running a recovery group for men who have experienced childhood sexual abuse. During that time, he partnered with Lynne MacDonell, a Toronto-based psychotherapist, to develop a group for men who have been sexually abused and went on to sexually offend against others. Program development is extremely important to address male specific issues and concerns. Craig is dedicated to recovery practice and implementation of new programs that help to prevent child abuse in all its forms.

Jim Clemente, J.D., is a retired FBI Supervisory Special Agent/Profiler and former Prosecutor for the New York City Law Department. He is a dynamic public speaker who delivers keynote speeches, lectures, and instruction on a variety of topics across the country and around the world. During his 22-year career with the FBI, he investigated cases from bank robberies to serial killers. He also investigated sex crimes, public corruption, white-collar and violent crime, and has worked as an undercover agent posing as everything from a street beggar to a broker on Wall Street. For over a decade he was an FBI Profiler investigating serial violent and sexual crimes. He is an internationally recognized expert in the fields of child sexual victimization, sexual homicide, and child abduction. Today he teaches and gives presentations around the world. He also consults on criminal and civil cases and does television commentary for multiple news and entertainment shows. In August 2014, Clemente authored his first novel, *Without Consent*, about his own experience as a survivor.

Christine A. Courtois, Ph.D., ABPP, is a Board Certified Counseling Psychologist recently retired from Independent Practice in Washington, DC and is now a consultant/trainer on trauma psychology and trauma treatment. Dr. Courtois has published three books on the treatment of complex trauma in adults, adolescents, and children, and one on the treatment of PTSD in conjunction with Dr. Julian Ford. She also co-edited *Spiritually Oriented Psychotherapy for Trauma* with Drs. Donald Walker and Jamie Aten and authored the consumer book, *It's Not You, It's What Happened to You*. Dr. Courtois recently chaired a working group that produced Clinical Practice Guidelines for PTSD for the American Psychological Association and for Professional Practice Guidelines for the treatment of complex trauma for several professional organizations. She is a recipient of a number of professional awards, among them, the American Psychological Association Award for Distinguished Contributions to Psychology as a Professional Practice, the International Society for Traumatic Stress Studies Sarah Haley Award for Clinical Excellence, and the American Board of Professional Psychology Award for Distinguished Service and Contributions to the Profession of Psychology.

Howard Fradkin, Ph.D., LICDC-CS, has counseled male and female survivors of sexual victimization in individual, couples, and group psychotherapy, as well as weekend workshops, in his 34-year career as a psychologist, and trained over 2,500 professional colleagues. He authored *Joining Forces: Empowering Male Survivors to Thrive*, published by Hay House in 2012. One of Dr. Fradkin's proudest achievements was appearing as an expert on Oprah Winfrey's "200 Men" shows in 2010. He was a founding board member of MaleSurvivor and an Advisory Board Member. As Chair and Co-Chair of the Weekends of Recovery program from 2001 to 2016, he directed over 50 Weekends of Recovery. He founded Affirmations: A Center for Psychotherapy and Growth, in Columbus, Ohio, in 1984, and is currently Partner Emeritus, where he provides psychotherapy in the areas of trauma recovery, depression and anxiety, alcoholism and drug addiction, sex addiction, sexual orientation confusion and acceptance, and HIV and AIDS.

Richard B. Gartner, Ph.D., is Training and Supervising Analyst, faculty, and Founding Director of the Sexual Abuse Service at the William Alanson White Psychoanalytic Institute in New York City, which has honored him with its Director's Award for his contributions to the psychoanalytic understanding of trauma. A pioneer in treating sexually abused men, Dr. Gartner has written and spoken widely about the subject and has been quoted in media throughout the world. He is the editor of this book's companion volume, *Understanding the Sexual Betrayal of Boys and Men: The Trauma of Sexual Abuse*. In addition, he is the author of *Betrayed as Boys: Psychodynamic Treatment of Sexually Abused Men* (1999), runner up for the Gradiva Award for Best Book on a Clinical Subject given by the National Association for the Advancement of Psychoanalysis (NAAP), as well as *Beyond Betrayal: Taking Charge of Your Life after Boyhood Sexual Abuse* (2005). He most recently edited *Trauma and Countertrauma, Resilience and Counterresilience: Insights from Psychoanalysts and Trauma Experts* (2017), and also edited *Memories of Sexual Betrayal: Truth, Fantasy, Repression, and Dissociation* (1997). He is a founder and Past President of MaleSurvivor: National Organization against Male Sexual Victimization (malesurvivor.org), which honored him by establishing an award in his name, the Richard Gartner Award for Clinical Contributions, and is a Fellow of the Psychoanalysis and Trauma Divisions of the American Psychological Association. www.richardgartner.com

Daniel Gensler, Ph.D., is Director of Training of the Child and Adolescent Psychotherapy Training Program as well as a Training and Supervising Analyst at the William Alanson White Psychoanalytic Institute. He is co-author of *Relational Child Psychotherapy* (2002) and has published 15 articles and chapters in the professional literature. He is a clinical psychologist in private practice doing psychotherapy, supervision, and psychoeducational evaluations in Manhattan and Great Neck, NY.

Steven N. Gold, Ph.D., is Professor in the doctoral psychology programs at Nova Southeastern University (NSU) and Director of NSU's Trauma Resolution & Integration Program (TRIP). In 2004 he served as President of the International Society for the Study of Trauma and Dissociation (ISSTD). He was President of the American Psychological Association (APA) Division of Trauma Psychology in 2009; inaugural editor of the Division's scientific journal, *Psychological Trauma: Theory, Research, Practice and Policy*, from 2008 through 2014; and in 2014 received the Division's Award for Outstanding Service to the Field of Trauma Psychology. Dr. Gold has published extensively on trauma-related topics, including authoring the book *Not Trauma Alone*, which details a model for treating adult survivors of prolonged child abuse and serving as Editor-in-Chief of the *APA Handbook of Trauma Psychology*. He has been an invited speaker throughout the United States and in Canada, Colombia, Argentina, Spain, and Austria.

Rick Goodwin, MSW, RSW, wears two hats: He is the Clinical Services Director of Men & Healing, a clinic focusing on men's mental health based in Ottawa, Canada, and also serves as a Trainer and Consultant for 1in6, Inc., based in Los Angeles, CA. Apart from managerial duties, he trains service providers on issues of male sexual trauma, gendered violence, and trauma recovery across Canada and in the United States through 1in6, Inc. He also facilitates group trauma treatment programs for men. His research and writing have been published in journals, federal publications, and edited books. His co-authored guidebook *Men & Healing: Theory, Research and Practice with Male Survivors of Childhood Sexual Abuse* (2009) has been used to formulate services internationally. He also co-authored the Australian publication *Foundations*: *A Group Program Manual* (2017). In addition, Rick was the author for Health Canada in their investigation concerning the correlation between men's experience of HIV and sexual violence. Rick is the inaugural recipient of the Attorney General of Ontario's Award of Distinction for his work in "developing and implementing innovative victim service programs" (2007). He has received other awards from The Canada Council and the Canadian Mental Health Association. He can be reached at rick@menandhealing.ca.

Don Greif, Ph.D., is a psychologist and psychoanalyst with a private psychotherapy and forensic practice in New York City. He is a faculty member and supervisor at the William Alanson White Institute and Emeritus Editor of *Contemporary Psychoanalysis*. He has written articles about recapturing the countercultural dimension of psychoanalysis by viewing it as "slow food" for the psyche and an antidote to electronic culture; countertransference and dissociation in working with violent offenders; the value of sports; mastering athletic demons; and good-enough parenting. Currently he is writing a counterpoint to *Civilization and its Discontents*. Don received his B.A. in philosophy at Yale College and his Ph.D. from Yeshiva University.

Francey Hakes, J.D., was the country's first National Coordinator for Child Exploitation Prevention and Interdiction, a post appointed by the US Attorney General. She was responsible for creating the inaugural US strategy addressing child sexual exploitation, titled *The National Strategy for Child Exploitation Prevention and Interdiction*, which was submitted to Congress in August 2010. Hakes oversaw all child exploitation efforts at the Department of Justice, testified before the US Congress and the United States Sentencing Commission, and briefed senior officials at the White House, Congress, and the Department of Justice on child exploitation issues. Prior to this appointment, Hakes was a prosecutor for more than 15 years, serving first as an Assistant District Attorney specializing in crimes against children and then as an Assistant US Attorney specializing in technology-facilitated child sexual exploitation. She is CEO of her own consulting firm, providing advice, counsel and expert witness services to firms, law enforcement, schools, governments, industry, non-profits, and others on national security and the protection of children.

Scott M. Hyman, Ph.D., a licensed clinical psychologist, is Associate Professor and Institutional Review Board (IRB) Chairperson in the Doctoral Clinical Psychology Program at Albizu University. He earned his doctorate from Nova Southeastern University in 2003 after completing his pre-doctoral internship at the Boston Consortium in Clinical Psychology-Boston VA Healthcare System. From 2003 to 2009, Dr. Hyman held appointments in the Department of Psychiatry, Yale University School of Medicine, first as a postdoctoral fellow (supported by a NIH National Research Service Award) and then as a faculty level Associate Research Scientist. From 2013 to 2016, he also held a research appointment in the Department of Psychiatry, University of Miami-Miller School of Medicine concurrent with his faculty position at Albizu University. His scholarly work has primarily focused on childhood traumatic stress and addictive disorders, and he has authored a number of peer-reviewed articles and book chapters in these areas.

Paul Linden, Ph.D., is a somatic educator, a martial artist, and an author. He is the founder of the Columbus Center for Movement Studies and Aikido of Columbus (www.being-in-movement.com) in Columbus, Ohio, and is the developer of Being In Movement® mindbody education. He has a B.A. in Philosophy and a Ph.D. in Physical Education, and is an authorized instructor of the Feldenkrais Method® of somatic education. He has been practicing and teaching Aikido since 1969 and holds a sixth degree black belt in Aikido as well as a first degree black belt in Karate. His work involves the application of body and movement awareness education to such topics as stress management, conflict resolution, performance improvement, and trauma recovery. Paul is a member of the

International Facilitator Team for Male Survivor Weekends of Recovery (MaleSurvivor.org) and was recipient of the 2010 Howard Fradkin Award for Creative Survivor support.

Lynne MacDonell has been in clinical practice since 1983. Working for 20 years in substance abuse, she designed and implemented an outpatient substance abuse treatment program. In this capacity, she became aware that often issue of addictions could be traced to childhood abuse and/or other trauma. Lynne began to devote herself to healing this trauma. She designed and managed a comprehensive support system for survivors of sexual abuse, including one-to-one, group, and clinical support. Lynne developed "Understanding and Responding to Male Victimization" conferences for the Ontario Provincial Police, held in 25 venues around the province of Ontario. She and her team were awarded the Queen Elizabeth II Diamond Jubilee Medal for contributions to the community. On October 27, 2014, she received a Commissioner's Commendation for her role in educating police and justice partners, community support, and child protection workers to enable them to address the unique and underrecognized needs of male victims. Lynne is a Therapist at Level I and II "Male Survivor of Sexual Abuse Weekend of Recovery Retreats" (MaleSurvivor.org). Recently she joined the Leadership Team of MaleSurvivor Weekends of Recovery. She is certified as a Compassion Fatigue Specialist, a Traumatologist, and a Trauma Group Supervisor.

Heather B. MacIntosh, Ph.D., is Associate Professor in the Masters in Couple and Family Therapy programme in the School of Social Work at McGill University. Dr. MacIntosh is a clinical psychologist and principal investigator on a number of funded research projects examining the difficulties faced by childhood trauma survivors in their adult relationships. She is specifically interested in emotion regulation and mentalizing and is in the process of pilot testing a manualized treatment for childhood trauma survivor couples: Developmental Couple Therapy for Complex Trauma. Dr. MacIntosh is the author of a number of peer-reviewed articles and chapters in the area of trauma and couple therapy. Dr. MacIntosh maintains a small private practice in Montreal.

Mikele Rauch, M.A., LMFT, has since 1983 worked with men and women specializing in the areas of sexual, religious, ritual and physical trauma doing relational psychotherapy utilizing EMDR, art, music, body, authentic movement, humor – and mindful presence. She has been a facilitator of MaleSurvivor.org Weekends of Recovery team since its inception, and is Founding Chair of Taking Back Ourselves Weekends of Recovery, committed to helping women who are survivors of sexual abuse, violence, and incest become whole, healed, and connected to others. Mikele has written for *CANDID*, the *Missouri Review*, the *National Catholic Reporter*, *Cross Currents Magazine*, *Healing Ministry*, and *The New Therapist*. She is the author of *Healing the Soul after Religious Abuse: The Dark Heaven of Recovery*. She practices in Brookline, Massachusetts.

Monica Roy, Ph.D., is a clinical psychologist at the VA Boston Healthcare System where she is an Instructor in Psychiatry at Boston University. Her research interests include Substance Use Disorders (SUD) and Posttraumatic Stress Disorder (PTSD) treatment outcomes. She is currently involved in a research team that is working on creating web-based interventions for veterans with SUD and PTSD. Her clinical interests include providing empirically supported treatment for substance use disorders and co-morbid disorders (e.g., Seeking Safety, Dialectical Behavior Therapy, Relapse Prevention, Acceptance and Commitment Therapy). Dr. Roy plays an active role in training in the treatment of substance abuse and provides supervision for trainees at the practicum, intern, and postdoctoral levels. Dr. Roy is the program manager for the Jamaica Plain Outpatient Alcohol and Drug Treatment Program (ADTP) and Substance Abuse Residential Rehabilitation Treatment Program (SARRTP). She received her Ph.D. from Nova Southeastern University in 2007 and trained at the Boston Consortium as an intern and postdoctoral fellow in the substance abuse treatment program at the Jamaica Plain campus of VA Boston.

W. Christopher Skidmore, Ph.D., works as a Staff Psychologist in the Department of Veterans Affairs (VA) and the National Center for Posttraumatic Stress Disorder (PTSD) and is an Assistant Professor in the Department of Psychiatry at Boston University School of Medicine. He is the Clinical Education and Resources Lead for VA's national Military Sexual Trauma (MST) Support Team, which works at a national level within VA to promote best practices in the field for assisting Veterans who experienced sexual assault or sexual harassment while serving in the military. He previously worked as the VA Boston Substance Use Disorders and PTSD Specialist and was heavily involved in the VA Boston supervision and training programs. His interests include supporting the recovery of Veterans who experienced sexual trauma and diversity issues in psychotherapy and psychology training.

Jim Struve, LCSW, has been a Clinical Social Worker since 1976, currently in private practice in Salt Lake City. With special attention to mindful presence in the healing relationship, Jim provides psychotherapy services to individuals, couples, and groups. He works with a wide range of client issues: trauma (including male survivors of sexual trauma), relationship enhancement (including intimacy, assertiveness, identity, gender, self-esteem, and sexuality), and dissociative disorders (including Dissociative Identity Spectrum). Jim is a founding member of MaleSurvivor.org. He was the recipient of the Richard Gartner Outstanding Clinical Services Award at the 2010 International MaleSurvivor Conference. He is also a founding member and Coordinator (since 2004) for the LGBTQ-Affirmative Psychotherapist Guild of Utah. Jim is the author of "Dancing With The Patriarchy: The Politics of Sexual Abuse," in *The Sexually Abused Male, Volume 1: Prevalence, Impact, & Treatment*, edited by Mic Hunter (1990) and co-author, with Mic Hunter, of *The Ethical Use of Touch in Psychotherapy* (1997).

Robert Weiss, LCSW, CSAT-S, is a digital-age intimacy and relationships expert specializing in infidelity and addictions, in particular sex, porn, and love addiction. Currently, he is Senior Vice President of National Clinical Development for Elements Behavioral Health, creating and overseeing addiction and mental health treatment programs for more than a dozen high-end treatment facilities. Previously, he developed intimacy disorder and sexual addiction treatment programming for both men and women at the Sexual Recovery Institute in Los Angeles and The Life Healing Center in New Mexico. He is the author of numerous books, including *Out of the Doghouse: A Step-by-Step Relationship Saving Guide for Men Caught Cheating, Sex Addiction 101: A Basic Guide to Healing from Sex, Porn, and Love Addiction,* and *Cruise Control: Understanding Sex Addiction in Gay Men*. He has served as a subject expert for multiple media outlets including The Oprah Winfrey Network, The New York Times, The Los Angeles Times, The Daily Beast, and CNN, among others.

Introduction

Richard B. Gartner

Since the turn of this century, attitudes toward male sexual victimization and trauma have shifted dramatically. At one time, many in both public and professional arenas did not even believe the problem existed except in rare, isolated cases. Then came revelations in 2002 that sexually abusive Roman Catholic clergy were systematically protected by their superiors from facing their accusers and answering for their crimes. And in 2011 Coach Jerry Sandusky at Penn State University was charged and convicted of assaulting numerous young boys from the Second Mile, a non-profit agency he founded to help disadvantaged youth. Male sexual victimization had entered the public discourse.

During this period, increasing numbers of cases gained notoriety:

- Male and female teachers having sex with underage male students.
- Coaches in a wide range of sports molesting or assaulting young athletes, or manipulating them into sexual relationships.
- U.S. Congressmen taking advantage of power relationships with young male pages.
- Schools and universities ignoring or actively hiding sexual exploitation of students or other underage boys. While the Penn State University scandal was the most notorious of these, there were numerous other well-publicized cases, such as those involving the elite Horace Mann School in New York City (Kamil & Elder, 2015) and the American Boychoir School in New Jersey (Schemo, 2002).
- Multiple reports about incidents of sexual abuse and assault of boys in ultra-Orthodox Jewish communities (e.g., Otterman & Rivera, 2012).
- Credible allegations by at least 450 individuals emerging, a year after his death, about beloved English entertainer Sir Jimmy Savile. These individuals contended that he sexually abused them as prepubescent boys and girls or as adults (BBC News, 2012).

At the same time, a growing number of male celebrities stepped forward to reveal histories of sexual abuse. These included:

- Musicians such as Carlos Santana, Jonathan Davis of Korn, Axl Rose of Guns N' Roses, Kirk Hammett of Metallica, Chester Bennington of Linkin Park, and Mike Patton of Faith No More.
- Athletes such as NFL player Laveranues Coles, NBA player Keyon Dooling, NHL player Sheldon Kennedy, MLB player R. A. Dickey, former Stanley Cup champion Theoren Fleury, three-time Tour de France champion Greg LeMond, boxer Sugar Ray Leonard, and Olympic diving champion Greg Louganis.
- Performers, actors, and comedians such as Gabriel Byrne, Derek Luke, Tom Arnold, Billy Connolly, and Barry Crimmins.
- Actor/directors such as Antwone Fisher and Tyler Perry.
- Newscasters such as CNN anchor Don Lemon and NBC anchor Thomas Roberts.
- Journalists such as Charles Blow of the *New York Times.*
- Politicians such as former Senator Scott Brown of Massachusetts.

Every time a case was spotlighted or a respected celebrity disclosed boyhood sexual abuse, other men who had suffered in silence about boyhood abuse for years or decades felt empowered to come forward. Some sought legal redress, but many wanted to get psychological or pastoral help for their trauma.

In this book and its companion volume, *Understanding the Sexual Betrayal of Boys and Men: The Trauma of Sexual Abuse*, I have invited a group of experts to write about specific areas involving the sexual abuse of boys and men. Each contributes a chapter in an area of expertise, and *in toto* the books constitute a nearly-20-years-later follow-up of my book *Betrayed as Boys: Psychodynamic Treatment of Sexually Abused Men* (Gartner, 1999). In that book, I made the case for considering male sexual victimization a serious problem with specific meanings, antecedents, consequences, and treatment goals. I also described how interpersonally oriented psychodynamic or psychoanalytic treatment helps traumatized men.

This volume focuses particularly on treatment issues, while its companion volume focuses more on underlying considerations. This book begins with descriptions of treatment from various perspectives (Gartner, Gensler, Barnard, Skidmore and Roy), then moves to specialized types of treatment

(Fradkin and Struve, Goodwin, Hyman and Gold, Courtois and Weiss, Linden). Several chapters then consider the role of women in etiology and treatment (Rauch, Adams, MacIntosh). The book ends with three chapters that concentrate on predators, whether or not they themselves were sexually abused (Clemente and Hakes, Greif, MacDonell and Bolton).

Together, the two books constitute a rich and thorough analysis of a complex field that remains "common, underreported, underrecognized, and undertreated" (Holmes & Slap, 1998, p. 1860).

References

BBC News (2012, December 12). Jimmy Savile abuse: Number of alleged victims reaches 450. Retrieved from www.bbc.com/news/uk-20697738.

Gartner, R. B. (1999). *Betrayed as boys: Psychodynamic treatment of sexually abused men.* New York, NY: Guilford.

Holmes W., & Slap, G. (1998). Sexual abuse of boys: Definition, prevalence, correlates, sequelae, and management. *Journal of the American Medical Association, 280*(21), 1855–1862.

Kamil, A., & Elder, S. (2015). *Great is the truth: Secrecy, scandal, and the quest for justice at the Horace Mann School.* New York, NY: Farrar, Straus & Giroux.

Otterman, S., & Rivera, R. (2012, May 9). Ultra-Orthodox shun their own for reporting child sexual abuse. *New York Times*. Retrieved from www.nytimes.com/2012/05/10/nyregion/ultra-orthodox-jews-shun-their-own-for-reporting-child-sexual-abuse.html?pagewanted=all.

Schemo, D. J. (2002, April 16). Years of sex abuse described at choir school in New Jersey. *New York Times*. Retrieved from www.nytimes.com/2002/04/16/nyregion/years-of-sex-abuse-described-at-choir-school-in-new-jersey.html?pagewanted=all.

Part I

Treating men and boys

Chapter 1

Treating men sexually betrayed as boys

Richard B. Gartner

I am a psychoanalyst in the Relational/Interpersonal tradition. In my work I emphasize the interpersonal context of a patient's life. Earlier in my career, I was in a leadership position as a family therapist at a partial hospitalization service where we borrowed from a wealth of traditions to discover what works with a given patient. I am therefore respectful of a broad spectrum of approaches to treatment.

This is reflected in the experts I have invited to write about the treatment of sexually abused and assaulted men in this volume. I also have great respect for, and have written elsewhere (Gartner, 2005) about, non-traditional methods of helping traumatized individuals, including journaling, meditation, yoga, exercise, spiritual practices, altruistic works, good health practices, maintaining personal networks, and art, dance, and music therapy.

Nevertheless, I am at heart a psychodynamic psychoanalyst/therapist who focuses largely on the co-created relationship between a patient and me. In that relationship I try to connect to a man through person-to-person contact, each of us attempting to stay the course as his traumas unfold, often for the first time, and we attempt to make meaning of his life (Grossman, Sorsoli, & Kia-Keating, 2006). Hopefully he learns to trust in the benevolence of interest while I try to respect his life journey.

This is written as prelude to the treatments of three very different men. Each benefited tremendously from his therapy while focusing, concurrently or in sequence, on his traumatic history; the aftereffects of that history in his subsequent and current life; and the meaning and influence of our relationship as all this unfolded.

Nate: father hunger leads to disastrous choices[1]

Nate's parents married soon after they met, but they were ill-matched. His father was gregarious in public, but remote and uninvolved with his wife. His mother was depressed and emotionally needy. This increased when her husband distanced himself from her as he experienced how much she wanted from him. By the time Nate was born his parents were leading nearly separate lives; his father got more and more involved in his business (and, as it turned out, his mistress) and his mother devoted herself to Nate and his younger brothers.

Nate grew up with what is sometimes called "father hunger" (Herzog, 1983): the hunger children may feel when their fathers are absent from their lives, either literally – through divorce, separation, desertion, or death – or psychologically. Nate's father was in the latter group, physically present much of the time and a good provider for the family, but "otherwise engaged" psychologically, uninvolved and uninterested in his child's inner life, unaware of his child's emotional needs.

Nate's father, a dedicated athlete who unfailingly exercised every morning (thus absenting himself from breakfast and other early morning routines with his children), was largely indifferent to Nate's own fledgling attempts to get involved in athletics. He rarely showed up at Nate's baseball or soccer games or showed enthusiasm when Nate's teams won. Indeed, Nate could hardly remember a meaningful conversation he'd ever had with his father as he grew up. Meanwhile, Nate's mother, who came from another country and had no family and few friends in the United States, relied more and more on Nate to fill her lonely life.

Looking back as an adult, Nate realized that during his early adolescence his father started a long-term affair with a business associate. He recalls going with his father to professional ball games where they sat with this woman and her children. The purported reason for these outings was that Nate and her children should become friends. But he had little in common with these children, and his father seldom took Nate to games without this woman. Nate retrospectively realized the situation gave his father an excuse to spend time with his mistress.

When Nate was 11, he went to a day camp, where he met a counselor named Leon. That first summer, Leon was appropriately friendly to Nate.

1 Throughout this chapter, names and identifying information have been changed.

But then Leon took a job as an assistant coach in Nate's school. From then on he became friendlier and friendlier to this father-hungry boy, often going beyond the bounds of most coach–athlete relationships. Leon groomed Nate for sexual abuse over an extended period of time,[2] taking an interest in Nate's studies, giving him special practice time to improve his sports abilities. By the time Nate was 14, Leon began inviting him to spend time together outside of school. He asked about Nate's friendships, which dwindled as Nate spent more time with Leon. Then he probed about Nate's feelings about girls and sex, pressing for more and more details about Nate's sexual fantasies.

Nate was a reticent teenager, bright but shy, and very insecure about whether he was attractive to girls. Capitalizing on this, Leon remarked again and again that other boys his age were far ahead of Nate in their dating and sexual activity. Nate, Leon said, would have to work hard to catch up so when he finally began to date girls they would not realize how backward he was about sex. Soon Nate was convinced that only Leon could help him master dating and sex. He considered Leon, who was about 15 years older than he, his best friend, the only one who understood his loneliness and insecurity and could save him from social disaster. To accomplish this, Leon proposed doing Nate a "favor" by offering to "practice" sex with him. Initial groping led to oral and anal sex.

Confused by his mixed feelings of guilt, shame, revulsion, and pleasure, Nate nevertheless came more and more under Leon's influence. Leon claimed he himself had a great relationship with his girlfriend, although in all the years they knew one another Nate never met this woman. Indeed, given Leon's morbid obesity, slovenly habits, and unfailing availability to Nate, it seems unlikely she existed. But in his naïveté Nate did not doubt Leon's skill with women until well into his own adulthood.

Leon demanded Nate tell him every feeling he had about girls, every attempt he made to talk to one, every tentative amorous move he made. He then critiqued Nate's "performance," undermining Nate's sense of confidence while seemingly trying to help him become a "better," more masculine young man. With time, Leon ordered Nate to take risks by, for

2 See Chapter 13 by Clemente and Hakes in this volume for a discussion of grooming.

example, exposing himself in public or having sex with Leon outdoors. Eventually he began to "toughen up" Nate by doing things like inserting safety pins into Nate's scrotum. "This way," Leon told Nate, "you will become brave and more attractive to girls."

Nate's mother was alarmed by the intensity of his relationship with Leon, and tried to talk to him about it, but Nate maintained nothing inappropriate was happening. She then tried to enlist Nate's father to intervene, but he was completely unresponsive and unconcerned.

The intensity with Leon continued until Nate went to college. Even then Leon maintained insidious control over Nate's life by trying to oversee Nate's college social life via phone, and demanded sex when Nate was home. Finally, when Nate was 22 he told Leon he wanted to stop the sex. Leon did not protest, but still tried to orchestrate Nate's relationships with women. When Nate got interested in someone, Leon would comment that she sounded nice but he was sure Nate could do better, that he should not tie himself down, that he had become a "good catch" and should not waste himself on someone unworthy of him. And so, Nate never had anything close to a real relationship with a woman until his late 20s.

When Nate started therapy in his late 30s he'd stopped all contact with Leon for about five years. He felt ashamed, not just about what happened with Leon, but also about how long he allowed it to continue. He spent years in treatment trying to forgive himself for having been such a fool as to idolize Leon the way he had. With time, he began to see the connection between his father hunger and his vulnerability to Leon's predation. And over the course of the treatment he made me a stepping-stone to adulthood, using our relationship to assuage his father hunger while sorting through the damage from his abuse.

He began to see the extent of his destructive bond with Leon. But it took much longer for him to recognize the effect Leon was still having on his relationships, especially with women. His parents had by then divorced; his father married his mistress almost immediately. His mother, claiming to be totally surprised by her husband's affair, was bitter and heartbroken. As her health began to fail Nate felt more and more compelled to be her caretaker and support. His father now tried to relate to Nate, who was suspicious of the sincerity of these efforts, which may well have been at the behest of his father's new wife. In any case, Nate felt conflicted about seeing his father in her company; it felt like a betrayal of his mother to be friendly with them.

By now Nate's depression was long-standing. He was suffused with shame about his relationship with Leon, which he had spoken about only to his most recent girlfriend, who urged him to seek treatment. He had a history of short relationships with women that ended because he began to obsess about whether she was enough of a "catch" and whether "someone better" was out there. These were catchphrases Leon had drummed into his head. His longest previous relationship with a woman had lasted about six months. He wrestled internally with his feelings about his current girlfriend, who he felt was a wonderful woman but for whom he felt no physical attraction. Yet he stayed with her for two years, eventually breaking it off when he realized he was painfully and unfairly trying to force an attraction to her.

Despondent and guilty about ending this relationship, Nate immediately began to date another woman, with whom he felt great physical chemistry. Yet he had objections to some of her other qualities. While the relationship lasted over a year, she eventually called it off, citing his depression, negativism, and the way he held himself back from her. He used work or other obligations to keep from spending time with her, rarely allowing himself enjoyment with her, never taking time off to vacation with her. He explained this by saying he never thought of himself as "the kind of man who deserves vacations," and suddenly realized this was penance for doing such shameful things when younger.

Nate despaired as it hit him how he'd sabotaged this relationship. She was the first woman to break off from Nate – he'd always been the one to pull the plug. He panicked, seeing the possibility of ever marrying and having a family slip away from him. He'd strongly resisted medication for anxiety and major depression, but now agreed to try it. He was barely sleeping or eating and could not stop his fearful obsessions about how he'd wrecked the relationship with the "love of my life."

At this point, Nate's father was suddenly diagnosed with a fatal illness. In the few months remaining to them, Nate worked to repair their relationship, accept what his father could offer him emotionally at this point, and forgive. It was a tumultuous time, as Nate was also beginning medication, desperately trying to get his recent girlfriend to give him another chance, starting to date other women, and caring for his mother, whose fragile health worsened with the news of his father's illness.

Shortly after his father's diagnosis, Nate met Karen. He was determined to not repeat his past mistakes, to make himself available to her both by his physical presence and his emotional availability, and to not use her flaws as an excuse to pull away. He planned with her the first real vacation of his adult life, and actually let himself enjoy it. That struggle continues as of this writing.

So, Nate's treatment over several years explored his feelings about his extensive abuse, but also focused on the familial relationships that led him to be vulnerable to Leon's predation. He acknowledged the aftereffects of abuse in his familial and love relationships as an adult. These included his fear of intimacy, coupled with his longing for it; his need to be a "good boy," taking care of others – as he did of his mother – while denying himself satisfactions because he considered himself bad; and his desire for a woman, co-existing with his criticality and restlessness in any long-term relationship. He asked me many times to give advice, tell him what to do, somehow save him. I tried to be a support without leaving him high and dry, as his father had, or running his life, as Leon had. While we rarely talked about this directly, it became clear that through our relationship he was healing the harm these men did to him.

Eventually Nate had an "aha!" moment when he noticed that he "felt forced" to spend time with Karen. He suddenly recognized how often he'd felt this with Leon. Despite their intense connection, he'd felt smothered by Leon's demands on his time and Leon's constant breaching of Nate's psyche and planting ideas there. Nate felt forced to be with Leon even as he sought Leon's further approval. This dynamic was replicated in some measure in many of his relationships with women: he wanted to be near them and gain their approval, but if they started to connect with him emotionally he felt suffocated and wanted his "freedom." Then he would find fault with them, consider whether there was a "better catch" out there somewhere, and plot how to spend more time away from them.

At one point I said, "You know, Karen is not Leon." Nate was still for a long time as this sank in. He paled, and started to consider how this pattern had been replicated with girlfriend after girlfriend. He was stunned to see how Leon had subtly affected and eventually ruined so many of his adult relationships. His struggle continues.

Luis: getting justice is not healing

As psychotherapists and psychoanalysts, we often hear about treatments that seem to go nowhere: patients seemingly make few gains, perhaps making internal but not external changes. Then, so we hear, after therapy ends everything comes together and transformation begins. This can be frustrating for the therapist because there is no sense the therapeutic encounter was useful unless they meet again. Until Luis I had not experienced such a re-encounter.

When I began running private groups for sexually abused men in 1991, I cast a wide net for appropriate referrals, since most clinicians rarely considered their male patients might have been sexually victimized. I networked with mental health professionals in private practice, in clinic settings, in rape intervention and crime victims' programs. I even put a small ad in a neighborhood paper. Luis answered that ad.

He came for a consultation, but it quickly became clear my group was not for him. The unpredictability of his job meant he could not commit to a consistent time slot. Equally important, though, was Luis's emotional constraint and terror about being open regarding either his history or his confusion about sexual orientation. He worried the victimization he'd suffered made him gay but was not ready to explore this fully, and he was certainly not ready to talk about it to a group of other men.

Instead, we decided to meet individually for psychotherapy. The story of his abuse came out in fits and starts. At one point long after his therapy ended he wrote about it:[3]

> It began when I was fifteen. I was just beginning to establish my independence from my family. I was a junior lifeguard at a CYO summer camp. He was the Director who ran the camp with a "Tough Love" kind of iron fist. He was a Man's Man.
>
> As the summer dragged on I was feeling more and more like a man. He asked me to stay on a few days after the summer to help him close up the camp. I was ecstatic. He made me feel special.
>
> Then he took me to a bar. He let me sit with him on a bar stool as if I belonged there. He ordered a beer and me a soda. Before we left he ordered two six-packs to go. He let me drive back to the camp. I didn't even have a license. He started talking to me about sex. I was shy – this was making me nervous. But I found myself very interested. He gave me a beer to celebrate the end of the summer and the hard work we had done. Then things got intense . . .

3 I am indebted to "Luis" for allowing me to reprint parts of the history he wrote about his abuse and therapy.

He said, "I know you masturbate several times a week." How did he know this about me? Was it written all over my face? I didn't know then about the peepholes he had in the bathroom and shower. Nor did I know about the thousands of Polaroid photographs hidden in his office. But I did know he was treating me special. I knew no other adult had ever talked to me about sex and masturbation before. I was extremely naïve about sex and needed to learn more. And he was willing to teach me.

He kept on talking and showed me porno magazines. By now the six-packs were half gone. This was unbelievable. He was actually telling me to look through Hustler and Penthouse! He said it was OK, normal, good for me. All the guilt my parents and the Church had foisted on me was wrong and destructive. I needed to explore my sexuality and have fun with it. I was excited. He told me he could see I was aroused. He ordered me with a conspiratorial smirk to "take that magazine into the bathroom and jerk that thing off!" I fought off my embarrassment. I tried to be a man about it. I stood up and walked to the bathroom thinking, "Damn, this feels a whole lot better than guilt!" And I did what he told me to do. When I came out, he handed me another beer.

Now the talk got even heavier and he produced more porno magazines. He told me to go to my room and take the whole pile with me. With them in one hand and my beer in the other I went into my room and closed the door behind me. I was sitting on the bed looking through the magazines when he came into the room. I was really embarrassed but he told me to forget about it. He sat down next to me and looked at the pictures over my shoulder. I had a deep feeling of foreboding.

That was when the realization hit me, at least on a subconscious level. The praise and special attention he gave me was all just a ploy. He knew I craved it and he used my needs to lure me in. It would be over a decade before I fully understood this. I started to shiver. To shake, really. My whole body. It was as if the temperature in this isolated cabin 60 miles from the safety of my home had plummeted to zero. At the time I couldn't understand it. In fact I was embarrassed by it. He pretended not to notice.

As I went from magazine to magazine they got more and more graphic, including gay sex. Startled, I looked at him. What's up with that? He said it was just sex, only natural, and I should get rid of my hang-ups. I was shaking even more now. Then he told me to lie down and he gave me a magazine to look at. I wanted to get under the covers and hide. That was when he touched me. Then he did more. This moment changed everything. How could I be feeling this combination of physical pleasure and emotional pain? Why was I even excited? Why was he doing this to me!?!

I rolled over into the corner, and withdrew deep within myself. I tried to fall asleep. He came back in the middle of the night and did it again. At first I thought it was a nightmare. But I opened my eyes and saw the leering look in his eyes. He was real. A vampire in the middle of the night.

In the morning he did it again. I asked him why he was doing this to me. Was he trying to make me gay? "Don't ever use that word!!!" he demanded. "It has nothing to do with that. I am just doing you a favor, teaching you about sex. Don't ever tell anyone. They wouldn't believe you anyway. . ." He didn't have to say more. I did as I was told.

Then he drove me home. But how could I go home when everything had changed? How could I face my parents? How could I look my brothers in the eye? I'd have to break up with my girlfriend. She would know what had happened. I would never be the same.

When we pulled into my driveway I wanted to get my father to beat him with a baseball bat. But I was too ashamed and embarrassed. I knew I could never tell my father. And I thought my mother would die if I even uttered the words. He worked for the Church after all. Where was God when I needed him?

I went directly into the bathroom, turned off the lights, and started the shower. There were no windows and it was pitch black. When the shower was steaming hot, I got in and huddled in a fetal position in the corner. My arms wrapped around my legs drawn tightly against my chest as the water hid my tears. I didn't understand . . . Why did he choose me? What defect had he recognized in me? The flaw that made him pick me out of all the boys in the camp, out of all the boys in the world. I thought I was the only one. No one told me this kind of thing could happen to a boy.

I kept the secret. I suffered in silence.

I had nightmares about it over and over again, dredging up the guilt and self-loathing like a storm churning the sea. Throwing me into isolation.

Luis's case is unusual because he succeeded in pursuing this predator and getting justice:

> A decade later, my older brother told me about the Polaroid pictures he'd found hidden in the Director's office years earlier. I was in shock and I couldn't believe what I said next. "He abused me too . . . I thought I was the only one."
>
> The floodgates opened and I told my family and close friends, glad to be relieved of that awful burden. Then I went to the Joint FBI/NYPD Sexual Exploitation of Children Task Force. When they interviewed me about that night in the cabin I began to shake again. I couldn't help it. I was a victim all over again.
>
> They took the case and began to track him down. He'd been kicked out of the seminary. He'd taught and coached at 13 different Catholic schools. He worked summer jobs handing out towels in boys' locker rooms and other places giving him access to boys. He'd been the subject of numerous allegations of sexual abuse against boys – each time he was confronted, then allowed to resign. Only to pick up at another school, another camp, another hunting ground.
>
> After eighteen months of hard work and dedication by the task force members . . . he was arrested and convicted for the first time after 26 years of molesting boys.
>
> When I confronted him at the sentencing hearing, he was not remorseful. He claimed he had been planning to stop teaching and stay away from boys. That jail was not necessary.
>
> I stood my ground. I finally saw him as the pathetic bastard he was. I told him he was going to jail but he should consider it just a slap on the wrist. A warning! I would be watching him for the rest of his miserable life. I would make sure he never got near another boy. I turned and walked away, slamming the courtroom door in his face. The judge sentenced him to a five year split sentence. It was finally over . . . or so I thought. In fact, the healing process had only just begun.
>
> He was still out there and it bothered me. He ended up spending less than a year in jail and the remainder on probation. No mandated therapy. No sex offender registry. No mention of the countless other victims. As a cover story he told his family he was going on sabbatical to Europe and had a friend mail them overseas post cards during that year.

Despite all the work he had done to bring this pedophile to justice, Luis experienced as much psychic pain as ever:

> It is very difficult to describe, in retrospect, the final toll caused by traumatic events from long ago. In the end, how disruptive and painful was it? What was the cumulative effect on my life? If you added up all of the hours, days, weeks, and months of guilt, sorrow, loneliness, shame, and depression, what sum would you reach? . . . I can tell you it had a profound effect on me for over a decade. My happy childhood ended. I closed off a part of myself. I became hypervigilant. I lived in fear of disclosure. I pushed away my family and friends. I had difficulty trusting others. I feared the world would know my secret. I was damaged goods.
>
> What he did to me caused me to close down emotionally and separate from the people I loved. My mother died before I could resolve the issue with her.
>
> Perhaps what I feared most was the effect the victimization would have on my sexuality. I needed to talk to someone professionally. But, I feared that if I did, it would negatively affect my career.
>
> I remember one sunny afternoon, picking up the community newspaper and browsing through it as I walked to Central Park. Something I read in the classified section stopped me cold. It was an ad for a group that was forming, of men who had been sexually victimized as boys. But what was amazing to me was that the group was being formed for men who lived in my own neighborhood. How could it possibly be true that there were that many men like me, living so close by?

Luis was happy in his work and hopeful about the career laying before him. But ultimately the abuser's trial and imprisonment left him disheartened and depressed. He'd put enormous energy into the legal aspects of his sexual trauma but virtually none into healing from its emotional aftermath. We needed to focus on this.

I remember Luis in the early days of treatment, hunched over in his chair, clearly in pain, constricted, unhappy, and hopeless about ever achieving a fulfilling personal life.

In particular, he wondered if his sexual victimization had influenced his sexual orientation. With difficulty, he slowly acknowledged having bad dreams about his victimization and thinking about men in a sexual way. Afraid to date women, Luis felt lonely and unhappy. He was frightened about being discovered as a man who had not recovered completely from sexual victimization and was questioning his sexuality. His fear was so great he decided not to use his insurance to pay for psychotherapy, and he asked me to keep my notes about our work as sparse as possible. He was ashamed and despairing.

We needed to address the issues looming in front of him separately. First we focused on Luis's sexual betrayal by a man he trusted, a man in whose care his parents had placed him because they trusted the Catholic organization that ran the camp. We talked through how his betrayal influenced his reactions to other authorities and institutions. His trauma had not completely stopped his ability to work with authorities – after all, he'd had a successful academic career and worked well with supervisors at his job. Still, he tended be a "loner," always wondering about angles people were not telling him about, always thinking he might be double-crossed in some way. This undermined and isolated Luis from family, friends, and potential partners.

As he put it:

> I remember slouching in that chair, so worried that exploring unresolved issues related to my victimization and sexuality might hinder my career. I remember feeling stuck behind the 8-ball. I didn't want to be alone, but I felt such a weight on my shoulders about relationships, stigmatized whichever way I turned. It was very difficult discussing all this in therapy. It was very difficult even saying the words. How could I face these momentous issues? How could I deal with what they meant for me and my future?
>
> The answer was in my therapist's patience and calm demeanor. He was not judgmental, he was a good listener, he was willing to help. I had made the gigantic step of asking for help and I wanted to get on with it in one marathon session. I was resistant to the 45-minute therapy hour. But he explained this was how things worked. I needed to take things one step at a time and contemplate what we discussed every week before moving on to the next area.
>
> Eventually, with his patience and guidance, speaking became easier. I listened to what he said: It was not my fault. It did not *make* me gay. It is not the end of the world. I contemplated his words between

> sessions and I kept a journal. I was very introspective, living in my head. The journal helped me organize my thoughts and feelings and made it easier to talk about them when the time was right.

I tried to help Luis articulate the distrust underlying his wariness, to differentiate between occasions when wariness was advantageous to him from those where it obstructed his capacity to live comfortably in relationship to others.

Luis's concerns about his sexuality were more difficult to analyze with him. His Catholic upbringing had inculcated him with fear and guilt about all sexuality. For him, even sexual *thoughts* about men were sinful. Equally important, his worry that his thoughts about men were caused by his abuse made it impossible for him to feel comfortable discussing his orientation.

Additionally, he worried that his history of sexual victimization by a male predator undercut his manhood. In his mind, being a man meant not allowing himself to be abused and not being sexually involved with other men. So, he continued to live a secretive and secluded life, unable to move beyond the pretzel-like life he had created.

I felt great compassion for his position and tried as gently as I could to help him sort through these difficult issues. Oddly, my recognition of his quandary relieved Luis psychologically, even as it added weight to his dilemma.

And so, we continued to work together. We talked about his family and the reasons he felt he couldn't tell them about his trauma. We talked about his betrayal and its aftereffects. We talked about his sexuality. We talked about how these issues were inextricably intertwined in his mind. And we talked about the impasse all this created for his career and his intimate life.

I felt a dilemma. I was very moved by Luis's predicament. He had tried so hard to take on a burden no one should ever ask of any child or teenager. And he had so many questions about himself, questions he was unable to face head on.

I tried to make our therapy sessions a place of solace and safety, but I couldn't always tell whether I was succeeding, if my words had an impact. So I didn't know whether I was helping him become more self-reflective or even whether I was planting seeds for his future growth. Luis became a bit more at ease in sessions with me, but basically remained depressed, unhappy, and emotionally constricted elsewhere. He moved to a new apartment. Whatever his new home really looked like, because of how he described his life, in my mind's eye it was empty and cold, meagerly furnished, with few visitors and no warmth. His constriction centered on his abuse and his sexuality, but there was a spread of effect so his entire emotional life was tight and restricted.

Then Luis told me one day that his employer transferred him to an out-of-state office and he had to stop treatment. We stopped our sessions with little time for preparation or a real goodbye.

In my own mind, I considered our work largely a failure on my part. I felt frustrated, thinking I had not been able to help him much but not sure what I could have done differently.

Later on, when I began to write about my work, I thought a lot about Luis. I did not write about him, but our work influenced how I thought about the effects of boyhood sexual betrayal, especially those related to masculinity, male sexuality, and sexual orientation. Over the years, I wondered what happened to him. Had he found a way to be himself, to heal from the double trauma of being abused and being confused about and at war with his sexuality?

Twelve years later, I was stunned when Luis contacted me. I could barely recognize him. He greeted me in a cheerful, upbeat, confident voice, and immediately thanked me for having changed his life. He remembered many specific interactions we'd had and gave me examples of how what I eventually gave him the courage to confront his fears and lead a more open, spontaneous life. He was now far more comfortable with his sexuality, had developed close and loving relationships, and felt closer to family and friends. He wrote down his thoughts, saying:

> You guided me through one of the most convoluted journeys my life would take. Though you couldn't accompany me along the entire journey, you gave me everything I needed for a safe passage . . . I recently realized that one of the most difficult, yet critical, aspects of recovery is reclaiming the lost experiences we separate ourselves from as a result of being victimized. I had forced out of my mind everything that happened at the camp, even the good things, fishing and hiking and campfires . . . but especially anything positive the director had said to me or taught me. But, by doing so I was cutting off part of my life. As a teen, I deserved to have the mentor the camp director should have been, and I deserved to enjoy camp and remember it fondly. Without

the violation of trust, without being taken advantage of and without being made to feel responsible for it. So now, I've reclaimed all of those good memories, and I've even replaced some of the bad ones with understanding and forgiveness.

Terry: Lazarus returns to life

After an emotionally grueling session, Terry got up from the couch and headed to the door. Turning, he said over his shoulder, "Sometimes I think there are many people inside me . . . and I think the one who comes into this room is the one who least needs to be here." As I considered this statement, he seemingly evaporated from my office.

A 53-year-old married man when he first came to see me, Terry had just ended a three-year-long therapy after a stormy altercation with his male therapist following a very minor incident. He'd used this argument to end treatment abruptly. Given my name before he even started with this other therapist, he'd felt he was "not ready" to work with me. While in that therapy, he read everything I ever published, parsing my words, trying to see whether he might possibly feel safe with me.

But all that information came out much later. Entering my waiting room to greet him the first time, I saw what seemed to be a very small man, curled serpent-like into a chair, wearing an oversized coat and hat, not looking up at me. He seemed to be coiled in the chair without any skeletal structure holding him up. In fact, Terry is taller than I am, but it was several years before my sense of him as child-sized faded.

It felt like this man was barely in the room. Uncharacteristically for me, I held out my hand to shake his. He paused and looked at my hand. After a moment he took it, shaking it limply and quickly. I immediately wondered if I'd made a mistake offering it to him.

He followed me into my office, sinking into a chair as far from me as possible, looking at the ground, never removing his coat. My inquiry became increasingly detailed – he seemed to need help telling me why he was there. He volunteered little and in a thin, reedy voice answered my escalating questions with sparseness and circularity. By the time we finished, I felt exhausted and discouraged, sensing I had not made contact with him. He told me he would think things over and call if he wanted another appointment. I didn't think I'd hear from him again, but to my surprise he telephoned two days later and said he would like to work with me.

Years later, having gained language to speak about such things, Terry spoke about my extending my hand to him in the waiting room:

> At that time, to be touched by a man in any way was terrifying, yet somewhere inside I knew I wanted to be touched. I saw you wanted to touch me, toxic though I felt myself to be. I had a moment to decide whether to shake your hand or not, and knew when I decided to do it that I would come back and discover whether I could stand to be touched by you in the treatment. I thought there was a good chance I would die if I really related to you, but also a good chance I could truly live. If you hadn't held out your hand I'm not sure I could have come back. It might have meant you felt it was too risky, that you didn't feel you could help me.

Of course, at the time the meaning of the handshake was unspoken and understood only instinctively by each of us. I could not have articulated why I extended my hand and he only realized later what it meant to him that I did.

In our second session Terry asked whether I could see him twice a week. I did not have time available for a second session but told him I would let him know if a slot opened up. When I did find time, about three weeks later, he said he did not want it. I looked puzzled and he said, "I know it sounded like I was asking to actually *have* a second session, but I'm not ready to use it." I was beginning to get a better sense of how complicated this man was.

His current problems started with the suicide of his older sister (four years his senior) 13 years earlier. He entered a profound, frightening depression, masked for several years, that eventually brought him to a suicidal state. He started taking antidepressants and began the treatment previous to ours. Nevertheless, he continued to work at a very high level in a field related to public health.

Terry had a lengthy analysis in young adulthood with a female analyst, as well as several shorter treatments, also with women, starting at age 11 when he attempted to kill himself by running out into traffic. Our treatment unfolded with fierce, venomous attacks on my trustworthiness, integrity, and character; terse and deadened accounts of years of appalling and weird paternal sexual abuse; tearful recollections of the sister – also abused by their father – who killed herself in midlife.

Terry's parents both came from working-class backgrounds, but his father's childhood was far harsher than his mother's. He was the youngest of several sons of a vicious father who physically and/or sexually abused them all. While handsome and appealing to women, he seems to have been insecure with men and afraid of women, especially his wife.

Terry said in a flat tone that his father sexually abused him from at least age 3 (the earliest he could remember) until it ended after his suicide attempt. His father "always had his hands on me, touching, fondling, or his lips, licking, kissing, biting, making big slurpy noises." He mentioned that his father "loved it" when Terry got hurt or wounded so the father could touch him as he cleaned him up and bandaged him.

Terry showered with his father until age 11, and much of the wildly inappropriate touching and assaults took place there or elsewhere in the bathroom. As a child, he assumed all boys showered with their fathers and were touched similarly.

> He would clean me lovingly, slowly. He would turn me around and I would feel his erect penis against my buttocks. I'm not sure if he ever penetrated me, but then I've made sure there are many details of my life I keep out of focus or awareness.

Terry said this tonelessly, with no overt emotion and seemingly little sense of the import of his words. I thought of the Biblical story of Lazarus, who was dead until Jesus miraculously raised him back to life. But I was no Jesus and could certainly not perform miracles! Could I breathe life into him, or perhaps perform artificial respiration until he could breathe on his own?

"My father would put food on his penis and have me lick it off. I remember the smell, the taste." His father walked around the house naked as a matter of course. "I tried to always keep myself covered, put my clothes on as fast as I could. Seeing my flesh excited him and he'd find an excuse to touch me."

I thought, "Where was his mother?" As if hearing my thought, Terry began talking about his mother's "mental illness." She was hospitalized for an extended period of time after Terry's birth, probably with a post-partum depression or psychosis, but was "mentally ill" earlier as well.

Terry's father married his mother hoping this would keep him from being drafted into the army. Her parents were appalled at the marriage – not because they were suspicious of Terry's father but because they knew their daughter suffered from major depression and felt she could not manage a marriage. When his father was drafted anyway, her parents tried to convince her to have an annulment. But for once his mother defied her parents and insisted on staying married.

Terry believes his parents never had a good period in their relationship; certainly by the time he was born they had little interaction. His mother was nearly totally withdrawn, spending most days in bed, sometimes reading but otherwise staring at the ceiling. She rarely got dressed, but sometimes got up in the evening. She was a "present absence" in Terry's childhood.

His maternal grandparents moved nearby to care for the children; essentially they raised Terry. He recalls his grandmother as a benign and efficient but undemonstrative caregiver: "I know she loved me, but she hardly ever touched me or smiled at me." His grandfather was warmer, and Terry has positive memories of him joking, playing games, teaching him things. But he died suddenly when Terry was 12. Terry was not told his grandfather was seriously ill, although he knew he'd been taken to the hospital. He is still bitter about never having had the chance to say goodbye.

Things changed briefly when his mother got pregnant with his younger sister: "For those nine months, she was totally different. I suppose there was a hormonal shift, but she was animated, loving, available. It was the only time I really had a mother."

Terry thinks of himself as having been a strange, difficult boy who never fit in due to his lack of athletic interest or prowess and his general "weirdness." He had one friend who was "normal," a popular boy who was quite attached to Terry. He joked with Terry, teased him, treated him "like a regular guy." Then this boy's family moved to a distant state. Terry was so stunned he could not talk to his friend in the weeks before the move, refusing to come to the door when he repeatedly came by to say goodbye. Terry made sure he was out of sight when the boy's family actually left; the friend sent Terry a thick letter after reaching his new home, but Terry threw it away unopened. He simply could not deal with the abandonment, instead completely cutting off his friend. This pattern of cutting off people with traumatic emotional pulls on him was repeated throughout Terry's life.

As treatment progressed, I felt Terry's eyes continuously on me, although he rarely made eye contact. He noticed everything I wore, any deviation from how I usually greeted him in the waiting room or walked to my seat, exactly how close my chair was to him. He criticized anything that revealed something remotely personal about me. Well-read in psychoanalysis, he fiercely held me to tenets of neutrality as he understood them: I should be blank, sphinx-like, unapproachable, unknowable. I eventually realized he was hungry to find and connect to my humanity. But in the first years we worked together he recurrently harangued me about my divergences from the "correct" set of rules for therapeutic work he had constructed out of the narrowest and most stereotypic possible reading of what a traditional Freudian analysis should be. To the extent I engaged with him about this I tried to make clear the differences between the clinical framework he thought I should be working in and the framework I actually use, which focuses on our co-constructed relationship, not solely on his intrapsychic dynamics.

Gradually, with stops, starts, and backward steps, Terry began to reconsider my active stance with him, to question his unbending belief systems. He came into sessions furious at some tiny interaction in the previous session that "proved" my boundaries were too fluid. We laboriously went over each interaction and what it did and did not mean. He gradually felt safer, sensing I was listening and willing to hear his point of view, maintaining my own but considering compromise. He then began to reassess his inflexibility.

Terry desperately tried to control what he experienced as a hostile environment, continually feeling he was in a war zone. He was exceptionally talented and skilled at his work, but related to colleagues, supervisees, and even supervisors in tight, unfriendly ways. He was feared and isolated even as his work performance got him promotion after promotion.

Then one day he called in a panic. A supervisee had lodged a complaint against him for harassment. "It's for sexual harassment. I have no memory of doing anything sexually inappropriate with her but I must have. I will be fired. My career is ruined. And I don't even remember what I did." As it turned out, the complaint was for harassment through criticisms of her. The woman had saved all his voicemail messages, and as he listened he recognized the hostility in them *even though he actually liked this woman and thought she was doing a good job*. While Terry was not immediately fired, his duties changed and, as he expected, he was let go in a few months.

This incident illuminated how Terry's hostility suffused his relationships, as it had ours. Chastened, he said, "I'm a victim and a perpetrator and something else I can't articulate. I was a perpetrator with her. I am so tired of being radioactive. Revenge is my self-medication. But it never works."

This incident revealed the extent of his dissociation, and how he filled in blanks in his memory and experience. He "knew" he was being charged with sexual harassment and assumed these charges were true even though he did not recall any incident that supported them.

Terry alternately glided and crashed through his life in a dissociated haze. For example, after a few years he asked if I had redecorated my office; he'd never noticed the fabrics, colors, or even furniture before. He often had little bodily sensation and might go a week without a bowel movement, feeling no internal signal that he was ready to void until he was in terrible pain or remembered it must be time to defecate. Similarly, he had little sensation during sex with his wife, often "leaving the room" just as he had done when, as a preschool child and later, his father fisted him in the shower or ordered him to lick food off the father's erect penis.

With time, it became clear that – even though he angrily confronted me about supposed loose boundaries between us – Terry had been perfectly aware of how I work from having read my published work. Indeed, he finally confessed it was the sense he gleaned there of my "humanity and emotional availability" that originally made him yearn to be in treatment with me. In retrospect, he acknowledged he'd misused the tenets of psychoanalysis, rigidifying them beyond recognition to serve his need to isolate and hide interpersonally: "My critiques of your technique were expressions of my terror of being in relationship to you."

As he opened up, he said more about his father: "He related to me in three ways: he'd tell me I am uncoordinated and lazy; he'd lick, bite, and devour me; or he'd beat me." He noted his father was sexually and physically abused by three older half-brothers while growing up, and later abused his own full younger brother. Later, after years of black-and-white thinking about his loathed father, he confessed,

> He treated me the way he was treated. This is a level of reality testing I didn't anticipate. His history doesn't excuse him from hurting me, just as my history wouldn't excuse me. But perhaps in some small

> way it wasn't completely about me. Even if I *were* the son he dreamed of having, nothing would have changed. He would have abused his children no matter who they were.

With difficulty, Terry acknowledged after years of therapy:

> There was an excitement with my father. I hate to admit it but I enjoyed the beginning each time. I was so hungry for his love! He'd start by making me feel good, holding, hugging, telling me how much he loved me. But then it didn't feel good any more. He was kissing me all over, sucking me, licking me, incredibly seductive. It didn't end pleasurably.

As an adult, Terry was hypervigilant about men, fearing them, eroticizing them even though his sexual interest was in women. He had vicious, frightening fantasies of raping men, cutting them up, cooking and eating them. These fantasies filled his day. While he never came even close to acting on them, he was unsure about this, terrified that one day he would lose control and act horribly.

> My fears of men were always there, and I kept my distance to keep myself safe. But on a deeper level, I was afraid they'd "flip a switch" in me and I'd act on my fantasies. At that point I'd be a monster. There would be no turning back. The monster is my father, someone I never want to be.

All this was amplified when men on the street exposed some skin in summer, wearing shorts, sandals, short-sleeve shirts. He linked his reactions directly to his father:

> When I see men's feet I feel a genital sensation, I breathe faster, my heart beats faster. I eroticize the feet. My father would suck on or bite my feet, try to put his big toe up my anus through my clothes while I was lying on my stomach. Or if I was on my back he'd press his foot on my chest. Or he'd grab my nose with his toes or stick his toes in my ear to tickle me. He would lick and bite my feet. I couldn't get away. He'd make noises – a combination of enjoying something you're eating and being sexually stimulated – grunting, slurping, moaning.

Trying to ward off his father, Terry said, “I became inhibited and closed off, but it didn’t stop him. My father was less likely to bite or suck on me if I was clothed, so I’d dress as fast as possible.” As an adult, “the need to be dressed stayed with me. In locker room situations, I dissociate. My body disappears, not theirs. I am a pair of eyes and a brain. If someone comes close I don’t have a body, so I feel protected.” But eventually, as treatment progressed:

> Sometimes at home I find myself walking out of the bathroom without any clothes on. I’ve never done that before in my life! I don’t even notice it until I’m doing it. I used to get completely dressed in the bathroom even when alone. I wouldn’t let my wife in while I was shaving until I got dressed. But I don’t like actually dressing in the bedroom. It’s too large, dangerous.

Later in the treatment Terry focused again on his fantasies of raping and cannibalizing men. Earlier, he’d attributed them to his fury at all men. This time he questioned why he fantasized about men he didn’t know when the one who traumatized him was his father. At my suggestion, he tried picturing his father when triggered rather than an innocent stranger who’d made no moves on him. He was exultant when this succeeded. He no longer worried about all the men he passed on the street, focusing instead on the father who’d hurt him so much.

Our relationship has shifted dramatically over the ten-plus years we have worked together as of this writing. After that initial period when he tested, attacked, argued, confronted, and harangued me, he began to change his tone. A turning point was when he cut his hand just before arriving at my office. I offered him alcohol and a Band-Aid, standing outside the lavatory door while he washed his wound and handing him what he needed. He later told me that he would have expected his father to come in, take over the cleaning process, touch him in unnerving ways. I’d handled appropriately a situation that was so fraught with disturbing meaning in his childhood.

Shortly thereafter he came into a session looking troubled and lay on the couch quietly. I eventually asked what was happening and he started to stutter, “I . . . I . . . I . . .” He could not continue. I said, “Yes?” He started again, “I . . . I . . .,” he gulped, “I . . . love you.”

He went on.

> I could never let myself bond to another man. You're the only one since my grandfather died 40 years ago. I can have a relationship with my body because of my relationship with you. You don't have any but benign interest in my body. I tested you when you gave me that Band-Aid. Now I'm able to take off my shoes without worrying the hole in my sock will turn you on. There are times you have terrified me. Like when I'm lying down and you get up to open or close a window. But I eventually learned nothing bad happens . . . . I love you. I really, really love you. You are so loveable! You have a sense of humor, you are kind, respectful. I accept you aren't perfect. It's all very comforting. Other than my grandfather, I've never let any man get this close to me. I didn't think any man had anything to offer me that was worth the risk.

This was one of the most moving moments I've experienced as a therapist.

Later he said,

> After I said that it felt like the moment before the world ends. I was afraid you wouldn't want me. I was ending the world before you could tell me that. I was afraid you'd misconstrue, feel I was asking for something inappropriate. I was desperate to believe my father wanted me, and he did, but his definition and mine were different. His definition obliterated mine. I needed a father, and now I have one.

He started to weep quietly.

This marked a sea change in the treatment, as he openly talked of his longing for his father's love, and for mine. For several years thereafter he gave me Father's Day presents, each thoughtfully chosen.

Over time, I've met so many Terrys: the highly competent executive; the attack dog eviscerating colleagues and strangers alike; the meticulous scholar; the angry man whose frightening fantasies made me blanch and consider whether I had another Jeffrey Dahmer in my office; the nurturer who cared about every lost soul he met; the sensitively humorous fellow able to communicate warmth and gentleness while making potentially hurtful points to others in his therapy group; the researcher who read everything I wrote before ever calling me. And later, I met the simultaneously frightened and brave patient facing a deadly disease.

I became concerned and tender as I saw how as a terrified boy Terry created horrendous fantasies to psychically protect himself from horrific events he could not otherwise escape. And he has inspired me with his capacity in light of his history to get several advanced degrees; win acclaim in his field; maintain an enduring marriage; and weather a very difficult and frightening analytic process.

References

Gartner, R. B. (2005). *Beyond betrayal: Taking charge of your life after boyhood sexual abuse*. Hoboken, NJ: Wiley.

Grossman, F., Sorsoli, L., & Kia-Keating, M. (2006). A gale force wind: Meaning making by male survivors of childhood sexual abuse. *American Journal of Orthopsychiatry, 76*(4), 434–443.

Herzog, J. (1983). *Father hunger: Explorations with adults and children*. New York, NY: Brunner/Mazel.

Chapter 2

Psychotherapy with sexually abused boys

Daniel Gensler

Treating boys who have been sexually abused requires a balance between letting them define the therapy relationship and staying focused on the fact of the abuse and its consequences. Children's needs are met neither by drifting without focusing on the abuse, nor by speaking only about it. Rather, children need to come to trust that they can focus with the therapist on the abuse and also move away from its shame, anxiety, fear, and anger. Developing this kind of trusting relation is vital for the success of a therapy, a point of view that emphasizes the therapeutic relationship. In this chapter I describe an interpersonal or relational approach to working with children (Spiegel, 1996; Altman, Briggs, Frankel, Gensler, & Pantone, 2002) as applied to work with boys who have been sexually abused. This way of working is compared with trauma-focused, empowerment, and dissociation approaches usually found in the literature.

Relational child psychotherapy

In relational therapy with children and adolescents, a therapist treats a child as someone who lives primarily in relationships and who gets most of the meaning in life from those relationships. These relationships include those with a child's own thoughts and feelings as well as his[1] therapist, family, friends, peers, school, neighborhood, ethnic or geographic background, and so forth. A child's bodily experience, including his urges, pleasures, and pain, is vital, not as a primary source of drives but as one of the places where the experience of these relationships is registered. Developmental experience is a record of all of these relationships from infancy (Stern, 1985) through adolescence.

1 Since I am writing about sexually abused boys, I will use the masculine pronoun when referring to a child in therapy.

Psychotherapy reviews all these relations, including the relationship with the therapist. A therapist sees a child's image of the therapist not only as transference—a projection of the network of relationships that structure the child's mind—but also as a response to the therapist's actual contribution to the relationship between them. Further, therapists recognize that as participants in the therapy relationship, their experience is subject to unconscious motives and feelings. They can be a part of enactments that occur between them and their young patients, enactments that are at first unwitting and dissociated (Bromberg, 1998). The therapeutic task is to use those enactments as examples of relationship paradigms that the child lives within, allowing the therapist to empathize more fully with the child.

Alongside individual therapy with a child, therapists meet with the parents. In relational child therapy, including the parents in the therapy is vital rather than secondary (Altman et al., 2002). Getting into relation with a child's parents helps a therapist know what it is like to have these parents, and what it is like to have this child. Working with parents also allows therapists to have their own relationships with parents, and allows parents and therapist to guide each other as therapy progresses.

In relational work with boys who have been sexually abused, a therapist tries to use the developing relationship with the boy to promote an atmosphere of safety flexible enough to include both serious and playful review of the abuse. The capacity to play is important for healthy development. A child's play is a way to master challenging new experiences, whether benign or malicious, by practicing different roles and experimenting with different attitudes. Trauma can distort play into a post-traumatic play that is grim, monotonous, obsessively repeated, and literal, rather than bubbly and lighthearted (Terr, 1981). Post-traumatic play is a way for a boy to show his therapist his most rigid ways of coping and defending himself from anxiety. These ways typically include dissociating, denying, avoiding, displacing, projecting, reversing, and wishing for magic. They appear in the treatment relationship when the therapist or the therapy brings up anxiety-provoking memories and feelings. The aim in a relational child therapy is to create an atmosphere that feels safe enough to restore the choice and flexibility that are central to successful play, with the therapist as a partner in it. As post-traumatic, dissociative, or maladaptive coping mechanisms become visible in therapy, they can be described and become less rigid. In this way, a boy who has been sexually abused learns to choose or discard his ways of coping, rather than have to adhere to them compulsively.

I propose that the relationship between a therapist and a child who has been sexually abused is the context and framework for all interventions described in the literature, including the trauma-focused, empowerment, and dissociation approaches described below. I intersperse descriptions of these approaches with cases describing relational work with sexually abused boys, in order to locate such approaches within the treatment relationship that supports them.

Alan

Alan, age 12 and in 7th grade when I met him, grew up in four different countries, moving with his parents because of his father's work. He had no siblings. His father had molested him since he was in 1st grade, starting with fondling him in the shower and moving on to anal penetration. By the time his mother learned of the abuse and got him to a doctor, he had some incontinence, anal itchiness, and an anal scar. His mother fled with him to New York the year before I started to work with him.

Alan was shy at first, but quickly showed a teasing, competitive, energetic side—as long as sexual abuse was not being discussed. After four months of treatment we had talked about his life and about the moves he had made with his parents, and then with his mother after she left his father. We spoke a little about the sexual abuse he experienced, but he told me he hates talking about it—"I don't want to talk about what my father did, I want to forget about it." Once he wrote me a note that said, "Under no circumstances shall any person in this 'therapy' talk about the 'thing,' even my mother." Mostly his attitude varied between denial, avoidance, secrecy, shame, and displacement. He withheld information he knew I wanted to know in order to feel control in relation to me, and to avoid shame. We learned how he avoided other kids when he wanted not to talk about his father.

We also learned about his strengths. For example, through creating a sociogram[2] we learned about his social competence, and about friends

2 A sociogram (Moreno, 1934) is a chart of a child's peers that provides a visual demonstration of friends, enemies, subgroups, kinds of relationships, and types of activities typical of a child's different friendships. It is created with the child during a session; it is frequently referred to, changed, or added to over the course of time.

who could cheer him up when he was upset. Through card games we discussed his pleasure in winning and his hatred of losing. Through games of chess we learned about his way of coping by planning revenge on me for beating him (specifically, he tried to distract me while staying determined to be clever and not be beaten). When he beat me in a game, he called me a girl, elevating himself in his view to a superior male position. I said, "When we play a game, sometimes we win, sometimes we lose. But for you, losing feels like being a girl." Privately I thought he was calling me a girl to project onto me (and therefore not have to feel) the humiliation of feeling like a girl whom his father dominated and penetrated. I did not think he was ready to hear me say this; my goal here was to see if he would elaborate on the link he'd made between losing a game and losing masculinity.

Throughout our play and talk, he tended to denigrate me as the loser, projecting his own low self-esteem from feeling helpless with his father. In one therapy session Alan looked at one of the books on my shelves (Drescher, 1998) and said, "You have a book called *Psychoanalytic Therapy and the Gay Man*? You're a pedophile." He told me how ashamed I would be if people knew I was a pedophile. We were playing the board game called *Life*, where he had his five warrior sons denigrate me and kill me. After a while I told him I knew of a real pedophile, namely, his father, who used to molest him. Somewhere between playfully and seriously he replied, "That's a terrible thing to say. You're the pedophile, and your wife is a pedophile-ette."

This exchange could occur because of the freedom he had developed in therapy to raise the subject of molestation; because of my freedom to refer that subject directly to his experience with his father; and because of the ease we both felt with his displacing the shameful image of the molester onto me and my wife. Projecting it onto me was an intermediate position (like the transitional phenomena described by Winnicott, 1971), allowing him enough distance and safety from shame to face the subject of child molestation and condemn it, while still avoiding the experience of fully admitting its relevance to him.

This freedom and ease did not exist at the start of our therapy, four months earlier. At that time, just being alone in the therapy room with me felt unsafe; the offer to play and talk about matters such as his father's sexual abuse of him felt unsafe as well. It was understandable that he would not feel, at first, that I would be any more trustworthy than his father. Over the months of therapy, by explicit statements and by my actions, I showed him my intention was to help him feel better about himself; I would not touch him sexually or aggressively; and I would rigorously maintain this framework through his therapy.

Therapy also included work with Alan's mother and school. His mother was considering returning to the country where Alan's father lived, and she had not yet completed the paperwork for asylum in the United States. She was not in her own therapy, and in parent sessions we could compare the likely consequences of returning to that country to the continuing difficulties of life in New York. We also examined the culture clash between the relative freedom Alan experienced at school in New York, compared to the authoritarian restrictions more common in his home country. His mother was ambivalent about continuing Alan's therapy. She depended on her own father for money, but he was antagonistic toward psychotherapy and in denial that Alan had been molested. My regular contact with Alan's mother helped her examine this ambivalence about continuing the therapy, rather than to act impulsively and leave the country.

Relational child therapy expects contact with other adults in the child's world, such as the school. In Alan's case, I initiated communication with the school guidance counselor, with the mother's permission, leading to a productive exchange of information regarding her resistance to therapy.

I describe below two other cases of relational psychodynamic therapy with sexually abused boys. First, however, I review the work of a leading exponent of a trauma-focused approach to this work, in order to make a comparison with relational therapy.

William Friedrich

William Friedrich's book *Psychotherapy with Sexually Abused Boys: An Integrated Approach* (1995), guides therapists to use three points of view in their work—attachment, self-regulation (emotional and behavioral), and self-perception and self-development. He considers each of these viewpoints as he describes individual, group, and family treatment of sexually abused boys. His understanding of the trauma and betrayal of sexual abuse comes from attachment theory (Alexander, 1992), affect regulation theory (Garber & Dodge, 1991), and theories of the development of the self (Crittenden, 1994; Harter, 1999), understood in a developmental and family context. His therapeutic interventions are diverse and cannot be simply categorized, but include cognitive-behavioral, trauma-centered, and family-based approaches. He provides a wealth of ideas for therapists of any approach who work with sexually abused boys, including relational therapists.

Regarding attachment, Friedrich suggests therapists work on forming an alliance specific to a boy's attachment style—secure, resistant, avoidant, or disorganized:

- Children with resistant attachment seek but also resist contact and interaction, relating with an angry, coercive quality that is intended to help them cope with anxiety about closeness. Friedrich urges therapists of these boys not to give in to provocations to reject the boy, and not to be provoked into aggression, guilt, or indulgence.
- Children with avoidant attachment ignore their parents, showing little emotion when the caregiver departs or returns. They have learned interaction is likely to be frustrating, and so inhibit their feelings and don't deal directly with people. For these boys, Friedrich urges the therapist to notice superficial compliance, or the boy's focus on the therapist's unavailability.
- Children with disorganized attachment have unpredictable, fragmented behavior, alternately approaching, avoiding, and freezing, perhaps to allow some degree of proximity to a frightening parent. For these boys, Friedrich advocates being clear about boundaries to reduce fear and promote a greater sense of safety.

For all attachment styles, Friedrich advocates that therapists refer to the sexual abuse history from the start as they try to help boys recognize their difficulties. He advises therapists to develop a sense of connection to the boy, to make treatment rewarding with small gifts, food, advocacy regarding the school, occasional between-session phone calls, and pictures of the therapist and boy together, and to note similarities between therapist and boy, all to create a sense of "us." He suggests therapists distinguish images held by the boy of the victimizer, of himself as the victimized boy, and of himself as a competent boy. Drawing, play, and dialogue are used to help boys articulate their experience—getting resistant boys to think about how they provoke their mothers, for example, or getting avoidant boys to talk about how things would be different if mother were more available.

Friedrich also recommends keeping attachment matters in mind when working with parents and families. He suggests parents try to connote things positively to promote a better attachment to their sons. Parents should remember times when the boy is not behaving badly, so they can more often see him not as bad or perverted, but rather as struggling to overcome the effects of having been victimized. Parents can create a new narrative about their provocative sons, focusing on their spunkiness, misplaced enthusiasm, or misguided assertiveness. They can also consider the value in recognizing they are the only ones the boy trusts with his feelings. Friedrich tries to increase parents' compassion for their sons by having them consider how they would feel if no one heard them in their troubles. He would have parents reframe their sons' negative behavior as loyalty to someone. Further, therapists can help parents identify similarities among family members in order to reduce their sons' sense of isolation and foster a sense of belonging. Psychiatric medication can be helpful not only for symptom relief but also to create small rapid treatment gains that make a child more likable to his parents.

Friedrich also notes the value of reviewing with parents the effect of their own families of origin. This kind of work can reframe parents' current behavior, even counterproductive behavior, as an effort to see themselves as different from negative memories of their own parents. Parents can let their sons choose and direct play at home, and parents can set aside time for this play. Parents can also make more positive statements to the child, and make loving rather than angry physical contact. Friedrich guides therapists to recognize the jealousy parents can feel over the growing closeness between son and therapist, and to support parents so they do not withdraw in jealousy.

Promoting attachment is the first kind of intervention Friedrich recommends in therapy with sexually abused boys. The second kind of intervention aims to improve a boy's self-regulation and to reduce feelings of being overwhelmed. First, he explains the process of therapy to boys in ways that demonstrate its safety. Abuse must be articulated for therapy to be most effective. The horror of disclosing and describing the abuse can be measured, scheduled, and controlled. Abuse can be referred to with a word rather than with a full description. Confidentiality and its limits should be made clear, and the therapist should make himself trustworthy about this.

Friedrich establishes specific goals regarding self-regulation. He tries to help modulate the intensity of therapy for boys by being indirect and using third-person interpretations rather than directly addressing him ("many boys in your situation . . ."), or by using play and drawings rather than only verbal descriptions. When it is time to verbalize things, role-playing and written exercises are helpful for providing words for feelings. He recommends dividing the session into thirds and saving the hardest work for the middle. Stereotyped post-traumatic play (Terr, 1981) can be modified by predicting it, drawing it, or writing its steps on a blackboard. Introducing imagery is useful, such as learning to turn down the intensity and frequency of flashbacks as if with a dimmer switch. Friedrich teaches boys who fear flashbacks to construe them as teaching them about the abuse they suffered. He guides boys to identify positive features in themselves as they coped with the abuse as it was happening. If the boy denies having been molested, "as if" techniques can be useful, saying, "if you had been molested . . ." or asking him to imagine how he would advise a same-age child with similar abuse experiences.

For boys afraid that speaking about abuse will cause it to flood every moment of their lives, stock questions can be used. The purpose of these questions is to help the boy identify that, although he has intrusive thoughts in a certain limited number of areas, these thoughts do not invade other areas of his life. Questions drawn from standard sources (e.g., Briere, 1989; Wolfe, Gentile, Michienzi, Sas, & Wolfe, 1991) may include:

- Do you try to stay away from things that remind you of what happened?
- Do you sometimes have trouble remembering what happened during the sexual abuse?
- Do you ever have trouble falling asleep because pictures or thoughts of what happened keep popping into your head?
- Do you have dreams or nightmares about what happened?
- Do you ever think about what happened, even when you don't want to?

Friedrich also recommends using techniques of cognitive-behavioral therapy (CBT) to help boys calm themselves. He teaches boys to monitor their levels of anxiety to correct the idea that panic happens all the time.

He helps them distinguish intrusive feelings from the panicky fear that these feelings mean they are actually being re-victimized. He teaches them to distract themselves from such feelings or flashbacks. With CBT techniques such as thought stopping, guided self-dialogue, and cognitive restructuring, boys can learn to identify and correct irrational thoughts such as "I'll never be able to handle this." Finally, boys can learn to attend to the sexual thoughts, fantasies, and feelings that occur in masturbation, peeping, or sex play. The goal here is specifically to learn how their histories of sexual abuse affect their sexual thoughts and feelings, and to consider the possibility of choice and alternatives.

Friedrich offers guidelines for helping parents and families improve the self-regulation of a boy who has been sexually abused. First, he guides parents to create a sense of safety from further re-victimization by explicitly permitting the boy or his siblings to disclose the abuse. Parents should promise that there will be neither recrimination nor subsequent mistreatment for disclosing abuse. They should not withdraw emotionally from the boy after such disclosure. Parents and family members should not emphasize the perpetrator's needs over those of the child, and should forbid reunification with an abusing family member until the perpetrator has done a lot of work on his or her own remorse and restraint.

Friedrich advises parents to reduce overstimulation, sexual behavior, tolerance of others' inappropriate sexual behavior, pornography, parental nudity, co-sleeping, and aggression at home. Parents should learn about appropriate physical touch and nurturance, compared to sexualized touch. If a boy engages in oversexualized behavior, parents should positively reinforce his time spent on nonsexual behavior, using such strategies to reduce crotch grabbing, swearing, or sexual posturing. Concurrently, parents can create places and times for their son where it is acceptable to behave sexually (e.g., when, where, and how long it is alright to masturbate). Friedrich advises parents to try to help their sons recognize that excessive sexual behavior or preoccupation can be a normal consequence of sexual abuse. Parents need to learn more about how victimization occurs, and its effect on children. They should accommodate a boy's need for support and soothing through family rituals and routines (church, birthdays, meals, bedtime, schoolwork). Friedrich teaches parents to normalize a son's concerns that a non-abusive parent was allied with the perpetrator, while raising the possibility that that was not necessarily the case. Other concerns parents can look for, and normalize as common among sexually abused boys, include upset that a non-abusive parent was not supportive or protective enough, that siblings will shame him about the abuse, or that the perpetrator will return. Friedrich teaches parents how to respond to their son effectively, supportively, and non-punitively through monitoring the child's behavior, setting goals for problematic behaviors or periods of the day (such as bedtime), using more consistent discipline, increasing praise and distraction, and teaching their son ways to soothe himself when anxious. Parents often need their own support to support the child through all this.

The third area Friedrich presents for helping boys who have been sexually abused is in strengthening their developing sense of self. He teaches boys to identify their feelings and those of others by using a feelings list, a basket with pens and paper for generating feelings and linking them to the abuse (James, 1989), and a list of thoughts that sexually abused children often have, such as the questions from the CITES-R (Wolfe et al., 1991). If the boy is reluctant to identify his feelings about the abuse, he can be asked how another boy who had a similar abuse experience would answer. Or the boy can be told facts such as, "Lots of boys think it's their fault that they were molested, but it's not your fault, you didn't ask for it to happen, grownups shouldn't treat kids that way, if he would have asked you for permission you would have said no." The boy's actions during or after the abuse can be reframed in terms of positive steps (for example, telling his mother). Friedrich teaches children to recognize how behavior that gets them into trouble follows predictably from feelings they are not paying attention to, rather than to conclude that their misbehavior only signifies there is something wrong with them. Projective methods can be useful, such as noticing when a child refuses to tell stories that might remind him of the abuse.[3] Projective methods are also useful in helping a child make up stories or draw pictures of himself,

3 One example is in the use of the Roberts Apperception Test (McArthur & Roberts, 1982), in which a child is asked to make up stories about pictures of children and parents in various situations. The child is asked to include what led up to the situation, what is happening, and how it will end, including the people's feelings, thoughts, and actions. In this context, one of the pictures the child is asked to respond to is of a boy entering a bathroom and seeing a woman in the tub (card 15), a scene an abused boy might want to avoid.

focusing for example on images from before and after the abuse to bring out how feelings about himself changed because of the abuse. Boys who will not refer to their own feelings might still respond well to indirect approaches, such as asking them to tell stories or draw pictures about another boy who was abused.

More generally, Friedrich advises therapists to support boys' development and strengthening of self by contracting with them for behavior that would lead to greater feelings of competency, efficacy, and hope. He does this by setting goals with a boy for taking initiative with friends or teachers, completing homework, interrupting negative or self-defeating thoughts, behaving more competently or assertively, taking more initiative, being less passive, and generally reducing victim behavior. To reduce negative feelings, he teaches boys to externalize the problem ("I don't take pleasure in thinking about the abuse, those thoughts sneak up on me, I want to keep those negative thoughts away from me, I don't want to pay attention to them"). Using CBT techniques, he confronts boys with their all-or-nothing thinking and overgeneralization about unwanted qualities in themselves. He tries to soften extreme and contradictory perceptions a boy has of himself, and to correct inappropriate cognitions. Finally, he examines a boy's sense of his sexual self, discussing for example a boy's concerns that the perpetrator chose him to molest because the boy appears gay; concerns about how other children think of him; and concerns about what to tell a girlfriend or boyfriend. He also inquires about whether he is behaving sexually in ways that duplicate the abuse.

Friedrich includes parents in his focus on helping a boy strengthen his developing sense of self. In parent meetings, he urges parents to get out in the open such unacceptable feelings as shameful dislike of their son. Ambivalent feelings about children are normalized and accepted in the context of feeling commitment to the boy and hope for his future. Parental attributions are examined, such as blaming the boy for being sexually victimized or blaming themselves for being inept. Friedrich tries to get parents to give more weight to their own effectiveness with small goals achieved over therapy, including reducing their all-or-nothing thinking and making their self-understanding more complex (for example, "Though I'm a wimp, I'm still a loving parent and I was able to put my foot down and get my son to therapy").

More generally, Friedrich tries to reduce stresses in the parents' lives, including depression, marital discord, or lack of support. He tries to give them permission and acceptance about getting married and having children despite the trouble that came with having children. There is value in looking at the sexual abuse objectively and discussing how it has affected their lives. Parents can examine how they tried to influence the problem whether for better (ignoring their son's negative behavior so as not to reinforce it, or rewarding its absence) or for worse (getting angry at their son or insulting him). If parents feel betrayed and angry that their son did not disclose the abuse earlier, Friedrich helps them see their underlying feelings of failure as parents. Yet parents also learn to project a positive future for their son (for example, that he will marry, work, or have children) rather than just to worry about negative outcomes. Generally the goal is to try to interrupt parents' self-critical thoughts about their parenting and pejorative thoughts about their son, and instead to parent their son from the most loving part of themselves.

Friedrich notes that although therapy is most effective if treatment can extend six to eight months (p. 16), "the time necessary to engage the boy and to develop rapport is frequently brief" (p. xi). Therapy may be interrupted when custodial parents move away with their children after a perpetrator gets out of prison, or when they run out of money and have to move somewhere where they have more support or lower costs. When therapy is brief, Friedrich's recommendations and descriptions for interventions can be seen as a menu from which particular techniques can be chosen, rather than as a plan to be completed with each boy. Even in longer therapies, his recommendations are so numerous that a therapist can choose among them, rather than follow them all.

Friedrich's work integrates a vast number of techniques and organizes them helpfully with his three points of view. Missing, however, is an overall emphasis on the relationship with the therapist that sustains the therapy and provides the framework where techniques take shape and meaning, as in the case of Otto.

Otto

Otto, age 4, was referred to me for therapy by the court because of his mother's neglect to report his father's sexual abuse of him prior to re-incarceration for drug-related crimes. Otto was preoccupied with knives, having tantrums, and feeling bad about himself after being expelled from his daycare center for fellating a boy. He was also licking his mother's hand and engaging in oral sex play with the daughter of his mother's female friend. He did not get along with peers and liked to dress as a girl. His mother told me his father had taught him to tongue kiss at age one and showed him pornography at age two.

Therapy sessions were variously with mother, mother and Otto, and Otto alone. When Otto came into my office he was quiet, looked scared, and clung to his mother. In the first two sessions I showed him the dollhouse and invited him to play with it. He took to it quickly and eagerly demonstrated who was and was not to be included in the family. In the play, normal daily events were interrupted by disaster from "horrible beasts on the roof," and then the family recovered and moved on. People climbed up to the roof of the dollhouse and fell off but magically did not get hurt. They were alternately reckless and careful with the beasts on the roof. Hiding, they tried to fit into a hole, but it was too small to hide in; or they tried to freeze like a statue to avoid notice, and then came back to life.

During this demonstration of assault, hiding, caution, escape, and recovery, I verbalized the play but did not interpret its relevance to the abuse I knew he had suffered. In fact, I did not know the direct relevance. Then I brought out sexually-anatomically correct dolls and invited Otto to play with them. He did so, undressing and redressing them. He put one doll's mouth to another doll's genital area, getting excited and anxious as he did so. He told me it was hard to talk about people's private parts, left the office to check in with his mother, went to the bathroom, and then returned. I asked him if he had ever had his mouth to someone else's genitals, or someone else's mouth to his. He said, "I couldn't breathe, it didn't smell good," and went on to tell me in a calmer but tiny voice about two girls, a year older than he, pulling down his pants at the daycare center and laughing. He also told me about another girl his age pulling down her own pants and making him put his mouth to her genitals, then pulling down his pants and putting her mouth to his, before teachers saw them, got angry, and stopped them.

I told his mother about all this and she was upset to hear it. Later she called me to say that after the interview, Otto told her that he had once seen his uncle ejaculating—"milk came from his penis." From her knowledge of when Otto had seen his uncle, she realized that reviewing the sex play with peers at the daycare center made him remember a much earlier abusive experience with his father's brother, an experience his mother had not known about.

In subsequent sessions Otto was angry at me for ending sessions. He also blamed his mother for his having to leave his old school, and was mad at his mother's friend for planning to move away with her daughter. He also expressed fear his mother would go away or die. He wanted to dress like his mother, feeling this could somehow keep her from going away, during the time his mother's friend was planning to move away. He offered some theories about why his father was in jail; after he was told it was because of an assault with a knife he stopped playing with knives. He played at using magic to undo former painful experiences, and became furious when told magic does not exist. Regarding his upset about his mother's friend moving away with her daughter, he learned about real (rather than magical) forms of connection over distance, such as mail or phone. Some age-appropriate forms of play started to appear, such as building with blocks.

I worked with his mother to make a short book of his life to read to him at home (one page with a few lines of text, facing a page with a relevant picture), using this kind of bibliotherapy to bring out both painful and pleasant moments and memories.[4] This intervention was intended to counter the fragmented nature of his memories by putting them into a temporal order, linking preoccupations and feelings with facts and memories, and presenting them in a familiar form through reading stories with a parent. With his mother and with me he reviewed facts about bodily fluids, namely, that semen comes from the penis of teenage boys and men, and that milk comes from the breast of new mothers. He and I were able to link his strange behavior (such as going under a rug) to trying to hide when his father wanted to bite his nails, and his anger and aggressiveness to memories of seeing his father beating his mother for not giving him money for drugs.

In separate meetings, his mother and I addressed her encouragement of his cross-dressing (he would come to sessions dressed like a fairy, wearing all pink and carrying a wand). We linked it to her longing to be a male,

4 Creating books like this dates back to the work of Judith Kestenberg, who cofounded the Center for Parents and Children in Port Washington, New York, in 1972: "If a significant event was happening in the family, such as a hospitalization, the birth of a new child, or a long business trip of the father, a special individualized book was written and illustrated to help the child understand and prepare for the event" (Kestenberg Movement Profile website). This kind of bibliotherapy continues more recently in the Social Stories idea, created by Carol Gray for parents of children on the autism spectrum (2007).

and got her to start considering its effect on him separate from her own feelings about herself. Again and again we reviewed her guilt and anger over the uncle's and father's sexual abuse of Otto. We created the bibliotherapy text, a chapter a week, and reviewed the memories it was helping Otto recover. Her anger over the abuse made her stronger in her determination to deny Otto's father any access to him when the father got out of prison. She came to see Otto's sex play with peers not only as a pathological symptom of having been molested, but also as a sign of his attachment to her friend's daughter, especially as this friend and her daughter prepared to depart. Finally, she accepted advice to stop initiating references to memories that Otto had by now recovered, verbalized, discussed, and stopped talking about.

None of this work would have been possible without the development of sufficient trust, both from Otto and from his mother, that being with me was safe (I was not going to judge, abuse, or leave), that I was interested in what they were going through, and that I could be useful to them. The therapeutic relationship was the silent basis for interventions such as play therapy, anatomically-correct doll interviews, bibliotherapy, and parent meetings.

Before continuing to focus on the relationship with the therapist as the foundation for therapy, I will review books by Camino and Waters on therapy with sexually abused boys.

Lisa Camino

In *Treating Sexually Abused Boys: A Practical Guide for Therapists and Counselors*, published in 2000, Lisa Camino uses an approach based on the idea of empowerment to reduce a boy's feelings of powerlessness, and to help a boy differentiate between negative and positive uses of power (for example, being powerful does not mean controlling others). She advises therapists to help boys see that the person who molested the boy, not the boy himself, is responsible for the molestation; but that the boy, not other people, is responsible for the consequences of his own behavior. Therapists should also keep the child in charge of deciding to talk about the abuse, while communicating the expectation that it will be important to discuss it at some point if not now. Camino suggests that therapists permit a boy to refuse therapy while also talking about treatment as a positive choice.

There are chapters devoted to initial assessment and treatment planning. Indications for individual and group therapy are described in detail. For example, Camino frequently recommends group therapy, especially when

- the boy acknowledges he was abused;
- the offender is someone known to the boy, rather than a stranger;
- the boy is willing to join a group;
- the boy's parent agrees to attend at least an assessment session.

Individual therapy is recommended under particular circumstances, such as when

- molestation is suspected but not disclosed;
- the offender was a stranger;
- the boy is resistant to group therapy;
- the boy was assaulted by a group;
- the boy has a thought disorder or developmental disability;
- no group is available.

Regarding individual therapy, Camino asks therapists to remember that the therapy setting (in a closed room, alone with a stranger, talking about secrets) may feel threatening to the boy. She reviews ways to build a relationship with him without constantly asking about the abuse. In keeping with the empowerment theme, sharing initial information about the abuse is left up to the boy during the assessment. The boy should be told about the therapist's confidentiality and its limits from the outset. Therapists should impart knowledge, for example, that the majority of sexually abused children do not become abusers. Camino suggests dividing the sessions into parts that include opening rituals, assessing the current situation, giving the boy time to choose what to work on before the therapist introduces an agenda, and wrapping up with a closing ritual or with relaxation exercises. The value of empowerment is present in all her technical suggestions.

Camino sees most problem areas in working with sexually abused boys as representing three responses to abuse: depression, denial or minimization, and anger. She guides therapists to see these responses as choices a boy makes, or as strategies to protect himself. For example, depression may represent thoughts such as, "If I pretend not to care about anything and if I keep myself distant from people, then I won't be hurt again or lose anything else important to me." Coping through denial or minimization can reflect messages from relatives such as, "Stop talking about it, the abuse is insignificant, I cannot tolerate hearing about it, it is your fault this happened." Coping through anger can be intended to regain a sense of control and power, to obscure other feelings, or to get some other payoff.

Camino also offers guidelines for therapists working with parents of boys who have been sexually abused, either in ongoing support groups for parents or in regular or occasional individual meetings. She discusses how to handle parents' resistance; fears of homosexuality; fears the child will abuse others; denial; and expectations for masculine behavior. Suggestions are made for parents to support their sons, protect them from further harm, restore their sense of personal power, validate their feelings, enhance their self-esteem, and manage their anger. Camino also describes 50 group activities (which can be adapted for individual work) to help restore boys' sense of empowerment, express their feelings, and explore their concerns about sexuality.

Frances Waters

Another approach described in the literature concerning work with sexually abused children focuses on the value of overcoming and integrating dissociative defenses and structures (Silberg, 2013; Waters, 2016). Frances Waters' book, *Healing the Fractured Child: Diagnosis and Treatment of Youth with Dissociation* (2016) begins by describing signs and assessment of dissociation, and differential diagnostic considerations. The concept of multiple self-states is central[5] as she describes the treatment of children who were sexually or physically abused, or children who were adopted after being severely neglected or abused when very young. In subsequent chapters she presents treatment principles such as:

5 "Self-states (also called parts, ego states, or alters) are segmented states of consciousness within the child that may present as different beings that can either take executive control of the child's body or influence the child from within. These states are instinctively created to carry unwanted disturbing traumatic-associated material . . . so the child can survive intolerable circumstances. Self-states can perform necessary functions for the child when the child is unable to cope; the child may view himself or herself as having a different age, gender, and viewpoint from those of the presenting child-client" (Waters, 2016, p. 6). Self-states have also been described by Bromberg (1998), Harris (2009), and other major contributors to psychoanalytic literature.

- focusing on trauma-related symptoms;
- maintaining safety;
- finding underlying meaning in disturbing behavior;
- educating about trauma and dissociation;
- aiming to return the child to developmentally appropriate activities;
- engaging all of a child's self-states;
- aiming for responsible behavior across all self-states;
- engaging parents;
- promoting a parent's attachment to all of a child's self-states.

These principles are applied over three stages of therapy—stabilization, trauma processing, and integration:

- In stabilization, the therapist aims to enhance a child's awareness of his self-states and to increase cooperation and communication among them, to calm his overactive stress response systems, and to manage traumatic triggers.
- In trauma processing, initial conditions are that the therapist is ready, safety is assured, and comorbid symptoms are being treated. Implicit somatic memories of trauma are recognized, the child's ways of surviving the trauma are recognized, and the child is reminded that the trauma was in the past and is no longer present. The child tells the story of his trauma in every one of his self-states, and across many modes of expression (puppet play, drawing, clay, dollhouses, and so forth). Unrealistically idealized abusive or neglectful attachment figures are mourned while rage is directed at them rather than at current caretakers.
- In integration, a therapist encourages self-reflection across all of a child's self-states through metaphor, suggestion, and using materials such as dolls or clay to increase the feeling of caring for a neglected self and harmony among self-states.

Through the book's many clinical examples, Waters' dedication to each child is apparent. Despite frustration, prolonged symptoms, and setbacks, she continues to seek out multiple self-states and to help a child come to terms with them. But she rarely addresses the impact of the therapeutic relationship on this work. It is mentioned briefly as the first guideline for trauma processing, namely, "therapist readiness" (p. 287). There she notes a therapist must be self-aware, comfortable dealing with trauma, attuned to the child, able to hold a child's affect empathically, and recognize and validate the child's suffering, in order to facilitate the building of the child's confidence and trust in the therapist. Most of the book's focus, however, is on skillful interventions that focus on integrating dissociated self-states.

Oliver

In contrast, a case recently published by a doctoral student exemplifies the primacy of using the therapeutic relationship, with its countertransference and enactments, in working with a sexually abused boy (Faber & Prout, 2015). In this case, an 11-year-old boy named Oliver was sexually abused by his male teacher and started to wet the bed, have nightmares, refer to his penis as his vagina, and sleep with his mother. The therapist focused on her countertransference as she experienced herself in the roles of rescuer, abuser, and victim (Ralph, 2001). At first she wanted Oliver to speak with her about his experience of the abuse, as if she could quickly rescue him from his distress. Instead she faced the boy's steady avoidance of the subject, as he focused instead on play about shopping, cooking, and eating. As she came to accept Oliver's avoidance of the abuse, she began to notice him occasionally holding his genitals during sessions.

Concurrently, she tried to imagine the teacher's motivation for molesting Oliver, and was horrified to find herself identifying as an abusive voyeur. This lasted until Oliver again interrupted her (when she was about to ask him about the abuse) by playing doctor, giving her a shot, and telling her to cry because the shot was hurting her. He was making himself into the abuser and his therapist into the victim. Once this play had become established, the therapist again tried to ask Oliver about the abuse; he again put off discussing it.

The therapist became encouraged that Oliver was getting attached to her (despite his avoidance of discussing the abuse) when he asked her to accompany him to another room to retrieve a toy. His attachment to her became all the more apparent when he told her that if he beat her in a board game, he would feel alone. A few more weeks went by. Then Oliver put on a construction hat, set up an elaborate, protective stage, hid behind its curtain, hugged a doll, and tearfully described the abuse. He went into more detail at the end of the next session, and then never spoke of it again. The therapist felt as if she were both rescuer and victim with Oliver, as he unburdened himself and as she became upset hearing him reveal what the teacher had done.

Thereafter Oliver angrily screamed at her, “Do not speak!” if she spoke about anything at all, making her the victim of his anger and regaining control over having to think about the abuse. As he regained a feeling of control, he came back to feeling trust in his therapist. Once, angry about his belt breaking, he took it off and used it to whip dolls and make them cry. Then he told his therapist, “The boy’s in the bathroom and he’s crying into the bathtub. He totally filled the bathtub with tears. Drink the tears!” The therapist pretends to do so, and Oliver said, “Thanks, he feels better now.” The therapist, containing Oliver’s sadness, helped him feel understood, and returned to feeling like his rescuer.

By the time therapy ended (because of the mother’s financial difficulties) most of Oliver’s presenting problems were gone. In this relational-psychodynamic therapy, the relationship between therapist and child was in the foreground, without other explicit trauma-based, behavioral, empowerment, or anti-dissociative interventions. The therapeutic action was in the therapist allowing the boy to create a therapeutic playground in the relationship; tolerating his avoidance of the subject of his abuse while also making clear her wish to talk with him about it; containing Oliver’s and her own feelings by staying aware of her own felt roles as rescuer, abuser, and victim; and maintaining a nonjudgmental, accepting demeanor. Her recognition and struggle to accept her countertransference feelings about Oliver, rather than to judge or ignore him, let him feel accepted enough to use the therapy sessions as a “playground” (Winnicott, 1971). Once this was established, Oliver could safely play out with a nonabusive and helpful therapist the traumatic feelings and roles he was experiencing, detoxifying the trauma and learning to experience it as something bad he was able to contain and replay in the safety of the relationship with his therapist.

Conclusion

Friedrich’s, Camino’s, and Waters’ contributions require the therapist to stay attuned to the child’s family, attachment, self-regulation, self-esteem, empowerment, dissociation, neurobiology, and development. Their therapeutic approaches equip therapists with a wealth of techniques for intervention. A relational approach adds a focus on the developing relationship with the therapist as someone the boy comes to trust as a facilitator and partner for play. In this context, the comfort and familiarity with the therapist becomes sufficiently strong to allow the therapy to go forward, whether or not therapy also uses the techniques described by Friedrich, Camino, and Waters. The several cases reviewed in this chapter illustrate this kind of basic support from the therapeutic relationship. Conceivably, much therapeutic action attributed to specific techniques might be due, at least in part, to the effect of relational factors when they are applied well in therapy with sexually abused children.

References

Alexander, P. (1992). Application of attachment theory to the study of sexual abuse. *Journal of Consulting and Clinical Psychology, 60*, 185–195.

Altman, N., Briggs, R., Frankel, J., Gensler, D., & Pantone, P. (2002). *Relational child psychotherapy*. New York, NY: Other Press.

Briere, J. (1989). *Trauma symptom checklist-children*. Los Angeles, CA: Department of Psychiatry, University of Southern California School of Medicine.

Bromberg, P. (1998). *Standing in the spaces: Essays on clinical process, trauma, and dissociation*. New York, NY: Routledge.

Camino, L. (2000). *Treating sexually abused boys: A practical guide for therapists and counselors*. San Francisco, CA: Jossey-Bass.

Crittenden, P. (1994). Peering into the black box: An exploratory treatise on the development of self in young children. In D. Cicchetti & S. Toth (Eds.), *Disorders and dysfunctions of the self*, Volume 5 of Rochester Symposium on Developmental Psychopathology (pp. 79–148). Rochester, NY: University of Rochester Press.

Drescher, J. (1998). *Psychoanalytic therapy and the gay man*. Hillsdale, NJ: Analytic Press.

Faber, L., & Prout, T. (2015). Cry, baby, cry. *Journal of Infant, Child and Adolescent Psychotherapy, 14*, 455–467.

Friedrich, W. (1995). *Psychotherapy with sexually abused boys: An integrated approach*. Thousand Oaks, CA: Sage.

Garber, J., & Dodge, K. (Eds.). (1991). *The development of emotion regulation and dysregulation*. New York, NY: Cambridge University Press.

Gray, C. (2007). *Writing social stories with Carol Gray*. Arlington, TX: Future Horizons.

Harris, A. (2009). *Gender as soft assembly*. New York, NY: Taylor & Francis.

Harter, S. (1999). *Construction of the self: A developmental perspective*. New York, NY: Guilford.

James, B. (1989). *Treating traumatized children: New insights and creative interventions*. New York, NY: Free Press.
Kestenberg Movement Profile website. www.kestenbergmovementprofile.org/center-for-parents-children.htm.
McArthur, D., & Roberts, G. (1982). *Roberts Apperception Test for Children, Manual*. Los Angeles, CA: Western Psychological Services.
Moreno, J. L. (1934). *Who shall survive?* New York, NY: Beacon House.
Ralph, I. (2001). Countertransference, enactment and sexual abuse. *Journal of Child Psychotherapy, 27*, 285–301.
Silberg, J. (2013). *The child survivor: Healing developmental trauma and dissociation*. New York, NY: Routledge.
Spiegel, S. (1996). *Interpersonal approach to child and adolescent psychotherapy*. New York, NY: Jason Aronson.
Stern, D. (1985). *The interpersonal word of the infant*. New York, NY: Basic Books.
Terr, L. (1981). Forbidden games: Post-traumatic child's play. *Journal of the American Academy of Child Psychiatry, 20*(4), 741–760.
Waters, F. S. (2016). *Healing the fractured child: Diagnosis and treatment of youth with dissociation*. New York, NY: Springer.
Winnicott, D. (1971). *Playing and reality*. London: Tavistock.
Wolfe, V., Gentile, C., Michienzi, T., Sas, L., & Wolfe, D. (1991). The Children's Impact of Traumatic Events Scale-Revised: A measure of post-sexual-abuse PTSD symptoms. *Behavioral Assessment, 13*, 359–383.

Chapter 3

Adult male survivors of sexual assault

Linda S. Barnard

When most people think of male sexual assault survivors, they think of young boys who have been sexually molested and, indeed, that is the most prevalent form of sexual abuse of males. However, in the past decade we have come to recognize that there is a unique group of men who were sexually assaulted but remain hidden. These are the men who are sexually assaulted as adults. Little is written about this group other than an occasional footnote noting that "adult males are also sometimes sexually assaulted." Most frequently this is mentioned as an afterthought or a politically correct inclusion, with nothing else said about it.

> Joe is a 20-year-old African American man who played football in high school. After he graduated from high school, he began working as a firefighter, specifically to fight California forest fires. During his training, several of his fellow trainees grabbed him in the shower and took turns sexually assaulting him. He didn't report this to supervisors and he told no one. He started having nightmares and was afraid to be around people. He became angry and physically violent with his girlfriend, who had him arrested and subsequently broke up with him. He was referred to me for mandatory therapy as part of his probation for the violence against his girlfriend. It took several sessions for Joe to mention that there had been a problem with his work and for him to ultimately disclose the sexual assault.

"Hidden survivors" like Joe are adult men who were sexually assaulted by other adult men. While some sexual perpetrators are female, they rarely assault adult men (Black et al., 2011).[1] Sexual assault, in general, continues to be one of the most underreported crimes in this country (Black et al., 2011). We have no idea about the accurate numbers of unreported sex crimes against adult men because they so seldom come forward to law enforcement or to anyone else. We do know that sexual assault against adult men is very infrequently reported to the police (Hodge & Canter, 1998).

It is estimated that about one in five women are raped during their lifetimes; about one in 71 men are raped in their lifetime (Black et al., 2011). Including men and boys, about 10% of sexual assault victims are male (Gartner, 1999, 2005; Black et al., 2011). In such cases, when referring to adult male victims of sexual assault, any unwanted sexual contact is included rather than only including situations fitting the legal definition of rape (i.e., penetration).

Many adult men are exposed to sexual assault as part of hazing and initiation rituals associated with athletic teams, fraternities, military, penal, and other institutions and organizations.[2] While they are often left with a feeling of victimization, it is often not encoded as such, both out of loyalty to the group and confusion about the acts that were committed. As in sexual assault against women, sexual assault against adult males is about power and control – not sexual gratification (Foa & Rothbaum, 1998).

> Alex is a 24-year-old white male. A family member called me to ask if I had any experience treating adult male sexual assault victims. The family had been trying for about two years to find a therapist to treat Alex. They were told by numerous agencies that they didn't treat male survivors. They were also told by several therapists that they had the background and experience to treat Alex; but once he started seeing them it was clear they did not have the proper training. Alex

1 Editor's note: Nevertheless, female-on-male adult rape is a significant but under-researched topic. For a discussion of rape of adult men by women see Fisher and Pina (2013) and Kulze (2013). For discussions of boys sexually abused by female perpetrators, see Gartner (1999, pp. 42–58) on encoding sexual abuse as sexual initiation and the case of Tucker in Gartner's Chapter 1 in the companion volume to this one, *Understanding the Sexual Betrayal of Boys and Men: The Trauma of Sexual Abuse*.

2 Editor's note: See Chapter 4 by Skidmore and Roy in this volume and Chapter 8 Burmester in the companion volume to this one, *Understanding the Sexual Betrayal of Boys and Men: The Trauma of Sexual Abuse*, for discussion of these groups.

was sinking deeper into depression, isolation, anger, and suicidal ideation. He had been sexually assaulted as part of a fraternity hazing, after the fraternity provided large amounts of alcohol to the pledges. He eventually reported the sexual assault to the campus police, who took a report and referred him to the city police, who also took a report. University officials said that they would investigate this matter, but no one was ever charged or disciplined.

In general, male victims of sexual assault do not report to law enforcement because they fear being judged for somehow provoking the assault in some way. There is a stigma and sense of loss of masculinity – they blame themselves for not having prevented the assault, and they fear not being believed by police or the judicial system. Additionally, if they identify as heterosexual, they may fear being perceived as homosexual because they believe only gays are assaulted by other men (Vearnals & Campbell, 2001; King, Coxell, & Mezey, 2002).

Some additional facts about male sexual assault include (King et al., 2002):

- Perpetrators of sexual assault against adult males are generally heterosexual.
- Most victims are heterosexual.
- Victims tend to be younger than their perpetrators.
- Victims are usually in their 20s.
- The majority of perpetrators had previously assaulted strangers using physical force, intimidation, or entrapment.
- Perpetrators are generally known to the victim.

Myths about adult male sexual assault

These are among the common myths about adult male sexual assault, along with the facts contradicting them (Gartner, 1999, 2005; Morral et al., 2016):

- *Men cannot be sexually assaulted.* Men *are* sexually assaulted, regardless of their size, strength, appearance, or sexual orientation.
- *Only gay men sexually assault other men.* Most men who sexually assault other men self-identify as heterosexual. Sexual assault is about violence, anger, and control, not primarily about lust or sexual attraction.

- *Erection or ejaculation during a sexual assault means you "really wanted it" or consented.* Erections and ejaculation are *physiological* responses that can result from physical contact. These responses do not imply that the sexual contact was wanted or enjoyed. It also means nothing about sexual orientation.
- *A man who is sexually assaulted is not "a real man."* In our societal beliefs, a "real man" should be able to protect himself. Because of this common belief, many believe a "real man" would have fought back and never allowed sexual assault to happen.

Because the primary features of stereotypical masculinity are toughness, fearlessness, and the denial of vulnerability, it is not surprising that men in our society have been slow to acknowledge that men can indeed be victimized and that, like all victims, they can suffer (Pleck, 1981; McCreary et al., 1996). It is very difficult for people to reconcile the contradictory views of masculinity as tough and invulnerable, on the one hand, and hurt and suffering from victimization on the other (Mejia, 2005).

The psychological impact of adult male sexual assault

Whereas women grow up with the clear knowledge that they can be raped and are taught this at an early age, men do not get that same cultural message. Many male victims of sexual assault have never even considered the fact that men can be raped (Ledray, 1999, p. 79). This contributes to the devastation male victims experience, thinking they are alone and that no one will understand if they disclose the assault.

Adult male victims experience sexual assault in many of the same ways that women victims of sexual assault do, with symptoms of traumatic stress being common (Walker, Archer, & Davies, 2005). Anxiety is the most common symptom, but they also report depression, suicidal behavior or ideation, anger, somatic problems, sexual dysfunction, and disturbances in peer relationships (Koss & Harvey, 1991). Some studies have actually shown that adult male victims of sexual assault have more severe psychological distress than their female counterparts (Kimmerling, Rellini, Kelly, Judson, & Learman, 2002).

It is common for both men and women to "freeze" during a sexual assault, making them incapable of physically resisting the perpetrator.

This primitive physical response is not a sign of physical weakness by the survivor. It is a neurological response for protection, resulting from the brain perceiving imminent and potentially devastating danger.

Adult male survivors of trauma are not only a risk to themselves, through self-destructive behaviors, but also to those around them (Lisak, 1994). They are more likely than women to externalize their pain and become the perpetrator of personal violence (Finkelhor, Hotaling, Lewis, & Smith, 1990). Some of that externalization is because boys are socialized and taught not to share pain and grief openly. Boys are made to feel ashamed of their feelings, and especially about any feelings of weakness, vulnerability, fear, or despair. The use of shame to control boys is pervasive and stops men from disclosing sexual victimization (Pollack, 1998). Experience of victimization causes intense biological states of fear, grief, and distress, the very states that are contrary to beliefs about masculinity (Levant & Pollack, 1995; Levant, 1996).

Many of the universal reactions to sexual assault will also be experienced by the adult male sexual assault survivor:

- emotional shock
- disbelief and/or denial
- embarrassment
- shame
- guilt
- depression
- powerlessness
- disorientation
- flashbacks
- fear
- anxiety
- anger
- physical stress
- mood swings
- hypervigilance
- panic attacks.

Other common psychological responses of adult male survivors of sexual assault include (Levant & Pollack, 1995; Gartner, 1999, 2005):

- sense of self and concept of "reality" are disrupted;
- profound anxiety, depression, and fearfulness;
- concern about sexual orientation;
- development of phobias related to the assault setting;
- fear of the worst happening and having a sense of a shortened future;
- withdrawal from interpersonal contact and a heightened sense of alienation;
- stress-induced reactions (problems sleeping, increased startle response, being unable to relax);
- psychological outcomes can be severe for men because they are socialized to believe they are immune to sexual assault and because societal reactions to their assaults can be extremely isolating;
- anger about the assault, leading to outward- (and inward-) focused hostility;
- avoidance of emotions or emotional situations, stemming from the overwhelming feelings that accompany surviving a sexual assault;
- fear the assault will make them gay;
- feeling like "less of a man";
- relationships may be disrupted by the assault;
- relationships may be disrupted by others' reactions to the assault, such as a lack of belief or support;
- relationships may be disrupted by the survivor's reaction to coping with the assault.

Men are more likely than women to initially respond with anger or try to minimize the importance or severity of the assault. Male survivors are also more likely to abuse alcohol or other drugs as a means of trying to cope with the experience and its aftereffects (Rochman, 1991; Scarce, 1997a, 1997b).

The male's physiological reactions during a sexual assault might make it more difficult for the survivor to recognize that he was actually sexually abused. Because he may have had an erection or had other physiological responses to the assault, it may be harder to believe he was not somehow complicit in the assault. A physical reaction of an erection or ejaculation during sexual assault in no way indicates that he did something to cause or permit it or that he enjoyed it. But it is difficult for a man to comprehend that he did not want or cause the sexual situation, perhaps was revulsed and made anxious by it, yet experienced some physical pleasure (Gartner, 1999, 2005).

Homophobia may cause men who have experienced being raped by another man to fear telling about what happened to them (Rochman, 1991). He may question his own sexuality, especially if he experienced an erection or ejaculation during the assault. If the survivor identifies as gay, he has additional fear that disclosure of the assault will "out" his sexual orientation. Because of stereotypes about men being sexually assaulted, he may fear that others will think it was consensual (Scarce, 1997a). Indeed, in some cases where coercion rather than violence is used (such as in some date rape situations), a gay man may question whether it was an assault at all. Sexual assault happens because the perpetrator is exerting power and control over their victim. Again, note that over 95% of sexual assaults against all people are committed by heterosexual men (Black et al., 2011).

The discrepancy between what society thinks a man should be (for example, men should be strong) and what male victims of sexual assault experience (hopelessness, fear, and anger), cause intense confusion for the victim from the time that the sexual assault occurs. Negative symptoms such as depression, shame, suicidal ideation, self-neglect, and anxiety are commonly related to the assault. A male victim of sexual assault can experience the same symptoms that are recognized in Rape Trauma Syndrome and Posttraumatic Stress Disorder (Lin, 2005).

Most survivors experience overwhelming states of fear, helplessness, and vulnerability (Levant & Pollack, 1995; Gartner, 2005). The symptoms are difficult for anyone to deal with, but they carry an added message and burden for male trauma victims because of the myths and stereotypes involved that make them question their very masculinity and manhood.

Male survivors frequently express tremendous personal doubt and confusion about the crime (National Victim Center, 1993). Male victims, if they do report it at all, may divulge they were assaulted but seldom say they were raped. They might seek medical attention for physical injuries but never disclose that they were sexually assaulted. There is a great deal of denial of this, given the pervasive societal belief that men don't get sexually assaulted, or that a "real man" would fend off any sexual predator. Men are raised to believe that a man should be able to defend himself and/ or that he should be willing to risk his life to protect his pride and male identity. These beliefs about manliness are deeply ingrained, leading to feelings of guilt, shame, and inadequacy for the adult male survivor.

Male survivors question whether they deserved or somehow wanted to be sexually assaulted because they failed to defend themselves. They may withdraw from relationships and end up feeling even more isolated. Adult male survivors often develop sexual difficulties as a result of the sexual assault (Koss & Harvey, 1991). Sexual contact may cause flashbacks as well as underlying feelings of sexual self-doubt regarding sexual identity (Foa & Rothbaum, 1998). It is also common for adult male survivors of sexual assault to become homophobic after their assault, mistakenly equating same-sex sexual assault with homosexuality. They may show extreme anger at gay men as a result (Vearnals & Campbell, 2001).

Suicide risk is exceptionally high for adult men who have been sexually assaulted. A majority express suicidal ideation and this threat must be taken very seriously (Kimmerling et al., 2002).

Research suggests these symptoms may last for years, with the most lasting symptom being doubt about their sexual identity because they failed to prevent the attack (Mezey & King, 1992). Researchers also find marked psychological disturbances, such as irritability, emotional distancing, and lack of self-respect, similar to findings for female sexual assault survivors (Burgess & Holmstrom, 1974).

Help seeking for adult male sexual assault survivors

One of the most frustrating realities for adult male survivors of sexual assault is that there are very few resources for them. You cannot simply substitute help from one group to another: programs for men who were molested as children do not necessarily address the same needs as adult men who were sexually assaulted. Similarly, we cannot apply the same interventions that are used with female sexual assault survivors to adult male survivors. While there are some similarities in terms of general trauma responses, there are major differences about the psychological impact on each of these groups. Similarly, while there are some commonalities in approach, there are treatment issues unique to each of these groups.

While the general awareness about women survivors of sexual assault has increased in the past 30 years, there are very few programs for adult male victims of sexual assault. Most rape trauma programs will assert that they also serve male survivors, but the reality is that they usually have no one on staff with any real expertise in working with this population. You cannot simply put an adult male sexual assault survivor in a group with women rape survivors, any more than you can put the adult male survivor into a group with men who were molested as children. The dynamics and social consequences are entirely different among these groups.

Underrecognition of male survivors has made it especially difficult for these men to get help (Flannery, 1999). Many male survivors of sexual assault have been turned away by rape crisis centers, sometimes being confused with perpetrators, and sometimes just being told there are no services for men. The treatment of male trauma survivors should incorporate an understanding of the interaction between trauma and masculinity, as well as the unique psychological effects of sexual violence on adult men.

One national program available to survivors is Rape, Abuse, and Incest National Network (RAINN). They have a national hotline at 800-656-HOPE that will direct the survivor to a local rape crisis center. However, since very few rape trauma providers have expertise in working with male survivors, the "local" person might be several states away, but available for regular phone therapy. Online, rainn.org also has instant messaging available for survivors. These services are free and confidential. There is also the MaleSurvivor website, which serves men with histories of both childhood and adult sexual abuse or assault.

If an adult male sexual assault survivor is looking for local support groups, he will likely find nothing. These services simply do not exist, for a variety of reasons, including the fact that so few men come forward that there is no available pool of men for them to select for a group format. Often men do network with one another online, anonymously, through the MaleSurvivor website. And, while there are many therapists who state that they have expertise in treating trauma survivors, very few have any knowledge or skills to work with the unique symptoms of adult male sexual assault survivors. Even most of the professionals with experience working with male survivors of childhood sexual abuse lack the knowledge and expertise for working with adult male sexual assault survivors. This is clearly an underserved population.

Counselors should acknowledge that seeking help, discussing feelings, and participating in an ambiguous and open-ended relationship with a stranger are generally perceived as "un-masculine" activities that can seem threatening (Levant, 1996). An objective of counseling is to help normalize the immediate problems.

As with other trauma survivors, one of the goals is to explore resilience as a source of strength. Resilience is the process of adapting well in the face of adversity, trauma, tragedy, threats, or significant sources of stress. It means bouncing back from difficult experiences. Being resilient does not mean that a person is not experiencing difficulty or distress. Emotional pain and sadness are common in people who experienced major adversity or trauma in their lives. Resilience is not a trait that people either have or do not have; it involves behaviors, thoughts, and actions that can be learned and developed through therapeutic intervention (Mejia, 2005).

Additional challenges

Most victims of sexual assault know the perpetrator. The majority of sexual assaults are by an intimate partner, former intimate partner, or acquaintance of the victim. These sex crimes are difficult to prosecute because they don't fit the stereotype: a stranger, with a weapon, and a seriously injured victim, who fought back. Male sexual assaults are nearly always counter to those beliefs.

Note that, according to Campbell (2012), 86% of all sexual assault cases are never referred by law enforcement to a prosecutor or ever charged; of those victims who do report to law enforcement, 68% disengage after initially filing a report. Only about 1% of sexual assault cases result in convictions (Campbell, 2012). And these are the numbers for all sexual assaults, which primarily have female victims. We do not have numbers solely for adult male sexual assault victims, although they are likely to be even worse.

Everyone who works in the area of sexual assault knows that victims often change their story or cannot remember certain aspects of the crime. While there is a growing body of information about the effects of trauma on the brain and on subsequent behavior, this knowledge is still not typically understood by juries, judges, or even the attorneys who are involved in the cases. Nevertheless, mental health professionals need to be informed about these issues.

If a woman client comes in seeking therapy, inquiring about possible sexual assaults is part of assessing her history. However, therapists seldom ask the same question about men and, if they do, it is about child abuse, and not adult sexual abuse. It is important for therapists to inquire about all of a client's history, including screening for adult male sexual assault.

Conclusions

In reality, victims of sexual assault can be and too often are adult men; they remain one of the hidden groups of victims. These assaults most often involve heterosexual perpetrators preying on heterosexual victims, although the crime, if recognized, is often viewed as a sign of homosexuality in one or both parties. The sexual assault may be in the context of hazing or other group rituals.

One in 71 adult males are victims of rape in their lifetime. They seldom report the crime but they are significantly impacted by it, often for the rest of their lives. The therapeutic community has a responsibility to be educated about this unique group of victims and to provide needed services for their treatment and recovery.

References

Black, M. C., Brasile, K. C., Breiding, M. J., Smith, S. G., Walters, M. L., Merrick, T. M., Chen, J., & Stevens, M. R. (2010). National intimate partner and sexual violence survey (NISVS). Atlanta, GA: National Center for Injury Prevention and Control, Division of Violence Prevention, Centers for Disease Control and Prevention. Retrieved from www.cdc.gov/violence prevention/pdf/nisvs_report2010-a.pdf.

Burgess, A. W., & Holmstrom, L. L. (1974). Rape trauma syndrome. *American Journal of Psychiatry, 131*, 981–986.

Campbell, J. (2012). *The neurobiology of sexual assault: Implications for first responders in law enforcement, prosecution and victim advocacy*. Washington, DC: National Institute of Justice.

Finkelhor, D., Hotaling, G., Lewis, L. A., & Smith, C. (1990). Sexual abuse in a national survey of adult men and women: Prevalence, characteristics, and risk factors. *Child Abuse and Neglect, 13*, 19–28.

Fisher, N. L., & Pina, A. (2013). An overview of the literature on female-perpetrated adult male sexual victimization. *Aggression and Violent Behavior, 18*, 54–61.

Flannery, R. B. (1999). Psychological trauma and posttraumatic stress disorder: A review. *International Journal of Emergency Mental Health, 2*, 135–140.

Foa, E. B., & Rothbaum, B. O. (1998). *Treating the trauma of rape: Cognitive behavior therapy for PTSD*. New York, NY: Guilford.

Gartner, R. B. (1999). *Betrayed as boys: Psychodynamic treatment of sexually abused men*. New York, NY: Guilford.

Gartner, R. B. (2005). *Beyond betrayal: Taking charge of your life after boyhood sexual assault*. Hoboken, NJ: Wiley.

Hodge, S., & Canter, D. (1998). Victims and perpetrators of male sexual assault. *Journal of International Violence, 13*, 222–239.

Kimmerling, R., Rellini, A., Kelly, V., Judson, P., & Learman, I. (2002). Gender differences in victim and crime characteristics of sexual assault. *Journal of Interpersonal Violence, 17*(5), 526–532.

King, M., Coxell, A., & Mezey, G. (2002). Sexual molestation of males: Associations in psychological disturbance. *British Journal of Psychiatry, 181*, 153–157.

Koss, M. P., & Harvey, M. R. (1991). *The rape victim: Clinical and community interventions* (2nd Ed.). Newbury Park, CA: Sage.

Kulze, E. (2013, October 30). The hard truth about girl-on-guy rape. *Vocativ*. Retrieved from www.vocativ.com/underworld/crime/hard-truth-girl-guy-rape.

Ledray, L. E. (1999, July). *Sexual assault nurse examiner (SANE) development & operation guide*. Minneapolis: U.S. Department of Justice, Office of Justice Programs, Office for Victims of Crime. Retrieved from www.ncjrs.gov/ovc_archives/reports/saneguide.pdf.

Levant, R. F. (1996). The new psychology of men. *Professional Psychology: Research and Practice, 27*, 259–265.

Levant, R. F., & Pollack, W. S. (Eds.). (1995). *A new psychology of men*. New York, NY: Basic Books.

Lin, D. B. (2005). *The traumatization of male sexual assault: An integrative literature review*. Dissertation: Wright Institute.

Lisak, D. (1994). The psychological consequences of childhood abuse: Content analysis of interview with male survivors. *Journal of Traumatic Stress, 7*, 525–548.

McCreary, D. R., Wong, F. Y., Weiner, W., Carpenter, K. M., Engle, A., & Nelson, P. (1996). The relationship between masculine gender role tress and psychological adjustment: A question of construct validity? *Sex Roles, 1434*, 507–516.

Mejia, X. E. (2005). Gender matters: Working with adult male survivors of trauma. *Journal of Counseling and Development, 83*, 29–40.

Mezey, G., & King, M. (Eds.). (1992). *Male victims of sexual assault*. Oxford: Oxford University Press.

Morral, A. R., Golre, K. L., Bicksless, B., Farris, C., Ghosh-Distidar, B., Jaycor, R. H., Kilpatrick, D., Kistler, S., Street, A., Taniellant, T., & Williams, K. M. (2016). *Sexual assault and sexual harassment in the U.S. military: Annex Vol. 2*. Washington, DC: Department of Justice.

National Intimate Partner and Sexual Violence Survey (2011). Atlanta, GA: Centers for Disease Control and National Center for Injury Prevention and Control.

National Victim Center (1993). *Looking back and moving forward: A guidebook for communities responding to sexual assault*. Manual developed with funding by the Office for Victims of Crime and the Bureau of Justice Assistance, Office of Justice Programs, U.S. Department of Justice (Grant #91-DD-CX-K038).

Pleck, J. (1981). *The myth of masculinity*. Cambridge, MA: MIT Press.

Pollack, W. (1998). *Real boys: Rescuing our sons from the myths of boyhood.* New York, NY: Random House.

Rochman, S. (1991, July 30). Silent victims: Bringing male rape out of the closet. *The Advocate, 30*, 38–43. Retrieved August 26, 2016 from http://after-words.org/silent.html.

Scarce, M. (1997a). *Male on male rape: The hidden toll of stigma and shame.* New York, NY: Insight Books.

Scarce, M. (1997b). Same sex rape of male college students. *Journal of American College Health, 45*(4), 171–173.

Vearnals, S., & Campbell, T. (2001). Male victims of male sexual assault: A review of psychological consequences and treatment. *Sexual and Relationship Therapy, 16*(1), 279–286.

Walker, J., Archer, J., & Davies, J. (2005). Effects of rape on men: A descriptive analysis. *Archives of Sexual Behavior, 34*(1), 69–80.

Chapter 4

Male Veterans' recovery from sexual assault and harassment during military service[1]

W. Christopher Skidmore and Monica Roy

This chapter describes the prevalence and impact of sexual assault and harassment during military service (MSA) on male Service Members and Veterans. It also summarizes evidence from the literature and the authors' clinical practice and explores some common struggles in recovery for these men, such as masculinity and sexuality concerns, anger, shame, sadness, and isolation. Next, we briefly review important treatment themes and therapeutic approaches. Finally, we summarize additional resources for both clinicians and survivors. We hope providers from a variety of backgrounds will find this information helpful to understanding the needs of all men who experienced MSA. We also hope it provides encouragement and hope to all male survivors, especially to those sexually traumatized in the military.

Sexual assault, abuse, and harassment occur with shocking frequency, yet we still do not talk enough about their occurrence or about survivors' many paths to recovery. These crimes are committed in all walks of life, against people of all ages and backgrounds, including individuals serving in the United States military.[2] Despite the large numbers of men who experience sexual assault and abuse, they are often left out of the public discourse (Stemple & Meyer, 2014). Men who experience sexual assault and harassment while serving in the military have many

1 The material and opinions presented here do not necessarily reflect the official position or policy of the Department of Veterans Affairs or the United States Department of Defense. We express our deep appreciation and support for the Veterans with whom we work and learn from every day, our colleagues in the Department of Veterans Affairs, and the resources of the VA Boston Health Care System.

2 Editor's note: See Chapter 3 by Barnard in this volume for a more general discussion of the sexual assault of adult men.

struggles in common with male survivors of other types of sexual assault and abuse. They also have some unique challenges and needs in their recovery. This chapter describes the experiences of these men, including common struggles in the healing process and helpful themes and approaches in recovery.

Two men's stories, Mr. T. and Mr. H.

Mr. T. is a Caucasian Veteran who joined the military when he was 25 years old with the hope that he would develop a career in the US Army. He had recently lost two jobs as a result of alcohol use and hoped the Army would provide the structure and accountability he felt he needed. Approximately eight months in, he was off duty and off base, drinking at a bar with friends. When his friends were ready to leave, he decided to stay out longer and continue drinking. Returning to base alone and intoxicated, he passed out outside his barracks. He awoke later and found a soldier he didn't know performing oral sex on him. He immediately felt terrified and froze for several minutes. Eventually, he fought off the perpetrator and ran to his barracks. He was haunted and disgusted by the experience but never told anyone.

Mr. H. is a Puerto-Rican-American Veteran who joined the Air Force to continue a proud family tradition of military service. He believed in the ideals of the military and thought it would make him stronger and successful. However, from the beginning, he was harassed and abused for being different. It was often racially motivated, but he was also gay, which he knew he had to keep secret. He did this by being private and performing his duties to perfection, and he also didn't make sexualized or derogatory jokes about women. Some of his fellow Airmen began to wonder if he was gay and thought that he needed to be taught a lesson about how to "be a man." They cornered him one day and began punching and kicking him, grabbing and pinching his genitals, and calling him sexualized and feminine names. He told himself to "suck it up" for the team, and that it was "just hazing." Then, about six months later, a female supervisor repeatedly touched him at work and asked him to have sex, hinting he would receive better duty assignments if he agreed. When he politely refused, she insulted his manhood and said he must be gay. He began to dread working and isolated himself more and more.

The stories of Mr. T. and Mr. H. are composites of many men's experiences that illustrate some of the challenges and complexities that men face. Survivors of childhood and adult civilian sexual trauma of all gender identities may relate to much of this chapter. However, we will focus on male survivors of sexual assault and harassment during military service to raise awareness about their needs and to increase hope and resources for their recovery. By focusing on one group, we recognize we are excluding others. Therefore, we also encourage readers to review other chapters in this book, publications on women and transgender Service Members and Veterans, and studies of Veterans of diverse sexual orientations and racial and ethnic backgrounds.

Terminology and military culture

The Department of Defense and active duty "Service Members." Sexual assault and harassment during military service (MSA) are crimes that occur in all branches of the military, to people of all genders, sexual orientations, ages, sizes, and racial and ethnic backgrounds. The United States Department of Defense (DoD) generally refers to and addresses sexual assault and sexual harassment through separate policies and programs (Stander & Thomsen, 2016). A review of the DoD's ongoing efforts is beyond our scope here, but in general there are initiatives, programs, and resources for prevention, reporting, and treatment (http://sapr.mil/).

The Department of Veterans Affairs and "Veterans." After an appropriate length of service and discharge, Service Members are generally considered "Veterans" and are eligible to seek care from the United States Department of Veterans Affairs (VA).[3] The VA treats sexual assault and harassment together on a continuum, referring to these collectively as "military sexual trauma." This definition includes sexual assault or repeated, threatening sexual harassment during military service, "regardless of geographic location of the trauma, gender of victim, or the relationship to the perpetrator" (as cited in Allard, Nunnink, Gregory, Klest, & Platt, 2011, p. 325). In other words, sexual assault is any sexual activity against one's will, including when pressured (e.g., with threats of negative consequences for refusing or implied better treatment in

3 There are exceptions, and to be eligible Veterans must not have a "dishonorable" discharge.

exchange for sex), unable to consent (e.g., when asleep, drugged, or intoxicated), or physically forced. This also includes feeling forced to comply out of fear or obedience to the strict military hierarchy (Hunter, 2007). Unwanted sexual touching, threatening and offensive remarks about one's body or sexual activities, and threatening or unwelcome sexual advances also count (United States Department of Veterans Affairs, 2016). Of note, men are more likely than women to have had multiple perpetrators of a sexual assault experience (Morral et al., 2016). They are also more likely to call sexual assault experiences "hazing" (Morral et al., 2016), but such experiences still count as military sexual trauma for VA purposes.

We use the umbrella term MSA in this chapter to refer to both sexual assault and harassment during military service. This allows inclusion of both Service Members and Veterans, and of men who experienced a wide spectrum of unwanted sexual experiences. We focus more on mental health here, but we note that many male survivors also have complex physical, medical, and sexual health needs that deserve addressing (Street, Stafford, Mahan, & Hendricks, 2008).[4]

The military environment and its impact. Military culture, structure, and organization must be considered to understand the full impact of MSA. They emphasize strength, hypermasculine toughness, and aggression (Bell, Turchik, & Karpenko, 2014; Hunter, 2007; Lisak, 1994; Polusny & Murdoch, 2005). The training also stresses the critical need to not feel or be affected by emotions, to accept violence, and to suppress compassion and objectify others (Hunter, 2007). These mandates make it possible for Service Members to perform optimally under dangerous conditions, though they also amplify gender socialization and stereotypes about men.

Other aspects of military culture also affect the experience of MSA. An emphasis on unit cohesion and loyalty fosters tight bonding and helps Service Members to sustain their will and commitment to each other and the mission, even when under extreme stress (Manning, 1994). The good of the organization is prized at all costs, even at the expense of the individual, and obedience is mandatory; freedom, privacy, and control are lost

4 Editor's note: These issues are addressed elsewhere in this volume and its companion volume, *Understanding the Sexual Betrayal of Boys and Men: The Trauma of Sexual Abuse*. See especially the chapters by Spinelli; Fradkin and Struve; Kort; Linden; MacIntosh; Struve, Fradkin, and Beckstead; Courtois and Weiss; Easton; and Gartner.

or greatly reduced (Hunter, 2007). In addition, Service Members have to work, eat, and sleep in close quarters with each other, including perpetrators, often in isolated locations far from support. In many cases, perpetrators are of higher rank or there is a power differential; survivors may have to depend on perpetrators to perform their duties, be evaluated, or even protect their lives.

While beneficial for performance, these factors can intensify the experience of MSA and create unrealistic expectations about men's ability to prevent and respond to trauma. For example, if men and warriors must be hyperaggressive and never vulnerable or victims, then MSA threatens their very identities. Extreme emotional control can be associated with suppressing reactions to trauma, which leads to longer-term problems in abuse survivors (Marx & Sloan, 2002). Unit cohesion and loyalty can make reporting MSA feel like a betrayal, even when the MSA itself, or the system's response to it, are betrayals of those ideals. MSA can also interfere with access to social support, a critical protective factor (Martin, Rosen, Durand, Knudson, & Stretch, 2000); fellow Service Members may react negatively to disclosure (Eckerlin, Kovalesky, & Jakupcak, 2016), or survivors may tell no one and try to be "strong" to protect their unit and themselves from further fracture. In these ways, MSA can disrupt one's ability to trust oneself, fellow Service Members, and the military system itself.

Mr. H., retraumatized

> About six months after the initial incidents, Mr. H. was raped by two unknown men in the middle of the night in his bunk. He initially panicked and froze, then tried to fight them off but was overpowered. During and after, they told him they would kill him if he ever told anyone. He was terrified and disgusted, but he also blamed himself, thinking he was targeted for being gay and maybe that it shouldn't bother him so much. However, his work performance started to suffer, and he felt angry all the time. He made several requests to change duty stations, because he didn't feel safe, but was denied. He was constantly alert and on guard, and he started to overeat to numb and escape. He gained weight and started failing his fitness tests. He felt like a complete failure. He was eventually pressured to accept a medical discharge due to his performance and fitness difficulties, losing the career he had dreamed of his whole life.

Prevalence and reporting concerns

Both DoD and civilian research groups find that approximately 1% to 7% of male Service Members experience sexual harassment or "sexually hostile" work environments, and 1% to 2%, or about 10,600 men in one estimate, experience sexual assault each year (Morral et al., 2014, 2016; Stander & Thomsen, 2016). The VA screens all Veterans seen for health care and finds similar results (Hoyt, Klosterman Rielage, & Williams, 2011; Stander & Thomsen, 2016). Some studies find even higher rates (Polusny & Murdoch, 2005; Turchik & Edwards, 2012). Given the greater proportion of men than women in the military, this means that almost half of all Veterans who screen positive for MSA in VA are men, a total of over 60,000 men in fiscal year 2014 (Schry et al., 2015). Regardless of the numbers, even one instance is too many.

These studies sampled men at different points in both their recovery and stage of separation from the military, so it is difficult to generalize from them. Varying definitions of sexual assault and harassment and different sampling methods across studies also affect estimates. Many survivors also fear the consequences of reporting and how systems will treat them, often with good reason (e.g., Morris, Smith, Farooqui, & Surís, 2014; Patterson, Greeson, & Campbell, 2009). This is especially true for survivors of MSA, as the system in which the MSA happened is also the system on which they must depend for justice, possibly without success (Hunter, 2007). Men and women also do not report MSA for other reasons, including (Burgess, Slattery, & Herlihy, 2013; Rosenstein, 2015; Turchik & Edwards, 2012; Turchik & Wilson, 2010):

- Fear of further assaults, especially if working or living with the perpetrator.
- Fear of retaliation, disciplinary action, forced or dishonorable discharge, or the threat of further violence or death.
- Fear of being blamed, ridiculed, or gossiped about, or fear of loss of career or professional reputation.
- Fear of not being believed or that no action will be taken, or having to file a report with the perpetrator(s).
- Shame, denial, or a wish to "be strong" and handle it on their own.
- Dependence on perpetrator(s) to approve medical and psychological care.

Of special note, men are even less likely than women to report or seek treatment (Bell et al., 2014; Burks, 2011; Morral et al., 2016; Rosenstein, 2015; Street, Gradus, Stafford, & Kelly, 2007).

Besides stigma and the impact of rape myths, which we explore later, men may avoid reporting MSA due to the military's historical stance toward homosexuality. Until 2013, homosexuality, including even a propensity or intent to engage in same-sex behavior, could be grounds for administrative disqualification or discharge (Alford & Lee, 2016; Hunter, 2007; Stiehm, 1992; Turchik & Wilson, 2010). Along with laws like "Don't Ask, Don't Tell," this stance treated lesbian, bisexual, and gay individuals as inferior, morally wrong, and possibly a threat to military readiness and operations (Alford & Lee, 2016; Burks, 2011; Hunter, 2007). Men of all sexual orientations may fear being labeled gay if they report MSA, particularly by male perpetrators. This could have resulted in discharge and a loss of career and benefits until "Don't Ask, Don't Tell" was repealed (Burks, 2011; Hunter, 2007). Even today, male survivors and lesbian, bisexual, and gay Service Members still may experience stressors related to this (Alford & Lee, 2016; Bell et al., 2014; Burks, 2011).

To support survivors and encourage reporting, the DoD established the Sexual Assault Prevention and Response (SAPR; http://sapr.mil/) Office in 2004 and two methods for reporting sexual assault. The SAPR website provides details, but in general survivors can file "restricted" and "unrestricted" reports; the former maintains greater privacy and protections. They also have access to Sexual Assault Response Coordinators and Victim Advocates (Turchik & Wilson, 2010; http://sapr.mil/). Reporting rates have improved, but many survivors still choose not to file a report due to the concerns discussed above (Ferguson, 2008; Morral et al., 2016; Turchik & Wilson, 2010).

Mental and physical health impact

Mr. T. and Mr. H., leaving the military

After the rape, Mr. T. began drinking heavily to block memories and nightmares and feel numb. He suspected he had PTSD, but didn't want to admit it, and certainly didn't want help. His tolerance grew, and the anesthetizing effects of the alcohol decreased, so he also began

> using heroin. He felt desperate for any escape from daily reminders, so he also chose to leave the military, but his symptoms did not go away. After working odd jobs for many years, he met and married a woman. They quickly had a daughter. They divorced three years later, but Mr. T. maintained longer periods of abstinence from substances during that time to "man up" and hold a job so he could provide for his daughter. However, he relapsed, lost his job, and became homeless. His ongoing anger about being assaulted often manifested as thoughts of homicide toward the perpetrator or others whom he perceived as threatening. He often thought that none of this would have happened if he hadn't been raped.
>
> Mr. H. struggled to maintain regular employment after his discharge, despite the many duties and skills he developed during his service. He avoided men altogether and became lonely and depressed. He also began to have panic attacks. Once he thought about disclosing his sexual trauma and associated shame about his sexual orientation to a civilian medical provider. However, he interpreted the provider's initial reactions to hints about this as blaming and insensitive, so he kept quiet and stopped going to appointments. Although he gained better control of his eating, he became more depressed and isolated, and his sense of loss and emptiness increased.

Men who experience MSA respond in many ways like civilian survivors of childhood or adult sexual trauma. Initial reactions often include shock, disbelief, denial, fear, shame, and disgust. Like Mr. T., many men initially try to forget in any way they can. Others like Mr. H. may try to be "strong" and perform their duties to perfection, but later resort to unhealthy or unsafe coping methods. These initial reactions sometimes last and become problematic over time.

MSA is an experience, not a diagnosis, and many men can and do respond to sexual assault and abuse without developing mental health difficulties. However, many survivors do struggle with specific mental health diagnoses. For example, data from Veterans in VA care show that male survivors most commonly have diagnoses of posttraumatic stress disorder (PTSD), depressive disorders, anxiety disorders, and substance use disorders (Eckerlin et al., 2016; Kimerling et al., 2010). Although PTSD is the most common diagnosis, many men do not develop PTSD. Like Mr. H., they may struggle instead with depressive or anxiety disorders. Depression may be associated with other diagnoses or with men's feelings of sadness and loss, negative beliefs about themselves and the world, physical health changes, or isolation and inactivity.

Many male survivors like Mr. T. use substances and other unsafe behaviors to manage symptoms, avoid reminders, or reaffirm their masculinity. Although this is not yet well researched, anecdotally male survivors of MSA anecdotally may also struggle with compulsive behaviors, hypersexual behaviors, excessive work or exercise, gambling, and disordered eating, like other male survivors of sexual abuse (Romano & De Luca, 2001). Substance use at the time of an assault is not uncommon (United States Department of Defense, 2004, 2005) and may result in additional barriers to recovery. For example, Mr. T. blamed himself for the rape and thought it would not have happened if he had been sober. Many men go on to develop longer-term problems with alcohol and substance use disorders and impulse control disorders (Eckerlin et al., 2016; Hahn, Tirabassi, Simons, & Simons, 2015). In our clinical experience, substance use may also be associated with increased risk-taking, decreased ability to make safe decisions, and increased risk for retraumatization, further complicating recovery.

Studies of both female and male MSA survivors also find other associated diagnoses and concerns. These include increased rates of dissociative disorders, eating disorders, suicide attempts, and personality disorders (Kimerling, Gima, Smith, Street, & Frayne, 2007). Research seldom focuses on men, but some data suggest that the association between MSA and mental health concerns may be even stronger in men (Street et al., 2007). For example, men in residential treatment for MSA have higher levels of PTSD symptoms and more severe personality pathology than women; they also show greater struggles with behavioral control and relationships (O'Brien, Gaher, Pope, & Smiley, 2008).

Male survivors also report numerous physical health complaints. These include sequelae from injuries during the MSA, although many men do not suffer major injuries at the time. They also appear to suffer from chronic health problems such as pulmonary and liver diseases, increased somatic symptoms, and poorer reported physical health (Kimerling et al., 2007; Morris et al., 2014; Street et al., 2008). These medical needs are further complicated by many men's understandable anxieties about medical procedures and encounters, particularly those that involve power differentials and physical contact (e.g., Dougall & Fiske, 2009).[5] For example, Mr. H. once avoided medical appointments altogether for ten years.

Other demographic factors are also relevant to the experience of MSA. A recent study found that men who experienced MSA were more likely to be younger, have less education, and be a past or current smoker than men who did not (Millegan, Wang, LeardMann, Miletich, & Street, 2016). MSA also had negative occupational and health outcomes for men in that study, even beyond their time in the military; 60% noted they left or were discharged earlier than planned after MSA experiences, and 76% reported that they were unemployed or disabled at the time (Millegan et al., 2016).

Common themes in recovery

Many male survivors tend to struggle with several key themes in their recovery. These are often a focus of treatment and are sometimes acted out there, too (see Gartner, 1997, 1999). This section reviews some themes identified by other authors and in our own work, though it is not exhaustive. We view these as understandable reactions that nonetheless can be worked through or overcome. In addition, men may struggle with different combinations of these, so providers should ask rather than assume how they affect clients.

The impact of rape myths. To understand the key themes, one must first understand male rape myths and their impact on Service Members. Men grow up inundated by powerful messages about what it means to be a man. Myths about what rape is and is not, who it happens to, and what it means are also common (Bell et al., 2014; Turchik & Edwards, 2012). These messages, though false, create significant challenges for men, particularly when amplified by military ideals (Hunter, 2007; O'Brien, Keith, & Shoemaker, 2015). As Turchik and Edwards (2012) note, "rape myths not only perpetuate the occurrence of sexual violence . . . but also serve to conceal and minimize male rape, which has devastating consequences for the male victim" (p. 213). Rape myths are associated with greater blame of male survivors than female

5 Editor's note: See Chapter 3 by Spinelli in the companion volume to this one, *Understanding the Sexual Betrayal of Boys and Men: The Trauma of Sexual Abuse*, for discussion of male survivors' difficulties addressing medical problems.

survivors; people also make more assumptions about men, such as that they must be gay or somehow enjoyed or wanted the experience (Rosenstein, 2015; Turchik & Edwards, 2012).

Several of these myths are particularly relevant for men who experience MSA. Many struggle with the myth, "*Men don't get raped.*" This myth implies that male rape never happens and that men should be able to fight off perpetrators; it also implies that men are weak, and in some ways not men at all, if they are assaulted (Coxell & King, 2010; O'Brien et al., 2015). Male rape violates a fundamental view of manhood, even more so for men trained as "warriors." This myth also implies an almost superhuman expectation of men being able to take control of any hostile situation and prevent trauma. In fact, men of all sizes, strengths, and ability levels can be sexually assaulted.

The myth, "*Male rape is about homosexuality,*" complicates recovery for many men. It suggests that only gay men are raped, only gay men commit rape, and rape by other men may even "make" men gay (O'Brien et al., 2015). Heterosexual men often struggle with confusion and fear about this. A related myth, "*Gay/bisexual men can't be raped by men,*" conflates sexual orientation with the concept of consent and can cause significant harm to gay and bisexual men. Like Mr. H., gay and bisexual men may blame themselves because of their sexual orientation or face others who doubt their report that the MSA was non-consensual. They may have been intentionally victimized or harassed for their sexual orientation, for being perceived as targets less likely to file a report, or for not conforming to hypermasculine, heterosexual norms (Alford & Lee, 2016; Burks, 2011). In fact, both women and men of all sexual orientations can be perpetrators, and men and women of all sexual orientations experience MSA. More importantly, no factors about the experience, including automatic physical reactions such as an erection or ejaculation, change or mean anything about survivors' sexual orientation.

The myths, "*(Real) men handle things on their own*" and "*Men are less affected by rape than women,*" discourage men from telling anyone or seeking treatment (Polusny & Murdoch, 2005). Both actions involve witnesses to their vulnerability and may make them feel even more ashamed. Men influenced by these myths may adopt hypermasculine or aggressive behaviors or physical ways of coping, such as intense exercise, to try to erase any signs of weakness or effects of MSA. In fact, evidence suggests that men may be even more affected by MSA than women and that men can benefit from support and treatment (Martin et al., 2000).

The myth, "*Men can't be raped by women*," causes significant problems for men with female perpetrators. This may be particularly true for men in the military, where masculine strength is prized and women may be considered the "weaker" gender (Bell et al., 2014; Hunter, 2007; O'Brien et al., 2015). Men with female perpetrators may have increased doubt or self-blame and may avoid reporting due to fears they won't be believed or will be accused of being "gay" for not "enjoying" the experience. In fact, women can be perpetrators, too, and men can have sexual experiences with women to which they did not consent.

Masculinity concerns. Perhaps the most fundamental concern for male survivors of MSA relates to masculinity. Sexual trauma and abuse violate men's most basic view of themselves and what it means to be a man. This may be especially true for military men (Bell et al., 2014). Men struggling with such a deep identity disturbance and disconnection from the self may neglect or abuse themselves. Alternatively, they may try to "prove" or regain their manhood through hypermasculine and aggressive behaviors (Lisak, 1994; O'Brien et al., 2015). Emotional restriction or suppression, hypersexual behavior, or glorifying prior or current violence are other ways men prove or reclaim their manhood. These behaviors can also emerge in both individual and group therapies.

Sexual orientation concerns. Men also commonly struggle with their sexual orientation after MSA. For example, they may get an erection or ejaculate automatically in response to physical stimulation (e.g., Bullock & Beckson, 2011; Eckerlin et al., 2016; Morris et al., 2014). This may be one of the most deeply shameful and hidden aspects of the experience. Some men see it as a betrayal by their own bodies. Some assume that it must mean they "somehow" enjoyed or wanted it. Confusion and fear associated with these concerns can make sex, relationships, and self-acceptance incredibly difficult.

Sexual functioning concerns. Many male survivors have persistent sexual functioning concerns, often for years after MSA. They commonly struggle with erectile dysfunction, ejaculation concerns, and anxiety about or a lack of interest in sexual intimacy (Briere & Runtz, 1989; Eckerlin et al., 2016; Turchik et al., 2012).[6] Alternatively, they may cope or reaffirm

6 Editor's note: See Chapter 12 by Kort in the companion volume to this one, *Understanding the Sexual Betrayal of Boys and Men: The Trauma of Sexual Abuse*, for discussion of sexually abused men's struggles about sexuality.

their masculinity through risky or compulsive sexual behaviors, which can lead to shame, relationship dysfunction, and sexual health risks (Bell et al., 2014; Elliott, Mok, & Briere, 2004). Some men may require more targeted treatment (Crowder & Hawkings, 1995; Maltz, 2012) with a sex therapy professional.

Anger and betrayal. Male survivors struggle with varying degrees of anger and a sense of betrayal. Lisak (1994) and Walker, Archer, and Davies (2005) identified several ways that anger manifests for male survivors of sexual abuse, and men who experienced MSA report similar struggles. For some, anger covers or distracts from anxiety or shame. For others, it may emerge as fury at potential betrayals of trust. Anger can also manifest in revenge fantasies or aggression (Lisak, 1994), or hypervigilance for future betrayal or abandonment. Some men try to suppress anger and fear its expression, or they insist that they must vent all distress or else explode. For others, anger at their perpetrators, which can rarely if ever be satisfied, becomes directed at others, such as strangers, therapists, or loved ones (Lisak, 1994).

Shame and self-blame. Feelings of shame, humiliation, and disgust haunt many survivors (Morris et al., 2014). These are understandable reactions, and rape myths may intensify them for male survivors. Men who experienced MSA may think they should have been able to stop it due to stereotypes that men should be strong enough to defend themselves and always have power in sexual encounters. In addition, men (about 60% in some reports) can exhibit a tonic immobility response during sexual assault. Coxell and King (2010) compare this freeze-like response to a defense in which captured prey become immobile instead of struggling, which may aid in escape if a predator assumes it is dead/unconscious. This type of response violates hypermasculine norms and can cause increased confusion, self-blame, and shame. Men may also struggle with "insufficient justification" guilt (O'Brien et al., 2015), which involves thoughts that one's actions during a trauma were not justified or that different actions should have been taken (Kubany & Watson, 2003; O'Brien et al., 2015). Finally, men may feel ashamed about how they reacted after the MSA or for being affected by it at all.

Sadness and loss. Like other male survivors (Lisak, 1994), many men who experienced MSA feel deep sadness, often for years or even decades. Sometimes this is associated with an inability to feel emotions like love or happiness. Alternatively, men may fear and deny such emotions because they think that danger or loss will follow or that they do not deserve them. For men like Mr. H., that sadness may be associated with a profound sense of loss: of security, trust, identity, and the career and future they had wanted. This may be particularly true for those who leave the military after MSA or are forced to leave due to emotional and behavioral struggles in its wake (Hunter, 2007).

Power and control. MSA often involves abuses of power and control. Men may struggle with this, particularly as warriors trained to always maintain both. Superior officers may have been the perpetrators, or someone may have used a disclosure of MSA against them, such as to coerce men into further victimization or being discharged against their will. They may thus expect others to coerce, manipulate, or hurt them. This includes clinicians due to the power they hold over diagnoses, medications, referrals, or medical procedures. Men may need clear explanations of confidentiality policies and regular discussions of how progress notes are written as a result. Mr. T. angrily viewed all VA clinicians as part of the government and military system, despite the VA being an entirely separate organization. Some men react strongly when feeling unheard or unsupported, especially if they needed help or support after the MSA and did not receive it. Some men try to regain a sense of control through isolation, domination, or hypermasculine behaviors.

Isolation and avoidance. Most men who experience MSA never hear about male sexual abuse and assault, so they feel alone in their recovery. In our experience, many men bear the burden in silence for years, not sharing it with family, friends, or partners. Some struggle with getting close to anyone. They may be especially private or avoid social activities because they fear that others will suspect or ask about the MSA or will not believe them if they tell. Paradoxically, this may increase their isolation and loneliness.

Trust and relationships. Along with isolation and avoidance, many men struggle with trust and relationships (Valente & Wight, 2007). The betrayal associated with MSA makes it challenging to trust others or feel comfortable with intimacy (Morris et al., 2014). It can be difficult to allow anyone to be close or to feel close to others, even partners, children, or family members. Men who experienced MSA often place heavy emphasis on confidentiality and secrecy, avoiding emotional intimacy, and maintaining emotional control. Like Mr. T., they may participate in treatment for years without disclosing the MSA, and may disappear from treatment when discussions of it seem likely. They may have conflicts in relationships with authority figures and at work (Stander & Thomsen, 2016), particularly if perpetrators were commanding officers or if the military hierarchy was perceived as unhelpful or even punishing of a survivor's reports.

Treatment and recovery

There are many treatment approaches and resources for men who experienced MSA. Regardless of the approach, we strongly recommend the principles of trauma-sensitive care as a foundation for clinicians (Substance Abuse and Mental Health Services Administration, 2014). First and foremost, allow choice and control for clients in all aspects of treatment whenever possible. This includes helping men identify their own individualized goals rather than assuming or dictating what those goals should be. Treatment should incorporate a recovery model that identifies men's strengths and works toward increasing quality of life, rather than just decreasing symptoms. This may help men to feel empowered and be more actively engaged in treatment. Careful assessment of diagnoses, behaviors, and beliefs about the MSA, the self, and the world is also critical to guide identification of appropriate treatments.

General treatment perspectives and approaches. Several authors have described the dynamics and themes of therapy with male survivors, and we strongly encourage review of their work, which is also relevant for men who experienced MSA. For example, Gartner (1997, 1999, 2014) has written extensively about the challenges and rewards for both clients and therapists in psychoanalytic and psychodynamic treatment of men abused as boys. Other transdiagnostic approaches can also inform conceptualization and treatment. Briefly, these include: the principles and themes discussed in Herman (1992), dialectical behavior therapy (Linehan, 2015; Linehan et al., 1999), acceptance and commitment therapy (Hayes, Strosahl, & Wilson, 2011), and cognitive-behavioral therapy (Beck, 2011). These treatment approaches and others can help men build skills, challenge unhelpful beliefs, learn new ways of relating and acting, and build a life worth living.

Disorder-specific treatments. Specific therapies designed to treat the mental health disorders commonly associated with MSA can help many men. For example, evidence-based, cognitive-behavioral therapies for PTSD include Prolonged Exposure (Foa, Hembree, & Rothbaum, 2007) and Cognitive Processing Therapy (Resick & Schnike, 1993), the latter of which has proven helpful for male survivors of MSA (Voelkel, Pukay-Martin, Walter, & Chard, 2015). Some men also report benefits from eye movement desensitization and reprocessing (EMDR; Shapiro & Solomon, 1995) in our experience. Exposure-based treatments for anxiety disorders can be empowering and effective. Treatments for depressive disorders such as cognitive-behavioral therapy (Beck, 2011), behavioral activation (Martell, Dimidjian, & Herman-Dunn, 2013), mindfulness-based therapy (Segal, Williams, & Teasdale, 2012), and interpersonal therapy (Klerman, Weissman, Rounsaville, & Chevron, 1984) can be effective. Motivational interviewing (Miller & Rollnick, 2013) and relapse prevention (Marlatt & Donovan, 2005) are also relevant for many survivors with substance use and behavioral health concerns. Medication management for various disorders and sleep and sexual functioning concerns can also help (Eckerlin et al., 2016).

Psychotherapy modalities and preferences. Both group and individual therapies can help, and no evidence indicates that either is superior. Some (e.g., Gartner, 1999) have argued for the value of concurrent treatment when available. Regardless, no one-size approach will fit all. Some men feel that they can only be safe in a men-only support group, while many others would drop out of treatment before doing a group. In our experience, men can benefit from group therapy if they are open to it, as they realize they are not alone. This decreases stigma and increases men's comfort with discussing MSA-related issues. Groups also create opportunities to learn to cope with triggers, as when men who had female perpetrators participate in a mixed-gender group. For Veterans, groups may help them connect with other Veterans and rebuild a sense of camaraderie and trust, though some male survivors understandably report strong distrust of other Veterans (Leskela, Dieperink, & Kok, 2001). Men also report a diverse range of preferences about provider gender (Turchik et al., 2013), gender of group members, and content and focus of treatment. Regardless of the modality, providers should give men as much control and choice as feasible about the modality, pace, and goals of treatment.

VA-specific services. It may not be widely known that Veterans who experienced MSA are generally eligible for free care through the VA. VA provides free, confidential treatment to Veterans for mental and physical health conditions related to military sexual trauma (MST). This does not depend on disability ratings or benefits, and Veterans do not need to have reported the MST or have any evidence or documentation of it to receive care. Every VA medical center also has an MST Coordinator who can help Veterans get connected and navigate the system. Veterans can access services simply by calling their local VA and asking to speak to the MST Coordinator. In addition, all Veterans seeking health care at VA are screened for MST (Hyun, Kimerling, Cronkite, McCutcheon, & Frayne, 2012), and VA policy emphasizes the importance of a gender-sensitive organization of services for both men and women. Many VA medical centers also have specialized sexual trauma treatment teams or clinicians (Allard et al., 2011).

Mr. T. and Mr. H., moving forward in recovery

After ten years of substance use treatment, Mr. T. decided to disclose the rape to his therapist. He had begun to develop some trust, as his therapist appeared to be understanding and knowledgeable about trauma. Mr. T. started Cognitive Processing Therapy for PTSD after several discussions in therapy and completed a course of treatment over six months that included relapse prevention for substance use. It was painful, and he wanted to quit sometimes, but he stuck with it. Afterward, his symptoms decreased significantly. He was then better able to work on other issues, too. Eventually, he and his therapist decided to try acceptance and commitment therapy to help him develop a sense of self that was separate from an identity as an "addict" and "victim." Over time, he defined his values and identified ways to engage in meaningful life activities. He also joined a therapy group for men who had experienced MSA at his local VA hospital, and he now participates regularly in a community-based advocacy group for men who experienced sexual trauma and abuse.

Mr. H. initially struggled to attend therapy sessions after he finally disclosed his MSA experiences, so he and his therapist began with motivational interviewing to help him clarify his goals and reasons to engage in treatment. He was terrified about discussing the experiences in detail, so he committed to a year of dialectical behavior therapy to help him build better coping skills. After that, he felt more ready to discuss and process his intense emotions and reactions in treatment. He also began to do more activities outside of sessions. Although this was never easy, he learned he could tolerate it and felt empowered. He got a steady job and eventually fell in love with a man who respected him and understood his struggles with MSA to some degree. Although there are conflicts when he feels triggered, they are able to work through them effectively. He still struggles with feelings of shame and sadness at times, but he works on it day by day.

Additional resources

There are outstanding resources and organizations that can help men who experienced MSA and clinicians who want to learn more. For example, active duty Service Members who experience MSA can contact the Safe Helpline anonymously at any time at 877-995-5247 or www.safehelpline.org/,or visit http://sapr.mil/ to learn about reporting options and care, including a specific section with information for men. In addition, male Veterans can contact their nearest VA medical center and ask to speak with the MST Coordinator. They can also visit VA's MST website (www.mentalhealth.va.gov/msthome.asp), and the Make The Connection website (maketheconnection.net) for more information. Clinicians must also understand military organization and culture, so we recommend Hunter (2007) and the Center for Deployment Psychology's military cultural competence course (http://deploymentpsych.org/online-courses/military-culture). In addition, MaleSurvivor (www.malesurvivor.org) and 1in6 (https://1in6.org/) are dedicated to empowering male survivors with hope, resources, and community. Finally, although male sexual assault and abuse are still greatly understudied topics, there are some valuable books that can help (Fradkin, 2012; Gartner, 1999, 2005; Lew, 2004, to name just a few).

Conclusions

Fradkin (2012) wrote eloquently about male survivors developing "loyalty to functionality" as part of the healing process (p. 170), a concept that can also help men who experienced MSA. For example, they may come to realize that perpetrators' acts do not define or negate their own masculinity. In addition, they may decide there is no one "right" or "real" way to be a man; it is a complex and multidimensional concept. They will hopefully discover that MSA connotes nothing about their sexual orientation, which can lead to greater self-acceptance and healthier sexual and relationship functioning. Men can also heal from anger by lessening its intensity, processing emotions behind it, and learning more constructive ways to manage it. As they move forward in their recovery, we hope men who experienced MSA realize that they are not alone and that MSA was never their fault. We also hope that they begin to recognize their own resilience, overcome self-blame and shame, and cultivate a peaceful, hopeful, and valued life.

We outlined information and resources here for clinicians, survivors, and those who support them. We tried throughout this chapter to balance a recognition of the seriousness of the crime and the often deep and lasting impact of MSA with a hopefulness about men's ability to recover. We encourage readers to actively work to raise awareness about male sexual trauma, to incorporate trauma-sensitive principles into your work and your daily life, and to remember that some of the most common reactions to trauma (ultimately) are resilience and healing (Bonanno, 2005).

References

Alford, B., & Lee, S. J. (2016). Toward complete inclusion: Lesbian, gay, bisexual, and transgender military service members after repeal of Don't Ask, Don't Tell. *Social Work, 61*(3), 257–265. doi: 10.1093/sw/sww033

Allard, C. B., Nunnink, S., Gregory, A. M., Klest, B., & Platt, M. (2011). Military sexual trauma research: A proposed agenda. *Journal of Trauma & Dissociation, 12*(3), 324–345. doi: http://www.tandfonline.com/doi/abs/10.1080/15299732.2011.542609

Beck, J. S. (2011). *Cognitive behavior therapy: Basics and beyond* (2nd Ed.). New York, NY: Guilford.

Bell, M. E., Turchik, J. A., & Karpenko, J. A. (2014). Impact of gender on reactions to military sexual assault and harassment. *Health & Social Work, 39*(1), 25–33. doi: 10.1093/hsw/hlu004

Bonanno, G. A. (2005). Resilience in the face of potential trauma. *Current Directions in Psychological Science, 14*(3), 135–138. doi: http://dx.doi.org/10.1111/j.0963-7214.2005.00347.x

Briere, J. N., & Runtz, M. G. (1989). The Trauma Symptom Checklist (TSC-33): Early data on a new scale. *Journal of Interpersonal Violence, 4*, 151–163. doi: http://dx.doi.org/10.1177/088626089004002002

Bullock, C. M., & Beckson, M. (2011). Male victims of sexual assault: Phenomenology, psychology, physiology. *Journal of the American Academy of Psychiatry and the Law Online, 39*(2), 197–205.

Burgess, A. W., Slattery, D. M., & Herlihy, P. A. (2013). Military sexual trauma: A silent syndrome. *Journal of Psychosocial Nursing and Mental Health Services, 51*(2), 20–26. doi: 10.3928/02793695-20130109-03

Burks, D. J. (2011). Lesbian, gay, and bisexual victimization in the military: An unintended consequence of "Don't Ask, Don't Tell"? *American Psychologist, 66*(7), 604–613. doi: http://dx.doi.org/10.1037/a0024609

Coxell, A. W., & King, M. B. (2010). Adult male rape and sexual assault: Prevalence, re-victimisation and the tonic immobility response. *Sexual & Relationship Therapy, 25*(4), 372–379. doi: 10.1080/14681991003747430

Crowder, A., & Hawkings, R. (1995). *Opening the door: A treatment model for therapy with male survivors of sexual abuse*. New York, NY: Brunner/Mazel.

Dougall, A., & Fiske, J. (2009). Surviving child sexual abuse: The relevance to dental practice. *Dental Update, 36*(5), 294–296.

Eckerlin, D. M., Kovalesky, A., & Jakupcak, M. (2016). Military sexual trauma in male service members. *American Journal of Nursing, 116*(9), pages unavailable. doi: 10.1097/01.NAJ.0000494690.55746.d9

Elliott, D. M., Mok, D. S., & Briere, J. (2004). Adult sexual assault: Prevalence, symptomatology, and sex differences in general populations. *Journal of Traumatic Stress, 17*(3), 203–211. doi: http://dx.doi.org/10.1023/b:jots.0000029263.11104.23

Ferguson, C. T. (2008). Caring for sexual assault patients in the military: Past, present, and future. *Journal of Forensic Nursing, 4*(4), 190–198. doi: 10.1111/j.1939-3938.2008.00033.x

Foa, E. B., Hembree, E. A., & Rothbaum, B. O. (2007). *Prolonged exposure therapy for PTSD: Emotional processing of traumatic experiences (therapist guide)*. Oxford: Oxford University Press.

Fradkin, H. (2012). *Joining forces: Empowering male survivors to thrive*. Carlsbad, CA: Hay House.

Gartner, R. B. (1997). Considerations in the psychoanalytic treatment of men who were sexually abused as children. *Psychoanalytic Psychology, 14*(1), 13–41. doi: http://dx.doi.org/10.1037/h0079722

Gartner, R. B. (1999). *Betrayed as boys: Psychodynamic treatment of sexually abused men*. New York, NY: Guilford.

Gartner, R. B. (2005). *Beyond betrayal: Taking charge of your life after boyhood sexual abuse*. Hoboken, NJ: Wiley.

Gartner, R. B. (2014). Trauma and countertrauma, resilience and counter-resilience. *Contemporary Psychoanalysis, 50*(4), 609–626. doi: DOI:10.1080/00107530.2014.945069

Hahn, A. M., Tirabassi, C. K., Simons, R. M., & Simons, J. S. (2015). Military sexual trauma, combat exposure, and negative urgency as independent predictors of PTSD and subsequent alcohol problems among OEF/OIF veterans. *Psychological Services, 12*(4), 378–383. doi: http://dx.doi.org/10.1037/ser0000060

Hayes, S. C., Strosahl, K. D., & Wilson, K. G. (2011). *Acceptance and commitment therapy: The process and practice of mindful change* (2nd Ed.). New York, NY: Guilford.

Herman, J. L. (1992). *Trauma and recovery: The aftermath of terror from domestic abuse to political terror*. New York, NY: Basic Books.

Hoyt, T., Klosterman Rielage, J., & Williams, L. F. (2011). Military sexual trauma in men: A review of reported rates. *Journal of Trauma & Dissociation, 12*(3), 244–260. doi: http://dx.doi.org/10.1080/15299732.2011.542612

Hunter, M. (2007). *Honor betrayed: Sexual abuse in America's military*. Fort Lee, NJ: Barricade Books.

Hyun, J. K., Kimerling, R., Cronkite, R. C., McCutcheon, S., & Frayne, S. M. (2012). Organizational factors associated with screening for military sexual trauma. *Women's Health Issues, 22*(2), 209–215. doi: 10.1016/j.whi.2011.09.001

Kimerling, R., Gima, K., Smith, M. W., Street, A., & Frayne, S. (2007). The Veterans Health Administration and military sexual trauma. *American Journal of Public Health, 97*(12), 2160–2166. doi: http://dx.doi.org/10 .2105/AJPH.2006.092999

Kimerling, R., Street, A., Pavao, J., Smith, M., Cronkite, R., Tyson, H., & Frayne, S. (2010). Military-related sexual trauma among Veterans Health Administration patients returning from Afghanistan and Iraq. *American Journal of Public Health, 100*(8), 1409–1412. doi: 10.2105/ AJPH.2009.171793

Klerman, G. L., Weissman, M. M., Rounsaville, B. J., & Chevron, E. S. (1984). *Interpersonal psychotherapy of depression*. New York, NY: Rowman & Littlefield.

Kubany, E. S., & Watson, S. (2003). Guilt: An elaboration of a multidimensional model. The *Psychological Record, 53*(1), 51–90.

Leskela, J., Dieperink, M., & Kok, C. J. (2001). Group treatment with sexually assaulted male veterans: A year in review. *Group, 25*(4), 303–319. doi: 10.1023/A:1014393032249

Lew, M. (2004). *Victims no longer: The classic guide for men recovering from sexual child abuse* (2nd Ed.). New York, NY: HarperCollins.

Linehan, M. M. (2015). *Cognitive-behavioral treatment for borderline personality disorder* (2nd Ed.). New York, NY: Guilford.

Linehan, M. M., Schmidt, H., Dimeff, L. A., Craft, J. C., Kanter, J., & Comtois, K. A. (1999). Dialectical Behavior Therapy for patients with borderline personality disorder and drug-dependence. *The American Journal on Addictions, 8*(4), 279–292. doi: http://dx.doi.org/10.1080/105504999305686

Lisak, D. (1994). The psychological impact of sexual abuse: Content analysis of interviews with male survivors. *Journal of Traumatic Stress, 7*(4), 525–548. doi: http://dx.doi.org/10.1002/jts.2490070403

Maltz, W. (2012). *The sexual healing journey: A guide for survivors of sexual abuse* (3rd Rev. Ed.). New York, NY: William Morrow.

Manning, F. J. (1994). Morale and cohesion in military psychiatry. In F. D. Jones, L. R. Sparacino, V. L. Wilcox, & J. M. Rothberg (Eds.), *Textbook of military medicine, Part I: Military psychiatry: Preparing in peace for war* (pp. 2–18). Falls Church, VA: U.S. Department of the Army, Office of the Surgeon General. Retrieved from https://ke.army.mil/bordeninstitute/published_volumes/military_psychiatry/MPch1.pdf.

Marlatt, G. A., & Donovan, D. M. (2005). *Relapse prevention: Maintenance strategies in the treatment of addictive behaviors* (2nd Ed.). New York, NY: Guilford.

Martell, C. R., Dimidjian, S., & Herman-Dunn, R. (2013). *Behavioral activation for depression: A clinician's guide*. New York, NY: Guilford.

Martin, L., Rosen, L. N., Durand, D. B., Knudson, K. H., & Stretch, R. H. (2000). Psychological and physical health effects of sexual assaults and nonsexual traumas among male and female United States Army soldiers. *Behavioral Medicine, 26*(1), 23–33. doi: http://dx.doi.org/10.1080/08964280009595750

Marx, B. P., & Sloan, D. M. (2002). The role of emotion in the psychological functioning of adult survivors of childhood sexual abuse. *Behavior Therapy, 33*(4), 563–577. doi: 10.1016/S0005-7894(02)80017-X

Millegan, J., Wang, L., LeardMann, C. A., Miletich, D., & Street, A. E. (2016). Sexual trauma and adverse health and occupational outcomes among men serving in the U.S. Military. *Journal of Traumatic Stress, 29*(2), 132–140. doi: 10.1002/jts.22081

Miller, W. R. & Rollnick, S. (2013). *Motivational interviewing: Helping people change* (3rd Ed.). New York, NY: Guilford.

Morral, A., Gore, K., Jaycox, L., Schell, T., Bicksler, B., Farris, C., . . . Williams, K. (2016). Sexual assault and sexual harassment in the US military: Volume 2. Estimates for Department of Defense Service Members from the 2014 RAND Military Workplace Study. Santa Monica, CA: RAND Corporation. Retrieved from www.rand.org/content/dam/rand/pubs/research_reports/RR800/RR870z2-1/RAND_RR870z2-1.pdf.

Morral, A., Gore, K., Schell, T., Jaycox, L., Dastidar, M., Farris, C., . . . Williams, K. (2014). Sexual assault and sexual harassment in the US Military: Top-line estimates for active-duty Service Members from the 2014 RAND Military Workplace Study. Santa Monica, CA: RAND Corporation. Retrieved from http://sapr.mil/public/docs/reports/FY14_POTUS/FY14_DoD_Report_to_POTUS_Annex_1_RAND.pdf.

Morris, E. E., Smith, J. C., Farooqui, S. Y., & Surís, A. M. (2014). Unseen battles: The recognition, assessment, and treatment issues of men with military sexual trauma (MST). *Trauma, Violence, & Abuse, 15*(2), 94–101. doi: 10.1177/1524838013511540

O'Brien, C., Gaher, R. M., Pope, C., & Smiley, P. (2008). Difficulty identifying feelings predicts the persistence of trauma symptoms in a sample of veterans who experienced military sexual trauma. *Journal of Nervous and Mental Disease, 196*(3), 252–255. doi: http://dx.doi.org/10.1097/nmd.0b013e318166397d

O'Brien, C., Keith, J., & Shoemaker, L. (2015). Don't tell: Military culture and male rape. *Psychological Services, 12*(4), 357–365. doi: http://dx.doi.org/10.1037/ser0000049

Patterson, D., Greeson, M., & Campbell, R. (2009). Understanding rape survivors' decisions not to seek help from formal social systems. *Health & Social Work, 34*(2), 127–136. doi: 10.1093/hsw/34.2.127

Polusny, M. A., & Murdoch, M. (2005). Sexual assault among male veterans. *Psychiatric Times, 22*(4), 34–38.

Resick, P. A., & Schnike, M. K. (1993). *Cognitive processing therapy for rape victims: A treatment manual.* Newbury Park, CA: Sage.

Romano, E., & De Luca, R. V. (2001). Male sexual abuse: A review of effects, abuse characteristics, and links with later psychological functioning. *Aggression and Violent Behavior, 6*(1), 55–78. doi: http://dx.doi.org/10.1016/S1359-1789(99)00011-7

Rosenstein, J. E. (2015). Military sexual assault prevention and male rape myth acceptance. *Military Behavioral Health, 3*(4), 207–211. doi: 10.1080/21635781.2015.1038404

Schry, A. R., Hibberd, R., Wagner, H. R., Turchik, J. A., Kimbrel, N. A., Wong, M., . . . Brancu, M. (2015). Functional correlates of military sexual assault in male veterans. *Psychological Services, 12*(4), 384–393. doi: http://dx.doi.org/10.1037/ser0000053

Segal, Z. V., Williams, J. M. G., & Teasdale, J. D. (2012). *Mindfulness-based cognitive therapy for depression.* New York, NY: Guilford.

Shapiro, F., & Solomon, R. M. (1995). *Eye movement desensitization and reprocessing.* Hoboken, NJ: Wiley.

Stander, V. A., & Thomsen, C. J. (2016). Sexual harassment and assault in the U.S. military: A review of policy and research trends. *Military Medicine, 181*(1S), 20–27. doi: 10.7205/MILMED-D-15-00336

Stemple, L., & Meyer, I. H. (2014). The sexual victimization of men in America: New data challenge old assumptions. *American Journal of Public Health, 104*(6), e19–e26. doi: http://dx.doi.org/10.2105/ajph.2014.301946

Stiehm, J. H. (1992). Managing the military homosexual exclusion policy: Text and subtext. *University of Miami Law Review, 46*, 685–710.

Street, A. E., Gradus, J. L., Stafford, J., & Kelly, K. (2007). Gender differences in experiences of sexual harassment: Data from a male-dominated environment. *Journal of Consulting and Clinical Psychology, 75*(3), 464–474. doi: http://psycnet.apa.org/doi/10.1037/0022-006X.75.3.464

Street, A. E., Stafford, J., Mahan, C. M., & Hendricks, A. (2008). Sexual harassment and assault experienced by reservists during military service: Prevalence and health correlates. *Journal of Rehabilitation Research and Development, 45*(3), 409–420. doi: 10.1682/JRRD.2007.06.0088

Substance Abuse and Mental Health Services Administration. (2014). *Trauma-informed care in behavioral health services: Treatment improvement protocol (TIP) Series 57*. HHS Publication No. (SMA) 13-4801. Rockville, MD: Author.

Turchik, J. A., & Edwards, K. M. (2012). Myths about male rape: A literature review. *Psychology of Men & Masculinity, 13*(2), 211–226. doi: http://dx.doi.org/10.1037/a0023207

Turchik, J. A., McLean, C., Rafie, S., Hoyt, T., Rosen, C. S., & Kimerling, R. (2013). Perceived barriers to care and provider gender preferences among veteran men who have experienced military sexual trauma: A qualitative analysis. *Psychological Services, 10*(2), 213–222. doi: http://dx.doi.org/10.1037/a0029959

Turchik, J., Pavao, J., Nazarian, D., Iqbal, S., McLean, C., & Kimerling, R. (2012). Sexually transmitted infections and sexual dysfunctions among newly returned veterans with and without military sexual trauma. *International Journal of Sexual Health, 24*, 45–59. doi:10.1080/19317611.2011.639592

Turchik, J. A., & Wilson, S. M. (2010). Sexual assault in the U.S. military: A review of the literature and recommendations for the future. *Aggression and Violent Behavior, 15*, 267–277. doi:10.1016/j.avb.2010.01.005

United States Department of Defense. (2004). Task force report on care for victims of sexual assault. Washington, DC: Author. Retrieved from www.sapr.mil/public/docs/reports/task-force-report-for-care-of-victims-of-sa-2004.pdf.

United States Department of Defense. (2005). Report of the defense task force on sexual harassment and violence at the military service academics. Washington, DC: Author. Retrieved from www.sapr.mil/public/docs/research/high_gpo_rrc_tx.pdf.

United States Department of Veterans Affairs. (2016). *Military sexual trauma*. Retrieved from www.mentalhealth.va.gov/msthome.asp.

Valente, S., & Wight, C. (2007). Military sexual trauma: Violence and sexual abuse. *Military Medicine, 172*(3), 259–265. doi: http://dx.doi.org/10.7205/MILMED.172.3.259

Voelkel, E., Pukay-Martin, N. D., Walter, K. H., & Chard, K. M. (2015). Effectiveness of Cognitive Processing Therapy for male and female US

Veterans with and without military sexual trauma. *Journal of Traumatic Stress, 28*(3), 174–182. doi: 10.1002/jts.22006

Walker, J., Archer, J., & Davies, M. (2005). Effects of rape on men: A descriptive analysis. *Archives of Sexual Behavior, 34*(1), 69–80. doi: 10.1007/s10508-005-1001-0

Part II

Focused treatments

Chapter 5

Empowering male survivors to heal through community and peer connections

Howard Fradkin and Jim Struve

Introduction

We have long advocated empowerment as a crucial component of the healing process for male survivors of sexual trauma. We further believe that empowerment is facilitated by connection with other survivors. With the expansion of grassroots services for male survivors and the growth of the Internet, networking amongst male survivor peers is becoming more accessible. In this chapter, we will review research that demonstrates that the effects of individual psychotherapy can be amplified when clients risk sharing their recovery with peers.

We have found that when male survivors interact with peers in a group setting, there are opportunities to grow beyond the isolation that often characterizes their lives. One example of such a group program is the Weekends of Recovery (WOR) program, sponsored by the non-profit organization MaleSurvivor.org.

The WOR program creates an effective healing milieu in which male survivors can develop healthy peer relationships and take steps toward self-empowerment. We have co-chaired these three-day experiential group events for the past 15 years. Feedback from participants in the weekends affirms our premise that group experiences provide an invaluable adjunct to psychotherapy. Male survivors report their healing journey is exponentially more transformative when contact with other survivors grows into ongoing healthy peer networking (Struve & Fradkin, 2014).

We will begin with a brief overview about the philosophy of our program. We will then review some research about the effectiveness of peer group support that has informed how we designed our program. We will then discuss the evolution and growth of our WOR program, elaborate the design of these events, identify special issues with which we have grappled, and assess the program's impact on the healing process for WOR alumni.

The WOR program philosophy

The WORs originated in 2001 to provide an additional service to assist the healing process for adult male survivors who have experienced any kind of sexual trauma as children and/or adults and/or who have witnessed the sexual victimization of others. The weekends are designed to co-create, with the participants, a safe environment in order to reduce isolation, discover the benefits of engaging in recovery while in the company of other male survivors, and acquire recovery tools they can use when they return home. The weekends are highly structured and are conducted with adherence to the highest professional standards. They were conceived as an adjunct to psychotherapy, using a variety of modalities and interventions to meet the needs of a wide variety of participants.

The programmatic goal of the WOR is to co-create an environment safe enough that each man feels sufficiently secure being vulnerable that he can tell his story and create emotional bonds with other male survivors that may endure far beyond the weekend. Safety is enhanced by a small client-to-staff ratio, 3.5:1. The program includes participation of both male and female facilitators. Including women facilitators provides an opportunity for men who were victimized by a female perpetrator to be able to confront the complexity of safety issues in the presence of women in positions of power and authority. This opportunity to have a different and healing experience with a woman in authority is a significant benefit to these men. On the other hand, for men who have only felt safe talking to women, having safe women facilitators present at the weekend helps them expand their comfort zone to include some men as well.

Our team shares the philosophy that healing from sexual trauma is amplified when survivors join together, sharing and witnessing each other's strengths, challenges, and successes. Inviting diverse participants has been an underlying strategy, as men from all walks of life benefit from finding commonalities while having their differences honored.

As this volume and its companion volume, *Understanding the Sexual Betrayal of Boys and Men: The Trauma of Sexual Abuse*, demonstrate, there are a variety of therapeutic interventions that are effective for working with male survivors. A number of them provide a critical foundation for our work.

Research on the effect of peer group support

There is significant research suggesting that interactions with peers is effective in addressing many mental health challenges, particularly in changing self-defeating attitudes and improving health and overall achievement. For example, Kyrouz and Humphreys (2002) demonstrate value from participation in community programs and support groups for clients who struggle with intense emotional issues such as shame. This same research reports an increased sense of empowerment and resolution of shame from group membership. In another study (Edmunson, Bedell, Archer, & Gordon, 1982), a ten-month patient-led social network enhancement group with former psychiatric patients successfully empowered 53% of the patients to function with no contact with the mental health system. For those patients who still needed mental health assistance, half did not need repeat hospitalization and those who did had much shorter average hospital stays (7 days versus 25 days).

A survey (Galanter, 1988) of 356 members of Recovery, Inc., (a mental health self-help group now known as Recovery International) found that, when compared with a community sample, participants in the group had very low re-hospitalization rates (8% of group leaders and 7% of recent members). Another study by Recovery, Inc. reported that individuals who participated in self-help groups for two years experienced no more anxiety than the general population (Raiff, 1984). Similar results of decreased hospitalization and increased coping ability were found in two other studies of self-help groups (Kennedy, 1989; Kurtz, 1988). In yet another study, involving 869 participants, seven randomized controlled trials of peer support versus usual care for depression found that peer support interventions were superior to usual care in reducing depressive symptoms (Pfeiffer, Heisler, Piette, Rogers, & Valenstein, 2011). Finally, a guided peer support group for people with psychosis demonstrated a positive effect on increasing their social support, self-efficacy, and the quality of their life as compared to those who did not participate in the group (Castelein et al., 2008).

Both authors of this chapter have worked with individuals grappling with HIV/AIDS. One author previously worked as a facilitator in a Healing Weekend for individuals from this population. When offered the opportunity to participate in such a weekend retreat, many were able to leave their isolation behind and find ways to build support for themselves. Their group experience allowed them to learn new skills for coping with the profound challenges they faced psychologically and physically. Self-help groups such as Alcoholics Anonymous (AA) and Narcotics Anonymous (NA) have also been found to be key in HIV risk reduction for high-risk injection drug users (Sibthorpe, Fleming, Tesselaar, & Gould, 1994).

Twelve-step groups have helped vast numbers of people facing challenges of various forms of addiction, compulsive behaviors, and emotional struggles. For example, attendance at NA has been shown to help drug-addicted members stay sober, feel less anxiety, and acquire more self-esteem (Christo & Sutton, 1994). A meta-analysis of more than 50 studies found that membership in AA helped members reduce physical symptoms and improve psychological adjustment (Emrick et al., 1993). A 1994 study (Humphreys, Mavis, & Stoffelmayr) reported that African American patients who participated in NA and AA groups, as compared with patients who did not attend those support groups, showed significantly more improvements over 12 months in six problem areas: employment, alcohol, drug, legal, psychological, and family. A similar study found that male substance abuse patients who participated in self-help groups after treatment significantly reduced their frequency of alcohol and cocaine use in a seven-month follow-up (McKay et al., 1994). In the authors' experience and in the research (Hartman, Ho, Arbour, Hambley, & Lawson, 2012), participation in 12-step meetings has also been found to be a vital component of recovery for men who are struggling with sex addiction. The clinical experiences of the authors similarly corroborates that many sex-addicted clients who are also male survivors report that connecting with others with similar histories of sexual victimization helps them in reducing their shame.

One of the most healing aspects of attending and participating in this type of group is finding others with similar struggles, thereby being inspired by another's successes in facing challenges. Participants often discover that connecting and reaching out for support empowers them to embrace hope, whereas isolation is a less effective strategy.

Male military personnel returning from the battlefield with the scars of PTSD and its accompanying shame have found that joining a group where they can be open about their struggles and find hope is healing (van der Kolk, 2014). The National Center for PTSD advocates participation in peer groups to help people feel more comfortable talking about their trauma and cope with memories and difficult emotions. In addition, they suggest that connecting with other people can help you feel better (Sloan & Beck, 2016).

Designing peer support for male sexual trauma survivors

Male survivors of sexual trauma often feel great shame about the abuse done to them, and often suffer in silence. They endure a range of psychological problems and are often unaware that others are suffering with similar problems and challenges. Further, they often feel very reticent to reach out for support (Fradkin, 2012a).

The WOR program seeks to incorporate 11 curative factors of group treatment articulated by Yalom (1995):

1. *instilling a sense of hope*: often male survivors enter their healing journey with a great sense of hopelessness;
2. *universality*: a profound sense of inclusion may replace feelings of seclusion when a survivor has an opportunity to share with and listen to other male survivors;
3. *imparting of information*: debunking myths, which is especially important for male survivors, who frequently have distortions about the common dynamics of their own sexual victimization;
4. *altruism*: finding they can help other men despite believing no one could benefit from their struggles;
5. *corrective recapitulation of the primary family group*: participants incorporate learnings more deeply when awareness emerges from safe and ethical re-creations of past dynamics and struggles that have different endings within the corrective milieu;
6. *development of socializing techniques*: as the participants risk connection;
7. *imitative behaviors*: as participants mirror successful strategies used by their peers;
8. *direct advice*: given as suggestions of new possibilities to take further steps in the healing process;
9. *catharsis*: permitting themselves to be vulnerable and share feelings on a deep emotional level;
10. *interpersonal learning*: experimenting with new behaviors and seeing the effect on themselves and their peers; and
11. *existential factors*: as participants explore the realities of the trauma(s) of what was done to them.

These core philosophies are well articulated by a WOR alumnus, John:[1]

> The WOR changed my life by providing me ways to express my pain, shame, grief, helplessness, and anger within a compassionate, loving group. Knowing I was not alone . . . helped give me strength as I witnessed others challenge themselves. I found courage and safety to move beyond barriers within comfortable parameters. The weekend gave me hope that I was not defined by my abuse. I had nothing to be ashamed of; it encouraged me to heal and grow. I can honestly say I would not be who I am today without WOR. You provided me with the tools and platform to do that.

Goals of a WOR

The Weekends of Recovery strive to provide an opportunity for male survivors:

1 to experience a safe environment in which participants can discover they are not alone;
2 to co-create and experience safety with other survivors;
3 to share their inner pain, strength, and hope with others who have been abused;
4 to safely share their narrative with others who will understand and offer support;
5 to safely experiment with letting go, opening up, and being vulnerable, and practice asking for the support they need;
6 to explore safe ways of moving beyond their comfort zones, releasing their blocks, and moving beyond their abuse to experience a greater sense of freedom in their minds, bodies, and spirits;
7 to reconnect with ethical, life-affirming power, exquisite self-compassion and self-expression (defined below), and learn how to use it to protect themselves; and
8 to provide a safe place where participants can experience a sense of community, brotherhood, and joy.

1 We thank the alumni who participated in our survey of the Weekends of Recovery in 2014. Quotes in this chapter were responses to the survey, and help us explain more fully the benefits of the weekends.

Overall structure of a Weekend of Recovery

Introductory weekends are limited to a maximum of 28 participants. Potential participants sign up online, often encouraged by a therapist, fellow survivor, significant other, or ally. A preponderance of participants report that support from their therapist or another helping professional contributes to the success of their weekend experience. Each weekend usually includes a couple of alumni who are attending a second introductory weekend for the benefit of their recovery. Many participants spend some time on the MaleSurvivor.org website prior to attending, reading other men's experiences or participating in peer-moderated chat rooms. For a large number of our survey respondents, it was this positive feedback on the website that helped them decide to register. Support from a spouse, partner, or family member also often encourages them to risk attending a weekend.

We do not require that a man concurrently participate in therapy to register; however, we strongly encourage each man to have a support system in place when he returns home. Once registered, they participate in a structured screening interview with one of the facilitators. We'll detail below how the interview is structured, but generally it is a chance to screen for readiness to benefit from the weekend and to screen out those who may not be ready or do not fit our criteria.

The weekend programs are located at retreat centers around the United States that we have identified as providing safe accommodations, adequate meeting space, and nutritious meals, and whose staff understands, values, and respects the work we do at the weekend. It is necessary that the retreat center can provide private spaces for us to conduct our program. We utilize settings that offer the options of single, double, or triple rooms to accommodate diverse needs: men can feel safe enough when they head for bed and those with tighter budgets are assisted economically.

Once the men arrive and get settled in their rooms, we begin at 12 noon on Friday with lunch. The first day is devoted primarily to orientation and safety, welcoming the men into the community and teaching them mind-body awareness skills they can utilize throughout the weekend. One of the first activities at each WOR is a structured safety exercise, during which we ask a series of brainstorming questions about safety. This, like other experiential activities, contributes to participants becoming "mirrors" for each other. They transition from believing they don't fit in the group to discovering there are unquestionably other men who have walked in their shoes, and they begin to feel inclusion in a community of men, perhaps for the first time in their lives.

The second morning is devoted to providing a safe enough space for them to tell the story of the abuse they suffered. In the afternoon and evening, we focus on helping them learn how to offer themselves exquisite self-compassion and how to "bust through their shame" (see below). The third day focuses on preparing them to return home with a plan of specific skills, tools, and resources they can utilize to continue their recovery journey. Numerous breaks are provided throughout the program for casual connecting, recreation and art, and self-reflection.

The strength of a weekend is that survivors participate in a variety of experiential modalities: large group activities, four small group sessions during the weekend, access to individual consultations, and many opportunities for social interaction and networking. We also use a variety of interventions to keep participants engaged, including brainstorming, mind-body awareness, group process, psychodrama, artist activities, and therapeutic recreation blended with authentic movement. We have learned that each man will benefit from being engaged in a wide variety of activities and that some interventions will impact some men more than others. We spend considerable time at the beginning of the weekend helping men understand as fully as possible how we envision the structure of the weekend. We then invite them to participate in as many different aspects of the weekend as possible, including taking the risk of doing some activities that may seem to be beyond their comfort zone.

Pre-weekend interviews begin the process of creating group cohesion

Group cohesion develops organically once bonds are established that are rooted in safety. We approach safety as a process, with several avenues for engagement. A pre-weekend phone interview, conducted by a member of the facilitator team, offers a routine structure for our initial contact with each participant. The task of gathering preliminary information provides an opportunity to develop interpersonal rapport between facilitator and participant. As the facilitator gathers information about positive experiences and challenges a man has encountered in his recovery journey prior to deciding to attend the WOR, there emerges a natural context to explore safety needs with the participant.

During this interview, we inquire about physical and mental health issues that may impact attending a weekend. For example, survivors who experience a severe level of social anxiety may anticipate more concerns about safety during a weekend. For survivors who have not yet learned the skills for managing chronic dissociation, there is a risk that attending a weekend may be destabilizing or disabling. We assess for suicidality and substance use, thereby alerting us to address any needs for prevention planning. In these circumstances, the facilitator team's knowledge of individual participants' vulnerabilities alerts them to look for signs of who might be struggling at some point as the weekend progresses.

We also use the interview to screen out those who may not be ready or who do not fit our criteria for inclusion. A weekend is contraindicated for survivors who are still in active states of substance abuse and may be contraindicated for those in early stages of addiction recovery. We also screen out any participant who has been convicted of a sexual offense as an adult. Participants who acknowledge any other history of sexual offending are required to have a second interview with one of the co-chairpersons to determine if they can appropriately participate in the weekend. We assess specifically the participant's ability to take responsibility for his offending behaviors and for his ability to honor the physical and emotional boundaries of other participants. In cases involving sexual acting out behaviors during childhood or adolescence, we evaluate whether this reflected the dynamics of "sexually reactive behavior" rather than predatory or pedophilic intentions (Johnson, 2009). Such incidents mirror the trauma that was experienced, which is then reactively inflicted on another person. We frequently are able to accept a participant who had an incident of sexually reactive behavior, whereas we would screen out someone who exhibited predatory or pedophilic behavior.

During our initial interview, we inquire whether registrants perceive themselves as different from other survivors. Each question is designed to help us prepare for the diversity of participants at the weekend, and to communicate our respect for diversity (e.g., sexual, gender, ethnic, and religious identity). We evaluate what these minority group members may need both from themselves and others to feel safe. We also assess for biases that may make it difficult for any potential participant to be fully welcoming and respectful of the diversity of peers with whom he will be sharing the weekend milieu. When necessary, we address such conflicts during the interview.

Many male survivors hesitate to register for a three-day intensive retreat. Alumni who have completed weekends have identified several issues that contributed to their reluctance: perceptions that they were emotionally ill-equipped to tolerate a WOR; fears of being with other survivors; and questions about safety (Struve & Fradkin, 2015). The pre-weekend interview allows us a forum to validate and normalize these fears while simultaneously providing reassurance about ways the weekend can provide an opportunity for positive growth and change.

Healing benefits of a weekend retreat format

While not considered therapy, the weekends often have therapeutic benefits. There are many restorative benefits to having a small group of male survivors gather for a weekend to connect with each other. Isolation is a primary life strategy for many of them. They rarely have talked previously about the abuse and/or assaults they suffered. Indeed, many men go to their graves without disclosing their secrets. Their shame may be so immense and their fears about sharing so intense that they protect their sexual trauma secrets at all costs. Unfortunately, for some the only way out of their pain is suicide (Healy, n.d.).

A participant who attends a weekend is challenged to shed his belief that he is "the only one" with a secret of sexual victimization. Letting go of this myth is a profound experience, since it has likely fed his internal shame. During the weekend, survivors have the opportunity to interact with one another in ways that convey acceptance, warmth, and empathy instead of the rejection they often anticipate.

Men are socialized to be competitive (Gartner, 2005). As a result, it is common for male survivors to compare aspects of the abuse they suffered to others' stories. Men often minimize the severity of their trauma, masking their shame and propping up their masculinity. Hearing about peers' trauma experiences helps them understand more accurately the gravity of their own abuse/assault(s). Furthermore, many of the men who question if their abuse is "bad enough" to even warrant attending a WOR (e.g., "I was only groped once") find they do indeed belong and find others struggling with similar challenges.

Listen to alumnus Chris (Fradkin, 2012b):

> There is no hierarchy of abuse. It was something I realized at the beginning of my first WOR as I looked around the room wondering if I really belonged there . . . So many guys must have worse stories than mine . . . But somewhere, in the midst of all that doubt, a little voice inside of me spoke up and told me that I had to be there in that place at that time, and I had the right to ask for the help that I had needed for so long. The facilitators asked us to say anything that we needed to ask for in order to feel safe, and that's when I spoke up. I said I needed to know that no one there would tell me that what happened to me didn't matter because it wasn't as bad as what happened to some of the guys there. I was amazed and humbled when almost every person in the room agreed with me. It was at one and the same time the most foreign thing I had ever felt, and the most knee-buckling, life-changing, and deeply, desperately needed feeling to warm my chilled heart.

Men get many mixed messages about what it means to be a "real man." For a survivor who feels his manhood was stolen, the WOR provides an opportunity to re-define what it means to "truly be a man" while in the company of other "genuine men." For example, many participants begin a WOR believing that "authentic men" deal with personal problems by denying and minimizing pain. Many have spent a lifetime getting high or drunk, addicted to sex or gambling, or shutting down the emotional parts of themselves. During the weekend, they are invited to suspend their addictive/compulsive behaviors and risk trying new behaviors. Many participants discover there are other paths to manhood, experiencing what deep courage it takes to face problems directly, all while in the company of other men. They learn that vulnerability and empathy are valuable tools that reflect personal strength.

Many men begin a WOR feeling terrified about issues of safety, perhaps never or only rarely having felt safe. If talking to a single therapist has been his only reference for a safe space, imagining being in a roomful of other survivors seems a huge leap. Considerations of safety within a predominantly male environment are especially complex for participants who were victimized by a male abuser.

Participants commonly vie for seats allowing access to the quickest exit. As the weekend evolves, men describe the feeling of "jumping out of my skin," the urge to run away, or a disbelief that the intensity of their anxiety can possibly diminish. Joe explains his process for opening up:

> While at my first weekend of recovery, I remember thinking that it was the safest place I had ever been in regard to my CSA. I experienced the fact that I was not alone in regard to this aspect of my life. Attending the weekend helped me establish a foundation and launched my journey of recovery . . . I've learned that I can safely rid myself of my protective shell.
>
> (Fradkin, 2012b)

Three days at a Weekend of Recovery creates a more holistic environment than one or more hours per week in a therapist's office. Men appreciate having a "safe enough" space so they can focus for an extended period on themselves, the sexual trauma they endured, and its consequences. Feeling, like Joe, safe enough to let down barriers, they can absorb the support and allow themselves to be vulnerable in ways they typically would not permit, especially with other men. Members of the facilitator team often report that when their own clients attend a WOR, they share more than they routinely do during individual psychotherapy.

The WOR program is structured to balance large and small group activities, thereby titrating how male survivors address core problems of shame. There are many sources of shame, largely emerging from the degree of responsibility men internalize about the trauma they experienced. Typically, male survivors have accepted responsibility for acting shamefully rather than understanding it was the perpetrator who acted shamefully toward them. Shame is reduced when a man discovers he is a victim of something that was done to him rather than something he did; fellow participants validate this through speaking their own truth about the abuse or assault they experienced. Bill shared this example of how his shame was manifested:

> Before the WOR I would stutter a lot when I got "too close" to the core of the abuse. When I told my story, it was only the second time. My therapist was the first. I stuttered and cried and didn't look up until I was finished. Everyone else was crying too. That's when I

> understood that I was in a room with other guys who "get it." I didn't have to clarify or explain. I was heard and validated. By the time the weekend was over, my stuttering was decreased. And bigger than that, I just did not care about the stuttering that remained.
>
> (Struve & Fradkin, 2014)

Dave underscored how attending a WOR helped him overcome and heal his shame:

> Where to start? I wasn't the monster I was so used to painting myself as. The ability to say the things I could only ever say to my therapist or wife and it was not only okay, it was encouraged. I felt "home." That may sound weird but there was no judgment, only loving support!
>
> (Struve & Fradkin, 2014)

The WOR can have long-term as well as short-term benefits. Alexander, a 48-year-old survivor of father–son incest and multiple rapes, reported several years after his WOR:

> The weekend helps you to take a good look at yourself and your behaviors that are hindering you from your greatness. It pushes the envelope and makes you cross the boundaries from self blame to self empowerment. It helps you to discover fears that you were not even aware of until you came to the understanding of how you have built up barriers to your own healing. Those old festering wounds are now healed and the sin-sick soul is renewed. Before coming to WOR, I was a classic self destroyer . . . Now, I am getting out of the house more. I have been able to hold my job for three years compared to the six months to a year attitude I have had before because I didn't want to be too close to others.
>
> (Fradkin, 2012b)

Diversity challenges at the Weekends of Recovery

Throughout the evolution of our program, we have sought to provide services to male survivors diverse in age, sexual orientation, gender identity, religion, ideology, ethnicity, and race. Because our facilitator team is more homogeneous than we prefer, education and training is an essential way for us to enhance our commitment to future inclusion of more diverse staff, which remains a priority. It also remains a priority to elicit feedback from survivors of color that can help us overcome whatever barriers are preventing them from attending. Although men of color who have attended a WOR have not directly reported to us any discriminatory behaviors or problems, we believe that a predominantly white facilitator staff inevitably influences perceptions from survivors of color.

Our staff has been vigilant about how differences could impact the experience of participants. Ongoing education and sensitivity training is a priority for our facilitator staff, as we want to insure the most comprehensive environment of inclusion. In turn, we have realized over time that participants are responsive to our ability to model acceptance and inclusion. We have witnessed extraordinary examples of the depth of acceptance displayed by these men.

We also have a long history of welcoming male survivors who exhibit alternative expressions of sexuality and gender. One endearing example was a homeless male survivor who identified as gender-queer. He arrived wearing a dress and exhibited minimal interpersonal social skills. Despite all of the ways he seemed different from the other men, the facilitator staff focused on supporting inclusion, and the other participants responded by warmly embracing this peer with similar inclusion.

Although we establish a norm of zero tolerance for sexual or gender prejudice and harassment, there are inevitable incidents that test this guideline. For example, participants may be triggered to use derogatory language about gays, propelled by their own insecure worry that someone has assumed they were other than heterosexual. Another participant may experience such comments or behaviors as a "micro aggression," a term that names and labels negative messages that target others based on their perceived marginalized identity (Pierce, Pierce-Gonzalez, & Wills, 1977). We attempt to deal proactively with the impact of such language. We further assist in the resolution of any wounding or victimization that may be consequentially experienced as sexual or gender prejudice by the recipient of that message.

Most gay and bisexual men who have attended a WOR feel the healing impact of inclusion. They often approach a WOR with the same trepidation they have in everyday life, fearing they will encounter rejection. Some sexual and gender minority men enter the weekend with their own set of heterophobic assumptions that can also create blocks. They are often surprised that even men from whom they expect rejection may, in fact, offer acceptance, empathy, and support. Indeed, even heterosexual men who have never met a gender minority person may find they have more in common than they have differences.

Our efforts at inclusion have recently led to outreach that ensures that female-to-male transgender survivors are welcomed and made to feel safe at WORs. Our attention to co-creating safety during the initial stage of a WOR has enabled other participants to extend respectful acceptance to male transgender survivors. Establishing clear norms for inclusion also contributes to an expanded capacity of participants to manage problems occurring outside our immediate view. This is illustrated by feedback from one transgender survivor who disclosed after a WOR that the overarching milieu of acceptance allowed him to deal constructively with the impact of inappropriate questions from another participant about his stage of surgical transition.

We have been less successful in attaining our goals of including a greater number of men of color in our weekends. Of the men who attend WORs, 90% identify as Caucasian, underscoring the lack of ethnic or racial diversity amongst male survivors we currently serve. We have initiated several outreach efforts to survivors of color. For example, we established a Men of Color Scholarship Fund, being mindful that men of color often experience financial hardship. We have conducted community awareness programs specifically in communities where men of color live and work, and we have reached out to spiritual communities that serve men of color. Several years ago an agency that provides services to indigenous men of color contracted with us to conduct two WORs for their male survivor clients. Utilizing our staff and their agency staff provided the means for the men to trust us enough to benefit from the experience.

Accepting men with a wide range of ages (18–80) has contributed to a very rich therapeutic milieu. Many younger men fail to recognize or accept the depth of their courage in dealing with their sexual trauma at a young age. However, older participants often admire their younger peers, with the effect of instilling positive self-esteem in younger participants as they accept, often uncomfortably, this truth about their courage and resilience. Older participants, many of whom have not in the past considered how helpful altruism can be for the "giver," find that helping younger peers strengthens their own self-esteem as well. Sometimes, older participants struggle with self-blame for not dealing with their abuse sooner, and contact with younger peers provides an opportunity to affirm their own path and schedule for healing.

Religion and spirituality are also significant aspects of diversity that influence the healing journey, as participants subscribe to a wide spectrum of beliefs. Immersion into an environment of multi-cultural religion/spirituality is unfamiliar for many of the participants. Understanding such diversity without prejudice can pose a challenge. But, as survivors find their voices, they can articulate both how they are different as well as how their experience transcends differing spiritual or religious backgrounds. Diminished prejudice sometimes allows an opportunity to establish close bonds across religious and spiritual divides, thereby offering yet another healing aspect of a WOR.

Clinical challenges for the facilitator staff

Developing group cohesion is a major challenge at any WOR. Participants represent a spectrum of diversity. In addition, and most importantly, the men are varied in the types of sexual trauma they were subjected to and in their pathways for recovery. It is inevitable that participants risk multi-faceted possibilities for being triggered by peers or staff.

For example, an 18-year-old participant was abused by a man in his 60s; another member of his small group is in his 60s. Or, a heterosexual participant was abused by a gay man; the presence of gay participants triggers internalized homophobia, thereby threatening his feelings of physical and emotional safety. Or, a female-to-male transgender participant struggles with risking disclosure of his authentic identity because he has experienced discrimination and anticipates the same at the WOR. Or, a gay man who left an Evangelical church so he could feel safe to come out, then finds himself in the presence of Evangelical participants and an Evangelical pastor. These all pose challenges requiring skillful handling by facilitators.

Another challenge for our facilitator team is that we enter the WOR with little information about participants other than what emerges in the interview. If the participant has a therapist, that therapist may submit a letter of support that gives us expanded feedback; however, this is entirely optional. All information we receive is shared with the entire

Weekend team as we place each participant in an appropriate small group of six to eight men before any given weekend. This process of assigning men to groups, which generally takes a few hours, is accomplished through careful evaluation of whatever information we have about each participant. One key consideration is diversity; we try to be very sensitive to dynamics that can arise when a person who identifies as different is the only one in a group. For example, when possible we assign more than one gay or bisexual man to the same group. We also consider all other aspects of differences related to stages of healing and stated goals, seeking to balance heterogeneity and homogeneity in the group composition. We have learned the rewards of more vibrant relationship dynamics because of the time we devote to this process of constructing the membership of small groups.

Resolving participants' challenges about feeling safe with men and women in authority is another challenge for the team. Each small group is led by two facilitators. Each facilitator team meets ahead of a weekend to decide who will be co-facilitators. We intentionally assign male and female co-leadership for small groups while always providing at least one small group with two male co-leaders for those participants who have communicated reservations about addressing their sexual trauma with a female. For some participants, interacting with staff of a particular gender may be intimidating and frightening, especially since facilitators are in positions of authority during the weekend. For men who have experienced trauma at the hands of a man, their trust of men may be so damaged that they only feel safe at a weekend knowing there are women present to provide an atmosphere of perceived safety. Men who had female perpetrators often report they want little to do with the women staff. These participants usually experience at least one corrective emotional experience interacting with one or more female facilitators. Participants frequently verbalize that having staff of both genders represented on the WOR team contributes to a greater level of safety. Our commitment to gender diversity on our team thus provides a gamut of opportunities to address – and help resolve – emotional struggles participants may have with women and/or men in authority.

The "mirror environment" created in the weekend is both a strength and a challenge for the facilitators. Seeing themselves reflected in fellow survivors, men are able to absorb validation and understanding in ways that may not be possible from a professional therapist's feedback. Hearing someone else describe aspects of his own story empowers participants to share hidden parts of their past or current struggles in new ways. Facilitators must remain cognizant that this mirror effect can also be overwhelming for those men who have kept so much hidden or buried. With this awareness, a structure/process is created whereby participants can ask for additional help from a facilitator at any time. Facilitators also maintain an attunement to the subtle or indirect ways participants sometimes communicate, or not communicate, requests for help or support, for example when a participant withdraws.

The WOR provides a unique environment where participants can experience corrective healing. Interactions with peers or facilitators may replicate distressing dimensions of their trauma. These interactions may be triggering to the survivor in ways the facilitator could not have known or prevented. In turn, the survivor may reenact with the facilitator some aspect of his trauma. These reenactments are expected, and facilitators must remain vigilant against personalizing these engagements. Indeed, such therapeutic transferences provide unique opportunities to create corrective responses within the community setting. Yet we must remain cognizant that, while it is never our intention to trigger any participant, such triggering is inevitable if our relationships are authentic.

Perhaps our biggest challenge is overcoming the reluctance of most male survivors to register. We have come to accept that despite its many benefits, a three-day WOR is simply too long, too costly, or too overwhelming for some potential participants. We continue to explore many different avenues to extend our outreach efforts.

The core of our model: team cohesion

Developing and maintaining team cohesion is an ever-evolving process. Each weekend has five to eight facilitators. They collaborate with different subsets of colleagues from the total facilitator team of 12 members. We are fortunate to have a team of facilitators who share a commitment to collaboration, consensus, and respectful conflict resolution. We have a collective milieu that is firmly embedded in genuine faith and trust in each other as colleagues and friends. We each contribute to the team through a diversity of therapeutic models, differing levels of experience, a range of ages, a spectrum of sexual orientations, some variety in ethnic and racial backgrounds, and divergent spiritual practices and lifestyles. Some facilitators also have their own survivor history and recovery path.

This team diversity allows us to share responsibilities for the community as a whole while attending to a multiplicity of participant needs. Team cohesion, which includes modeling respectful disagreement, has remained fundamental to our effectiveness. Maintaining authenticity when we encounter discord among ourselves about clinical interventions is another essential cornerstone to our success. Nevertheless, we have sometimes been challenged to find solutions to problems and differences between team members. Protecting the integrity of our work over the span of many years has required us to make some difficult decisions resulting in the departure of some members from the team.

Perhaps our most challenging struggle has been managing our personal emotions. The small participant–staff ratio allows us both to offer individual attention when, based on his interview, someone has greater mental health challenges, and to provide support to each other as we face the challenges the men bring to the weekend. Because many of us are survivors ourselves, managing the boundaries for emotional self-care has sometimes been tricky if we or other members of the team have been triggered while facilitating. Team members have learned the importance of monitoring the risk – to ourselves or others – of becoming embroiled in reenactment dynamics. It is important that we help one another be aware and grounded in each present moment. Facilitator meetings at the end of each day help the team sort out these dynamics and monitor the safety of all participants. We also meet at the end of each weekend and share our successes and challenges with the whole team online in a confidential Dropbox and also during our quarterly meetings.

Unique aspects of the weekend

Exquisite self-compassion and exquisite self-expression

On Saturday afternoon, after having told their story, many of the men have come face-to-face with their shame and acknowledged some of the most difficult challenges in their recovery process. It is important for them to use the tools of offering themselves what we call "exquisite self-compassion," defined as learning to love yourself on steroids or kicked up a notch, and "exquisite self-expression," which empowers participants to speak their truth and assert themselves to improve their sense of self-value. Using sociometry and psychodrama techniques,[2] we invite them to explore the childhood and societal messages that keep them loyal to dysfunctional self-images they learned when being abused, neglected, devalued, and/or unprotected. We teach them that recovery is a process of learning to be disloyal to dysfunction and loyal to functionality (Fradkin, 2012a), and invite them to share examples of both with a sociometric step-in exercise.[3] For example, we ask them to step in to the inside of the circle as they state a message they learned growing up that stops them from feeling worthy of self-compassion today; all others who heard the same message also step in and see they are no longer alone. We then invite each man to identify three mentors – personal, interpersonal, and transpersonal – with whom they will dialog using psychodrama role reversal so they can carry home functional inspiring messages to use when facing challenges.

Shame-busting

We start "shame-busting" on Saturday evening, exploring where in their bodies men store their shame. We invite them to use this workshop as an opportunity to experience how to be freer in their bodies as they make real connections with the other men in the room. We introduce the concept of "authentic movement," inviting them to be true to themselves and move only in ways that feel safe enough as they nonverbally experience a physically safe connection with another man. They have the opportunity to physically mirror and be mirrored so they know they are seeing and being seen as courageous, strong, and sensitive men. A powerful exercise involves inviting participants to take turns moving authentically to music with eyes closed while their partner provides protection from bumping into others. When men who arrived at the weekend frozen and scared can now freely and gracefully move around the room feeling safe, this is a testimony to the power of a community creating healing.

In the second half of shame-busting, we utilize therapeutic recreation methods to help men safely learn to be playful and spontaneous, while

2 Sociometry and psychodrama are clinical methods used to help people understand their relationships to themselves and others with whom they interact.

3 In this exercise, participants observe how similar or different their responses are to those of other men at the weekend. Knowing they are not alone in what they think, feel, and have experienced, helps heal shame.

taking into account that participants represent a range of introversion and extroversion. For example, at a recent weekend, we lost power in the meeting space; we had just asked the men to bounce a ball to each other in pairs. With the aid of a few flashlights, they discovered they could be spontaneous and playful, with no fears of being judged for their ability to catch or bounce a ball. One of the real joys of being on the team is watching the men transform themselves from being isolated to feeling alive and connected by the evening's end.

Bridges to home: transitioning back home

Throughout the WOR we constantly seek to balance empowering each participant to go deeper into his issues with providing enough time and support to help him find enough resolution to go home safely. We are ethically committed to facilitating some degree of closure before participants leave a WOR; therefore we engage them in a "Bridges to Home" segment during the final morning of each weekend.

This Bridges segment is a core component of each WOR. In it, we review tools and resources a participant can utilize to continue his healing once he returns home. During this review session, we identity the important skills that have been woven into the three-day experience so participants can specifically name and label the resources they have acquired. This empowers them to understand new internalized aspects of personal growth and energizes them to incorporate self-growth after the weekend. This process of integration and internalization helps reduce the risk of a "post-weekend let-down," a phenomenon in which participants in intensive retreat experiences are unable to sustain their experience beyond the boundaries of the retreat.

This structured process for closure includes having each participant complete a Bridges to Home worksheet where he identifies the skills he is taking home. We review the basic skills we have introduced to them during the weekend: mind-body awareness, exquisite self-compassion and exquisite self-expression, emotional risk-taking, affirmations, practice in sharing the sexual trauma narrative, authentic movement, conflict resolution, and releasing spontaneous parts of oneself. The structured worksheet also provides a place for each participant to note names and contact information for three other men. Each member of this quartet thereby commits to become a "human bridge" to support each other when they return home by promising to contact each other at two weeks and again at four weeks after the weekend via phone or video chat. We provide them with a list of questions to discuss during the calls. Each also identifies a message he wants to be reminded of when he returns home, and each member of the quartet includes that message when they make contact.

Other post-weekend resources

Peer-led support groups

One outgrowth of the WORs is that men leave the weekend feeling a sense of connection to peers living in far-flung geographic locations. Many participants develop an intense desire to experience a similar personal bonding with other survivors in their home community. Early in our history of offering WORs, attendees pioneered a model of post-weekend peer-led support groups. Because there is often at least one participant in each weekend who attends a support group in his home community, we include time during the Bridges to Home segment for these men to convey the value of post-weekend support groups. This often inspires and motivates other participants to go home and form groups providing outreach to other male survivors. Or, they may join an open ongoing group, if one exists in their area.

MaleSurvivor offers supportive guidance to any alumnus who wants to start a peer group in his community. Two facilitators are liaisons for peer-led group leaders and provide a number of written guidelines to help them get started. We recommend a very specific structured approach to these peer-led groups to enhance the safety of each member.

The MaleSurvivor website maintains a registry of peer-led support groups, sometimes listing 100 or more. Most groups face an initial challenge assembling enough members to start; maintaining regular attendance is sometimes an ongoing problem. Effective outreach requires peer organizers to feel comfortable being visible as survivors. This provides a growth opportunity and, at the same time, can be anxiety-producing for the peer leader, especially if he encounters negative judgment.

Survivors can be very sensitive to inclusion and exclusion, so this is an aspect of peer-led support groups that often requires attention. A peer facilitator needs to be mindful of possible rejecting or non-welcoming messages or behaviors from either himself or other group members. Peer facilitators can consult with our WOR facilitator liaisons to help them manage these matters.

We have not yet conducted research to document the benefits of attending peer-led male survivor support groups. However, anecdotal information from men who have attended them suggests they are beneficial adjuncts to therapy. Members of peer-support groups often report the value to themselves of helping other group members, especially those newer to the recovery process. Such altruistic behavior may increase feelings of self-esteem and personal worth. Peer relationships provide an important antidote to isolation and offer opportunities for giving and receiving support and for measuring a man's own recovery progress.

As with the WORs, there is the inevitable risk of reenactments and conflicts. Such incidents provide a test for participants to develop skills to address these problems directly.

Visiting the MaleSurvivor website

Visiting the MaleSurvivor website (www.malesurvivor.org) is often the first step a male survivor takes as he begins his journey of recovery. Frequently a significant other, advocate, or therapist makes this recommendation. Ideally, the survivor discovers through the website that he is no longer alone. The website offers opportunities for users to find reflections of themselves mirrored in the available resources, including stories from other male survivors, articles, postings in the Discussion Forum, and a peer-moderated chat room. Sometimes men visit for just a few minutes, sometimes for hours, and sometimes they return again and again. There is international user access to the MaleSurvivor website. Its platform nurtures networking among male survivors that transcends geographic boundaries and offers support to survivors in geographically remote places.

The MaleSurvivor website also lists well over 100 links to international peer resources for male survivors, family members and allies, and therapists (www.malesurvivor.org/partners-in-healing.html). The growth of these resources supports an underlying tenet of this chapter: accessing peer support is an ever-growing need for survivors of sexual victimization.

Closing thoughts

Healing is more dynamic when a male survivor is able to interact with peers. Isolating behaviors hinder effective recovery from sexual trauma. It is vital that clinicians understand that a core component of the healing process involves seeking resources that provide safe opportunities for survivors to engage with one another. The benefits of expanding beyond the boundaries of an individual therapeutic relationship are both immediate and long lasting.

Interactions with peers enhance the male survivor's ability to decrease internalized shame, increase self-esteem, instill hope, and enhance the quality of his life. With the growing number of avenues on the Internet that survivors can use to connect with each other, these interactions are becoming much more accessible, comfortable, and rewarding.

References

Castelein, S., Bruggeman, R., van Busschbach, J.T., van der Gaag, M., Stant, A.D., Knegtering, H., & Wiersma, D. (2008). The effectiveness of peer support groups in psychosis: A randomized controlled trial. *Acta Psychiatrica Scandinavica, 118*, 64–72.

Christo, G., & Sutton, S. (1994). Anxiety and self-esteem as a function of abstinence time among recovering addicts attending Narcotics Anonymous. *British Journal of Clinical Psychology, 3*, 198–200.

Edmunson, E. D., Bedell, J. R., Archer, R. P., & Gordon, R. E. (1982). Integrating skill building and peer support in mental health treatment: The early intervention and community network development projects. In A. M. Jeger & R. S. Slotnick (Eds.), *Community mental health and behavioral ecology* (pp. 127–139). New York, NY: Plenum Press.

Emrick, C. D., Tonigan, J. S., Montgomery, H. A., Little, L., McCrady, B. S., & Miller, W. L. R. (1993). Alcoholics Anonymous: What is currently known? In B. S. McCrady & W. R. Miller (Eds.), *Research on Alcoholics Anonymous: Opportunities and alternatives* (pp. 41–75). New Brunswick, NJ: Rutgers Center of Alcohol Studies.

Fradkin, H. R. (2012a). *Joining forces: Empowering male survivors to thrive.* Carlsbad, CA: Hay House.

Fradkin, H. R. (2012b). Interviews for unpublished chapter in *Joining forces: Empowering male survivors to thrive.* Carlsbad, CA: Hay House.

Galanter, M. (1988). Zealous self-help groups as adjuncts to psychiatric treatment: A study of Recovery, Inc. *American Journal of Psychiatry, 145*(10), 1248–1253.

Gartner, R. B. (2005). *Beyond betrayal: Taking charge of your life after boyhood sexual abuse*. New York, NY: Wiley.

Gartner, R. B. (Ed.) (in press). *Understanding the sexual betrayal of boys and men: The trauma of sexual abuse*. New York, NY: Routledge.

Hartman, L. I., Ho, V., Arbour, S., Hambley, J. M., & Lawson, P. (2012). Sexual addiction and substance addiction: Comparing sexual addiction treatment outcomes among clients with and without comorbid substance use disorders. *Sexual Addiction & Compulsivity, 19*, 284–309. doi: 10.1080/10720162.2012.735515

Healy, M. V. (n.d.). Column: The risk of suicide among survivors of child sexual abuse needs to be measured. Retrieved from www.thejournal.ie/readme/risk-of-suicide-among-survivors-of-child-sexual-abuse-1075540-Sep2013/.

Humphreys, K., Mavis, B. E., & Stoffelmayr, B. E. (1994). Are twelve step programs appropriate for disenfranchised groups? Evidence from a study of posttreatment mutual help involvement. *Prevention in Human Services, 11*(1), 165–179.

Johnson, T. C. (2009). *Helping children with sexual behavior problems: A guidebook for professionals and caregivers* (4th Ed.). San Diego, CA: Institute on Violence, Abuse, and Trauma.

Kennedy, M. (1989). Psychiatric hospitalizations of GROWers. Paper presented at the meeting of the Second Biennial Conference on Community Research and Action, East Lansing, MI.

Kurtz, L. F. (1988). Mutual aid for affective disorders: The Manic and Depressive Association. *American Journal of Orthopsychiatry, 58*(1), 152–155.

Kyrouz, E. M., & Humphreys, K. (2002). Research on self-help and mutual aid support groups. Retrieved from http://psychcentral.com/library/support_groups.htm.

McKay, J. R., Alterman, A. I., Koppenhaver, J. M., Mulvaney, F., Bovasso, G., & Ward, K. (1994). Treatment goals, continuity of care, and outcome in a day hospital substance abuse rehabilitation program. *American Journal of Psychiatry, 151*(2), 254–259.

Pfeiffer, P. N., Heisler, M., Piette, J. D., Rogers, M. A., & Valenstein, M. (2011). Efficacy of peer support interventions for depression: A meta-analysis. *General Hospital Psychiatry, 33*(1), 29–36.

Pierce, C., Pierce-Gonzalez, D., & Wills, D. (1977). An experiment in racism. *Education & Urban Society, 10*(1), 61–87.

Raiff, N. R. (1984). Some health related outcomes of self-help participation. In A. Gartner & F. Riessman (Eds.), *The self-help revolution* (Chapter 14). New York, NY: Human Sciences Press.

Sibthorpe, B., Fleming, D., Tesselaar, H., & Gould, J. (1994). Self-help groups: A key to HIV risk reduction for high-risk injection drug users? *Journal of Acquired Immune Deficiency Syndromes, 7*(6), 592–598.

Sloan, D., & Beck, J. G. (2016). Group treatment for PTSD. *National Center for PTSD: PTSD Research Quarterly, 27*(2), 1–4.

Struve, J., & Fradkin, H. R. (2014). Survey of MaleSurvivor Weekend of Recovery alumni. Unpublished raw data.

Struve, J., & Fradkin, H. R. (2015). Survey of GBT MaleSurvivor Weekend of Recovery Alumni. Unpublished raw data.

van der Kolk, B. (2014). *The body keeps the score: Brain, mind, and body in the healing of trauma*. New York, NY: Penguin Books.

Yalom, I. (1995). *The theory and practice of group psychotherapy* (4th Ed.). New York, NY: Basic Books.

Chapter 6

A requiem for a men's trauma organization

The Men's Project 1998–2015 R.I.P.

Rick Goodwin

This is the saddest story I ever have told. That being said, it is also an analysis of a community-based service organization dedicated to trauma recovery for male survivors, of one of the first outposts of free-standing trauma service agencies for men and their families in the world,[1] and of a potential harbinger for future efforts to build places of healing for men.

I don't want to get ahead of myself.

This is the story of the rise and fall of The Men's Project/Le Projet pour hommes, an Ottawa, Canada initiative to serve male survivors and their families. I co-founded the organization and served as its Executive Director until near the end. It is the organization's story, but it is also my story. And, as such, I take full responsibility for the personal lens to this chapter – it is the only way I can see.

Prologue

The Men's Project was born out of friendship. Here is the backstory: I lived in Ottawa for most of the 1980s – worked in residential treatment services for vulnerable youth (I think we called them emotionally disturbed back then), worked my way through a Bachelor's degree in Psychology, and then on to a Master's degree in Social Work. Along the way, I encountered leaders and agencies that impressed me mightily about the strides the women's and peace movements were making for their constituents. I determined to actively pursue efforts to end men's

1 It sounds like I am exaggerating. Being modest by nature, I often haven't stated that. But it's true. More on that later.

violence toward women in my new social work career. Out of a social work internship, I initiated a community-based service to work with men who were assaultive to their partners.

The year was 1985, and little was known at the time on how to engage with men who abuse their intimate partners.[2] This work was instrumental, though, in developing my chops as a practicing social worker. The era of radical feminism was just coming to the forefront, and there was lots of ideology to explain men's violence toward women – much more so than effective ways to intervene.

My soon-to-be-new-pal Larry Gauthier came to that initiative as an intern. I resigned from the program, as did he, as did others, when the service imploded over allegations of a colleague's abusiveness became known. I subsequently shifted my career identity and became a college instructor in social sciences – first in Aboriginal social services, then in the mainstream college system. While I moved away from Ottawa for a few years, I gravitated back in 1993, and subsequently picked up my friendship with Larry.

Over evenings of cool drinks, we commiserated about the failed promise of men's services for domestic violence, and the general lack of community resources for men. Through his role as a social worker for the Board of Education, Larry had a keen eye on where men could and could not access support services. Despite the myriad of community services funded for women by different levels of government, men in crisis were often left stranded – much like it is today.

After a period of necessary griping, we envisioned a community-based mental health practice focusing on the needs of men first and foremost. At his kitchen table, the genesis of The Men's Project (TMP) was formed. From our work with men who have been assaultive, we understood that to achieve success in men's anti-violence initiatives we had to first address old wounds in men's lives and then build resources to sustain their violence-free future. We planned three points of entry: services for male survivors of childhood trauma; a community-based resource for men with issues of rage and violence; and a personal growth program to support men in their lives.

We pictured ourselves running a group or two each week – our voluntary community service. A hobby, if you will.

2 We still don't, sadly, but that is another story.

The name "The Men's Project" struck us a useful framework of service. We wanted a "shame-free" name that would not label men as they entered its doors – as victims, offenders, or anything in between. After a period of reflection, we decided this service should be located in a broader institution that would be the most "guy-friendly" – not a hospital, not something labelled as "mental health," not as an adjunct of a women's service. To this end, we thought the YMCA-YWCA would be the perfect pick. For 18 years, it was.

When we first presented our concept to the Y's management team, they expressed both interest and caution concerning this unheard-of notion of community services for men. In other words, they wanted proof. Being the good college professor I was, I got a group of students to conduct a community needs assessment and environmental scan of the proposed service areas. Their report was presented to Y management. It provided a strong case statement for TMP.[3] To make a long story short, the Y concurred with the report's findings of systemic gaps in community-based services for men, and formally supported the initiative by granting us a singular office space to start the initiative. Larry and I threw in $1,000 each to buy business cards and brochures and to get a phone line in. In July 1998 we were in business, and by the fall we started with the first individual and group services. By the fall TMP fulfilled its mandate by offering full group programming in trauma recovery (Men & Healing), anger management/ending abuse, and emotional intelligence. In its first calendar year, we served about 50 men.

We started off as a therapist-cooperative in those early years, with an arrangement with the Y to "front" proposals and other work. In essence, they acted as a go-between for our services, the community, and potential funders. While this was a great first step arrangement, it soon became clear that this structure would not be able to sustain the growth, service demand, and maturation of the agency. In May 2001, the cooperative closed, and the next day TMP became incorporated as a non-profit organization, with our charitable licence coming a year later.

In 1999, we received our first provincial funding to engage with male survivors of a multi-victim, multi-offender sexual abuse crisis in the city of Cornwall.[4] Despite an existing sexual assault center in that town, men

3 They got an A for that paper.

4 Cornwall, Ontario, has often been referred to as Canada's Boston, given the parallels of child sexual abuse of boys, in part by Roman Catholic clergy.

were not being served because the center's mandate only served women survivors – a story we would be hearing again and again. Now, with some government funding, we were truly in business and fulfilling our mandate. This funding success also was a provincial first – the first agency dedicated to serve male survivors of sexual abuse. We were cooking.

So, out of friendship a notion was born.[5] Out of what was supposed to be a plan to volunteer an evening or two a week became a full-time social enterprise.[6] And this fledgling agency became one of the first faces of an emerging social sector, a movement of community-based service agencies supporting the healing of men. How to sustain the initiative would, in time, become our fundamental challenge over the years.

Building the case statement

Perhaps one of the most demanding steps for any new organization is the process of telling the world its purpose. As we shifted from a back-of-the-envelope type of organization to now being a provincially registered non-profit with national charitable status, we had to get serious about who we were. We had to grow up in a hurry.

Over the course of long-suffering meetings and retreats that focused on our self-definition, the formulations of our mission, vision, and values statement began to take place. We had to take this seriously – we came to realize that, sadly, women's services were suspicious of us (the overt concern that we seemed like a misogynist men's rights organization always was present, yet seldom voiced directly to us).[7] Equally disturbing was the incessant bad-mouthing of our work by family service agencies that perceived us as competition for their funding dollars (they frequently stated that they always served men in their mandate, so funders did not need to fund TMP). The whispering campaigns against us were increasingly active, and we had to assert ourselves accordingly.

5 And we are still friends! Larry and I have been working out lately. He is good at nagging me when I say I am too busy!

6 No lie! Larry's partner at the time called The Men's Project a "hobby gone bad!" It was a perfect analogy for our modest expectations of the service. The intention of a volunteer initiative was quickly eclipsed by the full-time demands it was making in our lives.

7 The first "feedback" we received from the women's community was that we should establish a "women's advisory committee" to oversee the agency!

The mission statement

The first task we had to undertake was defining our mission – the overall purpose of the organization. We needed words to describe why we provide counseling (or therapy)[8] – in other words, what we were already doing. This proved to be a tough haul.

Here is the mission statement we came up with:

> The Men's Project strives to support men, in a process of change, with structure and integrity.

Integrity became a big theme for us, so we had to explore that a bit more in our values statement as I will discuss below.

Despite the flowery language in our opening line, we needed to get concrete about what we did. So, our next line evolved:

> We provide mental health services to men and their families in the areas of childhood trauma recovery, recent sexual assault, emotional integrity, and anger management, among other service areas.

This line was our multifaceted presentation to the community: on one hand, we were a men's mental health center with a broad mandate. This served us well, giving us a broad perch from which our service mandate could operate. On the other hand, as with our name, we asserted our role as a men's sexual trauma recovery center without overtly identifying as a place with "sexual abuse" or "sexual assault" in its name. The last thing we wanted was for men to stay clear of our services, even if they fit our mandate, given the inherent shame many male survivors carry. Thus, we could morph easily, depending on who our audience was.

With that task complete, we moved onto defining the organization. Even in the early years, we were a complex entity. Our clinical services group was comprised of at least four mental health disciplines. We hired an office manager to keep us all in line. There were various unpaid folks working with us too – some because they supported our cause and some because they were interns and wanted experience in our clinical work.

8 This reminds me of an old joke: What's the difference between a flutist and a flautist? $30/hour!

Of course, we also had our newly minted board members to recognize as well. We came up with:

> We are a charitable non-profit organization with a diverse team of professionals supported by a roster of volunteers.

Next on tap was describing *how* we did our work. This became a source of debate. While most psychologists and therapists would assert that the focus of therapy should be cognitive and emotional intervention, we knew that trauma work requires a much broader and deeper engagement. How can one heal without embodying the physical realm of being? How could one heal without addressing the spiritual or ontological realm? Were we fooling ourselves in thinking we could meaningfully engage in this broader way? We wrote:

> We address men's psychological, emotional, physical and spiritual needs within a community-based framework.

Lastly, we needed to refer to our philosophy and approach to our work. Again, language proved to be difficult. If we wanted a parallel term to feminism that would speak to men in ways that depicted men's reality, then the term "masculinism" made sense. However, this wording was almost arcane in common parlance, and would likely have the connotation of misogynist – at least where it was used. Eventually we settled on the term "male-centered" as a way to describe our approach of working:

> The Men's Project provides innovative counselling and educational services through a male-centred approach that honours and respects the experiences of men.

Other challenges arose in developing our self-description. We wanted to assert our openness and inclusion of men of all sexual orientations, so including "gay and bisexual" into our mission was important.[9] Inclusion of other cultures was critical too – so we borrowed from the Y's mission statement for this part of the mission statement:

9 The term "queer friendly" was not in usage then.

> Our programs are open to straight, gay and bisexual men regardless of race, religion, creed or culture.

Lastly, we knew our task in life was more than psychotherapy – as good social workers, we wanted to change the world.[10] We had to take on the broader structures that govern the identity of men, and the systems in place that confine and restrict gender mores. Community presentations and workshops were not enough – our role had to be bigger. In this regard, we took on the role of advocacy:

> We are committed to education and advocacy for men through engaged communication with the wider community.

This identity of advocate became one of the core strengths of our "small yet mighty organization."[11] Advocacy eventually became one of the death knells of the shop. But I am getting ahead of myself again.

Core values statement

We believed we had to keep drilling away about who we were. Perhaps it was the whispering campaign in the community or perhaps it was out of our own fledgling organizational self-esteem, but regardless we wanted to define our values – both about who we were, but also who we served.

The broadest statement was the easiest statement to compile – perhaps something resembling apple pie to all:

> The Men's Project invites all men to live their lives with integrity. In a sanctuary of transparency, tranquility and safety, the professional services of the Men's Project provide insight and hope, offering men:
>
> - Compassionate, nurturing, and healing experiences;
> - Respectful, affordable, and confidential services;
> - Innovative, courageous, and inspiring programs;
> - Integrity and validity to speak as witnesses on behalf of men to the wider community.

10 MSW = Must Save the World!

11 This became my favourite expression in framing the mandate of The Men's Project.

It was then imperative for us to define integrity – for the organization, the staffing group, our working dynamic, and what would be the consistent glue of all of our services. We knew, intrinsically, that integrity was as great an aspiration for a man struggling in his trauma wounds as it was for a man struggling in his attempt to live violence-free. This core value had to be built into our identity. So we wrote:

> Out of the many interpretations of the concept of integrity, The Men's Project promotes emotional integrity in both its programming as well as a core organizational value. We define emotional integrity as living one's life and conducting oneself in relationships of significance based on the following three premises:
>
> - Being profoundly honest with oneself.
> - Owning one's own feelings and behaviour (taking responsibility).
> - Closing the emotional space with others.

It also seemed imperative to define our relationship to feminism. Despite our professional creds from years of working with offenders to end domestic violence, we had to assert our position to the broader community. Even our sponsoring organization, the Y, would report back on criticism they received from women-identified services asking why they supported a men's organization. While this in no way silenced those whispers, here is how we articulated it:

> How We Define Gender Equality:
>
> - The Men's Project uses the term "gender-just" to describe our dedication to building a world of equality between men and women.
> - We believe it is the responsibility of both sexes to take the necessary steps in this process of change. As an organization, we adhere to the principle of justice – that is, the fair treatment of all peoples involved.
> - We are shaped by many of the principles of feminism in guiding us to this place of understanding in terms of gender equality.

Despite our self-congratulations about coming to agreement with this tricky statement of gender equality, we managed to piss off some segments of both the women's community and the men's rights groups.

The criticism from the "violence against women" (VAW) community was hard to fathom. Of course, TMP reflected "men" as a whole. With men being the primary aggressors of women around the world, some projection must have been at play. Also, the perception (and reality) of competition for funding dollars creates deep distrust in the non-profit sector – and this seemed entrenched for both them and us. There was also an implicit politic that men speaking about sexual violence need to be deferential to the existing (read women's) services community. Still, as a Dad of two girls, I could not have been more supportive of a robust women's services sector – TMP even raised money as an agency for a women's sexual assault center in our early days. Ultimately though, support could not overcome distrust between TMP and many VAW organizations.

The disdain from the men's rights activist (MRA) community was more predictable, even if TMP would seem to be on their side of the page. While we were advocating positions like "funding for essential services should not be based on the gender of the victim," our core service to men was essentially therapy, not advocacy. This was seen by many MRAs as a convenient cop-out – we weren't standing up to government, or to women's services, in any kind of loud and public way. We were accused of being apologists for the women's community. Harsh words were said. Ultimately, we truly had no wish to align with the MRA movement, given the depths of anger and misogyny that seemed to be part of their discourse.

After eventually developing some thick skin, we took it that we were doing the right thing if we were hit with criticism from both sides.[12]

The building years

The 2000s provided much growth for the agency despite precarious (yet continued) project funding from the province. It was a juggling act of small grants, small donations, and time-limited projects that built the agency in terms of competency and stature.

Some of these highlights included:

- Delivering Canada's first gay-identified trauma recovery group program. In 2001, understanding that gay men often wish to pursue their healing in the safety and identity of a gay men's circle, we started this service. After announcing it in the local LGBT paper, we had 11 men sign up in two weeks.

12 Like standing in the middle of the street and getting whacked by traffic either way!

- Developing a pan-Canadian training service. As men's services were just starting to take hold in Canada,[13] we found ourselves in the niche of providing clinical training to community agencies, government services, and First Nations on how to work with male survivors. By the time of closure, TMP had provided training to most provinces, the United States, and Great Britain.
- Training, clinical supervision, and evaluation services of a cross-cultural men's healing program for the M'Wikwedong Native Cultural Resource Centre in Owen Sound, Ontario. The program, entitled Hearing, Healing, Hope, was the first program we knew of that blended Western psychology (our Men & Healing clinical model) with traditional Aboriginal ways of healing for men.
- The agency's clinical services were assessed through an Aboriginal lens and they were documented as a "Promising Healing Practice" in the Final Report of the *Aboriginal Healing Foundation Report, Volume III*.
- We developed a collaborative service with the Canadian Mental Health Association regarding a new group treatment program for male survivors who have concurrent disorder diagnoses.
- As Executive Director of TMP, I became active with MaleSurvivor[14] – speaking on a regular basis at its biannual conferences. From 2002 to 2004, I served on its Board of Directors, including a term as Board Secretary. Involvement with MaleSurvivor led me to engage with numerous international colleagues in this field – many connections I still cherish today.
- Further group program development occurred over this time – a therapeutic "Fathering" program[15] as well as the "Sexual Integrity" program for men with issues of compulsive or problematic sexual expression.[16]

13 To my knowledge, the first free-standing agency in the world dedicated to male survivor services was founded by colleague Don Wright at the British Columbia Society for Male Survivors of Sexual Abuse (BCSMSSA). In 2015, they celebrated their 25th anniversary.

14 See MaleSurvivor.org.

15 The program was conceived around the statement that "all fathers are sons," and explored ways to strengthen fathers' attachment with their children.

16 The model utilized by Sexual Integrity operated in contrast to a "sex addiction" model of understanding.

- The agency won a slew of awards and recognitions: the inaugural Attorney General's Victim Services Award of Distinction (for innovative service programming), the Canadian Mental Health Association's Mental Health Award, the United Way's Community Builder Award, and a similar one from Crime Prevention Ottawa.
- In 2008, the agency hosted the first provincial conference on male sexual trauma in Toronto. *Men of Courage* was a sold-out event for 325+ service providers and survivors, and included keynote speakers, such as Fred Mathews, Andy Fisher, Jim Clemente, Richard Gartner, Steve Sullivan, Sheldon Kennedy, and Art Lockhart. Grand Chief of the Assembly of First Nations Phil Fontaine was the keynote at a special lunch. Our Aboriginal Elder for the Men of Courage conference was Verne Roote.
- Also in 2008, TMP engaged in its first international partnership with 1in6, Inc., a new Los Angeles-based national non-profit organization whose mission "is to help men who have had unwanted or abusive sexual experiences in childhood live healthier, happier lives."[17] One of the first steps in this collaboration was their recognition of our Men & Healing model as part of their conceptual base of service provision. I was invited to serve on their Advisory Committee – a position I still serve today. A further international partnership was later built with Living Well in Australia.[18]
- We excelled in two peer-reviewed evaluations of our Men & Healing services. Our funder, the Ministry of the Attorney General, commissioned an outside evaluation of our services, which concluded that, in their eyes, the service was "highly successful" (Herring & Associates, 2002). Later, through research headed by Jennifer Hopton of the University of Ottawa (Hopton & Huta, 2013), a published quantitative study demonstrated the program's clinical success in reducing both clinical depression and post-trauma behaviours of its participants. Sadly, despite what we believe were the only two peer-reviewed studies of their kind concerning treatment outcomes of male survivors, the funders stated they "weren't convinced." They didn't elaborate.

17 See 1in6.org.
18 See livingwell.org.au.

The Cornwall Public Inquiry

To address the long-standing issues of the multi-victim, multi-offender child sexual abuse crisis in Cornwall, and the abject failure of the criminal justice system in bringing these crimes to justice,[19] the province (after much prodding) called for a provincial inquiry into the affair. In 2005, TMP succeeded in gaining official standing in the Cornwall Public Inquiry (Special Standing for Part I, Full Standing for Part II).

Our involvement, as the only victim treatment agency with standing at the event and the only men's agency in the province, gave us a unique perspective and voice in the Inquiry. Our involvement was robust, and achieved a number of objectives:

- We successfully advocated for all witnesses in the Inquiry, along with Inquiry staff, to have access to professional counseling services in order to address issues of both historical and vicarious trauma.
- We were successful in receiving granted monies to research and write a handbook on service delivery for male survivors (Fisher, Goodwin, & Patton, 2008).
- A similar research project was funded for an investigation into safe peer support services for survivors of sexual violence, as well as a concept paper on an ombudsman for victims of sexual violence (Goodwin & Patton, 2007).
- We requested a research grant to investigate whether the Ontario government was in violation of the Canadian Charter of Human Rights by not providing funding for victim services on the basis of gender (i.e., men's services as compared to their female counterparts). However, the request was denied.
- We consulted on a research project led by Circles of Support and Accountability Ottawa (COSA) on the provision of trauma recovery services to "victim/perpetrators" of sexual abuse (men who were sexually abused as children and who have sexually offended as adults).[20]
- We delivered nine training conferences for service professionals in Eastern Ontario through the support of the Inquiry.

19 In 1997, the Ontario Provincial Police established Project Truth, which eventually laid 114 charges against 15 people, but found no evidence of a pedophile ring. Only one person was convicted.

20 Editor's note: See Chapters 14 by Greif and 15 by MacDonell and Bolton in this volume for a discussion of treatment of survivor/offenders.

Over the course of the Inquiry, we challenged representatives of the provincial government in their assertion that they were addressing issues of sexual violence for all Ontarians. In our closing submission to Commissioner Normand Glaude, we made a slew of recommendations to the Inquiry, chiefly that services for male survivors of sexual violence, much like women's services, need to be made available on a province-wide basis (for many years, we were the *only* funded service for men in the province).

About a year after the close of the Inquiry, the Ontario government announced, for the first time ever, a competition for funding for services for male survivors – on a province-wide basis. We were ecstatic with this news – the first jurisdiction in North America with this mandate. You could hear the whoops from our office a block away. Apart from regional service mechanisms, there would also be a provincial 1-800 line established for referrals for men. So much the better.

The Fall

To make a long story short, despite vigorous proposals by TMP for both regional services and the provincial 1-800 service, TMP was shut out of all funding announcements! We were collectively flabbergasted by this news; however, the more cynical ones in our agency had predicted just this – that there was no way the province would fund an agency that advocated so hard for an emerging sector, for a sector that truly did not exist in free-standing form apart from TMP. The case statement for the agency was thus closed.

Instead, the province gave funding to a collection of family service agencies and women's centers to take on the work.[21] Not one men's organization was funded! To make matters more abhorrent, local funding went to a Catholic charity![22] The Church is perhaps the largest institution in the world that has aided and abetted the sexual abuse of thousands of children, primarily boys, and the Ontario government granted a Catholic organization funding! As one articulate letter to the editor said, "Edgar Allan Poe could not have written a better outcome for this story."

21 Funding that was "a mile wide, but an inch thick," according to one bureaucrat who shared this in private correspondence.

22 I recall facilitating our Cornwall program at a time when half the clients in our group services had been abused or assaulted by priests.

Some intense lobbying during this time only delayed the inevitable. Pursuing other funding streams helped but could not erase the writing on the wall. Increasing client fees, laying off staff, taking on more national work – none of these could turn the page either.

In the span of four years, we watched our money crumble to a third of our original funding basis. Then, after 16 years of project (aka "temporary") funding, the Ministry ended the funding for TMP in 2015.[23] Despite the many awards, the Attorney General's Award of Distinction, two peer-reviewed, evidence-based outcome studies, and TMP's status as a leader in this emerging sector, this was their stance. On October 30, 2015, the agency closed its doors. The "small yet mighty" organization was no longer.

The exposed underbelly of men's survivor services

Before we move onto the wake of TMP and get maudlin, I want to reflect on a few issues that plague organizations like TMP in the hopes that they can be attended to as the male survivor movement grows.

Unintegrated survivors in leadership positions

First, while the prevalence of sexual abuse in the broad population is well known, little is said about the high prevalence of victimization among helping professionals. Yet this, I believe, is a given. These "survivor-therapists" or "survivor-activists" bring inherent strengths to the work, yet they often have inevitable attendant vulnerabilities. There is variability in the extent that they have dealt with their own trauma, and so an unspoken given in the field is the presence of service providers and advocates who are relatively unwell, often un-integrated in their trauma and spreading their own dis-ease in their work and in the community, thereby often contributing to adverse consequences.[24]

Other survivors are active in the movement, often with great effect but sometimes to their own and the movement's detriment: Famous celebrities

23 The Ministry did not have to say why it was not renewing its funding – given our "project funding" status. They did comment about the provincial deficit – less money plus other bureaucratese – only to announce "new" money for women's sexual assault centers six months later.

24 Full disclosure: I experienced sexual abuse as a child.

making erroneous statements based on anecdotal experiences. Folks who demonstrate their rage, paranoia, or pain while wearing the guise of a professional. The damage they can do is consequential. Much like some 12-step advocates who see the world solely through abstinence-lenses, these folks, both male and female, often take up more than their share of space. From an ardent "violence against women" counselor who freaked out when I spoke of the linkage between men's victimization and subsequent partner violence, to leaders in the field publicly stating they felt "raped" when they experienced an organizational loss,[25] we collectively trip over ourselves as we walk hip deep in this dysfunction.

Dysfunction in the ranks

The broader field of trauma recovery is rife with problems due to troubles in the sector itself. While many service providers *say* they are trauma-informed, the nature of service delivery exposes their weaknesses. It could be funding parameters created by well-intentioned but ill-informed bureaucrats who believe a 12-week period of engagement is fine, despite every indication that childhood sexual trauma is complex and requires a sustained period of treatment. It could be therapists who, despite their knowledge of abuse in a client's life, choose not to attend to the issue, perhaps out of their own discomfort. It could be service providers with sloppy boundaries who are willing to see their ethical breaches in shades of gray. Or, it could be a well-meaning but totally inappropriate decision about what will heal. There was, for example, one agency that focused its "counseling" work with survivors on making crafts – no lie! While these stories generally don't make headlines, I can appreciate why many survivors lose faith that their wounds will be treated effectively – too often, they have been re-injured in their efforts at finding help.

Women's services are not necessarily allies

Could the development of men's trauma services like TMP have been different if the women's movement were indeed supportive of men? I am not convinced that the women's sector, or at least the "violence against

25 Raped? You'd think that of all people they would know the difference between feeling angry and being raped.

women" sector, is always an ally of this developing field. At first blush, one would think we should be close collaborators. But we are men – the same gender seen as having privilege, power, and control, not to mention the gender most often to blame for women's suffering. But how can society ever overcome abuse and violence if women and men cannot work together? TMP as a male-serving organization met closed doors in sexual assault networks, regional coordinating committees, and provincial coalitions simply due to our mission. It all was a bit too much.

While we have had strong women supporters over the years, and some great partnerships with women's services as well, the doors of the existing networks for victim service providers, including those focusing on sexual and domestic violence, remain tightly guarded. Some of these barriers are a product of government policy, and some exist because some women want to "own" the issues (the discourse of "rape culture" or "take back the night" would be such examples) and the funding dollars they contain. Men's services generally are not given a place at the table; instead they are too often met with hostility, suspicion, and indifference. (Mind you, in some cases this exclusion might have been warranted – see the discussion concerning "men's rights" organizations.) Yet, collectively, we fail both ourselves and the change we all want to see made.

Broader issues of governance

I think our sector – particularly community-based services and non-profit organizations – faces a variety of challenges. Some are possibly unique to male survivor serving organizations; others may have application to the wider sector.

Here are some reflections on those concerns and how they manifested with TMP and elsewhere.

Leaders who still need healing

Male survivors, or, more properly stated, partially healed (or unintegrated) male survivors are a bane to the functioning of healthy male-oriented anti-violence organizations. Sometimes these men inhabit Boards of Directors – often with devastating results. As with many community-based services (HIV/AIDS organizations are one such example) there is a history and expectation that service users, either present or past, can and should serve on Boards of Directors. When service users serve as Board members, they naturally are often advocates for the services they still need and/or continue to access; yet these services may not be what the larger community needs most. While TMP never had active clients on its Board, it did at times have past clients. This was, essentially, a mistake, despite the gems that some contributed. Having ex-clients on the Board of Directors is unhealthy to all parties – whether because of their personal take on service provision as seen from their new position, or because they themselves are unwell. Additionally, when implosions occur for such Board members, should the organization see them as loose cannons or as clients who need to return to care?

Apart from past clients, we need to examine the parallel issue of the presence in this sector of male survivors on Boards of Directors – period. As organizations generally cannot screen for the emotional well-being of such volunteers as a ticket to entry, the organization can be plagued by their dysregulated, dysfunctional thoughts and behavior of (some of) these wounded souls – adding to the malaise of such services. This is truly a catch-22 – how can these services be supported if it not from the male survivor community? – yet many of these individuals can pull down an organization given their unhealthy state of being. I have no solution to suggest here – just the need to have open and brutally honest conversation.

A frequent complaint by many non-profits is having Board members delve into operations – neglecting the fact that the purpose of serving on a Board is the nurturing of the vision of the organization and overseeing its financial well-being. The conceptual boundary between governance and operations becomes blurred – to the detriment of the organization. Poor personal boundaries are a common issue for trauma survivors, so there is often temptation to delve where the "action" is. Caveat is needed here – "non-survivors" are not always healthy, so this element of dysfunction cannot be avoided just by cursory Board candidate interviews.

The inability to fundraise

Men's issues are a hard sell. Think about it – do any organizations place the faces of men in their charitable pitch? And, despite the perennial quest for finding the "pink ribbon" that would mobilize the men's survivor cause, such a device remains elusive. But, while male sexual victimization is a difficult area for which to fundraise,[26] fundraising for services is the financial lifeline of small community-based agencies, particularly with the continued fraying of the social safety net. Despite this need, the TMP Board never fully acted on fundraising – with claims of not knowing how, not knowing why it was needed, and, perhaps most critically, not wanting to be the public face of the issue.

Organizationally, I am not sure we could have ever succeeded even if the Board of Directors gave it their best. But government funders frequently pointed out our failure – why weren't we like women's services, raising money on our own behalf? Again, unrealistic standards posed numerous challenges for ourselves, and, more broadly speaking, the movement. Nonetheless, significant privately raised monies – had we been able to obtain them - would have kept the doors of TMP open. This just did not occur.

Dependency on funding

While some readers of this chapter might be envious of TMP's history of receiving government funding, the withdrawal of government funding led to its collapse, which should provide a warning to all. Of all forms of social services, victim services is perhaps the sector that has the most difficulty achieving financial independence. After all, you work with the most vulnerable people, and folks expect services should be free of charge while the organization is run on a shoestring with good-hearted volunteers. Finally, let's be honest here: funding for victim services are the crumbs of the justice system – an afterthought, really – with little appetite for accredited professionals, sustainable funding, and service excellence.

Funding for non-profits creates dependency on government, and thereby generates substantial vulnerability for the viability of services. If the game plan is to develop a free-standing service, it should be a given that an organization avoids core government funding. Yet victim services cannot be run without core government funding. This is the catch-22 that TMP could not get out of.

26 Child-serving, pet-finding, and women's services all appear to be easier subject areas for fundraising – because men aren't accepted as victims, right?

Founder's syndrome

The last issue is a factor that I need to own. Yet, saying that, I am unsure in retrospect what I should have done differently. Let's let Wikipedia define this term:

> *Founder's syndrome* . . . is a popular term for a difficulty faced by organizations where one or more founders maintain disproportionate power and influence following the effective initial establishment of the project, leading to a wide range of problems for both the organization and those involved in it. The passion and charisma of the founder or founders, which was such an important reason for the successful establishment of the organization, becomes a limiting and destructive force, rather than the creative and productive one it was in the early stages.[27]

Given that the agency started with my tenure as Executive Director from the beginning, I know I unduly shaped the organization. Given that my training was initially in community development and later as a clinical therapist, I viewed the Executive Director role through these lenses. For example, I was more drawn to discussions about clinical models of service than to talking about financial forecasts. I took on the lion's share of the training work for the agency because of my teaching background and because the income was sorely needed by the agency. However, this eroded my time spent managing the agency, let alone working with the Board. Frustrations were frequent. I could go on.

In reflection, I should have stepped away from the Executive Director role much earlier and focused on my strengths of clinical service management and training. But the opportunity to move laterally did not present itself, and the full-time pay (and prestige) of being an Executive Director kept me there. When my job duties became too much, and funds were cut, I offered the Board much less hand-holding. They unfortunately did not step up to the challenge of doing things for themselves, and the spiraling downward continued.

I bring this up here because I don't believe Founder's Syndrome was unique to TMP. This sector is replete with examples of initiatives that

27 https://en.wikipedia.org/wiki/Founder%27s_syndrome. Retrieved May 9, 2016.

started from nothing but the good will of good hearted individuals stepping up and developing what was needed, often without regard to financial viability or even a sane work week. In so many organizations, this is a fact, and the resultant dynamic must be managed, not avoided.

> TMP served approximately 3,400 male survivors over its 18-year history.

Epilogue

I started out by saying this was the saddest story I have ever told. Here is the greater truth: I was only kidding![28]

While the agency "The Men's Project" may have died from gender bias, funder neglect, and a cultural disdain of supporting men's mental health, its mandate and vision has continued in a different form. As Albert Einstein said: "Energy cannot be created or destroyed, it can only be changed from one form to another." That applies to you and me, and even small yet mighty organizations.

Let me update this final section of the story.

As the agency limped toward ending its services in the fall of 2015, the staff was uniformly interested in ensuring the continuance of services. From this, the collaborative practice "Men & Healing" was born. Led by me, with the participation of all the therapists and our brilliant administrator (even our techie and bookkeeper!), we managed to pull a rabbit out of the hat: the day after TMP closed its doors, the new enterprise opened its doors.

As we replicated TMP programming in its entirety, the client group moved as a whole over to the new initiative. Low-income clients, who would not normally have been able to pay the near-market fees of the new service, were "grandfathered" into Men & Healing at fees they could afford. At this writing, nine months into the development of this new entity, the group programs we offer have expanded; we have taken on three new "purchase of services" of the program by community agencies (which ensure low-income men can access services free of charge); and our client

28 You gotta have a sense of humor doing this work!

numbers are rebuilding from where we were two years ago. This week alone, I am overseeing nine group programs as well as individual therapy.

It's a new chapter in the book.

This turn of events brings out some interesting questions in terms of community-based services for this sector. Is non-profit governance the best model for men's services? Our new social enterprise makes it impossible for us to receive government funding, as it is considered a for-profit enterprise.[29] Yet, given the paucity of funding available for men's trauma work, and the inherent dependency created by government backing, let alone the loss of autonomy and independence – should we even be bothered? When a Board of Directors has to spend $6,000 to insure its own operation in order to be considered for government funding, then has to spend $3,000 for audit fees, we must question which model of governance serves survivors best.

There are other advantages to this new model. Smaller, less administrative-heavy organizations can be nimble and quick. Whether taking on a new program area, a new collaboration, or a *pro bono* service, they are not tied by a dusty strategic plan, a self-absorbed Board of Directors, or a funder who may not approve of the new venture. Given that the work of developing community-based services for survivors is still in a pioneering stage, cumbersome models of engagement do not serve us well.

The deepening of collaborations

The partnerships developed with 1in6, Inc. and Living Well of Australia continued to deepen, despite the death of TMP.[30] This is not truly surprising – the nature of all partnerships rests with the souls who are doing this work – not the paper entities that were signed. With Living Well, we worked on a collaboration to co-write a treatment manual for male survivor services called "Foundations." This was recently finished for the Australian edition. We believe this is the first international collaboration of its kind.

29 When people refer to it as a for-profit model (versus a non-profit model), I laugh!

30 I am deeply indebted to Mr. Steve Lepore, Executive Director of 1in6, Inc. and Dr. Gary Foster of Living Well, both of whom were my collegial anchors during the demise of TMP. I owe them my professional sanity. Thanks, guys!

My work with 1in6, Inc. has deepened immensely – and in ways I could not have anticipated as TMP was sinking. I am now its Director of Training in its efforts to strengthen the American service sector – including training engagements with the American military.[31, 32] I also facilitate their online group support program – a cutting-edge program for male survivors who can access these services from anywhere. After TMP concluded, I never expected to contribute to the male sexual trauma services sector again as vitally as I am today.

And broader issues of international collaboration continue. After the success of the second South-South Institute on Sexual Abuse of Men & Boys and Men (SSI) held in Cambodia in 2015, there are new efforts to expand the fledgling international network of service agencies in the emerging sector of men's health issues. Systemic barriers to address the needs of boys and men who have experienced sexual trauma were documented at the conference, from conflict zone refugees in Uganda to the "dancing boys" of Afghanistan. These barriers paralleled in many ways obstacles to serving male survivors in First World countries. I have never met a finer, more courageous group of men and women, representing 40+ countries, than those I spent time with in Phnom Penh. I hope to assist in the next SSI gathering, scheduled for New Zealand in 2017.

So, you see, nothing really died – unless you call some bricks and mortar life. The phoenix does sometimes rise from the ashes. After trauma can come recovery. Good things, even careers, can be built over a kitchen table. This work has given my life great meaning, both personally and professionally. I believe that, modesty aside, TMP and its reincarnation have given hope and healing to many people. Of course, it is a team effort – no one is indispensable to making it all happen. My unsung heroes have been my mentors, my colleagues, my family, my friends, my staffers, our supporters, our Board members, and our volunteers – a list a mile long. Not an inch deep.

This, I know, is true: no survivor of sexual trauma should be *dispensable* – not for lack of services, lack of political will, or lack of money to pay for such services. Not for his (her, their) gender either. How we approach building places of healing for men in our communities remains a deep challenge for activists and professionals alike.

31 More men are sexually assaulted in the American military than women, but I digress.

32 Editor's note: See Chapter 4 by Skidmore and Roy in this volume for discussion of sexual victimization of men in the military.

A shingle saying "men are welcome here" should be hung in every community. That would be a great start. Yet nothing comes easily, and there is no recipe that can be found.

This story was about one such effort in one community. My deepest wish is that it will inspire others to do what's necessary where they live – for their fathers, brothers, sons, neighbors, and community – and write their own story. For if we can tell a story of suffering, we can just as well transform it into a story of healing.

References

Fisher, A., Goodwin, R., & Patton, M. (2008). *Men & healing: Theory research and practice in working with male survivors*. Toronto: Prepared for Cornwall Public Enquiry

Goodwin, R., & Patton, M. (2007). *Peer support guidebook: Tools for creating and maintaining safe and successful peer-led groups for adults with histories of sexual abuse*. Toronto: Prepared for the Cornwall Public Inquiry.

Herring & Associates. (2002). Evaluation *of The Men's Project*. A Pilot Men's Project of Cornwall & Ottawa. Unpublished study.

Hopton, J. L., & Huta, V. (2013). Evaluation of an intervention designed for men who were abused in childhood and are experiencing symptoms of post-traumatic stress disorder. *Psychology of Men & Masculinity, 14*(3), 300–313.

Chapter 7

Anesthetizing open wounds

Substance addiction in male survivors of sexual victimization

Scott M. Hyman and Steven N. Gold

Despite the many advances in addiction medicine and the growing consensus that substance addiction is a complex brain disease and chronic medical illness that seriously undermines the ability to judge the consequences of one's actions, impairs insight and rational decision-making, and disrupts learning/memory and adaptive self-control (American Psychiatric Association, 2013; Cami & Farre, 2003; Crean, Crane, & Mason, 2011; National Institute on Drug Abuse (NIDA), 2012; Schoenbaum, Roesch, & Stainaker, 2006; Volkow, Baler, & Goldstein, 2011; Volkow & Li, 2004), substance addiction continues to be vilified in many circles as a selfish manifestation of flawed moral character, poor willpower, and bad choices (NIDA, 2012; Volkow & Li, 2004). In effect, the daily struggles of people with substance addictions often go unnoticed, and many "healthy" individuals lack an understanding of or empathy for their plights, perhaps because the thought of continuing to engage in such a self-destructive behavior is baffling and unfathomable to those who have never known addiction.

Indeed, what many people fail to recognize is that many addicted individuals have experienced a tremendous amount of life stress and adversity and have genetic vulnerabilities and learning/coping deficiencies (e.g., social and coping skills deficits) that have contributed to the development and maintenance of their substance addictions. The human brain is susceptible to environmental insults just like any other organ, and the cumulative pounding it can take from chronic stressors and traumatic life events (e.g., sexual victimization) during critical periods of brain development can create a cascade of neurobiological problems that can severely alter cognitive, emotional, and behavioral functioning and influence the development of debilitating psychiatric problems, including addictive disorders (De Bellis, 2002; Heim & Nemeroff, 2002; Teicher, Anderson, Polcari, Anderson, & Navalta, 2002).

Purpose of the review

This chapter focuses on understanding the relationship between sexual victimization and substance addiction in males and the implications of this knowledge base for clinical assessment and treatment/care planning. We begin by discussing literature on the relationship between childhood sexual victimization and substance use outcomes in males. We follow by discussing how childhood sexual victimization can complicate the clinical picture in addiction and increase the severity of frequently co-occurring problematic behaviors (e.g., sexual/HIV risk behavior; co-morbid psychiatric problems) in males who are seeking treatment for substance addiction. We end by discussing how available trauma treatments for male survivors of childhood sexual victimization can be tailored to address substance addiction, and through a case illustration we provide recommendations regarding how addiction treatment programs may better assess for and address childhood sexual victimization in their male clients.

Throughout our discussion, we review empirical studies and well-constructed reviews that focus on male samples and/or which allow for the analysis of gender-specific relationships. We are cautious about making any definitive conclusions given the limited number of studies conducted on this issue with males as compared with females, the mixed findings when it comes to studies of sexual victimization and substance use outcomes in males, and the overall methodological shortcomings of the psychological research literature.

While the recently revised diagnostic system uses the term "Substance Use Disorder" to refer to the cognitive, behavioral, and physiological symptoms that accompany problematic drug-seeking behavior (APA, 2013), throughout the chapter we use the terms "substance addiction" and "substance dependence" to refer to the severe designation of Substance Use Disorders given that these terms are commonly seen in the literature and used in clinical circles.

Theoretical perspective on the sexual victimization/substance use relationship

The expected relationship between sexual victimization and various substance use outcomes may be best explained through the lens of stress-coping and self-medication models of addiction (i.e., negative reinforcement models), which posit that substance use and misuse will be heightened in stress-vulnerable individuals (i.e., those raised in high stress environments with inadequate models of adaptive coping), and that substances will be used to manage stress reactions and psychiatric symptoms that develop in response to acute and chronic life stress (Begle et al., 2011; Khantzian, 1985; Kilpatrick, Acierno, Resnick, Saunders, & Best, 1997; Wills & Hirky, 1996). An alternative perspective is that those who engage in risky substance use behavior may be more likely to place themselves in situations where they could be sexually victimized (Begle et al., 2011; Kilpatrick et al., 1997). Of course, a reciprocal relationship involving a vicious cycle of substance use behavior and sexual victimization may also be in effect (Kilpatrick et al., 1997).

Stress, traumatic stress, and vulnerability to substance addiction: a coping perspective

Both environmental and genetic factors have been implicated in the development and course of substance use disorders (Enoch, 2011; Sinha, 2009, 2011), and people report using substances for a number of reasons including to enhance social activities, to alter mental states, to gain an edge in athletic and academic performance situations, in response to peer pressure, and simply out of curiosity (NIDA, 2010; Volkow & Li, 2004). Germane to the current discussion is a wealth of research evidence pointing to the harmful effects of cumulative life adversity, chronic life stress, and particularly early life traumatic stress including childhood maltreatment-related stress on addiction vulnerability and course of addiction (Ansell, Rando, Tuit, Guarnaccia, & Sinha, 2012; Cleck & Blendy, 2008; Enoch, Hodgkinson, Yuan, Shen, Goldman, & Roy, 2010; Enoch, 2011; Goeders, 2004; Hyman & Sinha, 2009; Lijffijt, Hu, & Swann, 2014; Najavits, Hyman, Ruglass, Hien, & Read, 2017; Sinha, 2008).

Specific to maltreatment-related stress, De Bellis (2002) concluded that maltreatment-related changes to brain stress systems can increase the risk for psychiatric disorders such as posttraumatic stress disorder and major depressive disorder, which in turn can contribute to the development of substance use disorders. Enoch (2011) concluded: "experiencing maltreatment and cumulative stressful life events prior to puberty and particularly in the first few years of life is associated with early onset of problem drinking in adolescence and alcohol and drug dependence in early adulthood" (p. 17). Importantly, Enoch cautioned that a large proportion of stress-exposed children do not go on to develop psychiatric and substance use problems, suggesting that resilience factors are present and/or can be fostered (see Enoch, 2011 and citations within).

Nevertheless, it is evident that, at least for a subset of vulnerable individuals, substance use may be initiated and maintained as a maladaptive method to avoid traumatic memories, numb emotional pain, and escape from intolerable distress. Another possibility is that childhood maltreatment sets vulnerable individuals on a developmental trajectory toward delinquent and risky behavior that includes substance use. Unfortunately, chronic use of substances may only serve to increase the individual's risk of developing a substance use disorder which, upon taking on a life of its own, can further damage brain circuits and lead to severe cognitive and behavioral dysfunction.

Childhood sexual victimization and substance use outcomes in males

Simpson and Miller (2002) conducted a systematic review of empirical studies published between 1970 and 1997 that looked at relationships between childhood sexual and physical abuse and substance use problems in adults and adolescents. When looking at adult and adolescent males in treatment for substance use problems, rates of childhood sexual abuse (average of 16.3% for adults and 16.8% for adolescents) were comparable to the 14.2% to 16% rates found in the general male population (Briere & Elliott, 2003; Finkelhor, Hotaling, Lewis, & Smith, 1990). However, when looking at adult males with histories of childhood sexual victimization who were seeking mental health treatment, the authors found that rates of reported substance use problems were elevated compared to those without histories of childhood sexual victimization (65% versus 25%), suggesting that childhood sexual victimization is a risk factor for developing substance use problems. They indicated that these results could be an accurate reflection of reality, or that men who are seeking treatment for substance use problems may be particularly reluctant to disclose a history of childhood sexual victimization.

It is important to note that more recent studies using sensitive and validated methods of assessing childhood sexual victimization have found higher rates of childhood sexual victimization in substance addicted males. This may demonstrate that, over time, males may have become more willing to disclose childhood sexual abuse, that researchers have become more able to detect it, or that the rates are indicative of a real increase. For example, Hyman, Paliwal, and Sinha (2007) found that 28% of their severely cocaine dependent, treatment-seeking adult male sample reported childhood sexual victimization (which was still less than the 58% reported by women in the sample). Orellana et al. (2014) reported that 38% of men in their sample of methadone treatment seekers reported a history of childhood sexual victimization. Thus, while rates of childhood sexual victimization in drug abusing men in treatment are still much lower than those reported by women, and prior studies have found rates in substance abusing men comparable to those reported in the general population, these more recent studies seem to demonstrate considerably elevated rates of childhood sexual victimization in male, substance-addicted individuals in treatment.

In a more recent review, Butt, Chou, and Browne (2011) examined the relationship between childhood sexual victimization and illicit substance use of males in clinical and general population studies. They found mixed support for an association between childhood sexual victimization and illicit substance use outcomes in males depending upon the sample and particular outcome examined. Their major findings are summarized below:

> In sum, research on community samples demonstrated differences between CSA victims and comparison groups or controls in relation to drug use frequency, multiple drug use, risk of illicit drug use and use of crack cocaine, and severity of drug use. By contrast, significant differences were not reported between CSA victims and controls with regards to early experimentation with drugs, drug problems and illicit drug use at the time of study in general . . . A review of the research in relation to CSA using clinical/specialised samples demonstrated support in relation to an association between CSA and injection drug use, drug use disorder, substance use consequences, earlier drug initiation, drug abuse severity, perceived benefits of drugs, and greater frequency and variety of drug use. However, contradictory results are reported in relation to greater frequency of drug use.
>
> (p. 25)

Overall, their findings indicated that some aspects of illicit substance use were associated, albeit inconsistently, with childhood sexual victimization whereas others were not. The authors cautioned that firm conclusions could not be drawn due to inconsistency across studies and methodological limitations such as the correlational nature of the research and potential confounding factors.

With regard to substance use relapse outcomes (i.e., alcohol and cocaine), researchers have not found an association with childhood sexual victimization in gender-specific analyses of males (Heffner, Blom, & Anthenelli, 2011; Hyman et al., 2008). Greenfield et al. (2002), on the other hand, found that childhood sexual victimization predicted a shorter time to alcohol relapse following inpatient treatment in a mixed, but primarily male, sample (41 women and 59 men), but that the association was no longer significant once they controlled for background demographic variables. The authors suggested that one possible explanation for their findings is that "sexual abuse may heighten an individual's risk for social vulnerabilities that in turn worsen response to alcohol treatment" (p. 232).

While relationships between childhood sexual victimization and substance use outcomes appear to be stronger and more consistent in women, this absolutely does not mean that childhood sexual victimization is not having an effect on substance use outcomes in men. Certainly, a number of studies have demonstrated a significant association between childhood sexual victimization and substance use outcomes in males. It may be that greater variability of disclosure of childhood sexual victimization in male substance-abusing samples is affecting the results across studies or that the effects of childhood sexual victimization on addiction outcomes may be more indirect in boys/men than they are in girls/women. Intervening variables or more proximal factors such as impulse control difficulties, reactivity to conditioned drug cues, antisocial behavior, and greater affiliation with substance-abusing peers may play a more prominent role in mediating the associations between childhood sexual victimization and substance use outcomes in males. Clearly, more research is needed to better understand these relationships and come to firm conclusions.

Childhood sexual victimization complicates the clinical picture in substance use treatment-seeking males

Studies have found that when childhood victimization does occur it often complicates the clinical picture in male substance abusers. Male substance abusers with a history of childhood sexual victimization have been found to have a more severe clinical profile than non-victimized substance abusers, including greater substance use severity, greater psychiatric co-morbidity, greater psychiatric severity (e.g., suicidal thoughts), and increased levels of risky sexual behavior. For example, Schneider, Cronkite, and Timko (2008) assessed a sample of men seeking outpatient substance abuse treatment at intake and at six- and 12-month follow-ups. They found that having a sexual victimization history was associated with more severe substance use problems at intake and greater psychiatric severity at all three assessment points (i.e., intake, six months, and 12 months). Moreover, individuals with a sexual victimization history were more likely to report suicidality at intake and at the six-month assessment.

Orellana et al. (2014) found that having a history of childhood sexual victimization was associated with sex trading (i.e., buying and/or selling sex for money or drugs) and greater Human Immunodeficiency Virus (HIV) risk behavior in heterosexual men who were receiving methadone treatment, and that these relationships were mediated by substance use and psychopathology. They concluded that their study supports the notion that childhood sexual victimization "is strongly associated with increased odds of developing substance abuse and mental health problems, through which increased vulnerability to sex trading and HIV risks seems to evolve" (pp. 124–125).

Case vignette

Ralph, a successful 35-year-old businessman who worked for a large corporation, sought out therapy for alcohol addiction that, although severe, seemed to be secondary to intense social anxiety disorder. Having grown up in a strict religious home with parents who strongly disapproved of alcohol consumption, he had not begun drinking until around age 30, after his career took him several states away from his hometown. At first his alcohol use was well-controlled and allowed him to socialize more consistently and comfortably and, he claimed, to function better in general than he ever had before. However, after about two years his alcohol intake rapidly increased, so that eventually he was drinking up to two bottles of wine a night and two double bottles of wine plus two-fifths of vodka over the weekends. With his marked increase in drinking and his efforts not to let anyone find out its severity, his social anxiety escalated markedly as well.

At intake, Ralph's drinking and social discomfort were so debilitating that he stated, "I can't really enjoy anything." Despite these seriously debilitating difficulties, his skill at work had led to a series of promotions and relocations. However, many other areas of his functioning had become severely compromised. For example, although he had moved to his current residence four months earlier when he had relocated to start a new job, he was still living amidst unpacked boxes because as soon as his work day was over he headed home to drink. The disorganized state of his apartment also supported his avoidance of having anyone over.

Ralph indicated he had always felt shy and socially awkward, and he was often teased and bullied as a child. Although feeling belittled and socially ostracized was a source of anxiety during his growing up years, when he moved away from his hometown to attend college and as his job subsequently took him even further away in his early 20s, his social adjustment improved markedly, and he was able to establish and sustain a network of friends. Over a period of several years he became increasingly confident and convinced that the intense social discomfort he had been plagued by throughout his growing up years was behind him. He reported, however, that about two years after he started drinking and three years before entering treatment his social anxiety returned, escalated markedly, leading to extreme social avoidance and loss of control over his alcohol consumption.

Upon exploration in therapy it became evident that his problem drinking and social anxiety arose as his high school reunion approached, and he considered returning to his hometown to attend it. While a return to the environment in which he had been rejected by peers as a child might have contributed to his mounting distress, he eventually hesitantly explained to his therapist that there was another, more crucial reason for his apprehension. With considerable shame, he described a bond he had developed when he was 11 years old with a boy two years his senior, Craig. In the midst of ongoing ridicule and rejection by his peers, it was especially validating to Ralph that someone older than he had taken a liking him. He was so appreciative of the friendship and so used to maltreatment by his peers that at first he failed to recognize and later tried to deny to himself Craig's increasingly controlling and humiliating behavior toward him.

Ultimately Ralph revealed to his therapist that his anxiety was primarily driven by fear of the possibility of running into Craig if he returned to his hometown to attend the reunion. With intense apprehension and embarrassment, he revealed that one day when he was 13 years old, suddenly and without any warning, Craig wrestled him to the ground, physically overpowered him, and anally raped him. That was the last time they ever spoke to each other. As is frequently the case in instances of sexual assault, before telling his therapist about the rape, Ralph had never disclosed it to anyone. He felt he was at fault for his own victimization and that he should have somehow been able to protect himself, despite the fact that Craig was two years older and considerably bigger than he.

As the date of the reunion grew imminent, Ralph's anxiety rapidly spiked and "everything collapsed." He did not attend the reunion and started avoiding people in general, retreating to the Internet, and as much as possible working from home rather than going into the office. Simultaneously, his alcohol consumption intensified.

Ralph and his therapist set the following goals: (1) establish abstinence from alcohol; (2) increase his time at the office and stop avoiding casual encounters with his co-workers; (3) organize his residence and invite people over; and (4) become comfortable going out and engaging in recreational and social activities. Working toward reducing Ralph's alcohol intake, given both the medical risk it presented and the increasing toll it was likely to take on his ability to function, was the top priority of treatment. In exploring the costs and benefits of continuing to drink versus quitting, it was apparent that the main reason for Ralph's excessive drinking was to manage his extreme social anxiety. Although both his alcohol addiction and social anxiety were clearly trauma-related, arising in the wake of the reunion, which stirred up disturbing memories of the rape and having been teased and bullied, initiating intensely trauma-focused intervention early on would almost certainly have only served to precipitously increase his anxiety and consequently exacerbate both these problems.

In the initial stages, therefore, treatment was aimed at reducing the anxiety that was fueling Ralph's drinking. His therapist taught him an imagery-based relaxation technique that in session effectively reduced his anxiety level from 6 to 2.5 on a 10-point scale. Determined to overcome his difficulties, Ralph was conscientious about consistently practicing this exercise three times a day, logging his Subjective Units of Distress (SUDS) level before and after each instance of practice as instructed in order to work toward reducing his baseline level of distress.

As his anxiety decreased, Ralph was able to gradually increase the period of time during which he was able to maintain sobriety.

Simultaneously, he and his therapist negotiated a series of lifestyle changes he incrementally implemented: unpacking boxes from the move a little at a time; organizing and cleaning his apartment; exercising regularly, beginning with walking and gradually increasing the intensity, in part to lose the considerable weight gained as a result of his heavy alcohol intake; and moving toward resisting his tendency to avoid social situations.

Philosophically, Ralph was not strongly opposed to attending Alcoholics Anonymous (AA) meetings, but he was very hesitant to do so because of his social anxiety. By chipping away at his anxiety with consistent practice of the relaxation exercise and initiation of a course of graded *in vivo* exposure to social situations he would have previously avoided, Ralph was able to attend three AA meetings by the sixth therapy session. As a result of his reduced social anxiety, he also became acquainted with more and more of his co-workers; with cognitive intervention and encouragement to make a point to notice their reactions to him he was increasingly able to recognize that they liked him and sought him out. This recognition represented a major revision of the negative self-concept he had developed in response to having been teased, bullied, and sexually assaulted. With his increased self-confidence, he transitioned to consistently going into the office instead of working from home, and developed an active social life with co-workers and people he met at AA meetings.

After 28 therapy sessions that spanned the next two years, Ralph established sustained remission from alcohol dependence. With his sobriety and comfort in social situations solidly stabilized, his therapist concluded he was now equipped to more directly address the rape. Perhaps due to the gains he had made to this point, especially marked reduction of his anxious arousal and an appreciably augmented sense of self-esteem, after two sessions of imaginal exposure it was apparent that he was no longer triggered by thinking about or discussing the explicit details of the assault. However, he did continue to be disturbed by self-blame for his own victimization and a sense of shame that he had ignored and tolerated Craig's accelerated denigrating behavior toward him in the months preceding the rape and what he saw as a failure to fend it off.

During the next year in therapy, cognitive trauma processing was directed at targeting the beliefs that sustained these perceptions. Much of this work involved encouraging him to identify and examine the validity of the oppressive view of masculinity that permeated the social environment in which he was reared. Bolstered by his sense of security and social acceptance in the present, he was able to develop a much more empathic view of his younger self, recognizing that as a young man in a socially conservative community he was faced with the expectation of maintaining a wildly unrealistic stance of invincibility, confidence, and social adeptness. As he revised his masculine role expectations for himself in the direction of less rigidity and more self-valuation, his self-blame for his own victimization waned, and he became angry about rather than faulting himself for his abuse. He also was able to see how an unreasonable and unrealistic view of masculinity, in conjunction with his sexual violation, fostered pervasive self-deprecation and self-condemnation that fueled his uncontrolled drinking.

About halfway through his third year of treatment his social anxiety had diminished to the point that he was regularly chairing and acting as secretary at AA meetings. In a follow-up session over a year later he reported he had maintained total abstinence from drinking, continued a high level of social activity, was dating, had opened up to his AA sponsor about his sexual assault experiences as part of his fourth and fifth steps in the Twelve Step Program, and had reconnected with old friends from his hometown.

Discussion

The fact that a number of studies demonstrate a relationship between childhood sexual victimization and substance use outcomes in males, and findings that a history of sexual victimization in substance abusing males complicates the clinical picture, speaks to the need to address sexual victimization in substance abuse treatment. The presence of a sexual victimization history may influence treatment planning especially when the victimization is associated with the development of co-morbid posttraumatic stress disorder (PTSD). However, trauma may be associated with a number of psychiatric outcomes in addition to PTSD and substance addiction (Gold, 2008), and, as illustrated by Ralph's case, helping the client to establish a foundation of sobriety and emotional safety before engaging in extensive trauma processing can circumvent the risk of a severe exacerbation of substance abuse and symptoms of other co-occurring difficulties.

Yet, possibly due to masculine gender socialization, a significant barrier to receiving effective treatment for these men may be the fear and gender-role-related shame associated with disclosing sexual victimization to treatment providers or substance-abusing peers. Much of what occurs in substance addiction treatment (e.g., learning ways to identify and cope with cravings and relapse triggers) happens in a heterogeneous group setting with users of different substances and of different backgrounds. For individuals with a history of childhood sexual victimization who may have greater psychiatric co-morbidity and unique triggers of substance use behavior (e.g., hearing a news story of child abuse), treatment in such a setting may not be conducive to addressing the additional concerns and psychiatric comorbidity (e.g., posttraumatic stress symptoms) that may be associated with the sexual victimization history. Individualized treatments or homogeneous groups of substance abusers with histories of sexual victimization where greater confidentiality and trust can be established may be more effective.

Still, a significant barrier to effective care may be helping patients overcome the fear of disclosure even initially to determine where they should be placed for treatment. Direct inquiries about whether a man has ever experienced sexual violation are less likely to be effective than asking more specific questions, such as if he ever was sexually approached by someone older as a child or adolescent or at any point in life found himself in a sexual situation that was uncomfortable or felt forced upon him. In addition, motivational interviewing techniques with a strong focus on expressions of empathy may help to develop trust and elicit patient disclosure of a sexual victimization history, if present. Also, brief, easily administered, sensitive, valid, and reliable screening measures such as the Childhood Trauma Questionnaire-Short form (CTQ-SF; Bernstein et al., 2003), which asks about specific sexual abuse experiences that subjects rate with regard to the frequency with which they occurred, may be useful in detecting childhood sexual victimization in substance addicted males. Sensitive screening tools would be beneficial given that males may not even acknowledge that some of their victimization experiences qualify as sexual victimization (Artime, McCallum, & Peterson, 2014). The incorporation of peer-support interventions provided by male treatment providers with their own sexual victimization and substance addiction experiences may help to overcome this treatment barrier. It is also important for treatment providers to engage in discussions of stigma and shame associated with sexual victimization disclosure prior to asking about it during the initial assessment so it can be better identified and addressed. Moreover, therapists can directly challenge fallacies of masculine gender socialization in order to break down reluctance to disclose sexual victimization (Lisak, 1995).

Acknowledgements

The authors wish to thank Danielle Lewis, MS, and Autumn Birch, BA, for their assistance locating and screening literature for this chapter and Danielle Lewis for assisting with the preparation of the manuscript.

References

American Psychiatric Association. (2013). *Diagnostic and statistical manual of mental disorders* (5th Ed.). Washington, DC: Author.

Ansell, E. B., Rando, K., Tuit, K., Guarnaccia, J., & Sinha, R. (2012). Cumulative adversity and smaller grey matter volume in medial prefrontal, anterior cingulate, and insula regions. *Biological Psychiatry, 72*(1), 57–64. doi: 10.1016/j.biopsych.2011.11.022

Artime, T. M., McCallum, E. B., & Peterson, Z. D. (2014). Men's acknowledgement of their sexual victimization experiences. *Psychology of Men & Masculinity, 15*(3), 313–323. doi: 10.1037/a0033376

Begle, A. M., Hanson, R. F., Danielson, C. K., McCart, M. R., Ruggiero, K. J., Amstadter, A. B., & Kilpatrick, D. G. (2011). Longitudinal pathways of victimization, substance use, and delinquency: Findings from the National Survey of Adolescents. *Addictive Behaviors, 36*(7), 682–689. doi: 10.1016/j.addbeh.2010.12.026

Bernstein, D. P., Stein, J. A., Newcomb, M. D., Walker, E., Pogge, D., Ahluvalia, T., & Zule, W. (2003). Development and validation of a brief screening version of the Childhood Trauma Questionnaire. *Child Abuse & Neglect, 27*(2), 169–190. doi: 10.1016/S0145-2134(02)00541-0

Briere, J., & Elliott, D. M. (2003). Prevalence and psychological sequelae of self-reported childhood physical and sexual abuse in a general population sample of men and women. *Child Abuse & Neglect, 27*, 1205–1222.

Butt, S., Chou, S., & Browne, K. (2011). A rapid systematic review on the association between childhood physical and sexual abuse and illicit drug use among males. *Child Abuse Review, 20*, 6–38. doi: 10.1002/car.1100

Cami, J., & Farre, M. (2003). Mechanisms of disease: Drug addiction. *New England Journal of Medicine, 349*(10), 975–986. doi: 10.1056/NEJMra023160

Cleck, J. N., & Blendy, J. A. (2008). Making a bad thing worse: Adverse effects of stress on drug addiction. *The Journal of Clinical Investigation, 118*(2), 454–461. doi: 10.1172/JCI33946

Crean, R. D., Crane, N. A., & Mason, B. J. (2011). An evidence-based review of acute and long-term effects of cannabis use on executive cognitive functions. *Journal of Addictive Medicine, 5*(1), 1–8. doi: 10.1097/ADM.0b013e31820c23fa

De Bellis, M. D. (2002). Developmental traumatology: A contributory mechanism for alcohol and substance use disorders. *Psychoneuroendocrinology, 27*, 155–170. doi: 10.1016/S0306-4530(01)00042-7

Enoch, M. A. (2011). The role of early life stress as a predictor for alcohol and drug dependence. *Psychopharmacology, 214*, 17–31. doi: 10.1007/s00213-010-1916-6

Enoch, M. A., Hodgkinson, C. A., Yuan, Q., Shen, P. H., Goldman, D., & Roy, A. (2010). The influence of GABRA2, childhood trauma, and their interaction on alcohol, heroin, and cocaine dependence. *Biological Psychiatry, 67*, 20–27. doi: 10.1016/j.biopsych.2009.08.019

Finkelhor, D., Hotaling, G., Lewis, I. A., & Smith, C. (1990). Sexual abuse in a national survey of adult men and women: Prevalence, characteristics, and risk factors. *Child Abuse & Neglect, 14*(1), 19–28.

Goeders, N. E. (2004). Stress, motivation, and drug addiction. *Current Directions in Psychological Science, 13*(1), 33–35. doi: 10.1111/j.0963-7214.2004.01301009.x

Gold, S. N. (2008). The relevance of trauma to general clinical practice. *Psychological Trauma: Theory, Research, Practice, and Policy, S*(1), 114–124. doi: 10.1037/1942-9681.S.1.114

Greenfield, S. F., Kolodziej, M. E., Sugarman, D. E., Muenz, L. R., Vagge, L. M., He, D. Y., & Weiss, R. D. (2002). History of abuse and drinking outcomes following inpatient alcohol treatment: A prospective study. *Drug and Alcohol Dependence, 67*(3), 227–234. doi: 10.1016/S0376-8716(02)00072-8

Heffner, J. L., Blom, T. J., & Anthenelli, R. M. (2011). Gender differences in trauma history and symptoms as predictors of relapse to alcohol and drug use. *The American Journal on Addictions, 20*(4), 307–311. doi: 10.1111/j.1521-0391.2011.00141.x

Heim, C., & Nemeroff, C. B. (2002). Neurobiology of early life stress: Clinical studies. *Seminars in Clinical Neuropsychiatry, 7*(2), 147–159. doi: 10.1053/scnp.2002.33127

Hyman, S. M., Paliwal, P., & Sinha, R. (2007). Childhood maltreatment, perceived stress, and stress-related coping in recently abstinent cocaine dependent adults. *Psychology of Addictive Behaviors, 21*(2), 233–238. doi: 10.1037/0893-164X.21.2.233

Hyman, S. M., Paliwal, P., Chaplin, T. M., Mazure, C. M., Rounsaville, B. J., & Sinha, R. (2008). Severity of childhood trauma is predictive of cocaine relapse outcomes in women but not men. *Drug & Alcohol Dependence, 92*(1–3), 208–216. doi: 10.1016/j.drugalcdep.2007.08.006

Hyman, S. M., & Sinha, R. (2009). Stress-related factors in cannabis use and misuse: Implications for prevention and treatment. *Journal of Substance Abuse Treatment, 36*(4), 400–413. doi: 10.1016/j.jsat.2008.08.005

Khantzian, E. J. (1985). The self-medication hypothesis of addictive disorders: Focus on heroin and cocaine dependence. *American Journal of Psychiatry, 142*, 1259–1264. doi: 10.1176/ajp.142.11.1259

Kilpatrick, D. G., Acierno, R., Resnick, H. S., Saunders, B. E., & Best, C. L. (1997). A 2-year longitudinal analysis of the relationships between violent assault and substance use in women. *Journal of Consulting & Clinical Psychology, 65*(5), 834–847. doi: 10.1037/0022-006X.65.5.834

Lijffijt, M., Hu, K., & Swann, A. C. (2014). Stress modulates illness-course of substance use disorders: A translational review. *Frontiers in Psychiatry, 5*, 1–20. doi: 10.3389/fpsyt.2014.00083

Lisak, D. (1995). Integrating a critique of gender in the treatment of male survivors of childhood abuse. *Psychotherapy: Theory, Research & Practice, 32*(2), 258–269. doi: 10.1037/0033-3204.32.2.258

Najavits, L. M., Hyman, S. M., Ruglass, L. M., Hien, D. A., & Read, J. P. (2017). Substance use disorder and trauma. In S. Gold, C. Dalenberg, & J. Cook (Eds.), *APA handbook of trauma psychology* (pp. 195–213). Washington, DC: American Psychological Association.

National Institute on Drug Abuse (NIDA). (2010). Drugs, brains, and behavior: The science of addiction. doi: 10.1037/e596722007-001

National Institute on Drug Abuse (NIDA). (2012). DrugFacts: Understanding drug abuse and addiction. Retrieved from www.drugabuse.gov/publications/drugfacts/understanding-drug-abuse-addiction on February 18, 2016.

Orellana, E. R., El-Bassel, N., Gilbert, L., Miller, K. M., Catania, J., Epperson, M., & Wu, E. (2014). Sex trading and other HIV risks among drug-involved men: Differential associations with childhood sexual abuse. *Social Work Research, 38*(2), 117–126. doi: 10.1093/swr/svu012

Schneider, R., Cronkite, R., & Timko, C. (2008). Lifetime physical and sexual abuse and substance use treatment outcomes in men. *Journal of Substance Abuse Treatment, 34*(4), 353–361. doi: 10.1016/j.jsat.2008.01.001

Schoenbaum, G., Roesch, M. R., & Stainaker, T. A. (2006). Orbitofrontal cortex, decision-making, and drug addiction. *Trends in Neurosciences, 29*(2), 116–124. doi: 10.1016/j.tins.2005.12.006

Simpson, T. L., & Miller, W. R. (2002). Concomitance between childhood sexual and physical abuse and substance use problems: A review. *Clinical Psychology Review, 22*, 27–77. doi: 10.1016/S0272-7358(00)00088-X

Sinha, R. (2008). Chronic stress, drug use, and vulnerability to addiction. *Annals of the New York Academy of Science, 1141*, 105–130. doi: 10.1196/annals.1441.030

Sinha, R. (2009). Modeling stress and drug craving in the laboratory: Implications for addiction treatment development. *Addiction Biology, 14*(1), 84–98. doi: 10.1111/j.1369-1600.2008.00134.x

Sinha, R. (2011). New findings on biological factors predicting addiction relapse vulnerability. *Current Psychiatry Reports, 13*(5), 398–405. doi: 10.1007/s11920-011-0224-0

Teicher, M. H., Anderson, S. L., Polcari, A., Anderson, C. M., & Navalta, C. P. (2002). Developmental neurobiology of childhood stress and trauma. *Psychiatric Clinics of North America, 25*, 397–426. doi: 10.1016/S0193-953X(01)00003-X

Volkow, N. D., Baler, R. D., & Goldstein, R. Z. (2011). Addiction: Pulling at the neural threads of social behaviors. *Neuron, 69*, 599–602. doi: 10.1016/j.neuron.2011.01.027

Volkow, N. D., & Li, T. (2004). Drug addiction: The neurobiology of behavior gone awry. *Nature Reviews Neuroscience, 5*(12), 963–970. doi: 10.1038/nrn1539

Wills, T. A., & Hirky, A. E. (1996). Coping and substance abuse: A theoretical model and review of the evidence. In M. Zeichnec & N. S. Eudler (Eds.), *Handbook of coping: Theory, research, and applications* (pp. 279–302). New York, NY: Wiley.

Chapter 8

Early-life sexual trauma and adult-life hypersexual behavior (sex addiction) in males

Making the connection

Christine A. Courtois and Robert Weiss

The inclusion of the diagnosis of Posttraumatic Stress Disorder (PTSD) into the *Diagnostic and Statistical Manual of Mental Disorders: DSM-III* (American Psychiatric Association, 1980) was heralded by many as a significant development in the history of psychiatry. Primarily associated with the consequences of combat trauma, the diagnosis consisted of three main symptom criteria: (1) re-experiencing; (2) numbing; and (3) physiological hyperarousal, all with a number of manifestations. Not too long after publication, it became clear to many clinicians and researchers studying and treating childhood abuse that the diagnostic criteria for PTSD were not always an absolute fit for victims of childhood abuse, especially chronic abuse (i.e., "complex trauma") and certain other forms of relational and developmental trauma. In response, Herman (1992) differentiated the consequences of early-life complex trauma from those associated with adult-onset (particularly combat-related) trauma, and proposed criteria for the diagnosis of Complex Posttraumatic Stress Disorder (CPTSD).

Herman's proposed diagnostic formulation identified the developmental aftermath of early-life complex trauma, delineating seven sets of criteria above and beyond those associated with standard PTSD. These criteria include later-life challenges with: emotional regulation; identity and self-worth; dissociation; relationship with the perpetrator; relationships with others; somatization; and how one interprets life events/worldview/spirituality. Research supports the fact that when these consequences go unrecognized, untreated, and unresolved they can reverberate across the entire life span in acute, chronic, and/or delayed forms. Substance and behavioral addictions (including sex addiction) often arise as maladaptive coping mechanisms – misguided attempts to escape the emotional and psychological discomfort and pain wrought by unresolved childhood trauma. In this chapter, we elaborate on this association – in particular the relationship between early-life sexual trauma and adult-life sexual addiction – with an overview of efficacious treatment.[1]

To date, Complex PTSD is not included in the *DSM* as a free-standing diagnosis and, instead, is listed as an associated feature of standard PTSD. However, the PTSD diagnosis has been expanded to include some of the Complex PTSD criteria pertaining to changed beliefs and cognitions about self and others. And a new dissociative subtype of PTSD that closely resembles criteria for Complex PTSD has been included (American Psychiatric Association, 2013). Importantly, the diagnosis of Complex PTSD (built on Herman's original formulation) is to be included in the World Health Organization's soon-to-be-published *International Classification of Disorders* (Cloitre, Garvert, Brewin, Bryant, & Maercker, 2013).

Sexual trauma: the basics

If and when symptomatic victims of early-life sexual trauma enter treatment, they typically present with multiple, compounded, and complex clinical challenges (Courtois, 2010). Consider the case of Jason, a 25-year-old man:

> Jason grew up the only son of two alcoholics. His father sexually abused him from a very young age and his mother abused him verbally, emotionally, and sometimes physically. With both parents, the abuse grew worse when they drank. Now, as an adult, Jason is struggling to hold on to a job, to maintain his friendships, and to control his sexual behavior. He says that every night after work he logs on to half a dozen or so "adult friend-finder apps" and chats with people seeking sex. More often than not, he has sex with at least two or three different people, and sometimes more. As soon as one person leaves his apartment, he's online looking for the next one. Often he is awake and sexually acting out until three or four in the morning, which leaves him both tired and unproductive the next day at work – an issue that may soon get him fired.

1 Editor's note: See Chapter 12 by Kort in the companion volume to this one, *Understanding the Sexual Betrayal of Boys and Men: The Trauma of Sexual Abuse*, for another view of compulsive sexuality.

> Deeply ashamed of his behavior, Jason nevertheless continues to engage in it, stating in therapy that it's the only thing that makes him feel alive. At this point, he's convinced that he's nuts. While intellectually capable far beyond his current situation, emotionally he is fragile and depressive. He has no way of knowing or understanding that his compulsive adult sexual responses to any and all forms of emotional discomfort are in fact learned coping mechanisms that are relatively normal (or at least expected) given the degree and nature of the complex trauma he experienced in childhood. Therefore, he simply sees himself as bad, unworthy of love, and hopelessly broken.

Unsurprisingly, in the early stages of treatment Jason did not see a connection between his childhood abuse and his adult-life behavioral problems. This non-comprehension is both normal and understandable, as the obvious response to trauma is a desire to not think about it or relive it. As a result, adults like Jason with a history of early-life trauma, especially sexual trauma, typically are depressed and/or anxious and cope with their trauma by pushing it away – sometimes "numbing out" with addictive substances and/or addictive behaviors (compulsive sex, in Jason's case), other times alienating others and engaging in various forms of self-destructive activity, all without any understanding of their motivations.

Due to this lack of understanding and association, many sexually traumatized men whose issues manifest later in life think of themselves and their symptoms as crazy, as we see with Jason. These men simply don't understand that their upbringing was lacking and left them without a positive sense of self or needed life-skills, and that their problematic behaviors are an adaptive response to what they experienced. Instead, they develop negative and shamed views of themselves, becoming highly self-critical and blaming themselves for events and circumstances over which they had little or no control. In other words, the beliefs they developed as children about the cause and reasons for their abuse – and often what they were told by those who abused them – create a deeply ingrained shamed self and a negative self-concept, which in turn feeds a wide variety of later-life psychological issues (Courtois, 2010).

Sadly, research findings corroborate that traumatized children are more likely than traumatized adults to develop trauma-related disorders like PTSD, depression, anxiety, dissociative disorders, externalizing and internalizing behavior, substance and behavioral addictions, and the like

(Ford, 2009; Ford & Courtois, 2009, 2013). This is especially true when no relief or support is available and the abuse is perpetrated by someone in close relationship to the child, constituting a betrayal-trauma (Freyd, 1996). Research also suggests that the more times a child is traumatized, the greater the likelihood of adverse reactions later in life (Anda et al., 2006). In fact, young people with four or more significant traumatic experiences prior to age 18 are:

- 1.8 times as likely to smoke cigarettes;
- 1.9 times as likely to become obese;
- 2.4 times as likely to experience ongoing anxiety;
- 2.5 times as likely to experience panic reactions;
- 3.6 times as likely to be depressed;
- 3.6 times as likely to qualify as promiscuous;
- 6.6 times as likely to engage in early-life sexual intercourse;
- 7.2 times as likely to become alcoholic;
- 11.1 times as likely to become intravenous drug users.

(Anda et al., 2006)

In other words, there is an undeniable link between early-life complex developmental trauma and numerous adult-life psychological issues – including substance abuse and behavioral addictions (like sexual addiction).

Sexual addiction: the basics

Before further discussing the link between early-life sexual trauma and later-life sexual addiction, it is important to understand the basics of sexual addiction. For the most part, sex addiction looks a lot like any other addiction – the only significant difference being the addict's "drug of choice." In fact, the primary diagnostic criteria for sexual addiction closely mirror the criteria for every other addiction (Kafka, 2010; Weiss, 2015; Weiss & Schneider, 2014):

- ongoing obsession/preoccupation;
- loss of control (typically evidenced by failed attempts to quit or cut back and/or an inability to stop the behavior pattern once started);
- continuation with the behavior pattern despite directly related negative life consequences.

Thus, sex addicts engage in repetitive patterns of compulsive sexual fantasy and activity, and they continue to do so even as their clearly out of control behaviors (to an external observer) create significant problems in their lives – relationship issues, trouble at work or in school, physical risk, declining physical and/or emotional health, financial turmoil, legal concerns, mood disorders, and more (Hall, 2013; Kafka, 2010; Weiss, 2015; Weiss & Schneider, 2014).

Can a behavior (like sex) really be addictive?

At present, there is a general cultural consensus regarding addiction to substances – alcohol, nicotine, illicit drugs, certain prescription medications, etc. Less easily understood is the concept of behavioral addictions (also called "process addictions" or, sometimes, "behavioral compulsions"). Much of this confusion stems from the fact that behavioral addictions sometimes involve activities that are (for most people, most of the time) healthy and even life-affirming. For instance, eating and sex, two of the most commonly diagnosed behavioral addictions, are absolutely necessary to human existence, as they contribute to survival of both the individual and the species. In fact, these activities are so inherently necessary that the human brain is preprogrammed to experience them as pleasurable.

This experience of pleasure is evoked primarily by the release of the neurotransmitter dopamine into the nucleus accumbens, commonly referred to as the brain's "rewards center." The nucleus accumbens connects, via neural pathways, to other areas of the brain, including the hippocampus (memory), the ventral striatum (processing rewards), the dorsal anterior cingulate (anticipating rewards), the amygdala (the alarm center, processing the significance of events and emotions), and the prefrontal cortex (decision-making, judgment). Via these pathways the nucleus accumbens communicates to other parts of the brain the pleasurable sensations associated with being sexual (or eating). In this way humans remember the pleasure they've experienced related to life-sustaining activities, and thus are internally prompted to engage in the same or similar behaviors in the future.

Unfortunately, people with early-life trauma issues can learn to use/abuse the brain's dopaminergic response as a means of coping with and/or dissociating from stress and emotional pain (National Institute on Drug Abuse, 2007). For these individuals, the pleasurable dopamine response evoked by sexual fantasy and activity (or other highly pleasurable and therefore potentially addictive behaviors) is used as a way to tolerate and/or escape from stress, anxiety, depression, and the emotional discomfort wrought by unresolved early-life trauma. In other words, people who struggle with process addictions engage in their problematic patterns of behavior not as a way to have a good time, but as a way to emotionally escape and therefore control what they are feeling. These are *the exact same reasons* that alcoholics drink and drug addicts get high.

To further understand the similarities between substance addictions and behavioral addictions, it may help to consider the cocaine addict who, cash in hand, has found a source for the drugs he so desperately desires. In the moment, with little conscious thought, he will leave work early without informing his boss, hop in the car, and race to his dealer's house – all the while experiencing a sense of emotional euphoria and a tunnel-like focus on obtaining and using his drug of choice. Isn't he high already? After all, his thinking is impaired (he's making bad decisions), his heart is racing, his hands are clammy, and he feels compelled to purchase and use the drugs no matter the consequences. And the closer he gets to using, the harder his heart pounds, the more he perspires, and the more distorted and misinformed his thinking becomes. Put simply, this addict gets high on the anticipatory fantasy and euphoric recall his thoughts produce *long before he ingests the drug itself.*

Sexual addiction (and other behavioral addictions) operate on the same "anticipatory high" principle. For instance, sex addicts find as much (if not more) pleasure and emotional escape in sexual fantasies and the pursuit of sex as they do in the sex act itself (Carnes, 2001; Weiss, 2015; Weiss & Schneider, 2014). Sex addicts sometimes refer to this elevated, fantasy-driven state of neurochemical excitement as being in "the bubble" or "the trance" (Carnes, 2001; Hall, 2013; Weiss, 2015). In this state of fantasy-driven dopaminergic mood elevation, they will literally lose touch with reality for hours or even days at a time – high on the idea of sex, with little or no actual physical contact. Thus, for both substance addicts and behavioral addicts, the fantasies and actions that lead up to actually using/acting out (the ritualized *process* of the addiction) are every bit as compelling and desirable as the actual drug or behavior. In short, the pairing of intense fantasy and ritual produces a highly desired form of neurochemical arousal, which serves as a distraction from intolerable (to the addict) emotional discomfort.

Early-life sexual trauma, sexual shame, and sexual addiction

> Marcus grew up in a neglectful, emotionally abusive, and alcoholic home in which he was repeatedly reminded of his uselessness and stupidity by his father. At the same time, his mother clung to him as "her rock," using him as her confidant and for emotional support as a healthier mother would use her spouse (a pattern known as covert or emotional incest). Then, when adolescence set in, she incessantly and inappropriately commented on his developing body and found reasons to invade his personal space and his privacy – sitting too close, walking in on him when he was showering, etc.
>
> By age 14, Marcus was abusing alcohol and marijuana, quickly learning that getting high eased his confusion and the pain of feeling unlovable and defective. By age 15 he realized he was gay, which, in the small town he grew up in, was simply not acceptable. Feeling "different," with little mirroring or insight into his evolving sexual orientation, his feelings of isolation and shame escalated. Before long, he was getting drunk and high at school. He also developed a habit of sneaking out of the house late at night, looking for something or someone who could assuage his profound feelings of loneliness and isolation. It wasn't long before he found the places where gay men cruised for anonymous late-night sex.
>
> Though the outside observer might say that Marcus was being abused and taken advantage of (and he was, when sex occurred with an adult while he was still a minor), to him, each sexual experience felt like a powerful conquest. By engaging in the pursuit of sex, especially when drunk or high, he was able (in the moment) to feel as if he were (to these strangers) special, important, wanted, needed, and connected – all the things he never felt in his family of origin. In essence, Marcus learned to let men use him as an object (much as his mother did), which gave him a temporary sense of control over his unmet dependency needs. By the time he was 18, he had a fully evolved co-occurring addictive disorder – drug and alcohol abuse paired with compulsive sexual behavior.

Most addiction treatment specialists are relatively in-tune with the general connection between trauma, shame, and addictions. What often goes unrecognized, however, is the powerful role that *sexual trauma* and *sexual shame* play in the formation and maintenance of addictions, whether these involve substances, behaviors, or both. As early as the mid-1980s, when Browne and Finkelhor (1986) published one of the first reviews of the literature on the aftereffects of sexual abuse, the link between childhood sexual abuse, both overt and covert, and later-life issues with alcoholism and drug addiction was discerned. This finding has been replicated in numerous additional studies (Carnes, 2001; Rohsenow, Corbett, & Devine, 1988).

Without doubt, childhood sexual abuse, whether single-incident or chronic, often leaves its victims with feelings of both confusion and shame. This is true whether the abuse is overt, involving touch and actual physical intrusion, or covert, as occurs when a parent "emotionally partners" or becomes over-involved with a child (Adams, 2011).[2] Exacerbating matters is the fact that childhood sexual abuse can often be coupled with other forms of early-life trauma (Courtois & Ford, 2009; Ford & Courtois, 2013).

Oftentimes sexually shamed children begin to self-medicate their emotional discomfort relatively early in life – usually during adolescence but sometimes even before. This process of self-soothing typically involves alcohol and/or drugs. That said, many children also learn (or are taught) that they can self-soothe with sexual behaviors, most often sexual fantasy (not infrequently, fantasies that eroticize an aspect of their sexual trauma) coupled with masturbation. These associations may be reinforced through the stimulation of online pornography, where virtually any sexual scenario is available. While distracting in the moment, over time these fantasies and behaviors tend to intensify pre-existing feelings of sexual shame and emotional discomfort, thus creating an even greater need for emotional self-soothing, escape, and dissociation. A vicious cycle takes over and behaviors may escalate over time as it takes more stimulation (and possibly more risk) to experience the same "high."

Recognizing and assessing complex trauma and sexual addiction

Both sexual trauma and sexual addiction are under-recognized and under-diagnosed, partly because most clinicians have not been trained to properly assess and treat these problems (Courtois & Gold, 2009), and

2 Editor's note: See Chapter 11 by Adams in this volume.

partly because the *DSM* does not provide formalized diagnostic criteria for sexual addiction (American Psychiatric Association, 2013) or for complex developmental forms of PTSD, except for the newly added dissociative subtype. As such, it is unsurprising that clinicians rarely consider the relationship between early-life sexual trauma and adult-life sexual addiction. In recognition of this, we recommend that all psychosocial assessments and mental health screening tools include specific questions about past and recent traumatic events and experiences, asked in behavioral terms like, "Did such and such ever happen to you?" along with equally specific questions about both past and present sexual behaviors, such as, "Do you masturbate, and, if so, how often?" and "Are you sexually active, and is sex comfortable for you?"

Assessing traumatic events and sexual behaviors in this way indicates to clients that these topics are significant and gives them permission to talk openly about these often uncomfortable/embarrassing/shameful subjects. Such questions are analogous to universal precautions in medical treatment, where precautions are taken ahead of time as prophylaxes and in anticipation of possible conditions. Asking detailed questions during an assessment recognizes that many (perhaps most) clients, especially males, do not disclose sexual trauma histories or problematic patterns of sexual behavior unless directly asked. Instead, they tend to ask for help with symptomatic issues like depression, anxiety, intimacy disorders, and relationship problems. Without deeper exploration, these clients are likely to be treated only for their symptoms while their underlying sexual trauma and problematic patterns of adult sexual behavior go unassessed and therefore untreated.

For assessment of sexual trauma and sexual addiction, a variety of written/computerized assessment instruments asking about specific types of traumatic events and sexual experiences and aftereffects are available and can be combined with interviewing. It is important for therapists to understand that being asked about sexual trauma and sexual addiction is stressful and may evoke feelings of shame and self-loathing, and in some cases anger. Certainly some men are relieved to be asked about their trauma and sexual histories, but others are not. This means that therapists must always understand that questions about traumatic experience and sexual activity, even when asked with sensitivity, can cause pain and discomfort. As with all formalized assessments, the pacing and intensity of questions should be adjusted based on the client's individual needs and concerns – pausing or even stopping if the process is too stressful. Usually, when clients understand that the therapist is respectful, non-voyeuristic, nonjudgmental, attentive, and simply trying to uncover and understand the issues *with them*, they are more likely to accurately report their experiences and symptoms.

Therapists should also be aware that some clients will disown, deny, or outright lie about the nature and extent of their trauma history and their adult sexual activity even when asked about these directly (Courtois, 2010). Some of the more common reasons that sexual trauma survivors withhold or mislead include:

- They are not comfortable discussing their trauma.
- They don't understand what happened as traumatic or problematic.
- They are ashamed of what happened to them.
- They are under threat of retribution if they say anything.
- Disclosure feels disloyal, especially within the family or some other system where loyalty is expected.
- They don't trust authority figures or anyone in a helping role.
- They don't think what happened to them is relevant or connected to their current difficulties.
- They can't/don't/won't remember the trauma.

Sex addicts withhold and mislead for similar reasons, including:

- They are not comfortable discussing sexual fantasies and behaviors.
- They are embarrassed about the nature and/or the extent of their sexual fantasies and behaviors.
- They don't want to give up the consistent sense of power and control offered them by their addiction.
- They don't trust authority figures or anyone in a helping role.
- They don't view their sexual behavior as related to their depression, anxiety, or whatever else it is they've entered treatment for.

Treatment professionals should not make assumptions or judgments about motives for nondisclosure by complex trauma survivors, regardless of whether they are sexually addicted. For some, silence is in the interest of self-protection. For others, a degree of trust is needed before they are able to divulge such sensitive information. In such cases, disclosure will typically occur slowly over time as the therapeutic alliance develops. At times, disclosure is facilitated when the therapist explains that assessment is a collaborative effort with the client in control of the process. Clients should also be told they can ask for clarification if a question is unclear, and they can choose to not answer a particular question or questions (returning to that topic later in the therapeutic process as necessary or indicated). Some clients benefit from assignments to write about their experiences for later discussion with the therapist.

Treatment of sexually addicted sexual trauma survivors: the basics

Safety and sobriety first

It is a given that sexual trauma survivors cannot heal deep violations if/when they are still being traumatized (in any way). As such, risk assessment and safety planning are essential foundations of treatment. These involve an assessment of current risks, along with the development and implementation of specific actions and skills (i.e., emotional regulation and means of self-soothing) that can ensure personal safety in the present. When clients are actively at risk (i.e., still in an abusive relationship, engaged in sexually dangerous activities, engaged in self-harm, highly suicidal, etc.), establishing safety may take a great deal of attention and effort (Turkus & Kahler, 2006). Sex addicts cannot heal when they are still actively self-medicating via obsessive sexual fantasies and compulsive sexual behaviors. As such, a plan for "sexual sobriety" must be developed and implemented (in conjunction with safety) before other therapeutic work can effectively occur.

The treatment alliance

Therapy for complex trauma and related symptoms (including sexual addiction) requires an informed therapist with whom a trusting and meaningful "therapeutic alliance" is formed. Dr. Sandra Bloom has aptly described the building of a therapeutic alliance as "relational healing for relational injury" (Bloom, 1997). Typically this alliance develops over time and is based on the trustworthiness and attunement of the therapist, and the client understanding that he and the therapist are working together in the client's best interests. Establishing a therapeutic alliance in this way can help undo a lifetime of mistrust – a major therapeutic advance in and of itself.

Importantly, this process extends to not just the therapist but to others in the therapeutic environment, starting with the client's peer support group. Residential treatment settings, group treatment, 12-step support, and other peer support networks allow sexually addicted sexual trauma survivors to safely discuss their issues with supportive, empathetic, and nonjudgmental others, thereby extending their treatment alliance. These survivors learn that they are not alone in what happened to them and in the feelings and self-perceptions they developed, nor are they alone in the maladaptive coping methods they've relied upon. In time, they learn to give as well as take in group recovery settings, working for the benefit of all. Often these secondary treatment alliances are incredibly powerful from a healing standpoint.

Facing versus avoiding

Sexual trauma survivors typically use avoidance mechanisms in their attempts to emotionally self-regulate and self-soothe. They isolate, they keep secrets, they become people-pleasers, they get aggressive, they dissociate, they bond with their perpetrators, they "numb out" with substances and/or behaviors (including compulsive sexuality), etc. And while all of these mechanisms can shield these men from pain, they also prevent the experiencing, processing, and resolution of traumatic events. In contrast, *the core of complex trauma treatment involves exploring and processing traumatic experiences, memories, and emotions as a way to integrate and resolve them*. This means that sexual trauma survivors must over time engage with traumatic memories rather than avoiding or dissociating from them.

Unsurprisingly, dredging up painful memories can temporarily make symptoms of complex trauma worse rather than better, causing a return (or a desire to return) to tried-and-true coping mechanisms like sexual acting out. As such, addressing trauma must take place in an environment of safety with a focus on emotional and behavioral containment and healthy coping skills, including the ability to regulate emotions and to stay sexually sober. To this end, clients are taught skills to manage dissociative responses, to stay connected with physical responses, and to remain "present" and aware. To this end, the therapist helps clients separate the past from the present and to understand that remembered trauma is not occurring in the moment, even though flashbacks and other re-experiencing symptoms might make it seem as though it is.

Integrated and concurrent trauma-informed sex addiction treatment

Over the years, the authors of this chapter have independently (and now jointly) developed integrated models of treatment for addictions coupled with other psychological issues, including sexual trauma. This treatment approach, utilizing clinically proven methodologies for both sexual trauma and addictions treatment (some of which have empirical support and are evidence-based), recognizes the interconnected nature of unresolved trauma and addictions and the fact that they often have a negative synergistic impact. It is essential that, for full recovery, these conditions be treated concurrently so that clients heal from both issues simultaneously. This belief is well-supported by studies showing that addicts with extensive trauma histories have a much harder time maintaining sobriety than addicts without such histories (Najavits, 2002; Ouimette & Brown, 2003). In fact, sobriety may bring with it the return of posttraumatic symptoms and memories, rendering the addict vulnerable to relapse.

The stages of Integrated and Concurrent Trauma-Informed Sex Addiction Treatment developed by the authors are as follows:

- Pretreatment (Assessment): Assessment usually involves several clinical interviews in whatever the treatment setting (at the point of initial contact with the therapist or, in residential or hospital programs, at the time of admission with nursing, psychiatry, psychology, counseling, and other program staff). Psychological instruments might also be administered by computer or in written format, some of which might be re-administered later as a way to measure the client's progress. As discussed previously, assessment involves a wide-ranging psychosocial evaluation, including questions about trauma and other crises in the family or elsewhere, along with questions about sexual functioning, including fantasies and behaviors, relationships, other (nonsexual) addictions, and commonly co-occurring symptoms of trauma such as depression, dissociation, and anxiety. Based on the assessment, an individualized treatment plan is developed.

- Stage One: This stage is devoted to safety, meaning sexual sobriety and crisis management, often including a short period of sexual abstinence followed by a clearly articulated and co-created plan for healthy sexuality (i.e., the avoidance of problematic behaviors), similar to how we use contractual and behavioral methods to help contain addictive/compulsive patterns of eating. Emphasis is on crisis management, along with extensive psychoeducation about sexual trauma, sexual addiction, and their interaction. Twelve-step and other peer support groups are introduced as they relate to sexual sobriety and overall mental and physical health. The goals here are simple – to improve ego strength, to engage the client's observing ego, to contain any dangerous or self-harmful sexual behavior, and to improve social involvement and social functioning. Residential treatment settings may also incorporate a variety of alternative, experiential, and complementary modalities (meditation, yoga, neuro- and biofeedback, acupuncture), expressive therapies (art therapy, psychodrama), massage, mindfulness stress reduction, animal assisted therapies, etc. These can also be included as adjuncts to individual treatment. Sessions with family members might occur in this stage as a means of assessing relationship status, providing education, and providing support. Once the basics have been covered and the individual has achieved a reasonable degree of life-stability, functionality, sobriety, and a decreased risk of relapse, stage two can be implemented.
- Stage Two: This stage is focused on the processing of trauma and its impact using specialized trauma-focused techniques (Prolonged Exposure Therapy, Eye Movement Desensitization and Reprocessing, Cognitive Behavioral Therapy, etc.). The goal of this stage is to reintroduce and reintegrate trauma response in doses that are manageable through use of learned coping and emotional modulation skills. The therapist closely monitors the client's responses in order to keep the client in his "window of tolerance," helping him to face and process trauma without becoming overwhelmed. Typically, available therapeutic techniques are discussed in advance with the client so he may help choose one or more that suits his specific needs. All of the techniques involve some degree of exposure to what has been avoided/dissociated/suppressed, often resulting in a temporary intensification of distress. Clients are encouraged to discuss their reactions in detail with the therapist, who then offers both emotional

support and corrective information when problematic or erroneous interpretations and perceptions are uncovered. Shame, loss, anger, and grief are usually at the forefront during this stage. Over time, this emotional and cognitive processing of past traumas and associated memories to the point of changed perceptions and resolution results in the lessening of symptoms and, in turn, an easier time maintaining sobriety and living a more stable and satisfying life.

- Stage Three: In this stage, treatment focuses on the client's newfound ability to make life choices based not on his history of sexual trauma and sexual addiction, but on freedom from those bonds and a newly developed sense of self-worth and personal empowerment. Clients are encouraged to apply their newfound knowledge and skills to a life of sexual sobriety and safety from additional abuse and trauma. Many life changes may be in order during this stage – developing intimacy, recovering from sexual difficulties, improved parenting, developing new relationships and letting old ones go, discussing past abuse and trauma with perpetrators and others, determining whether to initiate a particular course of action (police report, further disclosure, confrontation, lawsuit, etc.), re-establishing a career or resetting a career path, and more. Twelve-step programs and group therapy can be especially useful as a foundation for these efforts.

Although the treatment stages are presented above in linear format, they are actually rather fluid in application, with clients engaging in the different treatment tasks and moving back and forth between the stages as needed. For example, if a client reports feeling unsafe and overwhelmed during the formal trauma processing that takes place in stage two, he returns to stage one's more cognitive safety planning and skill-building to re-stabilize and practice skills. Once stabilization and skills are reestablished, the trauma exposure work of stage two resumes. Furthermore, stage three is often implemented even though stage two is ongoing (and may continue to be ongoing for quite some time). Throughout the stages there is planning for backslides and relapse, with setbacks treated as problems to be solved rather than personal failures. At all stages, clients are encouraged to take risks with self-exploration in a safe and supportive environment and to engage in new behaviors based on newly acquired perspectives and skills.

Of note: Psychotherapy may be supplemented with psychopharmacotherapy – the use of medications to alleviate the symptoms of psychological disorders, including addictions. It should be noted that *psychopharmacological medications do not cure the underlying disorder*. Instead, they lessen the symptoms and their negative impact, sometimes making it easier for clients to tolerate things like re-experiencing trauma in therapy sessions. As such, these medications are best used in conjunction with a psychotherapeutic approach (or multiple psychotherapeutic approaches) and within a collaborative relationship with a prescribing psychiatrist who is knowledgeable about trauma treatment and addiction medicine.

For an example of Integrated and Concurrent Trauma-Informed Sex Addiction Treatment, consider the case of Moises, a 36-year-old man:

> Moises entered therapy after he met a wonderful woman, fell in love, and asked her to marry him (a proposal she accepted). It seems that after getting engaged Moises became extremely anxious and depressed, and he began to drink heavily (after nearly six years sober) and to act out sexually – primarily with porn and prostitutes found on hookup apps. Worried that his fiancée would find out about his cheating (and his relapse with drinking), he entered therapy, desperate for a solution.
>
> During assessment, Moises was asked about his sexual history, including any early-life abuse he'd experienced. Based on his reaction, it was immediately clear to his therapist that early-life sexual trauma would need to be addressed. However, it was also clear that Moises had not previously discussed this abuse and was reticent to do so now because of the emotional pain these memories caused him. Recognizing this, his therapist stretched this portion of the assessment over many sessions, getting the story piecemeal to the extent Moises could tolerate questioning.
>
> In the interim, Moises and his therapist developed a plan for chemical and sexual sobriety that included both addiction focused group therapy and 12-step recovery meetings (for substance abuse and also for sexual addiction). So Moises' treatment was able to move forward with stage one (safety) even though portions of the assessment were ongoing.
>
> In time, Moises was able to share in therapy about the full extent of his childhood abuse, which involved oral sex with his mother and an

aunt beginning at the age of 10 and continuing until he went to boarding school at 14. He also told his therapist that he did "the usual stuff" at boarding school, but he did not seem nearly as bothered by that behavior as what occurred within the family.

When Moises had a few months of chemical and sexual sobriety under his belt, he told his therapist that he felt ready to address his early-life trauma, and, after explanation and discussion, he and the therapist agreed on a combination of Prolonged Exposure Therapy and Cognitive Behavioral Therapy, conducted in both individual and group sessions. Moises also agreed to bring his fiancée into his process of healing. (By this point she was openly wondering what was really going on with him, knowing only that he'd relapsed with alcohol, returned to AA, and started therapy.) Both the therapist and Moises felt she deserved to know that he'd cheated on her, and about his underlying issues (the sexual abuse). They also felt that although she might initially be angry about his cheating, she would ultimately be supportive regarding his addiction recovery and trauma issues. And in fact this proved to be the case.

Unearthing and reliving the abuse Moises experienced with his mother and aunt was an emotionally difficult process that took well over a year, with numerous breaks to refocus on safety and sobriety (and to overcome one brief relapse with alcohol). He and his fiancée agreed to temporarily postpone their wedding while he dealt with these issues, and they also started in couples counseling – sessions that were incredibly enlightening and empowering for both individuals. Eventually, Moises developed a strong and wonderfully empathetic support network filled with other survivors of childhood sexual abuse, other recovering addicts, and his fiancée. Unfortunately, neither his mother nor his aunt were willing to participate in his process of healing, choosing instead to live in denial and to leave him to his own devices, to heal as best he could.

Today, Moises and his fiancée are married, and both feel that walking through his trauma and addiction issues is the best thing that could have happened to them as individuals and as a couple. Moises says he is currently reassessing his career goals, thinking about moving away from his sales job and into a helping profession. His wife supports this idea, and has encouraged him to take a few classes at the local college. Moises remains active in 12-step groups for alcoholism and sexual addiction, sponsoring other recovering men in both programs. And he continues to attend a weekly therapy group for male survivors of sexual abuse.

Moises says that at times he still feels depressed and anxious, and when he feels this way he thinks about drinking and relapsing with porn or a prostitute. However, because he has such a strong recovery support network, along with a wife who is fully aware of his issues and therefore tuned in to his emotional state, he has avoided relapse without much struggle.

Individualized treatment programming

Needless to say, every sexually addicted sexual trauma survivor's treatment arc is different. Each client arrives with specific problematic behaviors and a unique background, so each needs an approach tailored to his particular needs. Some will respond best to individual therapy supplemented by group work. Others will do best in group settings, making little progress one-to-one. Still others will struggle utterly until they are physically and emotionally separated from the people, places, and things that have perpetrated trauma on them or that remind them of their trauma.

If a sexually addicted sexual trauma survivor is struggling with core concepts of healing or can't seem to establish a footing in recovery and sobriety, then either intensive outpatient or inpatient residential treatment may be recommended to jump-start the process. These concentrated programs can last as little as a few weeks or as long as several months. In such settings, sexually addicted complex trauma survivors are removed from the people, places, and things that initiate and/or reinforce their trauma and drive their addiction. They are instead surrounded by supportive, empathetic staff members and other patients who are also dealing with traumatic re-experiencing, deep shame, and debilitating sexual addictions.

It is important to remember that there is no "cure" for either trauma or addiction, nor is there a "one size fits all" approach to healing. What treatment and recovery do is provide sexually addicted sexual trauma survivors with skills and tools that can reduce the power of both their trauma and their addiction. In all likelihood, unwanted memories of past traumas will persist to some degree even after extensive treatment, as will the desire to re-engage with compulsive sexuality. But these memories and desires need not be as debilitating and all-consuming if the client utilizes recovery skills, including reaching out for support before a crisis occurs.

Interestingly, the skills that are learned early in recovery typically become a sexually addicted sexual trauma survivor's go-to coping mechanisms. Many men recovering from sex addiction and underlying sexual trauma report feeling that their healthy coping mechanisms should evolve and become more sophisticated over time. And to a certain extent this does happen. But when the chips are down, when the sexually addicted sexual trauma survivor is hit with a powerful trigger out of the blue, it is almost always the basic skills that save the day.

It is also important to point out that recovery from addiction and trauma does not happen in a vacuum. A large part of recovery is dependent on relationships with other people who are also in recovery. These individuals can be found in therapy settings and various support groups, including 12-step groups. That said, many sexually addicted sexual trauma survivors will also remain in individual, one-to-one therapy, as this venue tends to provide a more directed approach to dealing with the emotions that past traumas continually bring up. Whatever the setting, it helps to have empathetic others who can and will provide support in times of distress and need. The significance of the client's healthy family and primary relationships cannot be overemphasized; however, these individuals have also been affected and they may also need ongoing support, education, and conjoint therapy.

In summary, treatment is now available that recognizes the synergy between early-life sexual trauma and later-life sexual addiction. Complex stress disorders consist of the classic symptoms of PTSD but also include other, more developmental criteria that require treatment for the individual to recover. This chapter offers an overview of these issues and outlines a treatment model that concurrently addresses issues of trauma response and sexual addiction. The model remains to be empirically tested; however, many trauma-focused strategies that are employed in the mid-phase of treatment currently are identified as evidence-based.

References

Adams, K. (2011). *Silently seduced, revised and updated: When parents make their children partners*. Deerfield Beach, FL: Health Communications, Inc.

American Psychiatric Association. (1980). *Diagnostic and statistical manual of mental disorders: DSM-III*. Washington, DC: American Psychiatric Association.

American Psychiatric Association. (2013). *Diagnostic and statistical manual of mental disorders: DSM-5*. Washington, DC: American Psychiatric Association.

Anda, R., Felitti, V., Bremner, J., Walker, J., Whitfield, C., Perry, B., . . . Giles, W. (2006). The enduring effects of abuse and related adverse experiences in childhood. *European Archives of Psychiatry and Clinical Neuroscience, 256*(3), 174–186.

Bloom, S. L. (1997). *Creating sanctuary: Toward the evolution of sane societies*. New York, NY: Routledge.

Browne, A., & Finkelhor, D. (1986). Impact of child sexual abuse: A review of the research. *Psychological Bulletin, 99*(1), 66–77.

Carnes, P. (2001). *Out of the shadows: Understanding sexual addiction* (3rd Ed.). Center City, MN: Hazelden.

Cloitre, M., Garvert, D. W., Brewin, C. R., Bryant, R. A., & Maercker, A. (2013). Evidence for proposed ICD-11 PTSD and complex PTSD: A latent profile analysis. *European Journal of Psychotraumatology, 4*. Retrieved from www.ejpt.net/index.php/ejpt/article/view/20706.

Courtois, C. A. (2010). *Healing the incest wound: Adult survivors in therapy* (2nd Ed.). New York, NY: W. W. Norton.

Courtois, C. A., & Ford, J. D. (Eds.). (2009). *Treating complex traumatic stress disorders: An evidence-based guide*. New York, NY: Guilford.

Courtois, C. A., & Gold, S. N. (2009). The need for inclusion of psychological trauma in the professional curriculum: A call to action. *Psychological Trauma: Theory, Research, Practice, and Policy, 1*(1), 3–23.

Ford, J. D. (2009). Neurobiological and developmental research: Clinical implications. In C. A. Courtois & J. D. Ford (Eds.), *Treating complex traumatic stress disorders: An evidence-based guide* (pp. 31–58). New York, NY: Guilford.

Ford, J. D., & Courtois, C. A. (2009). Defining and understanding complex trauma and complex traumatic stress disorders. In C. A. Courtois & J. D. Ford (Eds.), *Treating complex traumatic stress disorders: An evidence-based guide* (pp. 13–30). New York, NY: Guilford.

Ford, J. D., & Courtois, C. A. (2013). *Treating complex traumatic stress disorders in children and adolescents: Scientific foundations and therapeutic models*. New York, NY: Guilford.

Freyd, J. J. (1996). *Betrayal trauma theory: The logic of forgetting abuse*. Boston, MA: Harvard University Press.

Hall, P. (2013). *Understanding and treating sex addiction: A comprehensive guide for people who struggle with sex addiction and those who want to help them*. London: Routledge.

Herman, J. L. (1992). *Trauma and recovery: The aftermath of violence – from domestic abuse to political terror*. New York, NY: Basic Books.

Kafka, M. (2010). Hypersexual disorder: A proposed diagnosis for DSM-V. *Archives of Sexual Behavior, 39*(2), 377–400.

Najavits, L. (2002). *Seeking safety: A treatment manual for PTSD and substance abuse*. New York, NY: Guilford.

National Institute on Drug Abuse. (2007). Drugs, brains, and behavior: The science of addiction. Retrieved September 3, 2014, from www.drugabuse.gov/publications/topics-in-brief/drugs-brains-behavior-science-addiction.

Ouimette, P., & Brown, P. J. (2003). *Trauma and substance abuse: Causes, consequences, and treatment of comorbid disorders*. Washington, DC: American Psychological Association.

Rohsenow, D., Corbett, R., & Devine, D. (1988). Molested as children: A hidden contribution to substance abuse? *Journal of Substance Abuse Treatment, 5*(1), 13–18.

Turkus, J. A., & Kahler, J. A. (2006). Therapeutic interventions in the treatment of the dissociative disorders. *Psychiatric Clinics of North America, 29*, 245–262.

Weiss, R. (2015). *Sex addiction 101: A basic guide to healing from sex, porn, and love addiction*. Deerfield Beach, FL: Health Communications, Inc.

Weiss, R., & Schneider, J. (2014). *Always turned on: Facing sex addiction in the digital age*. Carefree, AZ: Gentle Path Press.

Chapter 9

Body awareness and self-protection training for male sexual abuse survivors

Paul Linden

As a somatic educator and martial artist, I address two core problems in my work with abuse survivors: the persistence of the distress response in the body and powerlessness. My body-oriented educational approach is a complement to psychotherapy. After discussing the core problems and addressing the logic of their solution, I will describe the modalities I use in working with them. Then I will describe some of the key exercises I have developed. I will conclude by outlining the ways this work can be applied before, during, and after therapy, either by psychotherapists or other practitioners.

Though much of the work can be easily learned and applied safely and effectively by any psychotherapist, other parts of it require very different training, expertise, and experience than psychotherapists usually have. For that reason, a team approach may be required. By informing therapists about the nature and use of these complementary methods, I hope this chapter will serve as a catalyst for therapists to seek further training and to find body awareness and martial arts instructors to team up with. Also, by showing somatic educators and martial artists a way to extend their expertise, I hope this chapter will serve them as well.

Problems and solutions

Distress response

The body responds to challenges or threats by contracting or collapsing. People make their breathing, posture, movement, and attention small, and this can take a number of related forms. It may take the form of tensing and bracing as a preparation for strength and effort. It may take a similar form of tensing and hardening in anger. It can show up as stiffening and constricting in fear. It may take the form of collapsing and becoming limp in defeat and resignation. It may manifest as reducing awareness in specific areas of the body or in an overall dissociative response.

Doing any kind of action when the body and awareness are made small (whether tensely or limply) will make the movement effortful, inefficient, and awkward. Beyond this, the distress response reduces one's ability to think flexibly; it reduces the ability to function calmly; and it can result in dehumanizing of the person threatening you and of yourself as well.

When the distress response stays stuck in the body, that is the trauma state.

Powerlessness

An effect of abuse is *learned powerlessness*. In the abuse, the victim learns that he is not powerful enough to protect himself. That learning becomes part of the self-structure and shapes the survivor's ways of dealing with life.

Instead of the more common term "learned helplessness," I use the word "powerlessness" because this focuses attention on what is needed: power! Abuse survivors learn in the assault that they *are* powerless, and that knowledge stays with them until new resources are learned.

Some survivors use various activities to feel powerful and in control of what happens to them – anything from anonymous sex to rock climbing to anorexia. Others, instead of finding counterfeit power, reduce the awareness of their pain by dissociation, drugs, compulsive exercise, and so on.

There is also a third way in which survivors attempt to experience power. In the moment of the abuse, many survivors tried to protect themselves, but were unsuccessful. In many instances, they continue to try, even years later. Unsuccessful, unfinished defense actions typically show up in a survivor's posture or movement as small, unconscious actions that repeat the survivor's attempts to protect himself in the original assault. Survivors keep doing those defensive actions in the unconscious but forlorn hope that they will succeed one day.

Centering

The solution for both the distress response and powerlessness must include replacing smallness with an expansive mindbody state and using that as a foundation for powerful and effective action.

Empowerment starts with awareness of one's body responses. Body awareness is the ongoing process of noticing and feeling your body as you perform actions. When you can feel what you do, you can evaluate its effectiveness and make changes if necessary. Body awareness is learnable and improves with practice.

Aikido is a nonviolent Japanese martial art. *Centering* is the Aikido term for the process of setting aside inner disturbances such as fear and anger and maintaining calm alertness and flexible strength. *Being centered* refers to the mindbody state created through this practice, and it is the foundation for effective Aikido self-defense. Centering is not a matter of stopping emotions/feelings. You cannot stop feelings any more than you can dig a hole in the water. It is a matter of starting something more effective and less costly with which to replace problematic emotions.

The centered state can be described in different ways. Speaking in structural language, in the state of center the musculoskeletal system is balanced and free of strain. Speaking functionally, this state allows stable, mobile, and efficient movement. Speaking in psychological terms, this state involves reaching out into the world with a symmetrical, expansive awareness and intentionality while simultaneously staying anchored in internal body awareness. Speaking in spiritual terms, this state is an integration of the body states of power and love. Speaking in ethical terms, this state creates an awareness of and concern for the effects of one's actions on the wellbeing of others. Whatever terms we choose to use, they refer to one and the same mindbody state.

Once survivors have experienced that they can center themselves in the present, that enables them to discuss the trauma they experienced in the past but change their relation to it in the present. Instead of re-experiencing their inability to deal with the trauma whenever they talk about it, they relate to it from a sense of calmness and capability. That is the foundation for breaking the chains to the old trauma.

Power

The distress response is a combination of movement reflexes and physiological responses. As such, it is logical that it would take body-oriented techniques to help a client manage the responses. In body awareness education, there are tools to change how people experience and act in and through their body. Body awareness, relaxation, alertness, kindness, and stability form a platform for undoing the distress response.

Power (in the context of abuse recovery) is having skills to manage the world around you to create safety and secure your needs. So it is logical that it would take instruction and skill building to overcome powerlessness. Whatever else abuse may be, it is fundamentally *combat*. Martial artists teach people to create effective boundaries and fight to save themselves when assaulted. Clients can learn to be powerful and use that power in an ethical, life-affirming manner.

Some therapists approach empowerment by having survivors use their strength in hitting a chair with a foam bat, for example, or pushing hard against a wall. That can be very useful in helping people feel their bodies, but it is not empowerment in the sense I mean.

Untrained strength pushing against the assault is how people normally fight back. At best that is difficult and harsh, and too often it will not work. Until you have had the experience of flow, elegance, and ease in executing self-defense movements, you won't even know what is missing in the common model of empowerment for healing.

Another element in empowerment could be called c*ognitive self-defense*, and it helps abuse survivors identify and expel the distorted thinking and the lies perpetrators injected into them. Cognitive self-defense includes the logic of various language processes. It also includes evidence-based thinking, the use of operational definitions, and hypothesis construction and testing. This will be discussed later in the chapter.

Modalities

For about 25 years, most of my body teaching has been with sexual abuse survivors. When I started doing this, I had to figure out how to use body awareness and martial art training for abuse recovery.

Aikido

My laboratory for exploring body awareness and empowerment training is Aikido, a nonviolent Japanese martial art. (For those not familiar with Aikido, my book *Feeling Aikido* [Linden, 2006b] will give a sense of what the practice is.) Aikido comes from a knowledge base developed over hundreds of years of civil war in Japan. The martial arts include very sophisticated and efficient methods of awareness, movement, and self-defense. Aikido is classified as a soft martial art. It uses relaxed, soft, cooperative, and harmonious movements to deflect attacks. That mind-body softness leads both to more efficient execution of self-defense techniques and a desire to avoid fighting if possible.

Aikido movements are healing. The smooth elegant movements feel better than the rigid efforts that are natural to us. Aikido techniques usually don't make survivors feel they are becoming violent and abusive by using harsh power against another human being.

Being In Movement

I started Aikido practice in 1969. I brought to it a lack of talent in physical activities but talent and training in the Western logical/analytic tradition. For my own learning, I needed to break down Aikido techniques into smaller chunks and more explicit principles – the antithesis of the Japanese non-intellectual style of teaching. This process of explicit awareness training is rare in Aikido instruction.

I discovered ways to vastly simplify teaching the centered posture, breathing, and movement of Aikido with the result that almost anyone can learn the Aikido way of being in the body relatively easily and quickly. I found the exercises could stand on their own as a body education system, which I called Being In Movement® (BIM) mindbody education. (The two books *Winning Is Healing* [2006a] and *Embodied Peacemaking* [Linden, 2007] show how I applied the body education processes to peacemaking and abuse recovery.)

BIM focuses on the detailed experiential awareness and understanding of the interaction among musculoskeletal structure/function; movement planning; thoughts, feelings, and beliefs; task performance; and ethics. The focus in BIM is on developing a state of body awareness, relaxed alertness, and compassionate power as a foundation for values, self-identity, and effective action.

Philosophy of science

In addition, having an academic background in philosophy of science, it was natural for me to include in BIM logical thinking exercises to help people evaluate the beliefs that structured their movements and actions.

When I started working with abuse survivors, I learned on the job what and how to teach survivors. My students showed me what they needed, and I figured out how to do it.

Case study 1

Chris (not his real name) came to me for bodywork. He told me his lower back was almost always stiff and painful. He had tried a number of different forms of bodywork; they often loosened his back for a while, and then it tightened up again. I asked Chris to walk around and then pick up a light object. I observed that he leaned forward from the waist as he walked, which strained his lower back. I showed him how to correct his posture, and he felt that his movement was smoother, better balanced, and easier to do. However, when he came back for his next lesson, his posture was as before, and his back was tight and painful again.

We continued working on his posture and movement, but he couldn't retain the relaxation and balance I helped him achieve. That was a signal to me that the problem was not merely tight muscles and inefficient posture. The fact that his inner "ecosystem" chose to re-tighten his muscles even though relaxation felt better, suggested to me that the stiff muscles might have had a function (whether he was consciously aware of it or not) that was too important in his self-structure to give up.

I had him dialogue with his body, asking his lower back to increase the tension and pain. I was careful to say that his lower back might or might not fulfill the request and that either response would offer a good starting place, so he would not feel that I as an authority figure wanted a particular response. Indeed, the tension did increase. I asked whether this sensation was familiar to him, and he replied it was. I requested he ask his body whether the stiffness had a job to do; his immediate reply was "protection."

When I asked Chris what he needed protection from, he immediately answered that he had been assaulted when he was 10 years old. He had been grabbed by the back of his neck and pushed down. He tried to push back and get the hand off his neck.

He never felt free and safe after that. He realized that the first moment of the attack, when he pushed back against the grip on his neck, was stuck in his body. He felt strong when he braced himself to keep from being pushed down.

At that point in the lessons, we role-played the situation in which he had been grabbed by the neck. As an Aikido instructor, I could show him relaxed, comfortable, powerful, and ethical ways of getting rid of the hand.

It took the combination of skills in body awareness work and martial arts to create the change in his back he was looking for. Massage or other bodywork could not succeed because they didn't recognize that the tight muscles had a purpose. Only a practitioner trained in combat could help fulfill that purpose. The muscles stayed tight because tension felt like protection. Without addressing that purpose and finding an effective but strain-free way to fulfill the function, efforts to reduce the strain on his back were doomed to failure.

Psychotherapy alone could not work for him either. His therapy had included valuable work with relaxation and self-regulation, but the real problem was not that he was tense but that he was defenseless. Eliminating the tension without teaching him to defend himself would not address the root issue.

I approached his braced posture by reframing it as a hypothesis and then testing that belief. We role-played the attack, and he experienced that the normal, human resistive ways of meeting attacks were not nearly as good as the "technology" of disciplined, trained Aikido skills. Chris very quickly realized that defending himself by becoming rigid and immobile was not the most effective or comfortable thing he could do. He experienced that as he became looser and more open in his body, he could move and defend himself better.

Having an effective and relaxed defense against the hand on his neck allowed him to give up the instinctive but relatively ineffective defense of just pushing back. It was only after he had better and less costly ways of protecting himself that he could give up his long-held coping strategy of rigid strength. And that allowed the pain in his back to subside.

Awareness exercises

So far, this chapter has been conceptual. But staying with concepts would be like going to a restaurant and eating the menu. In order to better convey what I teach survivors, I will briefly describe some of the exercises I have developed. My books and videos (e.g., *Embodying Power and Love* [2013] and *Talking With the Body* [2016]) describe them in much greater depth, and many others as well. If you are not familiar with somatic and martial art training, you may or may not be able to do these exercises without more information, but reading through them will give you a sense of what the training covers.

Soft tongue

I teach *relaxation* both for its own sake and as an opportunity to help clients take the first step in developing body awareness. As you read this, let your tongue get soft and loose in your mouth. What happens to your jaw, neck and shoulders? What happens to your breathing? Most people report feeling a comfortable softening and relaxation. (Other experiences are perfectly possible too.)

By starting with something easy to find and easy to control, I begin the process of helping people notice and feel the different areas of their body. There are a number of other exercises that step by step build the ability to stay relaxed under pressure.

It is important not to define relaxation as absence of tension. Relaxation is more usefully defined as *appropriate effort.* When you're lying on the beach resting, the needed effort approaches zero. When you're digging a ditch, it is appropriate to use a lot of effort – but using more than needed is wasted energy. Relaxation is using only the effort appropriate to the task at hand. Often survivors reject relaxation in favor of tension and heightened effort because they believe that relaxation means limpness and will make them vulnerable to attacks. This new definition of relaxation is crucial in developing power that is efficient and effective and acceptable to abuse survivors.

Sitting: The next step in the development of power is experiencing postural stability. Sitting, standing, walking, and running are all fundamental human movements, and all offer a way to experience how psychological stability is built upon postural stability.

Stand in front of a chair, and with each hand, touch your hip joints. (Not the hip bones – which are the top edge of the pelvis, but the hip joints – which are in the fold where the legs bend.) Use your hands to push your tailbone back and down to the chair. This will lean your torso forward, but not too much. It will take you down to a sitting position. However, this sitting process uses core muscles that most people do not know how to access, and this way of sitting down creates a posture that is calm, alert, and dignified. More than that, that, if someone stands in front of you and pushes on your shoulders to tip you backward, you will probably experience that this posture is very stable without much effort.

Language

Emotions are physical events in the body. Think of a sandwich. It is an *object*. The *word* "sandwich" is the sign that points to the object. When you eat it, there is a *physiological* action in your mouth. The *taste* is what is experienced when that body action happens. *Emotions* are body actions. *Feelings* are what the physical actions "taste" like to the person who does them.

The body events are actions that one does, whether with awareness or unconsciously. People may not be aware of the action in the body. They may or may not notice the feeling. And they may mislabel the emotion. Focusing on emotions as body actions, two questions that help people gain clarity are: Where in the body are you doing something? What actions are you doing there?

English moves us in the direction of passive acceptance of emotions as things that happen to us. Ordinary English language says "You make me angry," but a more useful structure would be "I choose to do the actions of anger at your behavior." Learning to speak this more precise (but perhaps cumbersome) way is very helpful in learning to gain control of one's life.

Anger and fear

Imagine you work for the Boss from Hell. He assigns you impossible jobs and dumps on you when you fail. And when you do succeed, he passes off your work as his own. You have tried every positive strategy for talking with him, but he says talking is a waste of time, and, in particular, that you are so stupid he won't talk to you. Feel the anger in you. Where in the body are you doing something? What actions are you doing there? And why?

Imagine that the Boss from Hell has threatened you with serious injury unless you help him embezzle funds from the company. Feel fear. What are you doing and where?

It is important to teach the client how to test actions such as fear and anger. By identifying what goals the client is trying to achieve in doing those actions, we can test different ways of achieving the goals. As a general rule, self-defense and most other actions are performed more effectively in the state of calmness.

Some people object to centering because they believe I am not respecting their feelings. On the contrary, I know that feelings are the essence of living, but I am recommending that if one's emotions are interfering with the task at hand, then he should respectfully set the emotions aside and concentrate on the task. And then return to the emotions and feelings later, when time can be set aside for working with them.

Pencil-wanting

Intention is the process by which we shape posture, movement, and action. For greatest efficacy, change must start on the fundamental level of intentionality. Helping people directly experience the intentional foundations of their actions is a way of both moving them to take responsibility for their responses and giving them tools to improve their responses.

To create an operational (tangible) definition of "intention," I put something, a pencil for example, down about three yards (or meters) in front of a student and I instruct him to want it. I ask the student to actually *intend* to go over and get the pencil. It must be an authentic wanting. It must be felt in the body.

Once people can establish this sensation, they usually feel themselves "involuntarily" tipping toward the pencil. For most people, this movement will be a slight drift toward the pencil, though some people will actually move quite a bit. Most people will feel as though the pencil were a magnet gently drawing them toward it. (Some people will move away from the pencil, and that usually is an expression of some need to reject their own desires.)

When you have an image of a movement and intend to execute the movement, the brain sends nerve impulses to the muscles that will do the movement. All you have to do is wish to begin moving in some direction and your body will begin to do that movement, either at a micro-level or in larger, more obvious ways.

The pencil-wanting exercise is a way to help people begin to feel and notice the micromovements that are the small beginnings of any voluntary action. There is no separation between the mind and the body.

Shining: Expansiveness is not just a metaphor. By aiming intention outward in this exercise, you will be literally making the body more open and spacious. This is the specific antidote to the smallness that is part of the distress response.

Imagine that you are a star or a firefly or a light bulb. What do you do? You shine. Feel every inch (or centimeter) of your skin glowing outward, as you shine in every direction – as far out as you wish. How does that feel? Most people experience this as spacious and calm.

Love: A further opening of the body is possible when you can approach a trauma in a spirit of love – not love of the trauma, but love *at* the trauma. If you can create a feeling of love in your body, you can think and act with freedom. Everyone has something or someone – perhaps a friend, a lover, a child, a flower, a piece of music – something that when they think of it makes them happy inside, makes their heart smile. Stand with your eyes closed, and spend a few moments thinking about whatever it is that makes you happy inside. What happens in your body? How is your chest affected? What happens to your breathing? What sensations do you feel flowing through you? Most people experience a softening and warmth in their chests, and a freeing up over their whole bodies.

Can you let your body stay in the loving state even as you speak about your abuse? This is a powerful part of breaking free from the abuse. I don't mean you should be happy about the abuse or love the abuser – but you should be happy because you choose to be happy – in spite of the abuse.

Frying words

Find a word or phrase that summarizes some painful situation you have experienced. Perhaps it could be a phrase: "I am worthless" or "I was raped." Notice what you do in your body and how that feels. Most likely it will be some variety of the distress response.

If you say, "I am not worthless," that puts energy into the statement you are denying. If you use an affirmation such as "I am valuable" you know you are saying that because you wish to believe it is true – in other words, you're saying it because you believe it is false. Agreeing with a negative statement strengthens the old stimulus–response connection. And so does protesting the statement.

However, saying negative words in an expansive/empowered body state breaks the old stimulus–response connection. In a state of expansiveness, kindness, and power, say your negative phrase clearly, loudly, and joyously. You are building a new stimulus–response connection in which remembering the old assault reminds you to be in your power and love in the present. Here is where you can use all the earlier exercises in stability and expansiveness. And once people have built the new connection, they can think and talk about an assault without the assault dominating their bodies.

Body numbness

Once people have developed center, it can be safe and helpful to investigate body numbness and dissociation. Body numbness is the process of withdrawing attention from one segment of the body. Dissociation is the process of withdrawing attention from the whole body by focusing attention onto something external.

Look at your hand. Feel it. Put your attention into your hand. Move your fingers and pay attention to the sensations of that. Now, imagine that you have to have an operation on your hand, but for some reason the surgeon cannot use anesthetics. Can you deliberately withdraw the attention from your hand and arm and deliberately place your attention in your shoulder and hold it there? What is that like? Try touching something with your hand, being very careful to have very little feeling/attention in your hand even as you touch something with it. And then come back into your hand. You don't have to stay numb.

Dissociation

Dissociation is the process of withdrawing attention from the whole body by focusing attention onto something external. Two common geometries are to focus up toward the sky, or to recede inward behind the eyes.

Stand up, breathe, feel your feet on the ground. Look up over you and pick a spot on the ceiling directly overhead. Next, slide the spot out to the side. Bring your eyes back down and look at something about your height in front of you, but continue to mentally focus on the spot on the ceiling. And then, to turn off the dissociation, come back into the center of your body.

Almost everybody has at one time or another played around with looking through the wrong end of a pair of binoculars. Try doing that now. Look at something in front of you as though it were far away and very small. Pull your vision back away from what is in front of you. Then come back into the center of your body.

Following the body

Another aspect of body awareness is a process that could be described as body-based almost-free association. If a student comes in with a puzzling or disturbing thought, dream, sensation, or action, I ask what body events take place when the student describes the puzzling theme. By using logically neutral language and taking care not to interpret or suggest anything to the student, meanings emerge.

The following example describes how to apply this process to dreams. I do not try to analyze the dreams in any way. They are full of images, but I don't try to ascribe meaning to the images.

I start the dream process by having the student recount the dream three times. The first time is an ordinary verbal account. The second time, I have him pay attention to his body responses to each dream image. We build up a parallel description of the dream as a flow of body reactions. The third time, I have him go through the dream again by retelling the progression of body sensations without reference to the dream images. Then I ask him to pick a dream image/body response to focus on. And I ask what is happening in his body. That starts a stream of sensations that will almost always take us somewhere important.

Often what emerges makes sense of the dream as a code. Sometimes the endpoint of the body association process may be entirely unrelated to the dream in any direct narrative sense, but the endpoint will be important for the student's life issues, whatever they may be.

Case study 2

A student came in very disturbed by a dream about being in a storm cellar, hearing the wind of a storm whistling overhead, and feeling the door to the storm cellar ripped open by the wind. As we went through the dream process, she felt a lot of fear around the image of the wind. As we stayed with that physical sensation, the image eventually resolved itself as hearing someone breathing, and that immediately turned into an awareness that she was reliving hearing her brother on top of her and breathing hard as he raped her. At that point she sat up suddenly and said that the door to the storm cellar that had been ripped open was her vagina. That awareness was very productive in the body learning that followed.

Self-protection exercises

The exercises on body awareness and empowerment are a foundation for exercises on self-protection. Self-protection is a much broader concept than self-defense.

Language use

Survivors often take in distorted or untruthful ideas from perpetrators. A key element in BIM is analysis of language elements as a form of self-protection.

Let's take an example. A number of my clients reported that when they were little their perpetrators said to them: "You are worthless!"

What does that mean?

An assertion is a statement about something in the world. For example, "The cat is on the couch." An assertion functions as a roadmap. It says this is what is happening in the world, and you can plan your behavior on the basis of this information. The evaluation of an assertion focuses on its accuracy.

Expressive language communicates emotions. Values language communicates that someone feels good or bad about something. Notice that statements that are expressive or value utterances are not about the putative subject of the utterance. They are about the person who made the statement. "You are worthless TO ME."

Without those last two words, the structure of this values statement makes it look like an assertion, and abuse survivors internalize it as a true statement about them. Explaining the different functions of language to an abuse survivor helps loosen the lies that chain them to the abuse. Once they realize that valuing is an action done by a conscious being, they understand that being worth something is not about them but about the person who is "worthing" them. Although they were not worth much to the abuser, survivors can find other people who will value them.

Hypothesis testing

Another element in my approach is *testing* assertions and/or movements. Rather than telling students to believe me because I am the expert, I teach students how to set up tests of my suggestions or their beliefs. That way they have the power to distinguish for themselves what is true and/or useful to them from what is not.

For example, survivors often think the feeling of defensiveness leads to effective defense actions. When I ask a client to show me defensiveness, the usual posture is to hold the arms against the chest or stomach, while stiffening the breathing and tensing muscles throughout the body. It feels like a good defense position. Reframing it as a hypothesis, we get, "A rigid barrier is a good way of keeping things out." However, when we test it, we find this position is so stiff that when I attempt to poke the student in the stomach, he cannot move well, and I can poke him easily. The defensive position is undefended! The hypothesis is disconfirmed.

To provide an alternative response, I invite people to stand with their arms wide open about shoulder height, while relaxing and paying almost casual attention in all directions. It always comes as a great surprise to them that when their arms are relaxed and held wide and their attention is wide open, they can move swiftly and effectively to block me when I try to poke them.

Safety

The idea that being wide open allows one (as a trained adult) to prevent being penetrated can be confirmed with tests involving a number of varied threats, anything from a punch to an insult. In fact, the commonality in all the different aspects of self-regulation and boundary management is that being open is necessary for effective decision-making about what to let in or keep out.

As a martial art instructor, I can teach abuse survivors how to achieve not just the *feeling* of safety but also the *actuality* of safety. When they experience that safety can come from their own skilled efforts, survivors usually light up with radiant smiles.

In Aikido, the self-defense techniques have to be grounded in awareness of the body and how to move with efficiency and kindness. Otherwise, at the least, the defenses would be inefficient and strain-filled.

Empowerment sandwich

I use self-defense instruction in two ways: as a generic preparation for contacting traumatic events and as a resolution of the specific attacks the student experienced. Bracketing the discussion of the trauma with power before and after contains the trauma.

Through gradual steps, building up power, survivors become able to talk about traumatic assaults without being overwhelmed by old feelings. Without that, talking about the assault often amounts to practicing being overwhelmed!

Only after the client practices staying centered do we discuss his traumatic experiences. Then we practice the specific self-defense needed to defeat the assault the client described.

Invading space

A way to start the practice of self-defense is to examine personal space. Have your client stand up. Your job is to walk over him like a steamroller over a frog. His job is to say “No” when he wants you to stop getting closer.

Often people are taught that when they say "No," that constitutes having a boundary. But what happens if someone chooses not to obey? If the survivor does not have skills to enforce his boundaries, then saying "No" is just a request.

We usually believe that when one person deliberately moves toward another with an intention to cause harm and gets very close, s/he is thereby invading the other's space. But try walking over your client again. This time ask your client to stretch out his arm in front of himself, so that as you walk forward, you will impale your throat on his outstretched hand. It doesn't seem right to say you are invading his space when you are the one getting injured or killed.

I suggest we can rethink the idea of the attack, and, further, that – though the grammar is terrible – it would be more accurate for the client to say, "You are invading your space upon me." In other words, the person who owns the space by virtue of having the tools to keep ownership of it is the one who is not being invaded.

Flowing improvisational Aikido

Aikido makes use of spirals of movement, both to generate power and to take over the movement of the attack. From my point of view, if a movement is not comfortable to do, then it isn't good Aikido. Movement should be graceful, upright, compelling yet gentle, and flowing. And joyful! Rather than start with defense techniques that survivors must memorize, I start with teaching improvisational Aikido self-defense. Once students can maintain emotional/postural balance, I have them practice sensing the trajectory of the attacker's movement and joining it with free-flowing movements. This unbalances the attack and allows the defendant to throw the attacker. Within a lesson or two, survivors start to feel comfort and confidence in their movements. They learn to stay present and strong when confronting an assault.

Self-defense

Aikido techniques are effective but intricate and difficult. Dedicated self-defense techniques are much simpler and easier to learn and use.

There is an equation: the simpler the technique, and the more attacks the technique is effective against, the harsher the technique is. So, for example, taking out an attacker's eye will stop almost any kind of attack.

There is a reason for learning self-defense techniques instead of depending on the flow to show you what moves to use. People spent a lot of time devising the most efficient solutions to specific attacks. It is hard to convey the nature of the many complex techniques, but here is an example of a simple movement:

If somebody is pushing you up against a wall and choking you with both hands, the urge is to get the hands off and push the attacker away from you. However, that frees up his hands for further attacks, and in any case it's hard to push against force. If, instead, you slide sideways along the wall, that nullifies the force. If at the same time, you pull one of the attacker's elbows down, that will spin the attacker and slam him up against the wall. If at the same time your free hand strikes his throat, that becomes a lethal technique.

When survivors are ready, I take them through the attacks they experienced and show them simple techniques by which they can defeat the attacks. Everyone lives in the present based on what they learned in the past. It is impossible to change the past, but with new information and experiences, it is possible to change what was learned in the past. By defeating now what they could not overcome in the past, survivors can replace the old learned powerlessness with capability and confidence. That will go a long way toward helping them break free of their abuse.

It is important that the student understands that Aikido and self-defense done within the context of recovery are limited to role-playing and breaking the connection to specific events of a student's past. It is not a full self-defense curriculum. A full self-defense course should probably wait until after the major trauma healing is done.

Earlier I made the point that Aikido techniques, by virtue of their gentle flowing nature, are acceptable to survivors, who often define destructive techniques as being violent and on that basis reject them.

When they are ready, I suggest a different definition of violence. I define violence as behavior coming from fear and anger with a desire to hurt and annihilate. But destructive force in the service of self-protection does not need to be violent. It can be done with kindness and regret, simply out of the need for self-preservation.

Love without power is weak and ineffective. And power without love is brutal and destructive. Integrating power and love leads to an entirely different way of functioning.

People often cannot imagine feeling kindness toward someone while focusing power against them in self-defense. To help them understand how that would be possible, I use the example of a beautiful dog with rabies approaching a dog lover. The dog lover would feel love and compassion and pity, yet shoot the dog to put it out of its misery and to prevent it from infecting other animals or people.

Experiencing their skillful power and their capacity to keep themselves safe allows abuse survivors to break the connection between the old attacks and their present lives. They no longer have to live in distress and learned powerlessness.

Somatic and combative work alongside psychotherapy

Let's consider how body awareness and martial art modalities function in conjunction with psychotherapy. They have different uses before the survivor begins psychotherapy, during psychotherapy, and afterward. The survivor should ideally have access to this material in all three stages if needed.

Therapists often ask whether the use of touch, both in body awareness education and in self-protection, is unethical or retraumatizing. My answer is that if a practitioner is trained and skilled, has a clear purpose in using touch as part of the recovery process, and has informed consent from the client, then it will not be unethical. And if it leads to greater empowerment and safety for the client, it will not be retraumatizing.

Remember, self-defense is not psychotherapy, and there is no reason that therapists and martial artists should have identical ethical rules. For example, a therapist should not lie down on top of a client. But if I as a self-defense instructor do not lie down on top of a client who has been pinned and hurt, I am not doing my job. If I don't pin him and teach him how to escape from the pin, who will?

Before

Awareness and centering exercises create a foundation for psychotherapy. BIM offers clear processes for helping people become aware of their bodies and thereby their emotions/feelings. And the self-protection work allows a client to *be* safe and thereby *feel* safe, which reduces resistance to dealing with painful feelings in therapy.

On the other hand, psychotherapeutic work is often a necessary foundation for survivors to be able to handle the immediacy of somatic work. In that sense, the psychotherapists in my network act as gatekeepers and send me clients who both need my work and are ready for it.

The material I work with does not stand on its own, any more than psychotherapy does. If someone who is not currently in therapy comes to me for trauma work, I will work with him only if he agrees he will enter psychotherapy whenever I feel it is important for his safety or his recovery to do so.

During

I believe that in many instances psychotherapy without body awareness and self-protection can be problematic. When people discuss a traumatic event without new resources, they recall and relive the trauma, thus reinforcing their powerlessness and their distress. In psychotherapy, survivors can use body awareness to be clear about what they feel, and on the basis of their newfound abilities to protect themselves they can afford to recall and re-experience their former vulnerability.

I have had a few clients who remarked that it was easier for them to work on their rage with me than with their therapists, and that was because they knew that they couldn't hurt me no matter how they lost control. They felt that they had to protect their therapists.

After

Body awareness and self-defense are not like antibiotics. With antibiotics, once the invading bacteria are killed, the effect is permanent. If body awareness exercises are part of the recovery process, then to maintain awareness, ongoing practice is necessary. There are many practices described in my books and training videos, and additionally there are many other martial arts and systems of body awareness to investigate.

To maintain and even increase proficiency in self-defense, a survivor could take a self-defense course. Or a martial art could be studied on a long-term basis. Self-defense courses generally teach only the simplest, most broadly useful techniques. Martial arts, even the most practical of them, are built on the idea that mastery requires practice over a substantial time.

For the therapist

There are some elements in the body or martial practice that could be helpful to therapists themselves. To begin with, if the therapists are themselves abuse survivors, if they have practiced centering, they would be less likely to be triggered by the work with abused clients.

Even without personal trauma, being human means we tend to mirror each other's body communication. And that means that therapists will often create in their own bodies the pain their clients bring. By using body awareness and centering techniques, therapists can avoid vicarious traumatization and burnout.

Practicing to better recognize the body underpinnings of feelings will improve the therapist's perception of clients. And being aware of what body experiences the therapist and the client each attach to the names they use for feelings will alert the therapist to instances when the two individuals use the same labels but refer to different experiences and meanings.

It would be wonderful if there were many therapists who were martial artists and somatic educators. However, there probably are not very many people who have skills in all three areas. I would encourage mental health professionals to build teams with body educators and martial artists and bring all three streams of knowledge to the clients we serve.

Many bodywork systems focus primarily on musculoskeletal change and improvement of movement. That expertise would be a good starting point for practitioners who want to learn to broaden their work.

Many martial arts focus on competition and tournaments or on destructive combat techniques. Some martial arts or self-defense systems derive their power from anger. However, it is important that the martial artists on teams be focused on centering and teaching ethical, compassionate self-defense.

One resource offering the possibility of enlisting Aikido practitioners is Aiki-Extensions (www.aikiextensions.org). This is an organization of Aikidoists who extend Aikido principles off the mat into areas of life such as fine arts, physical therapy, bodywork, business, and psychotherapy.

In turn, therapists may have to train martial artists and body educators on the nuances of teaching abuse survivors. My website (www.being-in-movement.com) has material that would help with that.

Final vignette

I remember a client whose mother phoned me and said that she was very dubious about someone who was not a mental health professional working with her adult son on issues of abuse. She was especially uncomfortable with my use of touch. Toward the end of my work with the young man, he invited his mother to come watch a lesson focusing on self-defense. I pinned my client to the floor. He threw me off with graceful power and sat up with a glowing smile. And his mother, with tears streaming down her cheeks, said: "Now I know why you work the way you do."

References

Linden, P. (2006a). *Winning is healing: Body awareness and empowerment for abuse survivors* (E-book). Available at www.being-in-movement.com/resources/books.

Linden, P. (2006b). *Feeling Aikido: Body awareness training as a foundation for Aikido practice* (E-book). Available at www.being-in-movement.com/resources/books.

Linden, P. (2007). *Embodied peacemaking: Body awareness, self-regulation and conflict resolution* (E-book). Available at www.being-in-movement.com/resources/books.

Linden, P. (2013). *Embodying power and love: Body awareness and self- regulation* (Video). Available at www.being-in-movement.com/resources/videos.

Linden, P. (2016). *Talking with the body: Body awareness for professionals* (Video). Available at www.being-in-movement.com/resources/videos.

Part III

Women in the picture

Chapter 10

The heart of the matter

A female therapist works with a male survivor

Mikele Rauch

I don't know you.
I don't trust you
I don't believe you
I want to trust you
I want to trust myself
I want to believe you
I want to believe myself
I remember and am afraid that I do
I'm beginning to trust
I'm beginning to believe that I can trust
Wait . . . but how can I trust . . .

And so we begin. I am a female therapist working with a male survivor. *We have a lot of stuff to cover*, he says. I tell him I will have to earn his trust. He pokes fun at my facial cues, my language, culture, perhaps even my wardrobe. I tell him I will under no circumstance break the ethical boundaries. I will be honest and straightforward. No games, no bullshit. No flinching. He asks me a personal question. We revisit what I said about boundaries. No bullshit, as I promised.

This is a laboratory, I say. We will experiment with a different template in the mind, the brain, and the heart, with the unspoken dynamics, preconceptions, and individual life experiences of two people in the room.

We go over the stuff: race, gender, health, sexuality, spirituality, religion (they are not identical), how we will work together. I tell him we won't have to agree. I encourage him to challenge his past experience and to test me.

He will.

He's a soldier or a cop. He is a priest, a lawyer, a contractor. He is homeless. He has a lot of initials at the back of his name. He has more tattoos than he has hair follicles. Or maybe he presents so clean-cut that nobody would guess what he's been up to. He is 25. He is 73. He is every decade in between.

He's here because of his wife. He's here because his world just fell apart. He's here because he has no friends. He has lost his children, and has lost his way. Or he is here because his friends have no idea what he is going through and he is so alone. He's here because he has been living a lie about his sexual identity—his sexual anything, certainly his sexual abuse. He's here because he can't stop the nightmares, the flashbacks, the rage attacks, the deepening addictions. He's here because he is sick and tired of carrying his secret.

He tells me he hates women. But actually, he says, he is afraid of women. Maybe he says that sometimes he wants to *be* a woman. Or he tells me this therapy has nothing to do with women at all. He may report that he was a woman once . . . Maybe it's all about his mother. Or, he says it has nothing to do with his mother; she was so depressed or drunk, she was never really there.

He may tell me that his perpetrator was a woman—his mother, his babysitter, his sister, his teacher, his commanding officer. Or he says that the person who didn't protect him was a woman. Perhaps the only person who ever tried to help was a woman. But maybe the women in his life never listen . . .

He can't be sure I am listening.

He is here because God betrayed him, and there is no hope.

He's so angry. He's so fearful. He is so shut down he can hardly move. He feels too much and it's terrifying to feel at all. He's ashamed to be this afraid. But he does not want me to talk him out of his pain, his doubt, or feeling shitty. He is furious that it matters at all.

> *Why do I have to prove myself in front of other men? In front of you?*
> *Why is it so important what other people think?*
> *Why do I care what* <u>*you*</u> *think?*
> *Why am I raging?*
> *What do I do with this goddamn shame?*
> *How do we begin?*
> *When will it end?*

He tells me that he has hurt people. He is ashamed to say what he watched others do, how he let things happen, what he participated in, what harm he managed to do. He is ashamed to admit what he continues to do. He tells me he wants to die from despair.

Sometimes he arrives on many prescription meds, antidepressants, stimulants, anticonvulsants, and mood stabilizers.

It's all too much, he says. *I'm not sure what I remember.*

In therapy, it is about memory, but not necessarily the linear time line. Even the present is linked to the past. Memory is supposed to be words in therapy, but words are mercurial. The mind remembers this and then forgets, like the quicksand of voice or face after dreams. The mind remembers with perhaps a force field of feeling and no explanation; a longing without recollection.

Memory is habit, thought, the clock, survival. Sometimes it seems blank.

But memory is a voice, a scream, or a sound in the night. Memory is the lips, the forehead, the genitals, chest, stomach, hair, the nose, the earlobe. Memory is a montage: potato bins, closets, broken bones, semen, abrasions, asbestos, unimaginable human debris, sulfur, blood on the tongue, the smell of garlic, sex, perfume. Memory is the red, the brown, the black.

Sometimes memory comes without access to the picture or the sound. It sees with the nose; it hears with the tongue: it's what has encoded when he encounters the quality of light in the afternoon, the open window, mildew on the sheets, a tea whistle, the dander of the dog, dehydrated breath, candlewax.

Memory is the mind waxing and waning: fluids, charred remains; body prompts. It is puffs of air. It is outside and inside.

Memory does not register those first cellular imprints—in utero and then at birth. But the body responds to the amount of cortisol pumping through the amniotic fluid, and later to the mother's first touch, whether for good or ill. This initial holding place is the introduction to the rest of a life. If he did not experience being wrapped, held, bonded early on, in and out of the womb, he has probably been in constant free fall ever since. In the words of Sebern Fisher (2014, p. 8), this is less a metaphor than a transcription of state—the nervous system in constant arousal—ambient fear his default position. It sets the template, encoding the system with a flood of information.

Then, the barrage of images, sensory experiences, faces and places. He recollects how it was to exist in his house, in his family, in the school, the town, and the church. Maybe there are no conscious memories at all, but as Freud says, what the mind has forgotten, the body has not—thankfully.

And so it goes. He is relieved. He is suspect. He dissects. He tests. He retreats. He opens.

He has been waiting for a long time to blurt out the whole story. Or he says that he cannot say with words what he went through, ever. Maybe he cuts himself, or bangs his head. Maybe he binges on sugar or sex, crack, porn, or alcohol. But there was always an "it" that preceded the addiction: the unrelenting hunger that could never be satisfied. Recovery is a steady and not so steady struggle. Eventually he comes to connect the dots in his relationships, his cravings, self-destructiveness and the past.

Sometimes he brings his guitar, his dog, a letter, a picture, or a text. Sometimes he brings nothing at all. Maybe today there will be nothing to say or do; or he will be present but not "in the room." He learns to cultivate an awareness of when he is here and when he checks out. Then, he has to contend with what happens next. At the first, he may not recognize himself without dissociating unless he *is* his fear or rage or humiliation.

In therapy, I tell him talk is only part of it. We might work with the sand tray; we will play music, do EMDR, or some kind of authentic movement. Sometimes we use weights. We make a body map. We go against the natural impulses: soften the belly instead of tighten the muscles.

There are many ways to go about this, so we try whatever works. It may take a while to get to the bottom of things. He gradually becomes aware of how much of his abuse he has repeated in his habits and relationships. But we can't just talk about it. That's where the bodywork, mindfulness exercises, and a bit of therapeutic nagging comes into play. I am pulling everything out of the bag here: engaging his body as he does EMDR; using Aikido as a metaphor when he thinks about confronting triggers or triggering people; I invite him to close his eyes and listen to a piece of music and move to it as he feels safe. *Work with me*, I say. *You can always say no, or just think about what I am suggesting*. He might roll his eyes at first or cry with relief, as his body opens up to something he has held in a black hole inside his gut, his throat, his groin, or his heart.

I ask him to shift his posture, breathe into his belly, track his attention, and move around in the room. He resists. We're working with his body to recircuit the skin and the disorganization within. I encourage him to respect his defenses; notice that constriction is an opportunity for awareness. He comes to realize some of what we are doing is like brain surgery, rewiring the circuits and decoding the script where trauma did its damage. We nuance the colors of life between the black and the white.

Something opens.

Respect. Movement. Stillness. Words. Push back. Pull in. Deconstruct. Risk. Remember. Recreate. Rework. Repeat.

He finds himself surprised when I laugh at his black humor, or what I find appalling that he considers natural.

He lets me see his inner parts. Some are women. Some are children. Some have no voice—they are too young. Some have been hiding all along.

His story of abuse is revealed layer by layer. He may not name what happened to him for what it really was. Maybe he romanticizes it: initiation, bad luck—"good" luck—or he cannot name it at all. It can be shameful to identify that what happened is something he could not control. He may still be blaming the child he once was for the abuse he endured. It is a struggle to have compassion for that child, and to recover the parts of himself that he learned to abandon. There is much to grieve.

If he was violated as an adult, he may be assailed by shame and powerlessness. After all, society says he was somehow supposed to be able to protect himself or enjoy any sexual activity that came his way. What if he enjoyed the abuse? Maybe it was the best sex he ever had. He may still love his perpetrator or hope for a resolution or reunion. How do we make sense together out of what might have felt like the kindest, most nurturing relationship he had ever known? What do we do when the devil's bargain between himself and his perpetrator has continued to bring him success or fame—or his livelihood or the family system depends on his secret? We sort through the weeds of this with a large and compassionate view. We look at all the sides and probabilities. That might be a first.

Some men blame their younger selves who reenacted their abuse with younger children. But others use their own abuse to excuse themselves from responsibility as adult perpetrators. It may take a long time for a man to admit that he himself has abused another, because he doesn't feel safe enough to reveal something so shameful. He may fear I will terminate with him if he tells me what he has done.

Treatment with an offender is different than traditional psychotherapy in terms of structure, mandates for values and limits, particular attention to accountability, and confidentiality. I consider his age when the perpetration occurred, as well the context. I have to make it safe enough for him to show himself and have a frame of reference in my mind for where therapy goes from there so I won't be blindsided if he does reveal a perpetration history.

Coming to a greater degree of truth about all of this may mean he will have to acknowledge how powerless or neglected he really was. He will have to grieve for all that he has lost, including some of the beliefs that helped him tolerate what was intolerable or do the unthinkable.

Rage, shame, yearning, intense loneliness, cynicism, engulfing fear—the confusing mishmash of emotion.

In time, he shares something he has never said out loud. *I can't believe I am saying this to a woman*, he says. Perhaps he could only tell this to a woman. Then, he tells me he's going to say something else . . . *nope*. He isn't going to tell me another damn thing. He says he is falling apart. He reports he has never felt more himself.[1]

I have to go around myself to get somewhere . . . he says.

Dreams, fragments, phantoms, triggers, perseverations, distilled despair, fierce loyalties.

Silence.

The sense of betrayal lurks at any moment, especially as the work deepens. He may diminish or embellish any attachment to me. He has to straddle the abyss between the familiar "comfort" of self-neglect, over-stimulation, and chaos with the possibility of connection and new interesting complexities that recovery may reveal. I am conscious of whatever physical or generational similarities I might have to the people who violated him, either with seduction or force. I constantly assess what imaginary role I may be playing in the process: mother, sister, buddy, potential lover, or perpetrator.

There are frustrations, accommodations, and resolutions of betrayal. At times, I miss a cue or say the wrong thing. Sometimes he goes on the attack about what just happened in the room. Therapy itself can be a trigger of past abuses. There's a lot to clean up. The misses themselves are as important as home runs, if we can work them through.

Transference may be the wrong word when working with a male survivor in its most traditional meaning. In the classical definition, transference implies the feelings exchanged are not real, when there is nothing more

1 "We come apart to leave, and also to join" (Hillman, 1999, p. 101).

real than this unconscious unmet need for contact, perhaps for his first intimate contact. And often what he experiences is something real and true. Hope against hope for this connection is why he might endure therapy at all. And, it certainly is not "resistance." In fact, it is inevitable. For my client it could be a question of arousal and survival.[2]

Entitlement, grandiosity, loneliness, responsibility, accountability, confusion, fear of abandonment, fear of engulfment, demons, hope . . . the relentless shame.

But shame is the operative word here for a male survivor. It is shameful for him to want more, to *be* more, or to appear less than he wants me to see. It has obliterated his sense of self, diminished his self-worth, his dignity, and the sense of his own goodness. Shame may dictate a black or white situation for a survivor—either he takes all the blame for what has transpired, or never owns even 50% of the responsibility for the harm or mistakes he has made. The legacy of shame spills directly into our therapeutic encounter; it is a true opportunity to rewrite the script.

But, there it is: that unconscious prompt to be his savior, mother, or a gratifier of some unrealistic need. I must tolerate what it means to represent these many elements of my client's inner landscape, even if I cannot or should not meet all his needs. His trauma can easily close in, especially when the raw material is near to the bone.[3] It means I need to accurately respond to the gravity of his story, which has often been dismissed, diminished, or denied. But what I communicate, whether I lean forward or cry, cannot be *my* personal drama around his unbearable pain. And, actions indeed speak louder than words. I assess what I communicate nonverbally. It is why I must be self-vigilant. When it comes to subtle signals, it may not matter so much what is said, but how it is spoken.

My client asks me about my own abuse history, or whether I am married. Sometimes the straightforward answer period, without embellishment,

2 "Motherlessness is the lowest ring of hell for a baby or a small child, creating a background of fear of death or obliteration. If this weren't enough it leaves these children feeling either insatiably hungry for this primary connection or so damaged that they can no longer feel the longing." See Fisher (2014, p. 249).

3 "Embracing all the aggressive, sexual and 'chthonic' energies which lie unredeemed under the 'nice' compliant false self of childhood-something easier said than done and often requiring the continued encouragement of the therapist, who, like the crone, has a faith in the complexities of life that the traumatized patient does not" (Kalsched, 1996, p. 212).

is more therapeutic than the game of "why do you ask?" which only fans the flame of speculation and mystery instead of getting back to the client and his therapy. Any personal information is only relevant if it is beneficial to him, not otherwise. But then, I wonder: am I always right in deciding about that?

I assess any personal agendas that may politicize the therapeutic encounter; especially when there is an undercurrent of misogyny in my male survivor client. I make use of my instinct, and what piques my responses. It is a useful barometer.

There are times when the story or the material is hard to sort out no matter how many years I have worked in this field. It is important for me to understand what in the process belongs to whom. It can be tricky especially if my client's story triggers something of my own. Supervision, consultation, and straightforward feedback are essential. But the key to staying on course is my support posse, those trusted colleagues with a deep backlog of experience in trauma, who I know to be safe if I talk these things through and who won't let me off the hook if I am missing something.

But there are other questions that might arise for me.

How am I to educate or help my male survivor client recognize the paradigms that he is playing out with me? Do I inform or inhibit his evolution in this area?

How can I tease out his different cultural markers from abuse-related material?

What does it mean to be a strong woman who also empowers my client without engaging in a power struggle?

How do I remain mindfully present, fully aware of my own thoughts, feelings and surroundings as I teach my client to be present to himself?

How can I remain non-defensive, curious, and consistent no matter what comes my way?

How do I help him look at his conflicts or double binds, his beliefs and his needs without shaming or silencing him?

If I assess at any time I am not physically safe, do I know how I will stop the treatment and get help?

Being a therapist is a bit like being a comedian: timing is everything. So how do I address the unspoken (if it is therapeutic) or the spoken (if addressed by the client) regarding any sexual energy in the room? This is such a potent and careful consideration in our work.

"Can I give you a hug?" he says.

Eventually, we might *negotiate* some kind of touch. Maybe we start with a fist bump. A hug, therapeutic touch in the course of bodywork, or even learning a principal of self-defense is not a casual contact. It must be mutually agreed on, and deliberate. For a male survivor, even eye contact can be overwhelming. Non-violent, non-sexual physical contact that is safe (no small thing) and nurturing can be a template for other relationships, including the choice to say *no*. But this is slow going, or no going—and always arbitrated. Touch is never a casual thing, especially when touch was where the trouble started in the first place. And, always, I must assess whatever energy, sexual or otherwise, belongs to me. I must carefully watch my own cues and gauge the razor's edge of intimacy as we bridge our connection with boundaries and care-filled energy.

I have the privilege of being the container and the mirror, to negotiate closeness and distance, and to facilitate my male survivor client in making meaning of the world, in and outside the therapy room.

In time, I might invite my client to join a mixed gender survivor's group: another laboratory. There he gets to experience the power of being safe with other men—and women. Group can be sandpaper or balm, or both. His old wounds are exposed to the air; they beg to breathe not with excuses or self-pity—but in community, with empathy for himself and one another.

It's a relief for him to know that nobody else wants to be talked out of their feelings either. He is surprised how much everybody laughs, sometimes at the expense of the facilitator! In time he is relieved how tender people are, how vulnerable he can allow himself to be.

Honest, deeply resonant, full of good humor, kind—nobody diminishes or embellishes the pain. The process does not change his story, but it can definitely transform what happens next. Something else has begun to unfold: a sense of respect for what is happening, and for the brotherhood that is developing.

I have the privilege of witnessing and bearing the pain with him—pain that perhaps cannot be reversed. It is humbling. But the steward of empowerment and recovery is the male survivor himself. It is the grace of his own resilience to be alive to himself, to feel himself, and to take new risks. This can be depressing, sorrowful, exasperating, threatening, frightening, invigorating—and joyful. I just have to have the integrity and authenticity to be consistent, blunt *and* kind, and utterly respectful of this extraordinary journey he is on.

Kinship, empathy, empowerment—and dare I use the word?—*love*. Words that have been bastardized from the original power of their definitions because of misuse.

And, so it goes.

The process continues. My client comes to recognize his own magnificence and his vulnerability, his power and his humanness.

Respect. Movement. Stillness. Words. Push back. Pull in. Negotiation. Risk. Remember. Laugh. Cry . . .

Love.

The portal to the places beneath the words, where he rewrites the script of his life.

Moving it out and letting it in.

I am a female therapist working with a male survivor.

Rework. Repeat.

References

Fisher, S. F. (2014). *Neuralfeedback in the treatment of developmental trauma: Calming the fear-driven brain*. New York: W. W. Norton & Company.

Hillman, J. (1999). *The force of character and a lasting life*. New York, NY: Ballantine Books.

Kalsched, D. (1996). *The inner world of trauma: Archetypal defenses of the personal spirit*. New York: Routledge.

Chapter 11

Covert seduction and its effect on boys and men

Kenneth M. Adams

In recent years, more attention and research have been given to documenting the impact of sexual abuse of boys and its effects on them as men (Gartner, 1999; Hunter, 1990; Lew, 1988). Much of that literature and documentation has focused on physical sexual abuse and assault. Dissociative disorders, addictions – including sexual addictions – gender and orientation conflicts, suicide, self-harm, depression, sexual dysfunctions, broken relationships, and traumatic reenactments of past abuse played out in high-risk sexual situations are just some of the problems now observed in men who were sexually abused as boys. As a result of this increased attention and validation (see other chapters in this volume), many of these men have now found help and freedom from the shame they have spent their lifetimes struggling with (Fradkin, 2012; Gartner, 2005).

Lagging behind, however, is the attention and validation needed for boys who have been exposed to covert forms of sexual violation and abuse. Although all sexual abuse might be considered covert in that it is hidden and largely done in secret, for the purposes of this chapter, covert seduction and abuse will refer to sexual violations that do not include physical sexual touch. Covert incest (Adams, 1987, 1991, 2011; Adams with Morgan, 2007) and emotional incest (Love & Robinson, 1991) are terms that have been used in an attempt to capture this type of abuse and describe its consequences in an adult man's life. While the symptom profile may not always appear as severe as with physical sexual abuse survivors, many covert survivors present with similar problems: sexual and other addictions, dissociative issues like excessive fantasizing and numbing, difficulty with romantic commitments (as well as other commitments), a lost identity or self, orientation and gender conflicts, trauma reenactments, sexual dysfunctions,[1] and depression (Adams, 2011).

There are two primary reasons for the lack of validation given to covert forms of seduction. One is, simply, the lack of understanding and documentation. This chapter will clarify the basic forms of covert seduction that occur to boys and the impact in manhood for them. The other reason is clinician countertransference. Even the most empathic and compassionate clinicians might be inclined to downplay this form of abuse due to a personal history of covert seduction that has not been dealt with or a history of physical sexual abuse that prevents the clinician from seeing covert abuse as significant. Additionally, a clinician's heavy caseload of physical-sexual-abuse clients might cause burnout and numbing, preventing him or her from becoming appropriately concerned when a covert survivor is telling his story. Countertransference issues will be discussed in more detail below.

Two separate forms of covert seduction will be described in this chapter. First is covert incest, where the boy (and later, the man) plays the role of a surrogate husband to his mother. Covert-incest seduction by mothers of both heterosexual and gay sons will be discussed. The second form of covert seduction to be considered involves the impact of parental affairs and other sexual violations (e.g., parental exhibitionism) on boys and their effects in adulthood.

Covert abuse and seduction

You can be sexually abused without being sexually touched. When sexual abuse is discussed, most people think of physical sexual contact. However, inherent in the definition of covert sexual abuse as used in this chapter is the observation that one's sexuality can be violated without physical sexual touch and that the impact of the violation is significant, with consequences carried into adulthood. This definition departs somewhat from other uses of the term "covert sexual abuse," where sexual intent and violation occur under the guise of other physical touch such as enemas or washing a boy's genitals too long (Gartner, 1999).

1 Editor's note: See Chapter 12 by Kort in the companion volume to this one, *Understanding the Sexual Betrayal of Boys and Men: The Trauma of Sexual Abuse*, for further discussion of sexual dysfunction.

Sexual development. How can there be sexual abuse without genital involvement? Sexual development is a key element of human development. A man's sexuality unfolds within his developmental and attachment history with his primary caregivers. Disruptions in healthy development may manifest themselves in an encumbered sexuality, whether there is genital abuse or not.

Sexuality is inherently linked to attachment and caretaking. Therefore, trauma, neglect, and other issues that disrupt development can significantly affect a man's unfolding sexuality. While the evidence is clear that being physically sexually violated skews and disrupts normal sexual development, leaving the survivor traumatized, it's also becoming increasingly clear that covert forms of seduction cause similar problems.

Since the development of sexuality is integral to early attachment and bonding experiences, it is part of the developmental process. This, then, is why covert seduction is violating. Sexuality is not just about genitals. Sexuality is a biological and experiential internal drive that is linked to a man's relationships to his caretakers. Its expression is influenced whenever there is significant violation, either overt or covert. The more violation there is in childhood, the more the damage and (later) the more the man has difficulties with his sexuality.

Developmental insults may leave a man able to be sexual but not able to bond. Parts of the self have been split off, and sexuality no longer serves to connect. Rather than enhancing intimacy and closeness, a dissociative or compartmentalized sexuality more often leads to loneliness, anger, and alienation. After all, sexuality is naturally linked to attachment. If it is dissociated, then trauma or disruption in attachment of some type has likely occurred. A healthy sexuality more naturally leads to love and connection.

The neurobiological component of attachment theory suggests sexuality is a neurobiological affective attachment mechanism (Creeden, 2004; Katehakis, 2009). Both overt and covert forms of sexual trauma can negatively impact this neurobiological mechanism, causing a gap between love and lust (Money, 1986) to develop. Erotic feelings now more easily merge with other feelings such as anxiety, anger, pain, and shame (Carnes, 1991). When this happens, arousal is full of anxiety, anger, pain, and shame, and the man may become dependent on control, power, and rituals in order for him to function sexually. We see this in sex addiction. Sex may become disconnected, dissociated from the individual, functioning on its own.

Then, sex is often used as a drug to medicate feelings rather than as an expression of connection with a partner.

Encumbered and unencumbered sexuality. When a child's sexuality unfolds free of major assaults to the developing self, it functions to serve his attachment needs. In adulthood, it serves to help him partner and bond and attach. It becomes a channel to initiate romance and sustain relationships. An *unencumbered* sexuality naturally supports loving and erotic connections. Assaults on development include, in particular, sexual assaults, but they also (or alternatively) might include neglect, physical abuse, or enmeshment. As these hinder and damage development, they also impact sexuality (Money, 1986).

When his sexuality is unencumbered, a man struggles much less with it. He finds it naturally and easily moves to attachment and love. In contrast, a man who has an *encumbered* sexuality struggles. His sexual focus has become truncated and dissociated. (For example, he might neglect his wife for porn.) Sex has become separate from the rest of his life, and he will often argue that a detached sexuality is normal or, in any case, something he must be resigned to.

So, we see that sexuality is naturally connected to attachment from early childhood. If childhood development is not seriously disrupted, then in adulthood sexuality is still connected to attachment and serves the needs of adult attachment in a very natural way.

If in early childhood the attachment figures are neglectful or abusive, then the individual may grow up with a sexual compulsion or addiction. Schwartz and Southern (1999) explain it this way: early attachment difficulties cause subsequent overwhelming experiences and feelings that the child is unable to assimilate. As a result, he has affect dysregulation issues – poor social skills, a lack of perceived efficacy in negotiating relationships, limited empathy and compassion, and difficulty with accurate attunement to cues from others. His self-development is impaired; he has split himself into parts. He may have difficulty with gender-related behavior; for example, he may not feel confident in his masculinity. Developing sexually compulsive or addictive behavior can be compensatory for an attachment disorder. He turns to addiction as a soothing agent. Now, a part of the self is sexually addicted, and this has all occurred without any overt sexual touch.

Research studies support the idea that various disruptions in attachment affect sexuality (Jore, Green, Adams, & Carnes, 2016; Money, 1986). Del Giudice (2009) notes that early stress leads to disrupted attachment and an increase in the number of sexual partners. Miller and Fishkin (1997), in a study that followed men over a 30-year period, found that men with anxious and avoidant attachment styles desire more sexual partners compared to those with secure styles. Both anxiously attached men and anxiously attached women have very high levels of love obsession compared to those with other styles of attachment (Stephan & Bachman, 1999). Allen and Baucom (2004) have noted that (1) males with dismissive attachment styles have the highest number of sexual partners; (2) females with preoccupied attachment styles have the second highest number; and (3) both groups have significantly more sexual partners than securely attached counterparts.

Sexual compulsivity and addiction. Further evidence that early trauma impacts sexuality is seen in trauma reenactment (van der Kolk, 2014). For example, trauma reenactment often leads to dissociative states of behavior, which facilitate sexual addiction. Van der Kolk (1989) notes that people who have been exposed to highly stressful stimuli develop long-term potentiation of memory tracts that are reactivated at times of subsequent arousal. Victimized people may neutralize their hyperarousal by a variety of addictive behaviors, including compulsive re-exposure to victimization of the self and others. According to Gartner (1999):

> Compulsive sexual activity can be a compelling way to soothe the unregulated affect that emerges when dissociation breaks down . . . [S]exually compulsive behavior is a dissociative solution to the problem of managing anxiety . . . Engaging in compulsive sex thus allows a man to re-experience directly the biochemical means his body used to calm his anxiety when the abuse first occurred.
>
> (pp. 165–166)

However, sexual acting out does not give long-term relief. Addictive highs can briefly help combat the numbness and depression that the victims of covert seduction have carried into adulthood (Schwartz, Galperin, & Masters, 1995). But this trauma reenactment may lead to a self-perpetuating sexual addiction (Schwartz, 1996). Van der Kolk (1989) puts it this way: "Compulsive repetition of the trauma usually is an unconscious process that, although it may provide a temporary sense of mastery or even pleasure, ultimately perpetuates chronic feelings of helplessness and a subjective sense of being bad and out of control" (p. 401).[2]

2 Editor's note: See Chapter 8 by Courtois and Weiss in this volume for further discussion of sexual addiction and its treatment.

How can we tell the difference between healthy sex and compulsive sex? Healthy intimacy leads to closeness and affection. Compulsive sex is linked to loneliness, anger, and alienation. Schwartz (1994) states, "Successful rehabilitation is as much about safely bonding as it is about genital sexuality. Eventually the individual needs to learn how to express and receive affection in both sexual and nonsexual ways" (p. 268). Courtship must go slow and be grounded in the pleasure of the other's company. Otherwise, the partnership cannot lead to true intimacy.

Shame. Covert abuse (like overt abuse) causes significant shame, which becomes rooted in identity formation. Children blame themselves for failures by their caretakers. This sense of failure is assimilated as their own personal inadequacy, which is reactivated in emotionally vulnerable/dependent states. Needs, feelings, and desires are now shame-based. The self is in contempt of the self. These victimized children grow up to be adults with a "shame core" and their sexuality encumbered with pain and conflict.

Covert incest

Covert incest, also referred to as emotional incest, occurs when a child plays the role of a surrogate spouse (husband or wife) to a parent (Adams, 1991, 2011; Adams with Morgan, 2007; Love & Robinson, 1991). This surrogate partnership is often carried into adulthood with significant consequences. "Wedded" to a parent, covert-incest survivors are unable to develop their own separate and autonomous identities. Even though there has been no physical sexual touch, they have become their parents' surrogate and "trusted" lovers. This "silent seduction" is a common dynamic in the development of addiction and sexual and relationship struggles (Adams, 1987, 2011).

While the consequences of physical sexual abuse of boys are readily identified by clinicians as harmful, the primary result of covert incest is a son who is over-protected and very "close" to a parent. What's wrong with that? In my book *Silently Seduced – Revised and Updated, When Parents Make Their Children Partners* (Adams, 2011), I address this confusion in the chapter "Frequently Asked Questions" in response to the question "Isn't it good to be close to your parents while growing up?":

> Yes, absolutely it is. When the relationship is primarily based on the needs of the child, children are free of the burden of inappropriate guilt and obligation to the parents. This early attachment becomes the gateway to successful adult relationships. Children are able to trust their own instincts and know their needs, which enable more healthy choices in friends and romance. But in a covert incest relationship with a parent, being close means feeling excessive responsibility toward the parent. Children lack the freedom to know their own needs and desires. The parent's needs become incorporated as their own. Constantly torn between demands from the parent and their own wishes, children learn to sacrifice themselves to satisfy the parent and temporarily escape the burden of excessive guilt and anxiety. This becomes a path to frustration and disappointment in adult relationships, particularly in romance. In the case of covert incest, being close with your parent is not in your best interest.
>
> (p. 152)

As adults, covert-incest survivors struggle to make commitments to romantic and sexual relationships; they fear engulfment and enmeshment, the very components of the entrapment with their parent. Instead, they often become ambivalent in their attachments, offering a part of themselves but never all. When they attempt to have their own life apart from their parent, they feel guilty, anxious, and disloyal. They have been burdened with excessive feelings of responsibility for the lonely and neglected parent. The implicit, and sometimes explicit, demands for companionship from the parent overwhelm the boy or man and draw him back to his parent as a dutiful son. These adult children become skilled caretakers and have trouble with self-care and boundaries. They are preoccupied with their parent's, as well as others', needs.

Case illustrations of covert incest

Victims of abuse have trouble finding their way to healthy sexuality. In the two stories that follow, we will meet two men who have stories that reflect the dynamics of covert incest, but with unique aspects to each. They illustrate how covert incest (i.e., covert seduction) can disrupt normal attachment and therefore disrupt normal sexual development.

Mama's little man

When Tom was 10, his alcoholic father left home to be with another woman. His mother was angry and grief-stricken, often crying and complaining to Tom about his father. His two younger siblings often turned to him for protection and comfort. One of the ways his mother seduced Tom for herself, was to negatively campaign against his father whenever she could. As a result, Tom's primary view of his father came from his mother. In his mind, he dismissed his father as "no good" and "just a drunk who liked carousing with other women," descriptions his mother often used. Tom viewed his mother as a "victim" and "someone to pity and feel sorry for." He recalls setting aside his feelings about his father's leaving so he could be there for his mother. Although he would eventually spend some time with his father in later years, he never felt close to or supported by him. All Tom had was his mother.

Tom would come home from school daily, sit with his mother on the couch, and listen to her talk about her loneliness and the difficulty she was having managing the household. Even though he wanted to see his friends after school, he felt guilty and too worried to leave his mother alone. He became her constant companion. He even gave up his desire to play baseball, which he loved, so he could stay home with her. At night, they would spend special time together, when the other children went to bed, watching her favorite TV shows and occasionally even holding hands. They shopped for groceries and clothes together, and he helped run the household and raise his siblings.

Sometimes he felt uncomfortable with this closeness, as when she would have him zip up her dress or she would ask him if she looked pretty in her new swimsuit, but his feelings of being special to her seemed to override that. He began to learn the art of ignoring the feelings that made him feel uncomfortable.

They argued at times, too, particularly when teenage Tom began to show an interest in girls. On a number of occasions after he had been talking with a girl on the phone, his mother would react angrily, grilling him about "who he was talking to" and complaining that she felt neglected. Torn between his strong interest in girls and his mother's need for him, he gradually hid his interest in girls and declared more loyalty to his mother. To avoid his feelings of guilt and her fits of anger, Tom promised to be there for her and assured her she would always be his "special girl." Angry that he felt trapped and smothered by his mother's neediness and jealousy, he began to masturbate compulsively to mental images of the girls he was attracted to as well as to online porn. Subsequently, he did not date in high school and felt embarrassed by this when he was around his friends. At one point, he entered his younger sister's bed wanting to be sexual with her while she slept. He stopped himself but always felt confused and tormented by this incident. Not until entering therapy did he come to understand that his mother's covert seduction set him up, provoking him to nearly act out overtly with his sister.

Because of his good grades and focus on achievement in school, Tom was able to get a scholarship to a college that was far enough from home that he finally felt some of the freedom from his mother that he had so desperately longed for. But even though the drive was four hours, Tom would often return home from college on weekends to spend time with his mother and give her comfort. This seemed like a good compromise to him between his wishes and her needy demands.

Eventually, though, this began to feel burdensome and smothering as well. Tom was desperate again to break free of his mother's increasing grasp on him. A line was crossed for Tom one night during a weekend visit when he returned from the store after picking up groceries and his mother was waiting for him on the couch wearing a see-through negligee. Shocked and disgusted, Tom went his room and closed the door. He went back to college the next morning and did not return for another weekend visit for the rest of that school year, despite his mother's pleas and protests.

Tom worked to push the memory of his mother's seductive behavior out of his awareness, but he became concerned when his porn viewing began to take on themes of older women and younger men and some mother–son sexual situations. Horrified, he vowed to never return to porn viewing and to begin looking for a girlfriend his age. Eventually, he met Susie in one of his classes and fell in love. She was pretty and smart. What really drew him to her, though, was that she came from a troubled family, and he felt comfortable and "right at home" providing her counsel and support. She felt she had found "her knight in shining armor" in Tom, and they began a passionate romance. Tom hoped to be rescued from his mother's grip and Susie from her troubled background.

Tom and Susie moved in together and worked to finish their college degrees. His mother struggled with Tom's decision to be with Susie and tried to talk him out of it. She said he needed to wait and make sure he had the "right girl." As his mother pushed him to end his romance with Susie, Tom became more determined to stay with her, though he also had ambivalent feelings about Susie that he fought hard to keep from surfacing. Even though he felt a replication with Susie of the familiar struggle between his desires and his mother's needy demands and jealousy, he and Susie enjoyed their first two years together and married when they graduated. Tom declared to Susie the kind of loyalty and devotion that his mother taught him: he set himself aside in order to be there for her, no matter how he felt.

However, he remained torn between the two women. As a way to deal with his mother's needs and demands for his attention, he worked out a compromise to spend time with her when he could during both weekdays and weekends, even though Susie and he had started a family and his stresses at home were increasing. Before long, Susie began to complain about his mother, and Susie and Tom would often fight about her. Tom complained she didn't understand his relationship with his mother; he was all she had after his father left and he owed her the love and support she needed. Tom began to feel trapped, smothered, and intruded on by Susie. Even though at some level he knew it was wrong, his guilt propelled him to spend more time with his mother and fiercely defend this when Susie complained.

When Susie found him watching live porn between an older woman and a younger man, she panicked, became enraged, and pleaded with him to get help. Instead, Tom turned to his mother for understanding and, to his surprise, found her supportive of his porn use. As she put it, "It's just what men do." When Susie discovered that he was turning to his mother for support and still using porn, she demanded he get help or she would divorce him. He agreed to enter therapy.

Tom's early therapy sessions were typical for covert-incest survivors. He defended his mother and complained about his wife, while minimizing his porn use. Tom's story had all the hallmarks of covert incest: he was his mother's surrogate husband, constant companion, caretaker, and "loyal lover." Though there had been no physical sexual touch between Tom and his mother, Tom's sexuality was greatly violated by this surrogate partnership. His sexuality was never his. Burdened with his mother's romanticized attachment to him he was drawn back to her through the porn that offered incestuous reenactments. Tom struggled to feel free in his manhood to own his desires and break free from his mother's seductive grip.

But he functioned like a boy. His priority was to please and placate his mother in order to feel of value. His sexuality became a place to hide and attempt to resolve the conflicting feelings he carried. In the isolation of his porn use, he felt free and unburdened by intrusive and inappropriate demands, first by his mother and then by his wife. He projected onto his wife the emotional template of "feeling smothered" that his mother engineered for him, ultimately making his wife the target of his anger and withdrawal. He began "divorcing" the wrong woman. He was more conformable masturbating to porn than being sexual with his wife, with whom he felt emotionally burdened, engulfed, and less free sexually. In his porn use, he escaped into a fantasy world where he could pretend to be free.

As Tom began to see how his mother's romanticized attachment to him had left him violated and obligated to her, he defended her less and began to set boundaries with her regarding his availability and the topics they could discuss. He gave up porn and reclaimed his sexuality and other aspects of his self, leaving him more available to Susie. Her complaints lessened, and he was able to reduce his projections that "she was just like his mother." Freer to be himself, he was able with Susie to rekindle aspects of the early romance they had once enjoyed.

Mom's best friend

Mike grew up close to his mother. He often attended social functions and visited family and friends with her. People "talked" about how he seemed too close to her and that it kept him from developing friends. Peers teased him for being a mama's boy, but Mike dismissed this. He was gay, and he just assumed it was normal for him to be close to his mother because of that. In fact, his mother acknowledged his gayness and assured him it would be their secret from his father, whom they both assumed would be disgusted by it.

Mike's father would rage often and emotionally abuse Mike and his mother. His older brother, a sports star, was the only one who seemed to escape his father's wrath and win his approval.

Mike's mother let him know that their "friendship" was "all he needed" and that they would always have each other. In his early years, he felt protected by her from his abusive father. Mother and son would have long talks in which she would confide in him about her loneliness and feelings of being trapped in the marriage. Often she commented that if it "wasn't for him and his brother, she would divorce his father." Her sacrifice only strengthened his desire to be there for her. Mike felt "special" being his mom's best friend, the one she turned to for comfort and companionship.

When Mike entered his teen years, he began to discover secret ways to connect with other gay teens that his father wouldn't discover. Mike had a crush on one boy in particular and couldn't wait to tell his mother. To his shock and disappointment, however, his mother was jealous and strongly discouraged him from seeing the boy. She used the excuse that his "father might find out." Feeling confused, angry, and guilty, Mike began to experience his mother as smothering and intrusive, feelings he had not felt before about her. She wanted to hug and kiss him more, leaving Mike for the first time feeling repulsed by her.

Not only did Mike keep his sexual orientation and desires secret from others, he began to keep his romantic crushes and sexual involvements secret from his mother as well. Over the course of his late teens and most of his twenties, Mike had a string of compulsive anonymous sexual encounters that left him with an STD and a handful of betrayed and angry partners with whom he was involved for short periods. He was unable to commit to these men for any length of time because he often felt engulfed and smothered by them, as he did by his mother, or saw them as untrustworthy, much as his mother viewed his father.

Mike entered therapy after a short period in a 12-step program for sexual addiction. His sexual sobriety left him reflecting about his relationship with his mother in a different way. He began to see that his feelings of engulfment and difficulties with commitment to his gay lovers were directly tied to his relationship with his mother, whom he had idealized for most of his life. Mike certainly understood that his father's rejection and abuse played a role in his difficulty bonding with men, but he never imagined that his mother's relationship to him was also a factor. He began to see that he had played the role of her companion in place of his father. What Mike had always thought of as a mutual closeness to protect each other from his father's abuse he now realized was more his meeting his mother's need for someone to empathize with her loneliness. Her jealousy and demands for loyalty left him feeling smothered and burdened when his boyfriends would seek more involvement from him.

Seeing other gay friends marrying or entering into long-term commitments, he broke down in one of his therapy sessions as he expressed his longing for the same. He worried he would never be able to get there because of his loyalty to his mother. In time, he began to feel anger toward her and set boundaries on their time together and what they could talk about. Though she reacted with self-pity, he held firm to his need to separate from his role as her surrogate companion and to let go of his idealized version of her. Free to be appropriately "disloyal" to her and not function with his lovers solely as a caretaker, he felt less smothered and freer to commit sexually and romantically.

Mike also discovered that his father was not rejecting of him in the way his mother always insisted he would be. Even though they had never talked at length about him being gay, Mike discovered openness in his father that had always been eclipsed by his mother's ownership of him. Mike faced his father on his own terms, not his mother's. While imperfect, their budding relationship gave him a confidence in himself to manage disappointments that he discovered with his male lovers.

Covert-incest survivors often idealize their mothers and have absorbed their mother's version of their fathers. Therapy must assist in de-idealizing the relationship to Mom in order to claim an authentic sense of self. Inherent in that process is separating the man's view of his father from the one he had learned from his mother. Therapy supports the man's journey to discover who he is outside the role of his mother's surrogate companion and constant caretaker. Therapy also assists the man to reconstruct the relationships to others that have taken on the hallmarks of his caretaking relationship with his mother.

Therapy with covert-incest survivors

For a covert-incest survivor, growing up as a parent's surrogate partner means having to "attune" to his parent's needs at a cost to his own. This is a reversal of the mandate of parenting. As adults, covert-incest survivors become caretakers and people-pleasers. Their primary source of identity is sacrificing themselves for others, hoping to receive something for themselves in return. But this is a false promise. They make poor choices in relationships, "burn out" in helping-profession roles, and develop physical and health problems as a result of long-term self-neglect and "over-attunement" to others.

The covert-incest client must shed the roles of people-pleaser and caretaker as an identity, so he has authentic feelings and responses available to him for important life experiences. This client needs to learn to manage feelings of guilt and disloyalty when expressing or acting on his own desires. He can claim his sexuality by owning his passion and decreasing his dependence on sexually addictive escapes or sexually avoidant patterns.

With proper identification and an appropriate treatment course, a covert-incest survivor can recover and build a life of his own choosing. Setting boundaries with parents and others, "divorcing" himself from the contractual demands to be loyal to a parent at any cost, learning to live within commitments of his own choosing, and recovering from addictions and excessive caretaking provide the basis for a life of contentment and satisfaction for the covert-incest survivor.

Note that while covert incest between son and father does occur, it is not as common as between son and mother. One circumstance that may cause this covert seduction occurs when the adult father is gay and living in a heterosexual marriage. He may turn to his son as a surrogate romanticized partner. These cases are similar to the other covert incest stories but with an added confusion regarding the boy's own orientation. Even though he may be heterosexual, he feels merged with his father and picks up on his father's sexuality, becoming fearful regarding his own. Or, if he is gay, he might struggle to feel free to positively affirm himself as gay because of the confusion resulting from his father's seduction.

Other covert forms of sexual abuse

Other forms of covert seduction can also be violating to a boy and leave a lasting impact on his sexuality and relationships. During a course of treatment many clients begin identifying early childhood exposure to sexually intrusive or overwhelming experiences by a parent or other adult that left them confused and feeling traumatized: a mother's exhibitionism, a father paying for a young son's first experience with a prostitute, witnessing a parent's affairs, and so on. In these situations, sons are drawn into their parents' sexual or sexualized behaviors but again without physical sexual touch.

The next story describes the impact on a man who as a boy was taken along when his father paid sexual visits to other women. The father insisted that the son help hide from his mother the affairs he had witnessed. So, together the son and the father were disloyal to the mother and the wife. When the son grows up, these experiences lead him to trauma reenactment, when he finds himself repeating the same pattern with his wife and hating himself in the identical way he hated his father for doing the same thing. He feels enormous guilt and shame but cannot stop.

I'm just like my dad. How did that happen?

Jeff came into therapy distressed that he was going to lose his second wife because of his compulsive pattern of extramarital affairs. He had lost his first wife for the same reason. His children from his first marriage wanted little to do with him, feeling betrayed by his disloyalty to the family. Jeff had hoped that his second marriage would be a fresh start, and he was desperate to understand why he found himself doing what he had long hated his father for doing.

Jeff remembers his excitement one Saturday when he was 10 years old, going off to work with his dad. But instead of work, Dad took him to lunch at a fancy restaurant, and Jeff's excitement turned to confusion as he watched his father kiss and grope a strange woman who joined them in the booth. The woman flirted with Jeff and said he was "cute." This left him not just confused but (as he remembers) literally made him sick to his stomach. He found himself feeling he was watching the whole scene unfold from the other side of the room. All he could think about was getting out of there.

On the drive home, Jeff's dad made him promise not to tell his mother. He explained that all men had other women "on the side," and when he was older he would, too. Jeff said nothing. He remembers feeling that he wanted to magically "leave" the car and disappear into his room at home. When they got home, his dad was excessively critical toward his mother for no apparent reason, and they began fighting. Jeff felt tremendous guilt knowing he was keeping a secret from his mother and pity for her over the betrayal he had just witnessed.

Jeff witnessed, or knew about, many of his father's affairs, always being sworn to secrecy. In time, he learned to block his guilt and pity for his mother, just so he didn't have to "think about it anymore." Over time, he also began to be confused because he was becoming excited at the prospect of being around his dad's other women, witnessing his father's prowess with them. Jeff felt a certain power in this and began to look forward to being with his father at these times. But this reaction also left him feeling guilty and confused. He tried to block this out of his mind as well, but found it difficult.

When he fell in love with his high school sweetheart, he seemed finally able to put his father's affairs behind him by refusing to go out with his dad anymore. It didn't take long, however, for Jeff to find himself straying with other girls. Confused, he rationalized that this was just what guys did, and besides he was still young. Even when his girlfriend found out and left him, he dismissed it as just what happens with "first loves." Thus, from the very beginning of his relationships with women, Jeff began a long and compulsive pattern of trauma reenactment that finally landed him in the therapist's office.

Therapy helped Jeff understand that he was repeating the same behavior his father had perpetrated on him and his mother. The blocking, numbness, and dissociation that he had used to cope in his childhood were the same defenses that allowed him to compartmentalize his behavior as an adult and rationalize the betrayal and hurt he inflicted on the women in his life. Therapy gave him an outlet to tell his secrets and to process his anger, pain, and guilt. He confronted his father, and he told his mother the secrets that, not surprisingly, she already knew. Now, Jeff finally felt he had a chance to start over.

Here, we see again that a covert form of sexual abuse has many of the same markers of overt sexual abuse: dissociation, numbness, compulsive sexual behavior, relationship and attachment failure or dysfunction, and despair and depression. Therapy must assist the client to validate his covert abuse and not distract by searching for overt forms of abuse to explain the symptoms (more about this in the section on countertransference). It also must help the client bring his story to consciousness and to "associate" the dissociative parts of self. If insight fails to bring about an arrest of the compulsive sexual behavior, 12-step programs for sexual addiction should be part of the treatment plan.

Transference and countertransference

A primary transference issue for covert abuse survivors is mistrust and the expectation that the authority figure (therapist) will violate or use them in some fashion. They will camouflage this with people-pleasing and a seeming willingness to do what the clinician expects of them. The clinician must be alert to this false self and not mistake it for treatment compliance. This will be especially true for the covert-incest client who is (unconsciously) adept at merging with the expectations and needs of others, including the clinician. The therapist must guard against the feeling of treatment success that follows this adaptive defense of the client.

It is critical that the therapist empowers the client with awareness and freedom, and guards against the dependency the client will offer to the therapist. If the therapist fails to disrupt this transference, the client will eventually feel engulfed and smothered. If this happens, the client will eventually "divorce" the therapist rather than the parent. Monitor clients who wish to recreate with the therapist the dependency they had with (usually) their mother and be aware of a possible temptation to become this object of dependency. Additionally, covert-incest clients may show ambivalence regarding the therapy process, projecting onto it their fear of being obligated and engulfed by the change process inherent in therapy. They may also fear that the therapist will push for separation from Mom before they are ready. Also, watch for countertransference issues: feelings of anger toward the parent or impatience with the client's ambivalence to separate. While these types of stories might easily provoke these feelings for many therapists, it is important that they not lead to interpretation before clients are ready.

A common complaint about therapy among covert-incest survivors is that they feel the therapist did not take them seriously. In some cases, therapists suggest that the complaint of covert incest or abuse is just a cover for overt sexual abuse. Clinicians must manage and deal effectively with their own countertransference issues that might interfere with proper differential diagnosis and treatment. This could include minimized or denied forms of covert sexual abuse in themselves or a history of overt sexual abuse that gets projected onto the client so that the therapist feels "that must be true for the client as well." The more a client's story causes distress or cognitive dissonance in the clinician, the more likely it is that the clinician will turn consciously or unconsciously to the model of diagnosis and treatment that regulates *their own* distress and allows a return to cognitive consonance, too often at the expense of the client.

Lack of proper attunement could also result from burnout caused by a caseload of intense stories of sexual abuse victims and the therapist's failure to track his or her own need for self-care. A therapist may begin to feel numb and fail to recognize and respond appropriately to cues that indicate covert sexual abuse and the client's need for validation.

It is critical that clinicians working with this population carefully monitor their own countertransference issues and recognize and respond to their own needs so the client's needs can be properly addressed.

Conclusions

Sexuality is a biological drive and is integrally linked to early attachment and caretaking relationships. As such, violating experiences that penetrate and interfere with the normal unfolding of sexuality have lasting consequences and should be categorized as sexual abuse. This abuse can be overt or covert or both. Covert sexual abuse of boys takes many forms and results in consequences similar to that of overt abuse. Issues with sexuality, intimacy, depression, dissociation, sexual dysfunction, and numbness are some of the problems that persist into manhood for boys who were covertly abused. Also common is traumatic reenactment involving sexual behavior that repeats the covert seduction and results in the shame-based and addictive arousal also seen in overt survivors.

One area not addressed in this chapter but critical as we move forward in identifying sexually abusive experiences that occur to boys is the potential of online porn as a form of abuse and violation. Many claim porn is only a "neutral actor" and that boys with backgrounds of dysfunction or vulnerability interact with porn and escalate already existing problems. But some clinicians are beginning to observe that today's porn (that is, all online representations of real-time sex, etc.) is *causative* in the trauma to a child and presents its own public health crisis (Anderson, 2014). Today's porn is not "your daddy's porn." The violent and degrading sex images in real time that young boys become exposed to at critical developmental periods in the unfolding of their sexuality may indeed be considered abusive. As we move forward in identifying and understanding covert seduction and abuse of boys, the impact of "today's porn" must be included in the discussion.

Future efforts by clinicians to identify and study covert forms of seduction will help to validate boys and men who need freedom from the shame and impact of all insidious forms of abuse.

References

Adams, Kenneth M. (1987). Sexual addiction and covert incest: Connecting the family roots of alcoholism, neglect, and abuse. *Focus on Chemically Dependent Families*. Pompano Beach, FL: Health Communications, May/June.

Adams, Kenneth M. (1991). *Silently seduced: When parents make their children partners – understanding covert incest.* Deerfield Beach, FL: Health Communications.

Adams, Kenneth M. (2011). *Silently seduced – revised and updated: When parents make their children partners.* Deerfield Beach, FL: Health Communications.

Adams, Kenneth M., with Alexander P. Morgan. (2007). *When he's married to mom: How to help mother enmeshed men open their hearts to true love and commitment.* New York, NY: Simon & Schuster.

Allen, E. S., & Baucom, D. H. (2004). Adult attachment and patterns of extra dyadic involvement. *Family Process, 43*(4), 467–488.

Anderson, C. (2014). *The impact of pornography on children, youth, and culture.* Holyoke, MA: NEARI Press.

Carnes, P. J. (1991). *Don't call it love, recovery from sexual addiction.* New York, NY: Bantam.

Creeden, K. (2004). The neurodevelopmental impact of early trauma and insecure attachment: Re-thinking our understanding and treatment of sexual behavior problems. *Sexual Addiction & Compulsivity, 11*(4), 223–247.

Del Giudice, M. (2009). Sex, attachment, and the development of reproductive strategies. *Behavioral and Brain Sciences, 32*(1), 1–21

Fradkin, H. (2012). *Joining forces: Empowering male survivors to thrive.* Carlsbad, CA: Hay House.

Gartner, R. (1999). *Betrayed as boys: Psychodynamic treatment of sexually abused men.* New York, NY: Guilford.

Gartner, R. (2005). *Beyond betrayal: Taking charge of your life after boyhood sexual abuse.* Hoboken, NJ: Wiley.

Hunter, M. (1990). *Abused boys: The neglected victims of sexual abuse.* Lexington, MA: Lexington Books.

Jore, J., Green, B., Adams, K., & Carnes, P. (2016). Attachment dysfunction and relationship preoccupation. *Sexual Addiction & Compulsivity: The Journal of Treatment and Prevention, 23*, 56–90.

Katehakis, A. (2009). Affective neuroscience and the treatment of sexual addiction. *Sexual Addiction & Compulsivity, 16*(1), 1–31.

Lew, M. (1988). *Victims no longer.* New York, NY: Harper & Row.

Love, P., & Robinson, J. (1991). *The emotional incest syndrome: What to do when a parent's love rules your life.* New York, NY: Bantam.

Miller, L. C., & Fishkin, S. A. (1997). On the dynamics of human bonding and reproductive success: Seeking windows on the adapted-for human-environmental interface. In J. Simpson & D. Kenrick (Eds.), *Evolutionary social psychology* (pp. 197–235). Mahwah, NJ: Erlbaum.

Money, J. (1986). *Lovemaps: Clinical concepts of sexual/erotic health and pathology, paraphilia, and gender transposition of childhood, adolescence, and maturity.* New York, NY: Irvington.

Schwartz, M. F. (1994). The Masters and Johnson treatment program for sex offenders: Intimacy, empathy, and trauma resolution. *Sexual Addiction & Compulsivity: The Journal of Treatment and Prevention, 3*, 261–277.

Schwartz, M. F. (1996). Reenactment related to bonding and hypersexuality. *Sexual Addiction & Compulsivity: The Journal of Treatment and Prevention, 3*, 195–212.

Schwartz, M., Galperin, L., & Masters, W. (1995). Sexual trauma within the context of traumatic and inescapable stress, neglect and poisonous pedagogy. In M. Hunter (Ed.), *Adult survivors of sexual abuse: Treatment innovations* (pp. 1–17). Thousand Oaks, CA: Sage.

Schwartz, M. F., & Southern, S. (1999). Manifestations of damaged development of the human affectional systems and developmentally based psychotherapies. *Sexual Addiction & Compulsivity, 6*(3), 163–175.

Stephan, C. W., & Bachman, G. F. (1999). What's sex got to do with it? Attachment, love schemas, and sexuality. *Personal Relationships, 6*(1), 111–123.

van der Kolk, B. A. (1989). The compulsion to repeat the trauma: Re-enactment, revictimization, and masochism. *Psychiatric Clinics of North America, 12*, 389–411.

van der Kolk, B. A. (2014). *The body keeps the score: Brain, mind, and body in the healing of trauma.* New York, NY: Viking.

Chapter 12

Working with male survivor couples

Heather B. MacIntosh

> *I was just like why, what the hell is wrong with me, what the hell is wrong with you? We are two young physically healthy people. Unless you are gay, why aren't you attracted? I've asked him that and he said he isn't. I just couldn't understand, I wanted to make it work and that's why I didn't want to leave.*

These are the words of Abigail,[1] a 34-year-old female partner of a male childhood sexual abuse (CSA) survivor, in the early stages of couple therapy. Abigail just couldn't understand why her husband wasn't attracted to her, didn't want her. She was filled with grief, pain, and fury over the many lost years of secrecy and silence finally broken by her husband's disclosure of his abuse history, at the brink of the dissolution of their marriage.

It is the goal of this chapter to review the impact of CSA history in males on their couple relationships and their partners, and to discuss some aspects of couple therapy specifically oriented toward working with what will be called male survivor couples. Clinical material will be drawn from male survivor couples participating in a study exploring Developmental Couple Therapy for Complex Trauma (DCTCT), an approach developed by this author to address the specific needs of childhood trauma survivors.

Male survivor couples typically fall into a cycle of distress distinct from the pattern for female survivor couples. The male CSA survivor desires the closeness and security of a couple relationship and is able to

1 Names and descriptions have been changed and clinical issues have been combined to create composites for the protection of the confidentiality of the couples participating in the research project.

initiate such a relationship, but experiences painful conflict between his conscious desire to engage with his partner emotionally and sexually, and a less conscious resistance to this connection that pulls the male survivor away into a pattern of chronic avoidance. This avoidance is often fed by dissociation, distractions such as overwork, or sexually compulsive behaviors. Avoidance is then reinforced by secrecy, due to lack of disclosure of his CSA history, and also from living multiple, segregated lives: the relationship with his partner is often devoid of sexual intimacy and full of tension, while hiding painful, compulsive, dissociative sexual reenactments through fantasies fueled by hidden pornography or illicit sexual encounters with "hookups," prostitutes, or individuals with whom he engages in extramarital affairs. This sexual secrecy leads to a rigid and inflexible division within the male survivor, fed by shame and dissociation directed at his hidden life, which creates deeper divisions within the couple as the male CSA survivor responds to this shame with further avoidance and, often, alienating interactions with his partner. Meanwhile, the partner struggles to figure out what is wrong, slowly falling into heightened anxiety and preoccupation with the relationship, observing the CSA survivor's trajectory of suffering and eventually, often, burning out. In these cases, the relationship typically falls apart. Many of the couples with whom I have worked in clinical practice and in research have followed this dynamic. This chapter examines the literature about male survivors and their relationships while exploring the most relevant concepts using examples from two research couples, Abigail and Alejandro, and Terrence and Thomas.

Couples

Abigail and Alejandro have been married for ten years after a long-distance courtship. They have one daughter, conceived through artificial insemination after a lengthy period of infertility. Abigail reported that physicians were not able to identify any particular physiological problems causing infertility and she believed that lack of intimacy and sexual frequency was responsible. This couple are both Spanish Canadians who came together from families of origin where each set of parents married spouses their own parents had chosen, and both grew up in intergenerational households. Abigail and Alejandro each dated outside their culture but, along with their families, they were happy to find a spouse within the culture. Both Abigail and Alejandro are very close to their families and treat their extended marital family as their own.

As the eldest child and the only boy in his first-generation immigrant family, Alejandro was raised to identify strongly with the role of eldest male, family protector, and caretaker. In the first session, Alejandro reported that his uncle, who lived with the family, sexually abused him from the ages of 10 to 12, until the uncle moved away to live with another family member. Alejandro did not disclose this to anyone. The abuse began with Alejandro being forced to sit with his uncle while he watched pornography and masturbated Alejandro. The abuse progressed to his uncle making Alejandro "jerk him off" while he forced him to watch pornography. Alejandro experienced a confusing combination of revulsion and arousal that has stayed with him as an adult. He found it difficult to discuss his abuse in early sessions, but was able to provide an outline of what he remembered, and to let me know that he had not told anyone—his parents, siblings, friends or, even Abigail—until the previous year when Abigail told him that she was going to leave if things did not improve.

Abigail was the elder of two girls in a first-generation immigrant family. She grew up witnessing her mother being emotionally abused day in and day out by her father's mother and reported her confusion watching her mother being so wounded by the same grandmother who was so kind and loving to Abigail herself. Over the course of Abigail's childhood, her mother fell into serious depressive episodes, which resulted in several hospitalizations and lengthy periods of recuperation. After her mother's fourth hospitalization, Abigail's father moved the family very far away, ostensibly for work reasons, providing them with a valid excuse to no longer house his parents. While saying that her mother's frequent hospitalizations were not traumatic or distressing for her, Abigail appeared to find it difficult to talk about these experiences.

For this couple, many aspects of development unfolded as they should, but the male survivor's CSA casts a long, dark shadow. Alejandro and Abigail have developed the capacity to regulate their emotional states, to develop and maintain basic attachments, and to mentalize well—to think about thinking, both their own and others. These essential developmental capacities helped this couple navigate the painful impact of CSA on their relationship. Both partners agreed that their marriage works in most ways; they are compatible, enjoy one another's company, complement each other as parents, and are devoted to their families. The couple also share basic values, are both well-educated and engaged in their careers, and have little conflict in relation to how they spend their time or money. The couple lives in a modest home, which they own, in a major city.

Terrence and Thomas have also been together for ten years, but their relationship has been rocky from the start, with many breakups and reconciliations throughout. This couple lives in a small subsidized apartment, and neither Terrence nor Thomas is employed full-time. Both struggle with significant mental health problems, yet neither has been able to access trauma-focused psychotherapy due to their limited finances and difficulty accessing help from social service organizations. In contrast to Alejandro and Abigail, Terrence and Thomas have not developed the capacity to regulate their emotional states, to develop and maintain basic attachments, or to mentalize well. In the absence of these essential developmental capacities, this couple is struggling to navigate the painful impact of CSA on their relationship or to deal with any meaningful challenges in their lives.

Terrence grew up with a violent mother who could be kind and loving at times but would fly into sudden, violent rages, hitting and kicking Terrence until he was bloody and cowering in a corner. His mother went through a string of boyfriends who could also be frightening and violent. Terrence has three sisters by different fathers and the family lived in severe poverty, always in situations where their housing was substandard and precarious. He was frequently hungry and frightened, and was left alone for long periods, even days at a time. Terrence did not see his father regularly, and when he did visit him on weekends and during holidays, his father violently sexually abused him. The abuse began before Terrence could remember, and continued until he was 14 and refused to visit his father anymore. Terrence paid a steep price for trying to avoid the violent abuse: his father stalked him relentlessly until he moved away from his mother's home at 16. Terrence was a poor historian in his sessions, appearing to be highly dissociative and struggling to provide any autobiographical detail, or even to recount what had happened the day before. He had little access to education, social support, or even the capacity to engage with work, due to such high levels of dissociation and symptoms of trauma. As an adult, Terrence continued to live in poverty, often on the streets, where he was physically and sexually assaulted.

Thomas is a person of color and an only child whose mother emigrated from Southeast Asia. His mother kept the identity of his father from him, and raised him largely on her own. Thomas reported constant conflicts with his mother during his childhood, as she wanted him to maintain a traditional cultural life while Thomas wanted to be a typical Canadian teenager. He indicated that his mother would regularly taunt and insult him, call him names, and physically abuse him by punching and slapping him, leaving marks. When Thomas came out at 22, his mother told him he was a disgusting aberration of nature and disowned him. Thomas has made several attempts to reunite with his mother but she has rebuffed all of his efforts. Thomas did not identify any of these behaviors as abusive, and was taken aback by my suggestion that he might have had a stressful childhood. Thomas works part-time in a diner and has completed some postsecondary education.

These two couples show many of the common themes of male survivors' experience, while representing diverse situations and experiences. Abigail and Alejandro are a heterosexual, cisgendered couple, where the abuse was external to the nuclear family—all potentially moderating factors. Both partners are functioning well in all other areas of their lives, but are struggling in their couple relationship. Meanwhile, Terrence and Thomas are same-sex partners, both with a history of trauma; they have experienced huge instability in their relationship without having had the benefit of many positive developmental experiences. In a recent study of couple therapy with CSA survivors and their partners, over 50% of the "non-trauma" partners had experienced other forms of childhood trauma (MacIntosh & Johnson, 2008). Dual-trauma couples have even greater challenges emerging from emotional dysregulation and attachment insecurity, and therefore have an even greater need for reliable treatment. Terrence struggles with complex trauma symptoms due to his experience of extensive, severe, and chronic CSA at the hands of his father, someone who should have protected him. Thomas is a person of color who experienced what most researchers and clinicians would describe as intergenerational cultural stress around acculturation, racism, as well as emotional and physical abuse in childhood. Neither Terrence nor Thomas functions well in their lives in any domain. They share with Alejandro and Abigail certain common issues related to CSA, but also represent distant poles of functionality in terms of emotion regulation, attachment security, and mentalizing (MacIntosh, 2013).

Impact of CSA on couple relationships

It is now well established in the literature, and clearly evident to those in clinical practice, that CSA has devastating and disabling impacts on survivors' capacities to form and maintain meaningful, intimate, close, and loving couple relationships. Survivors often find it impossible to trust or feel close to a partner, or to maintain consistent connections (Godbout, Runtz, MacIntosh, & Briere, 2013; Johnson, 2002; Styron & Janoff-Bulman, 1997). While CSA survivors continue to desire safe, satisfying, and consistent romantic relationships, they typically evidence pervasive and devastating challenges in their interpersonal relationships (DiLillo, 2001; Godbout et al., 2013; Rumstein-McKean & Hunsley, 2001).

Despite everything that is now understood about CSA survivors and their couple relationships, the impact of CSA on male survivors and their partners, in particular, has been virtually ignored. In what has been a growing literature, almost every article, chapter, and book mentions the existence of CSA among males but then moves on to provide case studies, empirical analyses, and clinical documentation of the experiences of female CSA survivors and their male partners; this portrayal assumes a female as victim and a male as perpetrator, and also presents only heterosexual, cisgendered couples. Male survivors are either overlooked, due to their small numbers within a mixed sample, or they are reported within a pool that includes female survivors, so that gendered differences are masked (Easton, 2012; Sorsoli, Kia-Keating, & Grossman, 2008). Higher rates of CSA among females, and a lack of attention to male survivors in the literature, have rendered male survivors and their experiences invisible (Kia-Keating, Sorsoli, & Grossman, 2010; Price-Robertson, Higgins, & Vassallo, 2013).

Clinical practitioners know female survivor couples are similar to couples with male survivors in the ways they are affected by trauma, such as CSA. However, in the impact of CSA on couple relationships, gender differences are significant. For male survivors, being violated is a fundamental transgression against the standards of masculinity—independence, self-reliance, strength, and even aggression—to be so vulnerable and overpowered by an abuser (Gagnier & Collin-Vézina, 2016; Tener & Murphy, 2015). The dissonance between social expectations of masculinity and the experience of being vulnerable and helpless can be highly destructive for male survivors, and is compounded by rape myths that communicate the idea that sexual abuse of men is harmless, even that the survivor is "lucky," or that the abuse is the fault of the survivor (Banyard, Williams, & Siegel, 2004; Denov, 2003; Mejia, 2005). Add to this the prohibition against expressing vulnerability, pain, or feelings of powerlessness, and male CSA survivors may feel like failures as men, which can lead to greater levels of shame and avoidance of disclosure (Hlavka, 2016; Lisak, 1993). And so, how can these gendered expectations not have a significant impact on male survivors' couple relationships?

Couple therapy and CSA

The literature about working with childhood trauma survivors in couple therapy is expanding, with more survivors seeking support in their relationships, feeling dissatisfied with therapists' limited understanding of the role of CSA in relationship distress (Zala, 2012). Up to one-third of couples presenting for therapy have a history of CSA in one or both partners (Anderson & Miller, 2006). However, in the literature for survivor couples the norm consists of a female CSA survivor and her male partner. As with other CSA literature, the studies pertaining to CSA survivor couples are virtually silent about couples with male survivors. While two articles mention that male survivors should be included in discussions about couple therapy, only Wells (2015) specifically discusses issues related to male survivors and their partners. This conceptual piece about gender and trust in CSA couples highlights the male survivors' confusion in maintaining the socially prescribed masculine role of power in intimate relationships, while coping with the vulnerability and powerlessness that they might experience as a result of childhood trauma. The study suggests that this may lead to high levels of anger and self-loathing (Wells, 2015).

Recent research concentrates on specific mechanisms through which childhood trauma survivors experience distress in their couple relationships, as well as in the process of couple therapy itself. Foundational interventions in couple therapy such as emotional heightening, exploring diverse perspectives, and expressing hurt and historical injuries in the couple relationship, require survivors to regulate their emotions while listening to their partner and assuming the partner's perspective while identifying and communicating their own feelings. These interventions, while transformative for couples without childhood trauma, may be emotionally arousing and dysregulating for childhood trauma survivors. The interventions may trigger collapses in basic capacities such as empathy and perspective taking—capacities that are vital for the success of couple therapy (MacIntosh, 2013, 2016). My current research explores a new model of couple therapy that includes interventions focused specifically on the essential developmental capacities that have been harmed by, or never developed in the context of, a history of CSA: emotion regulation, the capacity to form meaningful attachments, and the capacity to mentalize. This approach encourages these capacities to develop within the couple (MacIntosh, 2016).

Avoidance

The opening move in what appears to be a distinct dance of couple distress in male survivor couples is the conflict that many male survivors experience in developing and maintaining an intimate connection with their partners. Male survivors often report feeling a desperate conflict between their conscious desire to experience a close and intimate connection with their partner, and a deeper, less conscious force that they report feels like being stuck and held behind a wall. They feel unable to get close to their partners no matter how much they long for this kind of intimacy.

Very few studies have examined the specific experiences of male CSA survivors and their partners in their relationships. In a cross-sectional study, DiLillo et al. (2009) identified that for male survivors, maltreatment, not specifically CSA, was connected to high levels of distress in couple relationships. Godbout, Lussier, and Sabourin (2006) evaluated the role of gender in couple adjustment in a sample of 632 male and female CSA survivors. This study highlighted many similarities between male and female CSA survivors in terms of high levels of psychological distress and fears of abandonment. It found that CSA was not related to intimacy avoidance in men, but intimacy avoidance was related to higher levels of psychological distress and lower levels of couple satisfaction. In a larger sample of over 1000 participants, Godbout, Briere, Sabourin, and Lussier (2014) added the relationship of parental support into their assessment of the impact of CSA on survivors. Separate analyses suggested that male survivors who experienced strong parental support demonstrated lower levels of attachment avoidance in adulthood, whereas those who reported less parental support experienced higher levels of attachment avoidance and psychological distress. This was contrary to the results among female CSA survivors, who tended to express more attachment anxiety in response to lack of parental support following CSA. So, more simply, male survivors appear to turn off attachment, resulting in dismissal of attachment figures and avoidance of closeness, while female survivors appear to turn up their attachment-seeking and vigilance. This is certainly in keeping with clinical experience with male survivors, who tend to be very hard to engage with their partners and in the process of couple therapy.

For Abigail and Alejandro these themes were expressed in Alejandro's chronic lack of closeness, intimacy, and attachment-seeking behavior. His response to his sexual abuse was to shut down and avoid all reminders of the trauma. Alejandro spoke quietly in sessions about his longing for connection with Abigail and his confusion about why he could not break through the fog that seemed to separate him from her. He described long hours of talking to himself, of anxious self-loathing and of trying to push himself toward her. Alejandro avoided any kind of closeness; he could not articulate to Abigail why he was avoidant. Because this couple can regulate their emotional distress, they are able to talk about the complexities of their respective feelings. They can empathize with one another and see each other's perspectives; they have a basic attachment, albeit insecure, from which to explore these challenges.

For Terrence and Thomas, these themes are expressed with more hostility and less regulation. Terrence experiences very high levels of dissociation and finds that any kind of engagement sends him into a dysregulated state. As much as he wants to be in a relationship, he cannot tolerate Thomas's need for connection; it intrudes on his dissociative strategies for coping with chronic and overwhelming distress. When Terrence cannot engage with Thomas, the latter becomes overwhelmed with distress and despair, feeling that Terrence does not care for him and is not interested in him. Terrence reports he feels as though he is irreparably damaged and will never shift to a mode different from the abuse he experienced, stating that Thomas's demands for reciprocity in the relationship are impossible for him to meet. This couple cannot regulate their distress, lacking the capacity to see one another's perspectives or to empathize, and as such, cannot explore these ideas easily, clearly, and with curiosity.

Thomas: (crying) It's starting to feel unbalanced, I try to tell him like, actually caring about somebody feels really good . . . we talked about him practicing his active listening skills, and he said he appreciated me reminding him.

Terrence: (cuts in) Yeah but it's really exhausting and I'm tired, I'm tired. One part of me is like, it's good that he wants to talk to me and that he feels good when we talk but the other part of me is like, I've done too much work in my lifetime and I don't need to do this.

Therapist: What kind of work?

Terrence: Like caring about what's going on for my mother.

Therapist: Tell me about that.

Terrence: She's just was uh, pretty sick when I was growing up.

Therapist: How did that affect you, what was that like for you?

Terrence: Um, I feel like we don't have much time.

Therapist: We have lots of time.

Terrence: I mean I didn't get to be a child. I had to be concerned about people's emotions.

(Discussion of the experience of being parented by a mother so mentally ill.)

Therapist: There's a part of you that's saying, I had to work too hard when I was growing up paying attention to her and her needs, I'm tired of it, enough already.

Terrence: Yeah.

Therapist: So, your response of shutting down and shutting Thomas out is a part of that. On the one hand, it's a way of protecting yourself from getting into a situation like that again. When you were a child you had no control over that and now you have a little choice and control. And on the other hand, you miss out on a kind of closeness and richness of connection and your partner feels hurt and shut out.

Terrence: Yeah.

Therapist: It's a bit of a double-edged sword, there is something you need that you get but there's something that you want that you lose. I wonder if there would be a way to help the two of you learn how to feel connected to one another in the ways that are important to each of you that doesn't feel like a repetition of history. That it is something that you choose to do, not something outside of your control.

(Discussion of how Terrence's shutting Thomas out impacts both of them.)

Therapist: Dissociation can be like surfing on the wave and you're doing your thing and someone comes by and puts their foot under your board . . .

Terrence: Yeah, most people I can just get by with just pretending and not really paying attention.

Therapist: Yes, and that doesn't work so well in a love relationship. Dissociation is a very powerful protective mechanism but it also keeps us apart from other people. Thomas is saying that he needs more, more connection.

Thomas: I mean I haven't really thought about it as dissociation. It's interesting. I have a hard time thinking about it as anything but being self-involved and not interested in me. I mean, that's forgivable and I understand that it could be about trauma or about his mom. I know for myself, I have a hard time talking about myself and opening up to people and I need a lot of reassurance and trust and I've been trying to overcome that.

Therapist: So Terrence would be a perfect pick if the part of you that is afraid of opening up gets to be in charge.

Thomas: Yeah.

Therapist: At those extremes of self-protection the two of you fit lock and key. You're protecting yourself from being taken advantage of and you're protecting yourself from the vulnerability—perfect fit. But as you both try to do something new, you are trying to open up and you are trying to find your way through the fog then it becomes very painful and difficult. You are left feeling like you don't matter and you are left feeling like you aren't doing a very good job. You are both left feeling bad.

Disclosure

For many survivors, a turning point in their healing is the process of disclosing to others (Easton, Leone-Sheehan, Sophis, & Willis, 2015).

Male survivors appear to delay disclosure even longer than female survivors, on average 21 years (Jonzon & Lindblad, 2004). Avoiding disclosure means carrying a huge secret, which requires a lot of energy (Staller & Nelson-Gardell, 2005). Many factors serve as barriers for men to disclose, including the gendered socialization discussed above. Shame, guilt, self-blame, fears of being labeled pedophile or as homosexual, fear of being labeled weak, and a deeply socialized need to suppress the feelings that come with a disclosure all act as barriers in the lives of male CSA survivors (Alaggia, 2004; Easton et al., 2015; Gagnier & Collin-Vézina, 2016; Sorsoli et al., 2008; Tener & Murphy, 2015). This secrecy and avoidance of disclosure creates a barrier to intimacy (Tener & Murphy, 2015). "When you have a secret, like a heavy burden on your shoulders, there is always a kind of wall between you and the rest of the world" (Aakvaag et al., 2016, p. 234).

In our research on disclosure of CSA to romantic partners (MacIntosh, Fletcher, & Collin-Vézina, 2016), one theme concerned the reasons CSA survivors disclosed. A gender difference emerged within this theme: whereas the primary reason female survivors disclosed seemed to be a belief that they were damaged and that it would be wrong not to, men more often felt coerced to do so by external forces.

Alejandro only made his disclosure when Abigail was poised to leave. He hoped that all of the ways in which he was trying to be a perfect husband and father would somehow make up for his inability to get closer to Abigail.

Therapist: And what is it like to start to talk about it?

Alejandro: Oh God! I just felt like, I don't even know how, like I can't even describe to you, the emotion, I just remember that huge knot, like right here (shows his throat). [. . .] When I was actually able to say it, it was just like, a huge, like a huge, there was nothing sitting there, I just felt like a huge burden, like a ton of bricks coming off of my shoulders. [. . .] I'd been wanting to say for God knows how long, but it would go into this fuzzy area where I would kinda forget about it and then when we would have our issues, when she would bring it up, it would just kinda explode, it would come back, again.

Terrence was very open about his experiences of CSA right from the beginning of his relationship with Thomas, but he limited his disclosures to the barest outline. Thomas wanted more details, but Terrence was unable to tolerate telling him without becoming completely dysregulated. Unlike Alejandro, who had no intention of disclosing his CSA until forced, Terrence had never been able to hide that he had been traumatized due to the extent of his mental health difficulties.

Our research on couple therapy with female CSA survivors and their partners has identified that disclosing, and in fact, telling the story of what happened in their CSA experiences, facilitated positive outcomes (MacIntosh & Johnson, 2008). For couples to engage fully in the therapeutic process, and to build intimacy and closeness in their relationships, their partners must be brought into the story of the trauma. For couples in the preceding study, all of the partners were aware of their partner's history of CSA, but none of the partners knew any of the details of the abuse. For couples where therapists facilitated disclosure and exploration of details of the CSA survivors' traumas, outcomes in terms of trauma symptoms and couple satisfaction were stronger than for those where this process was not included in the therapy (MacIntosh & Johnson, 2008).

For Alejandro, telling the story of his abuse was a painful but necessary step in moving closer to his wife and, in the end, opening himself up to the dissociated, more complete story of his own abuse. However, as Alejandro began to share more about his experiences and to read more about CSA, his own dissociative disavowal began to slip and he started to have more flashbacks about other experiences of CSA that he had not been able to hold in his mind while he remained in his avoidant protective stance. Alejandro then found it easier to disclose the new memories to Abigail and to talk about the process of recovering these memories:

Alejandro: I don't know why it didn't come to me at that time (when he first disclosed), I think, a couple of days before, I was just reading the book Heather asked me to read (*Betrayed as Boys*[2]), all that's written in the book, it just kinda, reminders, images, it was perfectly clear that it happened, but the exact

2 Alejandro is referring to the book *Betrayed as Boys* (Gartner, 1999), which was assigned as reading to help him begin to understand that he is not alone in his experience of CSA and to start to understand the impact of CSA.

> images of what specifically happened, that wasn't there clearly. The events occurred and it just blew to the forefront. Like, I hadn't told anybody until I told the last time. That was the first time, I actually told somebody about those two new memories.

However, the process of disclosure was painful for Abigail who struggled with the mixed emotions of anger at Alejandro's perpetrators, at his parents for not protecting him, and at Alejandro for not disclosing earlier and for leaving her to feel that there was something wrong with her.

Therapist: (to Abigail after disclosure) What are you thinking, feeling?
Abigail: (crying) I feel horrible. It's not a good feeling. I feel hurt for him. I feel angry at his parents though. I don't know why, I have so much anger for them, against them. I feel like they should have known. I know exactly where my kid is all the time, or what's happening with her. I know she's still young, but still . . .

It was only when Alejandro was able to tell Abigail, with my help, more of the details of his traumatic experiences, that he was able to begin the painful and challenging work of breaking through his wall of avoidance. With the truth out in the open, he was able to start moving toward Abigail, pushing through the wall that was keeping them apart.

Alejandro: It's been, it has been extremely hard. I mean, I started feeling better about myself after I was able to finally get it out in the open. There was the relief of being able to tell somebody, that made me feel better. That didn't fix all feelings of my difficulties and I just kinda let it, pile up, too much.

For Terrence, it was necessary to work on developing skills in emotion regulation and grounding techniques before he could tell Thomas more about his experiences. For CSA survivors with extensive trauma histories who display high levels of complex trauma, the telling of the story cannot happen until the survivor is able to tolerate the telling and the partner is able to respond with empathy and compassion rather than reactivity and anger. For Terrence and Thomas, this was not until well into the first phase of the process of DCTCT, establishing safety and psychoeducation (MacIntosh, 2016). For Thomas, it was necessary to work on developing emotion regulation and mentalizing capacities so he could imagine the experience of Terrence, tolerate his distress at hearing such difficult stories, and not collapse into his own preconception that Terrence was avoiding engagement with him by withholding these stories. Thomas needed to understand that Terrence's failure to share his story with him was about survival and not about intentionally shutting him out.

The process had to be tailored to the capacities of both partners. Partners of CSA survivors struggle with the painful awareness that something is wrong, the feeling of distance from the CSA survivor and the certainty that there is something they should know, but somehow cannot. And so, while it is a great relief to know more about the reasons for the divide, partners also experience anger at being left out for so long, anger about feeling responsible for what has been wrong in the couple, and deep grief about lost time.

Sexuality and secrecy

Issues with sexuality in male survivors have been well covered in other chapters in this book,[3] so this section will focus on the specific challenges for partners of male survivors, for these couples, and for their couple therapy. The limited literature that addresses the impact of CSA on male survivors' sexuality suggests the greater the use of force and the more invasive the abuse, the more significant the sexual challenges in adulthood for male survivors (Banyard et al., 2004). This literature also suggests that CSA leads to traumatic sexualization and sexual behaviors, and conditioning in adulthood that may not reflect the conscious desires of the survivor, but could be more of a coping mechanism than a healthy expression of sexuality (Crawford & O'Dougherty Wright, 2007; DiLillo et al., 2009; Zala, 2012).

In female survivor couples, most partners described imposed periods of celibacy as painful but necessary (Bacon & Lein, 1996; Chauncey, 1994; Feinauer, Callahan, & Hilton, 1996; Firth, 1997; Harway & Faulk, 2005;

3 Editor's note: See especially Chapter 8 by Courtois and Weiss in this volume and Chapter 12 by Kort in the companion volume to this one, *Understanding the Sexual Betrayal of Boys and Men: The Trauma of Sexual Abuse*.

Reid, Taylor, & Wampler, 1995; Reid, Wampler, & Taylor, 1996). Research on female survivors indicates that reduced levels of desire are the norm, and periods of celibacy are required to heal their sexuality outside of any pressure from the partner for sex before they begin to reintroduce sexuality into their relationships (Traeen & Sorensen, 2008). However, anecdotal and clinical reports suggest that male survivors tend to experience a bifurcation of their sexuality: hyperactivation and reenactments "outside" of intimate relationships, and hypoactivation and suppression within intimate relationships. This bifurcation in their sexuality leads to a disconnected relationship with their partner and painful disavowal of sexuality that is held away, secret and separate. Another reason for helping survivors tell the story of their abuse to their partners is to help male survivors begin to bring together these two aspects of their sexuality, and to bring their sexuality back into the primacy of the couple relationship. Disclosure and exploration helps non-CSA partners understand and empathize with the struggles their partner is having in their sexual relationship.

Without disclosure and sharing, partners are left to try to figure out the mystery of why male survivors appear to be sexually disconnected or disinterested, a phenomenon that goes against the common belief that men always want sex (regardless of whether this is a myth). As discussed in the chapters on male survivors and sexuality, survivors may find themselves in compulsive cycles of sexual reenactment. For some, these struggles lead to a double life: an avoidant, unresponsive and artificially deadened sexual relationship with a spouse (often female) and a secret, chaotic, compulsive, or even traumatically reenacted sexual life lived through fantasy in online pornography, or in bars and through Internet hookups.

Alejandro was no exception to this trend. He could not find his way to initiating any kind of sexual contact with Abigail. He described feeling completely overwhelmed with anxiety and fear about losing her and then just turning off, going into a state of avoidant dissociation and not thinking about the issue until she brought it up again, in an angry state of despair. He described finding her very attractive and yet not being able to approach her. At the same time, Alejandro would wait for Abigail to go to bed and then descend into the basement and slip his way into a dissociated state of compulsive masturbation to Internet pornography. Like many male survivors, Alejandro found himself going deeper and deeper into this morass, masturbating for hours and hours in a semi-conscious dissociative state to darker and more extreme pornography over time.

Also, like many male survivors, Alejandro identified as heterosexual but was drawn primarily to homosexual pornography. His interests started with pornography depicting adult men engaged in consensual vanilla sex; over time, his habits evolved such that he needed to watch men engaged in rough and painful sexual acts and positions to become fully aroused and to reach orgasm.

Terrence was able to have sex with Thomas when Thomas initiated it, but he could only maintain his erection, penetrate him, and achieve orgasm if he imagined that Thomas was a small boy he was sodomizing. Terrence reported, in individual sessions, that he felt horribly ashamed of these fantasies but that he could not have sex with Thomas any other way. He would keep his eyes closed and drift into his fantasy; when sex was over, Thomas would long for close connection, but Terrence would fall into a dissociative stupor and become unresponsive. Terrence's secret sexual life was filled with the kinds of violence that characterized his abuse. Thomas had an idea that there was a secret life, because his intense anxiety about Terrence led him to hack into his emails, read his texts, and even follow him when he went out. While Terrence was filled with shame about the things he did in his compulsive sexual dissociation, he was unable to stop himself. In his secret sexual reenactments Terrence could be both perpetrator and victim. He engaged in sexual reenactments, finding intense sexual satisfaction in being penetrated anally by older men who are rough with him; he found these men on the Internet on sites for gay men seeking quick, anonymous sex.

Impact on partner

For Abigail, Alejandro's seeming sexual disinterest in her had a deeply painful impact. For years she fluctuated desperately between wondering what was wrong with him, and then what was wrong with her. She wondered whether Alejandro was gay, whether he was not attracted to her, or what was wrong with her that he remained so sexually distant. Abigail felt sad, lonely, sexually frustrated, and filled with anger at Alejandro for seemingly abandoning her. Eventually, she issued an ultimatum: get help or get out. It was at this point that Alejandro made his disclosure. Abigail was filled with sadness and anger about Alejandro's abuse experiences and toward his uncle, and at the same time was furious with Alejandro for not telling her previously, and leaving her with the belief that there was something wrong with her. Because this couple has the basic capacities for emotion regulation and mentalizing, and a fairly consistent attachment bond, they have been able to talk openly about the complexities surrounding their sexual struggles and begin to heal.

For Thomas, who knew that Terrence had a secret life but who could not talk with Terrence about it due to the secrecy, lies, and conflict between them, the pain of knowing and not knowing was devastating. Thomas knew about Terrence's CSA history, and subsequently discovered sexually explicit texts and emails from men, but never knew the extent of his partner's secret sexual life. He feared that Terrence was involved in dangerous or risky sexual contacts with men, and worried about his own health and well-being as Terrence's sexual partner, given that Terrence would not consistently use condoms. Thomas felt as though he could not confront Terrence, because he had violated his partner's trust through "hacking" and surveillance, but was immobilized by fear, anger, and betrayal. Unlike Abigail, Thomas had a history of overt childhood trauma, which added another layer of complexity, with reenactments overlaying reenactments. Thomas's own reenactment, at the beginning of therapy, looked like paralysis in the face of abuse as Terrence continued to avoid and stonewall, and eventually responded with disdain and anger to Thomas's increasing demands for engagement.

Holding individual sessions in the context of couple therapy is contested in the literature, with some authors arguing that individual sessions can be an important way to build the therapeutic alliance and to bridge points in the therapy that are highly conflictual. Other authors assert that the couple relationship is the client, and that individual sessions are dangerous to the therapeutic relationship and the treatment process (Leone, 2013). However, in the case of male survivor couples where information-sharing within the couple may be obstructed by sexual secrecy, individual sessions may be necessary and helpful. Therapists may find themselves trying to navigate discussions about sex and sexuality in a minefield of undisclosed compulsive sexual behaviors or extra-dyadic sexual contacts. With Abigail and Alejandro, and with Terrence and Thomas, I held individual sessions at the outset, and these continued throughout the treatment when it seemed important to have a space for full disclosure, where the partner was not present, and to help partners prepare, on their own, for difficult discussions to come in the therapy.

For Alejandro the individual sessions provided an opportunity to share newly resurfaced trauma memories in preparation for disclosing them to Abigail, as well as to discuss the secret parts of his sexual life. Feeling sexually neglected, Abigail could have been devastated by the initial presentation of these disclosures, and this also has the potential to make couple therapy a place where further damage is done to the relationship—therapy can become an unsafe space for healing. For Terrence, the individual session was a space for him to tell someone, for the first time, about the ways in which he was stuck in a spiral of compulsive reenactments and to discuss his inability to stop these reliving experiences in spite of his desire to be monogamous with Thomas. It was also an opportunity for me to be fully present for him, to help him with his emotion dysregulation and dissociation so he could make these disclosures in as safe and contained a manner as possible. Given the likelihood that male survivors will have a secret sexual life, it is important to create an environment for disclosures that protects the partner and allows for a thoughtful and conscious process of disclosure within the couple to allow for processing at each step of exploration. In Abigail's session, she was able to disclose the extent of her rage at Alejandro's abusers and at Alejandro, in a way that Alejandro would not yet have been able to tolerate. She was able to describe her ambivalence, hurt, pain, and despair and her frequent desire to leave him. She talked openly about her conflict, feeling that because he was so wounded she should not leave him, but at the same time believing she could not possibly continue living in the marriage as it was. Abigail and Thomas were able to express their feelings of anger, hurt, and betrayal openly, without concern about hurting their already-pained partner, and to return to the couple sessions ready to continue the work.

When the couple is ready to begin working in the minefield of sexuality, it is necessary to go slowly and to calibrate the explorations to the couples' ability to tolerate them. Psychoeducation forms an important basis from which to begin work with the couple. Exploring the impact of CSA on the development of healthy sexuality and the ensuing challenges for couple relationships is an important starting point. Much of the work is about balancing discussions of the couples' current sexual life and shifting avoidance, reducing dissociation, and reengaging healthy sexual contact as the couple communicates openly about triggers and their origins, develops the skills to communicate directly about sexual needs and preferences, incorporates sensate focus exercises during periods of conscious sexual abstinence, and learns how to reconnect through gradual shifts from non-sexual to sexual touch (Maltz, 2002).

Given the devastating impact of too-sudden disclosures of secret sexually compulsive behaviors, it is important to work with any partner engaged in sexually compulsive reenactments both in individual and in couple sessions to limit the exposure of the partner to potentially destructive disclosures. Attempting to help CSA survivors stop being aroused by stimuli connected to early abuse may be unsuccessful but helping survivors learn to turn toward their partners for sexual satisfaction is an important therapeutic goal. For many partners who have been kept in the dark about the extent of the secret reenacting sexual life, these extra-dyadic activities constitute too great a betrayal and they do not feel that they can remain in the relationship. Other partners can tolerate what has happened and continue to heal their relationship with their male survivor on the condition that future communication be open and honest. A number of resources are available to couples as they attempt to rebuild their sexual relationship (Maltz, 2002; Maltz & Arian, 2001; Maltz & Maltz, 2009). The role of a couple therapist may shift between facilitating exploration, moderating conversations, and even providing support around separation and seeking of individual therapy in the wake of a breakup.

Shame and its many faces

Shame, pervasive and painful in its impact on male survivors, leads to distance, detachment, and dissatisfaction in couple relationships (DiLillo et al., 2009). Gender norms reinforce the tendency of male survivors to blame themselves and to feel ashamed about the abuse, which contributes to the ongoing invisibility of male survivors (Alaggia, 2004; Dorahy, 2010; Easton et al., 2015; Hunter, 2011). Living in constant fear of being found out, many male survivors isolate themselves, leading to further drifting apart in their couple relationships. Sexual secrets reinforce the survivor's desperate need to keep vital parts of himself separate from his partner. Add to this the confusion that comes when a male survivor experiences conditioned sexual responses to men, while living in a heterosexual relationship, and then more avoidance, secrecy, and distance within the couple ensues.

While women are conditioned to internalize their shame, and many female CSA survivors engage in self-abusive behaviors, men are more conditioned to externalize. Men who have been sexually abused are more likely to engage in interpersonal violence in their relationships (DiLillo et al., 2009; Finkelhor, Hotaling, Lewis, & Smith, 1989; Mejia, 2005) with higher intensity of abuse being related to higher levels of interpersonal violence (Anda et al., 2006). Strategies to cope with shame can involve anger, reactivity, and controlling and suspicious behavior (Wells, 2015). Considering the impact of CSA on couple relationships in a large sample of both male and female survivors, Walker, Holman, and Busby (2009) highlighted some aspects unique to male survivor couples. These couples reported higher levels of negativity than couples in which the CSA survivor was female. Additionally, male survivors expressed higher levels of defensiveness and contempt toward their partners than female CSA survivors. These responses to shame and secrecy can further accentuate the distance between partners and reduce the potential for intimacy (Cole & Putnam, 1992; Millwood, 2011).

Shame drove Alejandro inward, holding back his disclosure for almost 30 years and isolating him from Abigail and his daughter. Like many survivors (Gagnier & Collin-Vézina, 2016; Tener & Murphy, 2015), he feared he would become a perpetrator and abuse his daughter, in spite of having never had any fantasies or urges to abuse her.

Alejandro: After we had our daughter, as she is growing, I never felt comfortable giving her a bath. I've told her, I don't feel that I can feel like I can touch her.

Therapist: You didn't trust yourself.

Alejandro: I can't say didn't trust myself, it was more of fear of, it's not the right thing, maybe it's wrong, I am her father, but you know like, if it was a son, maybe it would be easier, but I couldn't feel like, I was young at that time. I didn't want to have that. I guess you can say, I think [of] it more as a fear. It's just never felt right. I don't want something wrong to happen.

Alejandro feared his sexuality, and feared losing his wife and daughter, at the same time as feeling paralyzed and unable to do the things he needed to do to be close and intimate with them. He simply kept trying to be the best husband and father he could, from a distance, and hoped that this would be enough. Alejandro was never aggressive or reactive with Abigail; he simply withdrew.

Terrence, however, could be vicious and punitive in his reactions to his shame. His most frequent response was to completely shut down, reject any engagement, and treat Thomas like an intruder who was not welcome in his space. This left Thomas desperately exposed, needing to connect with Terrence but terrified of his anger and disdain. Meanwhile, it was difficult for Terrence to tolerate how much he could impact Thomas, and his sense of feeling responsible for Thomas's pain.

Therapist: What is it like for you, Terrence, at those times when things are difficult and you're . . .
Terrence: Well, I'm used to it.
Therapist: What does it feel like?
Terrence: Boring, stupid.
Therapist: What is that like?
Terrence: I just feel stupid, like I don't care.
Therapist: So, when you're feeling that way and you are with Thomas and there isn't a lot of interaction between you and you aren't talking and in those times you start to feel stupid and disconnected.
Terrence: OK.
Therapist: Hmmm, is that how it feels?
Terrence: Not really.
Therapist: Can you tell me how it does feel?
Terrence: What?
Therapist: What it's like when you are together and having trouble engaging?
Terrence: No, I can't tell you. I'm just not doing well and it's not really about you.
Thomas: I didn't say it was about me, I just want to know how you felt at the time.
Terrence: I suppose I felt lost.
Therapist: In those times it's hard for you to even hold Thomas in mind.
Terrence: Yeah.

With careful attention to his dissociated states of shame and anger, along with gentle acknowledgment of his pain and vulnerability, Terrence was gradually able to shift into a position of greater openness. He was willing to develop strategies to deal with times when his dark emotions made it hard to be civil and in contact with Thomas. Efforts to help these partners take each other's perspectives, and understand the pull of the past on the present, helped the couple to interrupt the destructive dance of reenactments and to move in new directions.

In my clinical experience, shame has a major deleterious impact on the therapeutic process, shutting down capacities for emotion regulation and potentially leading to a total shutdown of the therapeutic process. In some cases, shame eradicates the capacity for empathy and perspective taking; when overcome by shame, survivors are unable to tolerate the needs, feelings, and hurts of their partner. In these cases, it is necessary to slow the process down and help survivors regulate their distress so the therapeutic process can continue. My original findings concerned female CSA survivors, who tended to internalize their distress and became flooded and shut down in sessions. In the recent study looking at DCTCT, male survivors tended to externalize their shame, becoming agitated, angry, and at times, aggressive in sessions. The effect is the same; the therapeutic process shuts down.

To work effectively with male survivors steeped in shame, and their partners, it is necessary to contextualize their responses, to help partners understand that agitation and aggression reflect an underlying shame and vulnerability—an affect with which partners are more able to empathize (Wells, 2015). Psychoeducation about sexual abuse, its impact on male survivors, and the role of shame in perpetuating avoidance and secrecy in relationships, is a necessary starting point. Beyond this initial externalization and contextualization of shame as an aftereffect of CSA, therapists can then help male survivors tolerate and express their vulnerability, fear, and, eventually, their shameful secrets.

Conclusions

In working with male survivor couples the therapist is faced with a number of unique challenges. The therapist must integrate an understanding of gender and the specific impact of CSA on male survivors who are surrounded by the messages that to be vulnerable and violated is to be a failure as a man—failing to protect himself, failing to be strong, failing to be powerful, failing to be untouchable. The therapist must understand the overwhelming obstacles to disclosure and how these compound the impact of sexual secrets on the relationship with the partner. The therapist must also be able to support the distressed partner as the partner tries to traverse a very rocky path through secrets, possible infidelities, and heart-breaking sexual betrayals, back into relationship with the survivor, or into the decision to end the relationship.

Within the clinical setting, the therapist must understand the particular cycle of distress into which many male survivor couples fall as the male survivor struggles with the contradiction between a desire for closeness and challenges in tolerating and engaging with intimacy. Avoidance and secrecy mark the relationship as unstable and unsafe for both partners, while sexual compulsivity and acting out also take their toll on both members of the couple. Therapists should respond by contextualizing behaviors, impulses, and patterns while wading into the deep morass of shame and pain held by the couple, trying to break down the secrets and the barriers of avoidance separating them. Throughout all of these gentle yet firm interventions aimed at helping the couple come into conscious connection with one another and dispelling the power of the secrets, therapists work with the trauma survivors to help them develop the capacity to regulate their emotions so that they can tolerate their partner's distress, take responsibility for their impact on the relationship and their partner, and manage the shame they feel in relation to their partner and themselves. Additionally, therapists help trauma survivors develop the capacity to mentalize so they gradually become able to put themselves in their partner's shoes, reduce dissociative defenses, and pull themselves out of the stranglehold of avoidance in which they have been stuck.

This work is not for the faint of heart: training in couple therapy, expertise working with trauma survivors, and an understanding of the unique impacts of CSA on male survivors and their partners, are all required to engage successfully with these couples. However, the process can be extremely rewarding, as couples formerly entrenched in a painful and intractable cycle of avoidance, secrecy, and betrayal are able to shift out of dissociation, dysregulation, and disconnection, to share through disclosure and breaking secrets and to build a new and vibrant relationship empowering the male CSA survivor to go out into the world and continue in his healing work.

References

Aakvaag, H. F., Thoresen, S., Wentzel-Larsen, T., Dyb, G., Røysamb, E., & Olff, M. (2016). Broken and guilty since it happened: A population study of trauma-related shame and guilt after violence and sexual abuse. *Journal of Affective Disorders, 204*, 16–23. doi: http://dx.doi.org/10.1016/j.jad.2016.06.004

Alaggia, R. (2004). Many ways of telling: Expanding conceptualizations of child sexual abuse disclosure. *Child Abuse & Neglect, 28*(11), 1213–1227. doi: http://dx.doi.org/10.1016/j.chiabu.2004.03.016

Anda, R. F., Felitti, V. J., Bremner, J. D., Walker, J. D., Whitfield, C., Perry, B. D., . . . Giles, W. H. (2006). The enduring effects of abuse and related adverse experiences in childhood. *European Archives of Psychiatry and Clinical Neuroscience, 256*(3), 174–186.

Anderson, S. R., & Miller, R. B. (2006). The effectiveness of therapy with couples reporting a history of childhood sexual abuse: An exploratory study. *Contemporary Family Therapy: An International Journal, 28*(3), 353–366. doi: http://dx.doi.org/10.1007/s10591-006-9015-x

Bacon, B., & Lein, L. (1996). Living with a female sexual abuse survivor: Male partners' perspectives. *Journal of Child Sexual Abuse: Research, Treatment, & Program Innovations for Victims, Survivors, & Offenders, 5*(2), 1–16. doi: http://dx.doi.org/10.1300/J070v05n02_01

Banyard, V. L., Williams, L. M., & Siegel, J. A. (2004). Childhood sexual abuse: A gender perspective on context and consequences. *Child Maltreatment, 9*(3), 223–238. doi: http://dx.doi.org/10.1177/1077559504266914

Chauncey, S. (1994). Emotional concerns and treatment of male partners of female sexual abuse survivors. *Social Work, 39*(6), 669–676.

Cole, P. M., & Putnam, F. W. (1992). Effect of incest on self and social functioning: A developmental psychopathology perspective. *Journal of Consulting and Clinical Psychology, 60*(2), 174. doi: http://dx.doi.org/10.1037/0022-006X.60.2.174

Crawford, E., & O'Dougherty Wright, M. (2007). The impact of childhood psychological maltreatment on interpersonal schemas and subsequent experiences of relationship aggression. *Journal of Emotional Abuse, 7*(2), 93–116. doi: http://dx.doi.org/10.1080/10926770903539433

Denov, M. S. (2003). The myth of innocence: Sexual scripts and the recognition of child sexual abuse by female perpetrators. *Journal of Sex Research, 40*(3), 303–314. doi: http://dx.doi.org/10.1080/00224490309552195

DiLillo, D. (2001). Interpersonal functioning among women reporting a history of childhood sexual abuse: Empirical findings and methodological issues. *Clinical Psychology Review, 21*(4), 553–576. doi: http://dx.doi.org/10.1016/S0272-7358%2899%2900072-0

DiLillo, D., Peugh, J., Walsh, K., Panuzio, J., Trask, E., & Evans, S. (2009). Child maltreatment history among newlywed couples: A longitudinal study of marital outcomes and mediating pathways. *Journal of Consulting and Clinical Psychology, 77*(4), 680. doi: http://dx.doi.org/10.1037/a0015708

Dorahy, M. J. (2010). The impact of dissociation, shame, and guilt on interpersonal relationships in chronically traumatized individuals: A pilot study. *Journal of Traumatic Stress, 23*(5), 653–656. doi: http://dx.doi.org/10.1002/jts.20564

Easton, S. D. (2012). Understanding Adverse Childhood Experiences (ACE) and their relationship to adult stress among male survivors of childhood sexual abuse. *Journal of Prevention & Intervention in the Community, 40*(4), 291–303. doi: http://dx.doi.org/10.1080/10852352.2012.707446

Easton, S. D., Leone-Sheehan, D. M., Sophis, E. J., & Willis, D. G. (2015). "From that moment on my life changed": Turning points in the healing process for men recovering from child sexual abuse. *Journal of Child Sexual Abuse, 24*(2), 152–173. doi: http://dx.doi.org/10.1080/10538712.2015.997413

Feinauer, L. L., Callahan, E. H., & Hilton, H. (1996). Positive intimate relationships decrease depression in sexually abused women. *American Journal of Family Therapy, 24*(2), 99–106. doi: http://dx.doi.org/10.1080/01926189608251023

Finkelhor, D., Hotaling, G. T., Lewis, I., & Smith, C. (1989). Sexual abuse and its relationship to later sexual satisfaction, marital status, religion, and attitudes. *Journal of Interpersonal Violence, 4*(4), 379–399. doi: http://dx.doi.org/10.1177/088626089004004001

Firth, M. T. (1997). Male partners of female victims of child sexual abuse: Treatment issues and approaches. *Sexual & Marital Therapy, 12*(2), 159–171.

Gagnier, C., & Collin-Vézina, D. (2016). The disclosure experiences of male child sexual abuse survivors. *Journal of Child Sexual Abuse, 25*(2), 221–241. doi: http://dx.doi.org/10.1080/10538712.2016.1124308

Gartner, R. B. (1999). *Betrayed as boys: Psychodynamic treatment of sexually abused men*. New York, NY: Guilford.

Godbout, N., Briere, J., Sabourin, S., & Lussier, Y. (2014). Child sexual abuse and subsequent relational and personal functioning: The role of parental support. *Child Abuse & Neglect, 38*(2), 317–325. doi: http://dx.doi.org/10.1016/j.chiabu.2013.10.001

Godbout, N., Lussier, Y., & Sabourin, S. (2006). Early abuse experiences and subsequent gender differences in couple adjustment. *Violence and Victims, 21*(6), 744–760. doi: http://dx.doi.org/10.1891/vv-v21i6a005

Godbout, N., Runtz, M. G., MacIntosh, H. B., & Briere, J. (2013). Childhood trauma and couple relationships. *Integrating Science and Practice, 3*(2), 14–17.

Harway, M., & Faulk, E. (2005). Treating couples with sexual abuse issues. In M. Harway (Ed.), *Handbook of couples therapy* (pp. 272–288). Hoboken, NJ: Wiley.

Hlavka, H. R. (2016). Speaking of stigma and the silence of shame: Young men and sexual victimization. *Men and Masculinities*, Online First, 1–24. Retrieved from http://journals.sagepub.com/doi/abs/10.1177/1097184X16652656.

Hunter, S. V. (2011). Disclosure of child sexual abuse as a life-long process: Implications for health professionals. *Australian and New Zealand Journal of Family Therapy, 32*(2), 159–172. doi: http://dx.doi.org/10.1375/anft.32.2.159

Johnson, S. M. (2002). *Emotionally focused couple therapy with trauma survivors: Strengthening attachment bonds*. New York, NY: Guilford.

Jonzon, E., & Lindblad, F. (2004). Disclosure, reactions, and social support: Findings from a sample of adult victims of child sexual abuse. *Child Maltreatment, 9*(2), 190–200. doi: http://dx.doi.org/10.1177/1077559504264263

Kia-Keating, M., Sorsoli, L., & Grossman, F. K. (2010). Relational challenges and recovery processes in male survivors of childhood sexual abuse. *Journal of Interpersonal Violence, 25*(4), 666–683. doi: http://dx.doi.org/10.1177/0886260509334411

Leone, C. (2013). The unseen spouse: Pitfalls and possibilities for the individual therapist. *Psychoanalytic Dialogues, 23*(3), 324–339. doi: http://dx.doi.org/10.1080/10481885.2013.792187

Lisak, D. (1993). Men as victims: Challenging cultural myths. *Journal of Traumatic Stress, 6*(4), 577–580. doi: http://dx.doi.org/10.1007/BF00974326

MacIntosh, H. (2016). *Developmental couple therapy for complex trauma*. Unpublished Treatment Manual. McGill University. Montreal, Quebec.

MacIntosh, H., Fletcher, K., & Collin-Vézina, D. (2016). "I was like damaged, used goods": Thematic analysis of disclosures of childhood sexual abuse to romantic partners. *Marriage & Family Review, 52*(6), 598–611. doi: http://dx.doi.org/10.1080/01494929.2016.1157117

MacIntosh, H. B. (2013). Mentalising: An exploration of its potential contribution to understanding the challenges faced by childhood sexual abuse survivors in couple therapy. *Journal of Couple and Family Psychoanalysis, 3*(2), 188–207.

MacIntosh, H. B., & Johnson, S. M. (2008). Emotionally focused therapy for couples and childhood sexual abuse survivors. *Journal of Marital and Family Therapy, 34*(3), 298–315. doi: http://dx.doi.org/10.1111/j.1752-0606.2008.00074.x

Maltz, W. (2002). Treating the sexual intimacy concerns of sexual abuse survivors. *Sexual and Relationship Therapy, 17*(4), 321–327. doi: http://dx.doi.org/10.1080/14681990210000017173

Maltz, W., & Arian, C. (2001). *The sexual healing journey: A guide for survivors of sexual abuse*. New York, NY: Quill.

Maltz, W., & Maltz, L. (2009). *The porn trap: The essential guide to overcoming problems caused by pornography*. Toronto: HarperCollins Canada.

Mejia, X. E. (2005). Gender matters: Working with adult male survivors of trauma. *Journal of Consulting and Development, 83*, 29–40. doi: http://dx.doi.org/10.1002/j.1556-6678.2005.tb00577.x

Millwood, M. (2011). Empathic understanding in couples with a female survivor of childhood sexual abuse. *Journal of Couple & Relationship Therapy, 10*(4), 327–344. doi: http://dx.doi.org/10.1080/15332691.2011.613310

Price-Robertson, R., Higgins, D., & Vassallo, S. (2013). Multi-type maltreatment and polyvictimisation: A comparison of two research frameworks. *Family Matters, 93*, 84.

Reid, K. S., Taylor, D. K., & Wampler, R. S. (1995). Perceptions of partner involvement in the therapeutic process by patients who experienced sexual abuse as children. *Journal of Sex Education & Therapy, 21*(1), 36–45. doi: http://dx.doi.org/10.1007/s10591-006-9015-x

Reid, K. S., Wampler, R. S., & Taylor, D. K. (1996). The "alienated" partner: Responses to traditional therapies for adult sex abuse survivors. *Journal of Marital and Family Therapy, 22*(4), 443–453. doi: http://dx.doi.org/10.1111/j.1752-0606.1996.tb00219.x

Rumstein-McKean, O., & Hunsley, J. (2001). Interpersonal and family functioning of female survivors of childhood sexual abuse. *Clinical Psychology Review, 21*(3), 471–490. doi: http://dx.doi.org/10.1016/S0272-7358%2899%2900069-0

Sorsoli, L., Kia-Keating, M., & Grossman, F. K. (2008). "I keep that hush-hush": Male survivors of sexual abuse and the challenges of disclosure. *Journal of Counseling Psychology, 55*(3), 333. doi: http: /dx.doi.org//10.1037/0022-0167.55.3.333

Staller, K. M., & Nelson-Gardell, D. (2005). "A burden in your heart": Lessons of disclosure from female preadolescent and adolescent survivors of sexual abuse. *Child Abuse & Neglect, 29*(12), 1415–1432. doi: http://dx.doi.org/10.1016/j.chiabu.2005.06.007

Styron, T., & Janoff-Bulman, R. (1997). Childhood attachment and abuse: Long-term effects on adult attachment, depression, and conflict resolution. *Child Abuse & Neglect, 21*(10), 1015–1023. doi: http://dx.doi.org/10.1016/S0145-2134(97)00062-8

Tener, D., & Murphy, S. B. (2015). Adult disclosure of child sexual abuse: A literature review. *Trauma, Violence, & Abuse, 16*(4), 391–400. doi: http://dx.doi.org/10.1177/1524838014537906

Traeen, B., & Sorensen, D. (2008). A qualitative study of how survivors of sexual, psychological and physical abuse manage sexuality and desire. *Sexual and Relationship Therapy, 23*(4), 377–391.

Walker, E. C., Holman, T. B., & Busby, D. M. (2009). Childhood sexual abuse, other childhood factors, and pathways to survivors' adult relationship quality. *Journal of Family Violence, 24*(6), 397–406. doi: http://dx.doi.org/10.1007/s10896-009-9242-7

Wells, M. A. (2015). Gender, power, and trust in couple therapy with survivors of childhood abuse. *Journal of Couple & Relationship Therapy, 15*(3), 1–18. doi: http://dx.doi.org/10.1080/15332691.2014.962210

Zala, S. (2012). Complex couples: Multi-theoretical couples counselling with traumatised adults who have a history of child sexual abuse. *Australian and New Zealand Journal of Family Therapy, 33*(3), 219–231. doi: http://dx.doi.org/10.1017/aft.2012.27

Part IV

Perpetrators and perpetrator/survivors

Chapter 13

Profiling real-life child sex offenders

Jim Clemente and Francey Hakes

Most real-life child sex offenders do not look, sound, or behave the way the general public expects them to. Popular culture often portrays child sex offenders as dark-clad evil figures lurking in the shadows awaiting an opportunity to seize a child and perpetrate a violent assault. In fact, educational programs like "Stranger Danger" (Kulkofsky, n.d.) distract the community from reality. Strangers actually pose a rare risk to children, although when strangers do offend, the consequences can be very serious. But such offenders are by far in the minority. The vast majority of sexually victimized children are offended against by men and/or women they know. The most insidious offenders are those we willingly hand our children over to because we know, trust, and even love them. Using real-life examples, this chapter will describe who child sex offenders really are, how they actually operate, how child victims are targeted, and how to protect children from sexual victimization.

Offender typologies

Child Sexual Victimization[1] is a common phenomenon. Studies indicate that one in four girls and one in six boys are sexually victimized before the age of 18 (Centers for Disease Control and Prevention, 2005). Retired FBI Supervisory Special Agent Ken Lanning, an expert in this area, has developed a sex offender continuum to help in the study and understanding of what motivates child sex offenders (Lanning, 2001). His continuum aids in recognition of offender behavioral patterns and motivations. It

1 In this chapter Child Sexual Victimization will be used as the umbrella term that encompasses all forms of sex crimes committed against children.

therefore helps protect children through a more complete understanding of child sex offender behaviors. These behaviors are broken down into typologies. At one end of the spectrum we find situational child sex offenders. At the other end we have preferential child sex offenders. In between the two extremes exists a gray area encompassing varying degrees of overlap.

Situational child sex offenders are those who commit sex crimes against children even though they do not have a definitive sexual attraction to children. This category includes, among others, impulsive individuals who may have lowered inhibitions due to substance abuse; stressed individuals who may have lost a job or relationship or are undergoing some other traumatic event(s); and opportunistic individuals who seem to always take advantage of any situation or person they encounter, including taking advantage of children for sex. Offenders in this last group may be adept at assessing situational risk and will take advantage of any opportunity to sexually victimize a child where they feel the risk is low and the reward high. They may be aroused by adult pornography yet choose to offend against a child to whom they have easy access and control, or over whom they have authority. They tend to be less successful than the general population in relationships and work, as well as less intelligent, so, while they may accurately assess the risk of offending, they may also make mistakes. Stressed or intoxicated offenders may fall into this situational category because their inhibitions are lowered, which means they may act more impulsively and offend against a child while they wouldn't when sober.

Preferential child sex offenders have a definitive sexual attraction to children. Many people in law enforcement and the public think all child sex offenders are pedophiles, but pedophiles only represent the subset of preferential offenders who are exclusively sexually attracted to pre-pubescent children. In contrast, the term preferential offender includes those who are sexually attracted to both pre-pubescent and post-pubescent children. Preferential offenders can be obsessive and compulsive when it comes to children, meaning they constantly spend time, effort, and energy thinking and sexually fantasizing about children, as well as developing ways to gain access to children for sex. They can also be fixated on the pursuit of, being around, and relating to children, meaning children can become their life's focus.

The four hallmarks of preferential offenders are:

1 *A long-term and persistent pattern of offending behavior*. That is, they typically discover their attraction to children in adolescence and begin some form of offending shortly thereafter, generally continuing it throughout their lives.
2 *Specific sexual criteria for their targets*. These may include age, gender, physical characteristics or body-type, personality type, specific vulnerabilities, or some combination of the above. However, although these specific sexual interests may be the offender's ideal, there can be a high degree of crossover into other categories based on availability, vulnerability, and desirability.
3 *Well-developed techniques for finding victims and grooming*[2] *them*. This often includes targeting parents, guardians, and/or the community in order to ensure avoidance of detection by law enforcement.
4 *Fantasy and desire-driven behavior*. Producing, collecting and/or viewing child pornography is a major factor in establishing an offender's sexual fantasies and preference for children. They use these images of child sexual victimization to fuel their fantasies, usually reinforced by masturbation. They also rationalize and minimize their deviant sexual interests, which helps drive their desire and loosens any inhibitions about offending against children.

Although Preferential Child Sex Offenders (PCSOs) all share a definitive sexual attraction to children, for some that attraction is exclusive, while for others it is not. That is, some PCSOs are in a sub-category called *sexually diverse*, meaning they can be sexually attracted to children and simultaneously sexually attracted to adults and/or other entities. This can make sexually diverse offenders more difficult to identify and thus protect against. When an offender is identified as having one form of sexually deviant interest (paraphilia[3]), which might include offending against animals, incapacitated adult victims, children, etc., they typically are found to have a cluster of other paraphilic interests as well.

2 Grooming will be discussed in detail later in this chapter.
3 Paraphilia is defined here as a sexual interest in non-consenting parties or inanimate objects.

David Westerfield was a perfect example of a sexually diverse preferential offender. He was arrested after Danielle Van Dam was abducted from her San Diego, CA home in the middle of the night in 2002. Although he was sexually attracted to, sexually active with, and even engaged in stalking behavior with several adult women, he nevertheless abducted, sexually assaulted, and killed 9-year-old Danielle. When his computer was searched post-arrest, his collection of pornographic images was discovered. He had divided his collection into multiple categories of sexual material indicating his interest in various paraphilias that included voyeurism, bestiality, and rape fantasies of pre-pubescent girls.

Female offenders

In popular culture, we most commonly see child sex offenders depicted as men and victims as girls. While this archetype is based in reality, it does not represent the entire class of offenders or victims. There are offenders and victims of both genders. In fact, female child sex offenders and male child sex victims are much more common than our culture represents.[4] Often female offenders are teachers engaged in serial sexual victimization of male students, although they may also offend against female children. Mary Kay LeTourneau is a well-known example. In 1996 LeTourneau serially sexually victimized a male sixth grade student of hers who she had also taught in second grade. He was just 12 years old when she began taking advantage of him sexually. She was 34, married, and the mother of four children at that time.

Clearly there was a serious power and maturity differential between LeTourneau and the child she victimized. This case is a prime example of what the media often terms a teacher/student "love affair." Convicted of second degree rape of a child after getting herself impregnated by the child victim and later giving birth to their daughter, LeTourneau served a short term in prison as a result of a plea agreement. Upon her release she was instructed by the court to cease any contact with the victim, who was still a child. But she almost immediately violated her probation by continuing the sexual "relationship" with the same victim and becoming pregnant again. She was then re-sentenced and imprisoned

4 One study (Lisak, Hopper, & Song, 1996) found that of the men in their sample who acknowledged having been sexually abused, 61% said they were abused by a man, 28% by a woman, and 11% by both.

for seven years. Her victim was so convinced of their love that when she was released from prison he married her.

Studies show that women are responsible for 4–5% of child sexual victimization (Cortoni & Hanson, 2005; Cortoni, Hanson, & Coache, 2010). A female offender often targets children as sexual objects due to her own prior victimization, low self-esteem, poor self-confidence, or inadequate peer social skills (Janus & Prentky, 2003). These offenders are often referred to as "seducers" or "lovers" and rarely as rapists. However, the resultant effects on their victims can be just as detrimental, far-reaching, and long-term as effects on victims of male offenders. In a 2015 interview with Barbara Walters (Walters, 2015), LeTourneau's victim complained that he did not realize how unprepared he'd been for early sexualization until his children reached the age he was when first victimized by LeTourneau. He also indicated that he has struggled with long-term depression and substance abuse issues, both hallmarks of the effects of child sexual victimization.

In another case, Rachel Holt, also a 6th grade teacher, was prosecuted in 2006 for raping a 13-year-old male student. Like LeTourneau, Holt's victimization of the child occurred over a period of time. Holt took things a step further, however, and allowed a friend of the child to watch at least one instance of sexual assault. The record from the investigation of this case showed that Holt had engaged in a pattern of favoritism with the boys she victimized. This behavior occurred inside and outside her class, including her sitting on their laps, kissing them, driving them alone in her car, and acting like their girlfriend (*Thomas and Pitts* v. *Board of Education Brandywine School District*, 2008).

Holt was repeatedly admonished and disciplined by the school district for her behavior toward students. However, a federal court dismissed the victimized boy's civil claims against the school, finding it had no knowledge that her behavior "would" lead to sexual assault, but only that it "could" have. This ruling supports the strong need for training educators and others about grooming and other warning signs and behaviors indicative of current or future victimization (see below). Holt's behavior toward her male students was a glaring caution sign that those in charge of protecting students ignored. This seems to reveal a hidden bias in the legal and educational systems against recognizing female teacher on male student victimization. After all, would a male teacher caught sitting on the laps of and kissing young female students lead authorities – and courts – to the same benign conclusions?

Contact offenders versus online offenders

Law enforcement and treatment professionals alike have had a difficult time studying the differences and similarities between contact offenders (those who commit hands-on sexual offenses against children) and so-called "Internet only" offenders (those who commit online related sexual offenses against children). Research on whether those who traffic in the images of child sexual victimization are likely to engage in hands-on offenses against children has increased in the last decade as courts and treatment professionals struggle with the question of appropriate punishment for online offenders as it relates to future risk. A recent study conducted by the Department of Justice in cooperation with others found that 57% of those in contact with law enforcement solely for online child exploitation offenses (largely trafficking in the images of child sexual victimization to include trading, manufacturing, distributing, possessing, and viewing these images) admitted they had committed contact offense(s) against at least one child and that those offense(s) had gone undiscovered (Bourke et al., 2015). This suggests that the majority of online offenders have a similar "motivational pathway" to that of offline offenders. Both, then, are motivated by a sexual interest in children and given the opportunity there is a high probability the majority will commit hands-on sexual offences against children. It is logical, therefore, to conclude that those who traffic in these images – and use them for sexual gratification – are a clear and present danger to offend against children in the real world.

Our combined law enforcement experience tells us that online offenders not only create a market for the material that depicts child sexual victimization, but they also drive the actual sexual victimization of children. Child sexual victimization images cannot be created without the sexual victimization of a child. Practical case experience demonstrates that those who traffic in these images and who gain sexual gratification from them thirst for new or "fresh" and ever-more-explicit images. Given the ease of transferring large data files in today's technologically advanced society, these images can often include high-definition videos with sound in addition to still images. This thirst for new material drives those with a sexual interest in children to amass large collections of these images for their own gratification as well as to share with others. The sharing aspect of these crimes can be a method of bartering for new images as well as forming a sense of community with like-minded offenders.

A federal investigation based in Atlanta proves this to be more than a theory. James Bartholomew Huskey was an undetected online trafficker in images of child sexual victimization. He ran out of images to trade and so turned to a 5-year-old child to whom he had unfettered access. He violently sexually assaulted her for years before he was caught. He admitted that he assaulted her, in part, in order to create child sexual victimization images he could use to trade for more such images. Cases like Huskey's show that there are more commonalities than contrasts between those labeled "online" and "offline" offenders.

Grooming

Grooming is the constellation of behaviors designed to secure compliance and silence from victims as well as access from their families and communities. Grooming – a major factor in why children fail to disclose victimization – is an Acquaintance Offender's (see below) unique skill and weapon. Victimizers' demeanor, generosity in the community, and rapport with children all add to their ability to convince others they are "normal" and have no deviant sexual interests in children. Grooming ensures that it is unthinkable to consider such individuals potential child molesters.

As s/he grooms a child, an offender undertakes a campaign of charm, offering the child special treatment, gifts, affection, and/or extra attention. Sometimes these offenders allow the child to engage in conduct a parent wouldn't allow, like using sexually explicit terminology or profanities, using drugs or alcohol, driving without a license, and/or viewing pornography. In this way, the child becomes drawn into behavior the child knows would result in punishment if disclosed to a parent. The offender deftly uses the child's encouraged misbehavior as a tool for manipulating the child into further illicit conduct lest the previous "bad" behavior be revealed to parents or other authorities.

Grooming is a dynamic process, and successful acquaintance offenders exhibit a high level of ability to manipulate children. The gifts, intoxicants, sexual materials, and extra attention provided by a grooming offender are designed to lower the child's inhibitions and establish what appears to the child to be a special relationship between them. A key component of grooming is breaking down the barriers that usually exist between adults and children. This is a process that can take time – to the offender, time well spent. Indeed, the offender often gains sexual gratification from the grooming process itself.

As a result of grooming, the offender can ensure not only the child's compliance with his/her own sexual victimization, but often also the child's silence due to feelings of guilt, shame, and embarrassment, or ambivalence, gratitude, and love. The silence itself may become a conspiracy between the offender and the child that can last for decades. It may also lead to denial of the sexual victimization even if the child is confronted with evidence thereof. If a child in this situation does disclose, it is often incomplete or incremental. That is, the child may "test the waters" by disclosing some of the victimization, then gauge the reaction of friends, parents, guardians, or officials. The wrong reaction could cause the child to recant and retreat back into the conspiracy of silence.

Offenders with skill in grooming compliant victims often have multiple victims over a long period of time. The grooming process could take place over a matter of minutes, hours, weeks, months, or even years before the sexual victimization begins, as well as while the victimization continues. "This process not only gains the victim's initial cooperation, but also decreases the likelihood of disclosure and increases the likelihood of ongoing, repeated access" (Lanning, 2005, p. 2). Offenders who groom are often those in positions of power and trust, like coaches or youth leaders. They work or volunteer around children so they have access to a target pool of potential victims. Colleagues usually describe these offenders as having some kind of remarkable connection to the children they interact with and are noted to go "above and beyond" in their duties with children. These behaviors should actually be seen as red flags, but are rarely noted until after the victimization is uncovered when, too late, they are glaring examples of warnings unheeded. Much of this may be due to a serious misperception on the part of most members of the public that child sex offenders are "monster predators" who don't look, act, or sound like "normal" people. This could not be further from the truth. Most effective grooming offenders blend into the community to such a degree that parents trust them implicitly and willingly hand their children over to them.

Nice Guy/Gal Acquaintance Offenders

As noted at the beginning of this chapter, popular culture often suggests that those likely to sexually victimize children present as strangers lurking in the shadows. But in truth most child sex offenders are known to their victims. Such offenders are called Nice Guy/Gal Acquaintance offenders. Male and female schoolteacher sex offenders may fall into this category, along with coaches, clergy, youth leaders, and others in positions of trust. Many are "pillars of the community" and excel at their professions, whether they work with children or not. These offenders are particularly adept at putting forth a public face completely at odds with their sexually deviant behavior. They spend years building community credibility that makes it seem impossible they could be sexual predators. Indeed, people closest to Nice Guy/Gal Acquaintance offenders are often most taken in by their grooming tactics because they are believed to be good people who love children and would never take advantage of them.

A well-known example of a Nice Guy Acquaintance offender is Jerry Sandusky, the now-notorious former assistant coach at Penn State University who was arrested in November, 2011, and convicted of multiple counts of sexual assault of boys from 1994 to 2009. His victimization of vulnerable boys from the Second Mile, a non-profit charity he founded for at-risk youth, went unrecognized for decades. His charity work provided him with access, authority, and control over his targets, and his impeccable reputation for helping children provided cover for his serial sexual assault of numerous boys. Sandusky's criminal sexual victimization of boys took place over many years. He was so successful in building a reputation as a "nice guy" that when allegations surfaced against him, they were largely dismissed as absurd and unfounded, certainly by his circle of friends and family, but also by law enforcement, child welfare professionals, and a counselor. Of course the allegations must not be true, they thought. Some considered Jerry Sandusky a saint.[5]

Offender priests

Another high visibility example of this type of offender is the Catholic priest offender,[6] some of whom have been revealed over the last five

5 Editor's note: See Chapter 8 by Burmester in the companion volume to this one, *Understanding the Sexual Betrayal of Boys and Men: The Trauma of Sexual Abuse*, for further discussion of the Sandusky case.

6 Editor's note: See Chapter 9 by Gartner in the companion volume to this one, *Understanding the Sexual Betrayal of Boys and Men: The Trauma of Sexual Abuse*, for further discussion of the impact of sexual abuse by priests on their victims.

decades to be among the most prolific serial sexual victimizers of young boys in history.[7] John Jay College of Criminal Justice in New York City (2004) has published a study on this topic that spans decades of instances of sexual victimization by priests. It found that the vast majority of their child sex crime victims were post-pubescent boys, and that the offenders spent significant amounts of time socializing with both their victims and their victims' families. This socializing often included singling out the victim for gifts or extra attention.

Catholic priests have a unique authoritative position in their community, which often allows unsupervised contact between priests and children. Well-meaning parents generally encourage this contact, lending the priest further authority and status in the mind of their child victims. The John Jay study concluded that very few cases were reported to police, and only one in three of those that were investigated resulted in charges. In those cases, only 3% of offenders were sentenced to prison. This lack of accountability and punishment surely led to children remaining silent because they understood the futility of disclosure. There are many reasons children fail to disclose their sexual victimization, including fear, shame, guilt, and embarrassment. But in any case where an offender who is a respected authority figure victimizes children and disclosure appears futile, silence may be a child's only known viable choice. Many vulnerable children victimized by offending priests are old enough to understand that the Church and criminal justice system are ignoring their victimization and internalize this as betrayal by the institutions they have trusted.[8]

Compliant Victimization and "sextortion"

Successful prosecution requires investigators and prosecutors who understand the dynamics of child sexual victimization as they relate to offender and victim behavior. Especially problematic can be the fact that, because

7 The *Boston Globe*, through investigative reporting, first revealed the extent of these offenses in their 2002 accounts of abuse by priests and its subsequent cover-up by Church authorities. The process by which the investigative team documented these scandals was later depicted in the film *Spotlight*, which won the Oscar for Best Picture of 2016.

8 Editor's note: See Chapter 8 by Burmester in the companion volume to this one, *Understanding the Sexual Betrayal of Boys and Men: The Trauma of Sexual Abuse*, for discussion of institutional betrayal and its impact.

of effective grooming, children often submit to victimization or even cooperate in it. This is known as "Compliant Victimization."

Sometimes offenders capitalize on a child's misbehavior by blackmailing the child into further forbidden sexual behavior. This is often called "sextortion."[9] Unknown and Acquaintance offenders alike may take advantage of a child's guilt, fear, trust, or shame to induce cooperation in the first acts of sexual victimization. Further compliance may be ensured by blackmail. The offender threatens to reveal the initial sexual acts. The child's shame about these acts is often compounded by feelings during the victimization; those feelings can range from fear, to anxiety, to ambivalence, to sexual pleasure. And so, the child complies again, often with more serious sexual violations.

The largest "sextortion" case in FBI history provides a clear example of this blackmail scenario. It also shows that not all offenders are known to the victim, nor do they necessarily seem like nice guys. Patrick Connelly and Ivory Dickerson collaborated to hack into the computers of nearly 4,000 young girls around the world. They were able to turn on the webcams of these girls and obtain explicit images of them. They used these images to blackmail the girls into complying with their demands, which usually consisted of taking further images of themselves engaging in sexually explicit conduct, with the promise of destroying the original images if the girls would comply with this "final" request. Of course, the blackmail did not cease with these "compliant" acts. The girls were blackmailed into engaging in more and more explicit behavior, until one girl finally disclosed the victimization and authorities subsequently arrested both men. Many of the victims told authorities they were too ashamed to tell their parents and were afraid of the consequences, including the possibility of having their digital devices taken away.

Delayed disclosure and affect or sensory details in victim statements

Criminal investigations into child sexual victimization often turn on the word of the child, and so become a classic "s/he said, s/he said" scenario

9 Sextortion is the use of a threat to expose sexual behavior on the part of the victim in order to force that victim to engage in additional or more extensive sexual behavior.

where physical evidence to corroborate allegations is lacking. Unlike murder scenes, where DNA, fingerprints, or other physical evidence may be discovered, child sexual assault takes place behind closed doors, and often occurs over time. It is rarely disclosed in a contemporaneous way that lends itself to the collection of physical evidence. In fact, the John Jay study found that in the priest offender cases it took an average of 20 years for victims to disclose. Indeed, 20% of the victims delayed disclosure for 30 years or more. Thus, unless the victims are very young and/or the sexual assaults are violent and physically damaging, it is uncommon that physical evidence in child sexual victimization cases can be collected in order to prove the cases. This necessitates corroborating the child's disclosure in other ways such as via multiple consistent complaints from other victims.

Because of these dynamics, it is critical that investigators and mental health professionals recognize and understand the compliant victim. They must also be able to discern indicators of veracity that support the eventual disclosure of victimization. Since disclosures are often delayed, there is little possibility of corroborating allegations with physical evidence.

An allegation, therefore, may be corroborated by measuring the signs that indicate truthfulness. Studies on affect and the importance of sensory details support using these measures to discern the veracity of a child's disclosure. They measure the affect shown and details given in children's disclosure in corroborated versus false accounts of sexual assault.

One study noted that children giving real disclosures of sexual victimization are able to give physical, sensory details they noted at the time of the victimization (Jones & McGraw, 1987). They also provide age-appropriate language and use of pronouns in their disclosure, while those making false allegations do not. The level of detail, appropriate to the child's age, is a leading indicator of veracity (Faller, 1984). In addition to sensory details, victims are able to give details of events surrounding the sexual victimization as a way of giving context and supporting the allegations.

However, victims who have suffered traumatic experiences do not necessarily remember and recount those experiences in a linear or cohesive manner. Therefore, children who are suspected of being sexually victimized should be interviewed by a trained and experienced child interview specialist, preferably at a Child Advocacy Center.

The allegation of sexual victimization against Hollywood director Woody Allen by his daughter, Dylan Farrow, provides a useful example of how to measure veracity by assessing the disclosure of the victim. Farrow accused Allen of abusing her when she was a child. Her statement (in part) follows:

> [W]hen I was 7 years old, Woody Allen took me by the hand and led me into a dim, closet-like attic on the 2nd floor of our house. He told me to lay on my stomach and play with my brother's electric train set. Then he sexually assaulted me. He talked to me while he did it, whispering that I was a good girl, that this was our secret, promising that we'd go to Paris and I'd be a star in his movies. I remember staring at that toy train, focusing on it as it travelled in its circle around the attic. To this day I find it difficult to look at toy trains.
>
> For as long as I could remember, my father had been doing things to me that I didn't like. I did not like how often he would take me away from my mom, siblings and friends to be alone with him. I didn't like it when he would stick his thumb in my mouth. I didn't like it when I had to get in bed with him under the sheets when he was in his underwear. I didn't like it when he would place his head in my naked lap and breathe in and breathe out. I would hide under beds or lock myself in the bathroom to avoid these encounters, but he always found me. These things happened so often, so routinely, so skillfully hidden from a mother that would have protected me had she known, that I thought it was normal. I thought this was how fathers doted on their daughters. But what he did to me in the attic felt different. I couldn't keep the secret anymore . . .
>
> That he got away with what he did to me haunted me as I grew up. I was stricken with guilt that I had allowed him to be around other little girls. I was terrified of being touched by men. I developed an eating disorder. I began cutting myself.
>
> (Farrow, 2014)

Her statement is full of the kind of sensory details we typically find in truthful remembered accounts. She describes how she was led to the location of the victimization, the lighting, how it felt, how she felt, things he said to her, and even the spatial relationship between her, her father, and the toy train in the attic. She also describes grooming behaviors on the part of her father, as well as the feeling of "normalcy" this engendered in her. These details suggest a true memory as opposed to a false allegation.

Similar sensory details can be found in the case of Bishop Eddie Long, the senior pastor of a Baptist mega-church in DeKalb County, Georgia, against whom civil law suits were filed in 2010 by a number of young male parishioners who alleged he'd had sex with them over a number of years. The victim statements contained affective and sensory information indicating veracity. Although the known victims of Bishop Eddie Long were sexually assaulted shortly after they reached the age of 18, victim statements reveal that Long began grooming them years earlier, when they were children. The case against Long can be evaluated based upon the content and level of detail contained in the statements of one of his victims. This victim described how he couldn't get the sound of Long's voice out of his head or take enough showers to wash away the smell of his cologne after he was assaulted by Long. He also described how Long had manipulated them from childhood and the love they felt for him along with the betrayal of trust they felt. False allegations do not typically contain such a complex combination of ambivalent, affective, emotional, and other-sensory detail (Johnson, Foley, Suengas, & Raye, 1988).

Stranger abductors

As noted at the beginning of this chapter, cases involving strangers abducting children and engaging in violent assaults do exist. They represent a small but dangerous subset of child sex offenders, who are at the other end of the offending spectrum from groomers. Stranger offenders are typically motivated to engage in sexual activity with children but do not have the social or intellectual skills to groom children into compliant victimization. These offenders resort to abduction and sexual assault of children via coercion and/or force. Of the approximately 160 long-term non-familial child abductions in the United States annually, 50% are sexually motivated (Boudreaux, Lord, & Dutra, 1999). Sadly, in approximately 67% of these cases the child victims are killed. In those cases where children are abducted and killed, 44% are killed within the first hour, 73% are killed within three hours, and 99% are killed within 24 hours. It is therefore critically important for law enforcement to be prepared to respond to reports of missing or abducted children immediately.

In one such case, a 6-year-old boy living outside of Seattle, WA, was playing with friends in the parking lot in front of his apartment complex. An adult male approached the children in a white truck and asked the children to help him find his lost children. No children went with the man at that point. Within the hour, a man and vehicle fitting the same description were seen a short distance away, in front of a grade school. Then he went back to the original parking lot. This time the 6-year-old boy offered to help the man find his lost children. He was last seen walking to the white truck, hand-in-hand with the unknown man.

Twenty-three hours later, there were no leads, and prospects for the boy's survival were very grim. By this time, law enforcement was searching for the child across state lines and they reached out to the FBI's Behavioral Analysis Unit (BAU) for assistance. The children had described the offender as a white male, 20 to 50 years old, with a bump on his head and a white truck. The problem was, the police had made a statement to the media that they were looking for a "predator" who had abducted the boy. No one called into the tip line.

At this point the BAU advised the investigators to change the media strategy to one of a "missing child," and the man they were looking for as a potential hero in the neighborhood because he was the last person to see this child who had wandered off. This change in strategy produced two calls leading to men in that neighborhood who drove white trucks. One of those men, Richard Allen Dunn, did not answer his apartment door during the initial neighborhood canvass. The police were advised to forcibly enter that apartment and when they did, they found the child inside, tied to a bed. The boy had been beaten and sexually assaulted but was still alive 28 hours after being abducted. He had definitely beaten the odds. A later search of Dunn's computer revealed a collection of child sexual victimization images. Dunn eventually was convicted of the abduction and sexual assault of the boy and was ultimately sentenced to 21 years in prison.

Protecting against child sex offenders

Given what we know about offender typologies, acquaintance offenders, grooming, and compliant victimization, we can employ strategies to help protect against child sex offenders.

First, we must learn to recognize the risk factors for grooming so we can protect those most vulnerable to it from those in their circle of trust who would employ it against them. Some common external risk factors include: poverty, lack of supervision, poor communication with parents or guardians, and prior victimization. Children with certain internal risk factors are also more likely to be targeted: low self-esteem, rebelliousness, drug/alcohol abuse, sexual curiosity, and prior victimization. A child being sexually victimized becomes both an internal and external risk factor if known to potential offenders. Also, while poverty is considered a risk factor, it is important to note that some offenders target victims irrespective of their financial status. Thus, children who fall into the middle or upper classes can also become victims of grooming and sexual victimization. Also, some offenders target confident, outgoing children because their vulnerability may be that they are adventurous risk takers.

Second, it is critical to understand and identify the lures that child sex offenders use to groom children into compliant victimization. This will enable schools, churches, clubs, sports teams, and other youth serving organizations to develop and implement contact and behavior policies that can prevent opportunities to utilize those lures. Gift-giving, favoritism, rewards, one-on-one contact, physical contact, contact outside of the group or organization, overnight travel or camping, sexualized jokes or conversations, and texting, calling, emailing, or other contact through social media should be prohibited behaviors between adults and children in youth serving organizations as a rule.[10] Administrators, employees, volunteers, children, and their parents or guardians should be trained and made aware of these rules and the reasons for them. Any report of violation of these rules should be taken extremely seriously and investigated as possible grooming or offending behavior.

Third, the markers of a child who has been victimized are known and should be shared with parents, mental health professionals, school personnel, and all members of youth serving organizations. These signs include depression, mood swings, promiscuity, secretive behavior, sudden sexual knowledge or focus, unexplained money or gifts, and self-harming or suicide attempts. Youth exhibiting these characteristics should be encouraged to receive mental health counseling from a professional trained in recognizing and treating possible sexual victimization.

It should be noted, however, that some sexually victimized children show little or no behavioral signs of their victimization. In fact, they may

10 See Safe4Athletes.org for more information and sample policies.

overachieve in an effort to hide or disassociate from their victimization. Therefore, any allegation of impropriety or violation of adult/child prohibited contact rules should be taken seriously and investigated thoroughly whether or not the markers are evident.

Lastly, adults should learn to listen to their instincts about suspicious behavior. In many cases of child sexual victimization, adult colleagues of offending teachers, coaches, and scout leaders later noted they had always felt uncomfortable watching that colleague's interaction with children. The offender gave off a "vibe," or was "too close" to the children, or seemed "unusually" interested in socializing with children, or was "the most popular" teacher with students and had no outside interests or age-appropriate relationships. In such a situation, hesitation to further investigate or accuse someone of illegal conduct might put children at risk. The cases of Sandusky and abusive Catholic priests show that "nice guys" can be the most insidious and dangerous child sex offenders of all. And we must discuss all these issues with the children we are charged with protecting.

Conclusion

Can you imagine a world in which we "protect" children from the perils of crossing a busy street by *not* telling them about those dangers? Would we ever think that they would be safer if we kept them "innocent," by failing to warn them that they could get hurt if they don't look both ways? Of course not. We recognize the risks associated with crossing streets, so when they are young we hold their hands while crossing. We discuss the reasons we do that, and the dangers associated with this activity. This is how we empower our kids to go out into the world and how we enable them to participate in their own protection.

Unfortunately, we don't employ the same logic when dealing with sex and sexual victimization. Instead, we try to keep our children sheltered from sexual information. The problem is, if they don't even know a threat exists, they will not be prepared for it and won't know how to deal with grooming or how to prevent victimization. Children need to know they can talk to their parents about sexual topics. Parents should have a calm, supportive, age-appropriate, and loving discussion with them about the fact that even people who seem "good," and who they and their parents love and trust, could try to groom them into sexual activity.

If children feel comfortable having this discussion with their parents, they will be less vulnerable to offenders and be much more likely to tell their parents if victimization has happened or is happening to them. Children also need to know that no matter what happened or what they feel they have done wrong, being sexually victimized is never a child's fault. They need to know their parents want to protect them, will always love them, and will believe and not punish them for telling the truth about this kind of victimization.

In summary, when dealing with child sexual victimization, it is critical to understand the type of offender (situational or preferential), the methodology of access (grooming or abduction), and the victim's role (forced, coerced, or compliant). Recognizing these behavioral characteristics of offenders and victims – and adopting the tips delineated above – will aid in the detection and prevention of child sexual victimization.

Remember, the very best way to protect your child from sexual victimization is to set rules that minimize the opportunities for related or unrelated adults to be alone with your child, to educate everyone about these rules, and to enforce them. When that is not possible, you can add a layer of protection by giving your child empowering knowledge about the real risks associated with sexual victimization and the confidence that they can talk openly with you about sexually related matters.

References

Boudreaux, M. C., Lord, W. D., & Dutra, R. L. (1999). Child abduction: Age based analyses of offender, victim, and offense characteristics in 550 cases of alleged child disappearance. *Journal of Forensic Science, 44*(3), 539–553.

Bourke, M., Fragomeli, L., Detar, P., Sullivan, M., Meyle, E., & O'Riordan, M. (2015). The use of tactical polygraph with sex offenders. *Journal of Sexual Aggression, 21*(3), 1–14.

Centers for Disease Control and Prevention. (2005). Adverse childhood experiences study: Data and statistics. Atlanta, GA: Centers for Disease Control and Prevention, National Center for Injury Prevention and Control.

Cortoni, F., & Hanson, R. K. (2005). A review of the recidivism rates of adult female sexual offenders (Research Rep. No. R-169). Ottawa: Correctional Service Canada.

Cortoni, F., Hanson, R. K., & Coache, M. E. (2010). The recidivism rates of female sexual offenders are low: A meta-analysis. *Sexual Abuse: A Journal of Research and Treatment, 22*(4), 387–401.

Faller, K. (1984). Is the child victim of sexual abuse telling the truth? *Child Abuse and Neglect, 8*, 473–481.

Farrow, D. (2014, February 1). An open letter from Dylan Farrow. *New York Times*. Retrieved from http://kristof.blogs.nytimes.com/2014/02/01/an-open-letter-from-dylan-farrow/.

Janus, E., & Prentky, R. (2003). Forensic use of actuarial risk assessment with sex offenders: Accuracy, admissibility, and accountability. *American Criminal Law Review, 40*, 1443. Available at SSRN: http://ssrn.com/abstract=687231.

John Jay College of Criminal Justice. (2004). The nature and scope of sexual of minors by catholic priests and deacons in the United States, 1950–2002. Washington, DC: For the United States Conference of Catholic Bishops.

Johnson, M. K., Foley, M. A., Suengas, A. G., & Raye, C. L. (1988). Phenomenal characteristics of memories for perceived and imagined autobiographical events. *Journal of Experimental Psychology, 117*(4), 371–376.

Jones, D., & McGraw, E. M. (1987). Reliable and fictitious accounts of sexual abuse to children. *Journal of Interpersonal Violence, 2*(1), 27–45.

Kulkofsky, S. (n.d.). Stranger danger: An assessment of the effectiveness of child abduction education. Cornell University. Retrieved from www.human.cornell.edu/hd/circ/publications/upload/HE-CIRC-pb-KulkofskyPDF.pdf.

Lanning, K. V. (2001). *Child molesters: A behavioral analysis* (4th Ed.) (pp. 19–30). Alexandria, VA: National Center for Missing & Exploited Children.

Lanning, K. V. (2005). Compliant child victim: Confronting an uncomfortable reality. In E. Quayle & M. Taylor (Eds.), *Viewing child pornography on the Internet* (pp. 49–60). Dorset, UK: Russell House.

Lisak, D., Hopper, J., & Song, P. (1996). Factors in the cycle of violence: Gender rigidity and emotional constriction. *Journal of Traumatic Stress, 9*, 721–743.

Thomas and Pitts v. *Board of Education Brandywine School District*, Case No 08-205-LPS. United States District Court for the District of Delaware (2008).

Walters, B. (2015). Interview with Mary Kay Letourneau and Vilii Fualaau. 20/20, ABC. Retrieved July 7, 2016 from www.youtube.com/watch?v=aP6T3sAHAFs.

Chapter 14

The challenge of viewing sexual offenders as both perpetrators and victims[1]

Don Greif

Evaluating sex offenders' risk for sexually reoffending involves unique psychological challenges. It forces us to grapple with a difficult task, described by F. Scott Fitzgerald as the "ability to hold two opposed ideas in mind at the same time, and still retain the ability to function," which Fitzgerald referred to as "the test of a first-rate intelligence" (Fitzgerald, 1936). Evaluating sexual offenders is complex and challenging precisely because it requires the ability to experience opposite feelings and perceptions toward the same person, in this case, the offender himself.

Psychological evaluators (as well as therapists who treat perpetrators) must be receptive to experiencing vicarious trauma (McCann & Pearlman, 1990) or countertrauma, Richard Gartner's two-person or intersubjectively based term for the transformation that results from listening empathically to stories of trauma (Gartner, 2014, 2017). Evaluators must be receptive to a wide range of emotions – horror, outrage, and sadness when encountering details of a perpetrator's offenses – and receptive to these very same emotions when listening to or reading about the offender's experience of trauma as a child. In other words, it requires the capacity to understand that the offender is – in many cases – both a perpetrator and a victim.

Evaluators must understand this because offenders themselves, in order to deeply change, must recognize they are both perpetrators and victims. Offenders must understand how and why they perpetrated – how and why

1 This chapter is dedicated to the late Abby Stein, whose passion and lucidity about the precursors to violence and its psychological underpinnings deepened my understanding of sexual aggression and inspired me to write about my experience. In it I will use the masculine pronoun to refer to sex offenders because men comprise the very large majority of those charged with sexual offenses.

sexual aggression became not just thinkable but doable. They must understand that they were traumatized as children and know the harm done to them in order to recognize, in a visceral way, the harm they did to others. This recognition is pivotal for not perpetrating in the future. Only if an offender empathizes with himself as a child victim can he empathize with other people – including those he offended against and potential victims. The ability to put oneself in the mind, heart, and soul of another human being is an essential bulwark against violence. Therefore, evaluators must understand the perpetrator as a whole person in order to assess whether the perpetrator recognizes himself and others as whole people.

Viewing the perpetrator as victim as well as perpetrator is emotionally and intellectually challenging. What do we do when we hear, as often happens, that the same individuals who committed these horrific acts were victims of horrible acts themselves? As I have written, "It is not easy to feel horrified and angry towards a person for what he has done to another person and also feel sympathetic and sad for what he endured as a child" (Greif, 2010, p. 277).

Fear, revulsion, and rage are powerful, expectable reactions to sexual violence. It is tempting to dismiss one dimension of offenders' reality and, concomitantly, one side of our own reactions to their reality.

Because it is hard to view sexual offenders as human beings who have suffered severe trauma and deficits and have also perpetrated evil, it is very easy, for the forensic professional and the layperson alike, to see sex offenders (and other violent criminals) as intrinsically bad or evil, as monsters or psychopathic deviants who are somehow not human, a view that Abby Stein (2007) referred to as "bad seed theory." Demonizing sexual offenders protects us from seeing the humanness of the person who offended while shielding us from recognizing our own potential for committing violence.

Perhaps it is more tempting to vilify sex offenders in the United States – where our criminal justice system is heavily weighted toward punishment – than in countries that emphasize rehabilitating people who commit violent crimes and helping them reintegrate into society. Moreover, in American culture sexual offenders are often reviled, making it that much harder to view them as damaged – though dangerous – human beings. Viewing them as human violates a culturally normative view, and therefore requires overcoming the culturally shaped and reinforced tendency to see them as monsters.

Receptiveness to the full range of one's emotional responses – and being able to see sexual offenders as badly damaged human beings who developed into people who badly damaged other human beings – means resisting or overcoming dissociation when listening to overwhelming stories about the offender and his offenses. This can be difficult, since dissociation is as normal a response to hearing devastating stories as it is to enduring trauma. Parenthetically, dissociation, as Stein elucidated in her book *Prologue to Violence* (2007), played a large role in the lives of many violent offenders, both in their response to trauma and in their offenses, and overcoming it is critical for their growth.

Forensic institutions deemphasize sexual offenders' histories of trauma, which can promote and encourage evaluators – as well as judges and juries – to dissociate or simply ignore this dimension of offenders' experience. In the forensic settings where I've evaluated sex offenders – prisons and secure treatment centers for civilly committed offenders – their records give scant attention to their histories as victims of abuse and neglect. Sometimes it is not even mentioned. Treatment for abuse and its psychological sequelae is minimal at best in these settings.

Viewing sexual offenders – any violent criminals, for that matter – "as having been seriously maltreated and injured humanizes them, and forces us to see perpetrators as more like us than otherwise" (Greif, 2010, p. 276). When one listens empathically and hears the terrible details of the early lives of many violent criminals, we identify with their early innocence and vulnerability, and this deeply shakes us and makes us wonder how our lives would have turned out had we been subjected to the same conditions.

Among the first sexual offenders I evaluated was a man who had been incarcerated for sexual offenses against children, serving his criminal sentence and then civilly committed because he was deemed a high risk to reoffend. My job was to assess his readiness to leave the secure treatment center where he had been held for years. Responding to my questions, he told me that as a child he was forced on a number of occasions to have sex with his parents' friends while they and other friends watched. I was shocked. A part of me did not want to know any more about this; it would have been easier for me to dissociate, perhaps not even discuss his childhood. But I was also curious and thought it important for me to know what happened in order to understand how he developed into someone who could sexually violate children. He answered my questions in a matter-of-fact, emotionally muted way, which I also found shocking (but later realized was probably a manifestation of dissociation). But he also looked very sad. As he told me the gruesome details of these sexual encounters I felt sickened, horrified, and outraged. He straightforwardly told me, too, about his own sexual abuse of children – not his own – while continuing to look sorrowful.

After meeting with him I went to my car and began driving home. I felt shaken by what I'd heard. My eyes welled up as I realized the evil some parents can perpetrate upon their children. I realized that if I had grown up in his home and had his meager internal resources I could have easily wound up in the same place he was. In fact, I could think of no reason I wouldn't be. I realized luck plays an incredibly important role in how our lives turn out. "There but for the grace of God go I" seemed an irrefutable conclusion.

Despite realizing I could have ended up in prison had I been as unlucky as he, I also recognized he knew right from wrong and was capable of choosing to not sexually offend, even though his choice to offend was powerfully influenced by his terrible experiences as a kid. Although sexual offenders' histories usually go a long way to explaining their actions, viewing sexual offenders simply as victims of bad circumstances, severe trauma, and abuse when they were children is as simplistic as is viewing them as monsters.

While I empathized with this man, I also knew he groomed children to engage in sex with him. I felt sad for his victims and disturbed that he did to these children what was done to him. In evaluating his sexual dangerousness, I saw his understanding of the links between his history and his offenses was still rudimentary and his internal resources were still sparse in spite of many years of treatment. Ultimately I considered him at high risk to reoffend and I expressed the opinion that he was not ready to be released into the community. It saddened me to think he could very well spend the rest of his life inside the barbed wire.

Following are vignettes of two men at different stages of treatment when I evaluated them. They illustrate how important it is that offenders connect their offenses to their trauma histories.

Mr. A, now in his mid-50s, was sexually and physically abused by his father beginning at age 5. He remembered the physical pain he felt when his father anally penetrated him. I asked him if he thought there was any connection between having been sexually abused by his father and his sexual abuse of others. He said he never thought about it that way. But then, he reflected, "I could have wanted my victims to experience what I experienced." Although he had not previously made connections between his offenses and his childhood trauma, when I asked him to consider the link he made this sophisticated psychological interpretation, one many psychoanalysts take for granted. But for this man – and many other sexual offenders who are extremely concrete and limited in their ability to symbolize their experience in words – it represents a meaningful achievement.

Mr. A had also taken responsibility for 22 offenses against children, many of which he had not been charged with, meaning no one would have known about them had he not reported them. He disclosed many details about the offenses, acknowledged he was addicted – as early as 9 years old – to the feeling of having an orgasm, and expressed the thought that he may have offended against younger children instead of having sex with peers because he wanted to find someone more vulnerable with whom he could feel dominant, powerful, and in control.

Yet, this man clearly had much more work to do to access what he felt about his abuse, develop a greater capacity to empathize, and build other psychological capacities and resources. One of the formulations in my report to the court refers to the type of transformation I hope Mr. A and other sexual offenders aspire to, and at least partially achieve:

> [M]any of Mr. A's victims were close to the same age as he was when he was sexually abused by his father. This is not coincidental; rather, it represents Mr. A's attempt to cope with the trauma he suffered as a little boy and it represents his cry for help. So too, in my professional opinion, did Mr. A's false reports of sexual abuse, in which he fabricated having sexually abused other children, represent an enactment or role-play of the help and protection he wished for when he was being sexually abused by his father. Instead of being protected, however, his mother failed to protect Mr. A from his father's sexual and physical abuse. It is imperative that Mr. A's experience as a child victim of sexual abuse, the extent of which is unknown, be the focus of as much clinical attention as possible. The link between childhood sexual trauma and perpetration of sexual abuse is well known, and the road to rehabilitation must involve skillful therapeutic work around

> trauma. It is likely that Mr. A, similar to many other victims of childhood sexual abuse, learned to use the pleasurable feelings associated with sex to manage and escape from profoundly distressing feelings, including vulnerability, betrayal, helplessness, shame, rage, hatred, guilt, anxiety, and depression. He may have also used sex as a way to seek contact, connection, affection, and affirmation with others.

Mr. S, in his early 50s, was the fifth of six children whose parents separated when he was 2. His mother moved with her children to another part of the country and afterward he only saw his father annually. He was kidnapped and anally raped by an older man when he was 10 years old. His mother told him not to tell anyone about it. A few weeks later, an older woman seduced and fellated him, then coerced and shamed him into performing cunnilingus and having intercourse with her. Mr. S became socially withdrawn, confused about his sexuality, and unable to express his feelings. He looked at other children and tried to see if any of them went through what he'd experienced. He felt jealous of kids who had fathers. His teachers wondered why he was "spaced out." When he was 10, Mr. S turned to alcohol and at 13 began using marijuana and cocaine. At 14, Mr. S sodomized another 14-year-old boy; at 16 he tried to anally sodomize a 6-year-old boy; at 17 he anally raped an 11-year-old girl; and at 26 he tried to anally rape a 7-year-old girl.

After refusing treatment for many years and displaying little remorse for his offenses, in his early 40s Mr. S embraced treatment, developing self-awareness and insight into the reasons he offended and displaying what his group therapist called "striking empathic participation." After his initial offense, Mr. S told me, he was "off to the races" and "felt power and control and wanted more of (it)." He said, "I wanted someone to do as I wanted them to do, as someone had me do. It was vengeful. Putting people through what I went through." He recognized his wish for a father who could provide comfort, support, and guidance, teaching him right from wrong and to care about others. He understood that children are innocent and "need to be protected," and he thought of himself as a "wounded coward" when he offended.

By examining his history of trauma and neglect – and its connection with his sexual offenses – Mr. S achieved substantial psychological growth. I recommended his release to a strict and intensive supervised treatment program in the community but the judge decided to keep him civilly committed as a "dangerous sex offender requiring confinement."

In sum, for many sexual offenders, in order to change it is vitally important to understand the connections between their childhood trauma and their offenses. In turn, viewing offenders as victims as well as perpetrators is a difficult but essential challenge in evaluating their recidivism risk.

References

Fitzgerald, F. S. (1936, February). The crack-up. *Esquire*. Retrieved from http://isites.harvard.edu/fs/docs/icb.topic1069083.files/Unit%20II%20Readings/The%20Crack-Up.pdf.

Gartner, R. B. (2014). Countertrauma, resilience, and counterresilience. *Contemporary Psychoanalysis, 50*, 609–626.

Gartner, R. B. (2017). Trauma and countertrauma, resilience and counterresilience. In R. B. Gartner (Ed.), *Trauma and countertrauma, resilience and counterresilience: Insights from psychoanalysts and trauma experts* (pp. 13–26). New York, NY: Routledge.

Greif, D. (2010). Explaining the inexplicable, review of *Prologue to violence: child abuse, dissociation, and crime (2007). Contemporary Psychoanalysis, 46*, 272–279.

McCann, I. L., & Pearlman, L. A. (1990). Vicarious traumatization: A framework for understanding the psychological effects of working with victims. *Journal of Traumatic Stress, 3*, 131–149.

Stein, A. (2007). *Prologue to violence: Child abuse, dissociation, and crime (2007)*. Mahwah, NJ: Analytic Press.

Chapter 15

Dual histories of abuse and perpetration

Lynne MacDonell and Craig Bolton

Sex offenders are regarded with great disdain in our society, and most others. Child sex offenders in particular are considered the most heinous, irremediable, untreatable predators. While some females sexually offend against children, 97% of persons convicted of a sexual offense are males (Statistics Canada, 2007). The general revulsion with which predators are viewed has resulted in stringent laws and punishments (Quinn, Forsyth, & Mullen-Quinn, 2004). These directly impact perceived validity of any treatment options for these men.

A misconception further complicating their treatment is that males who have been sexually abused as children will go on to sexually offend against others in adulthood. While this happens at times, it is not a natural progression.[1]

While most sexually abused boys do not offend in later life, this chapter focuses on men who do have such dual histories.[2] We will discuss the efficacy of group therapy for those with dual histories and the lack of services for them. We will offer case studies[3] illustrating the dynamics and impact of sexual abuse, and the necessity of treating perpetrators' victimization to reduce the potential for what we call "reactive offending." That is, some male sexual abuse survivors who go on to offend against children are not pedophiles. Rather, they are acting out their own abuse in order to make sense of it. This does not in any way excuse their actions, but in treating their early trauma we effectively treat their offending behaviour.

1 Salter (2003) notes that 12% of sexual abuse victims may become sexual offenders.

2 Editor's note: See Chapter 14 by Greif in this volume for discussion of countertransference with this population.

3 Names and identifying characteristics are changed to protect privacy.

We will also differentiate between pedophiles and non-pedophilic men who sexually offend against children.

Who we are

One of us, Lynne MacDonell, worked at an agency that treated male survivors of sexual abuse. On occasion, she received calls asking for services for survivors who also offended sexually. The agency's policy was not to accept clients with offending histories. Later, when she started her own practice, she again received calls from men with dual histories looking for services. Although she could see these men individually, she could not bring them into the non-offending survivor groups she offered. Lynne also volunteered for MaleSurvivor's Weekends of Recovery program[4] and they too had a policy not to accept men who were also sexual offenders. In response to this gap in service MaleSurvivor put names of such men on a waiting list until there were enough to develop a program. To date, MaleSurvivor has not run such a group.

Experienced in both individual and group therapy, Lynne recognized that healing in a group works differently than in one-to-one counseling because it eliminates the dyadic relationship of individual therapy. During her years of running survivor groups and offering individual therapy for offenders, she noted that men with dual histories had no access to services to treat both experiences concurrently. Recognizing the benefit of group therapy, and its unavailability to those with dual histories, Lynne discussed her thoughts with her colleague and co-author of this chapter, Craig Bolton.

Craig works full time as a mental health clinician at a community mental health agency. In his practice, he counsels people with severe and persistent mental illness. Over the period of a year, two male clients disclosed to him they had been sexually abused in childhood. Craig hypothesized that their mental health symptoms were a direct result of the childhood sexual abuse. As these men were of limited income, it was difficult to find suitable recovery options. Craig approached Lynne, and she suggested that he start a group at his agency. Craig then began training with Lynne and started a group for sexually abused men at his office.

4 Editor's note: See Chapter 5 by Fradkin and Struve in this volume for discussion of the Weekends of Recovery program.

He has been facilitating this group for several years now in 12-week segments, cycling several times per year. During outreach to probation and parole offices and detention centers, Craig was often asked if men who were convicted of a sexual offense but had also experienced childhood sexual abuse would be eligible for his group. The answer was "No," as the safety of the survivor group would be compromised.

Together, Craig and Lynne considered offering sex offenders with sexual abuse histories a place to recover in a group setting. They believed that by treating men's trauma they would also be treating their offending behavior, thereby potentially reducing instances of childhood sexual abuse.

Impact of sexual abuse on males

Child sexual abuse (CSA) is one of the most debilitating forms of trauma because it challenges what children believe about the world. Attachment theory suggests that psychosocial development may be interrupted when a child's needs are unmet. This may manifest in socially destructive behavior, impacting the ability to form secure attachments, both in childhood and adulthood (Calvert, Kellett, & Hagan, 2015). Usually sexual abuse is perpetrated by a person known to the child, "which therefore shatters his fundamental assumptions of security, trust and invulnerability" (Sweig, 2000, p. 255). Seager and Thümmel (2009) note that if the perpetrator is someone in a position of trust, the ability to form emotional attachments in adulthood is further skewed. Addressing CSA as early as possible is imperative to reduce the likelihood of lifelong impact and rippling effects from the individual into society.

While both male and female victims of CSA often display symptoms of PTSD, depression, and suicidal tendencies, males typically present first with other symptoms: addictions, relationship problems, angry acting-out behavior, suicide attempts, difficulty with authority figures, and other symptoms discussed elsewhere in this book. Because of social norms, men are less likely to seek out emotional support (Berger, Levant, McMillan, Kelleher, & Sellers, 2005, 2008), but to minimize the lifelong impact of boyhood sexual abuse and work toward healing and recovery, psychological treatment is essential.

Sexual abuse occurs in secrecy; often children do not disclose until they find safety in adulthood or are in such a crisis situation that they must seek help. Statistics consistently show that one in four girls and one in six boys is sexually abused by age 18 (1in6.org). Although already alarming, those statistics need to be understood in the context of CSA often being underreported, especially by male victims. Wilken (2011) believes that, because of expectations about maleness, male sexual abuse is underreported 90% of the time. This inevitably leads to underestimating the need for services for male survivors of sexual violence.

Abuse does not always involve pain, coercion, or obvious manipulation. Individuals in positions of trust and authority sexually abused a number of our group members. These non-familial abusers, not having existing connections with these children, frequently groom victims[5] by developing "relationships" with them. They often start treating the victims as special, cared about, and loved. This grooming causes some male victims conflict later, because they enjoyed some aspects of the abuse and/or had caring feelings for the person offending against them. These children may not know that the abuse that followed involved abusive and harmful acts against them until they discover it through other social interactions.

Richard

Richard was a drug-addicted survivor of childhood sexual abuse. He had lived near the Maple Leaf Gardens, a hockey arena in downtown Toronto. "The Gardens," built in 1912, became home to the Toronto Maple Leafs in 1931. This hockey "shrine" was a magnet to boys living in the area of Church and Carlton Streets in the 1970s and 1980s.

Like many others, Richard came from a family with limited finances, limited supports, and an absentee father. When a man holding "access power" to "The Gardens" gave 12-year-old Richard attention and kindnesses, he was delighted. He would do anything to keep that attention. And so, he was abused.

Scandal hit "The Gardens" when the first of many victims of sexual abuse came forward in 1993, prompting other victims to disclose. Several employees were charged in over 100 counts of sexually abusing young men and boys over three decades.

After the scandal broke, many victims were provided free counseling. Richard, then in his early 30s, was one of them. He used drugs to

5 Editor's note: See Chapter 13 by Clemente and Hakes in this volume for a discussion of grooming behavior.

cope with the memories, betrayal, and pain of the abuse. He initially did well in treatment and became clean and sober. However, when he disclosed he had offended against children while an adolescent, the counseling was withdrawn. Counseling was funded for victims only; once Richard admitted to offending he was no longer eligible.

After counseling abruptly stopped, Richard, now in his mid-30s, felt there was no hope for him and relapsed into drug addiction. He later said that in adolescence he had not understood his actions. He thought he was just doing the "grownup thing" by paying attention to younger children in ways he himself had experienced. But he felt damaged, guilty, and unworthy of any support or understanding.

At one point, someone unexpectedly came up behind him while he was drugged out and paranoid. Richard "freaked out," stabbing the man to death. He pled guilty, receiving a custodial sentence of 25 years to life. While incarcerated, Richard reflected on his past history and deeply regretted sexually abusing other children. He called Lynne for support and used bi-weekly calls as therapy sessions. Lynne provided these sessions *pro bono*, but in order to connect with her he used a phone card, which was costly, and calls were time-limited. This complicated service and increased his personal risk; should he enter a crisis during the session, he and Lynne did not necessarily have time to fully debrief. Richard was assigned a social worker in prison, as Lynne's sessions were logistically difficult to sustain. He hoped the social worker would provide similar support, but was informed they would only provide treatment for his offending behavior, not his victimization. At this point, Lynne suggested he use the social worker's resources to find support so he could heal from his childhood abuse.

Richard, like many others who have sexually offended against children, suffered with regret and shame. Without holistic treatment, he had no opportunity to understand and come to terms with any connection between his own sexual abuse and his "reactive perpetration" (see below).

Men sexually abused as boys by another male often experience guilt, shame, and excessive worry about why they were chosen by a man for sexual abuse. This often results in fears of being homosexual or of committing sexual offenses themselves (Morrison & Treliving, 2002). Neither belief is necessarily accurate.

Males who were sexually abused may or may not be homosexual; abuse does not define one's sexuality. However, the experience can be especially confusing when the victim is the same sex as the offender. The struggle that some men experience with sexuality after sexual abuse by another male may be due to having development of sexual identity interrupted at such a young age (1in6.org).[6] If a man is heterosexual, he may be leery of any emotional relationship with other males, fearing another "seduction." If he is homosexual, he may either connect his sexual orientation to having been abused by a same-sex offender, or he may reject his homosexuality altogether (Lew, 2004).

The fear of becoming offenders themselves stems from the common belief that abused boys inevitably grow up to be abusing men. However, research does not support this myth. In a study by Glasser et al. (2011), researchers assessed the link between being a victim and becoming a perpetrator; the victim-to-victimizer cycle was present in only a minority of male perpetrators. Simons (2007, as cited in Richards, 2011) argued that being offended against is not causal for going on to offend, although he notes a possible correlation between the two.

Masculine gender socialization's effects on sexually abused men

Social expectation about maleness signifies that "men on the surface bear no resemblance to the picture of a victim" (Morrison & Treliving, 2002, p. 64). Because of such masculine gender socialization, many men with sexual abuse histories feel that, being male, they should have been able to stop the abuse or tolerate it. Seager and Thümmel (2009) outline how the societal construction of maleness lays the foundation for traumatic impact to be deeply ingrained and internalized in male victims.

Addis and Mahalik (2003) identify role socialization as a barrier to men seeking support. The social construction of maleness and the expectations that men are more sexual than females and cannot be sexually offended against by females mean that sexually abused males experience social stigmatization if they disclose. This limits their ability to report offenses or talk about the impact on them. If he had a female offender, the likelihood

6 Such struggles about sexual orientation rarely happen with female victims (Sable, Danis, Mauzi, & Gallagher, 2006).

of a male victim reporting is even further diminished (Sable et al., 2006). Additionally, these men feel tremendous guilt if they acknowledge that at times it felt good.

While there have been some gains overall in decreasing gender role stereotyping, much of these focus on reducing feminine inferiority, with less emphasis on reducing the bravado of masculinity. "Our culture still views with deep suspicion any man owning his softer feelings alongside more traditional masculine attributes" (Seager & Thümmel, 2009, p. 252).

Male sexual abuse survivors often struggle internally with their emotional pain. They are more likely to act out their emotions in a physical manner than to address them through words and feelings (Biddulph, 1998). Men's experiences are no more or less impactful than women's, but they are different. Whereas men often act out their distress through aggressive interactions with others, sexually abused women tend to internalize their distress, manifesting depression or self-harming behavior (Briere & Runtz, 1993).

Research suggests that criminality and anti-social behavior can be linked to past trauma, especially those traumas experienced in attachment relationships (Seager & Thümmel, 2009). Attachment theory suggests that psychosocial development may be interrupted when a child's needs are unmet. This may manifest in socially destructive behavior, negatively affecting the ability to form secure attachments, both in childhood and adulthood (Calvert et al., 2015).

Currie and Tekin (2013) have found that maltreatment doubles the probability of criminality in adulthood. Children who experience CSA often develop survival strategies that are maladaptive in adulthood (Sweig, 2000). Much of Sweig's research is on female participants, but Currie and Tekin (2013) note that both male and female children who have been sexually abused have an increased risk of maladaptive behaviors in adulthood, including criminal behaviors. They found that those adults who were maltreated as children were twice as likely to engage in criminal behavior, and that sexual abuse as a form of maltreatment had the largest effect on increased criminal activity.

Men with histories of sexual abuse are often in a confused position about their vulnerability and need for safety. Fleeing from the idea of being a victim, they may instead identify with the offender. They may try to take back the control that was taken from them, putting them more at risk of offending themselves. Again, we would like to emphasize, first, that understanding why a man might identify with his abuser in no way excuses offending behavior, and, second, that because any man has been offended against does not in any way mean he will offend sexually as an adult. But it is a risk supported by the research and is a frightening reality for some of these men.

Group therapy for sexually abused men

Group therapy is an ideal place to address sexually abused men's problems because it decreases isolation, increases interpersonal learning, and creates cohesiveness with other adults because of the commonality of the problem being addressed (Yalom, 2005).

Omar

A 52-year-old single man, Omar immigrated to Canada from Mumbai at age 23. The youngest of seven children, he did not know his mother, as she died when he was very young. When his father remarried, he was sent to boarding school. There he was sexually victimized by a Catholic priest and some older boys. Omar "accepted" this as simple bullying. This helped him withstand an otherwise unbearable experience.

In Canada, Omar was lonely, with no close friends. He joined a Hare Krishna faith community, where he was responsible for children's care during spiritual gatherings. Omar started watching pornographic images, including images of child sexual abuse. Addicted to pornography and unable to control himself, he fainted when the police came to arrest him. He was charged with downloading images of child pornography and given a 12-month custodial sentence. Although devastated about being arrested, Omar reports he was partly relieved, as he knew he was doing wrong; his obsession was out of control and he recognized he needed help.

When released on bail, Omar confided in an acquaintance from the Temple about the charges against him and was subsequently barred from attending meetings. Omar felt isolated and rejected by a community that preached forgiveness. He came to our group and found he was able to connect with the other men. Talking about his life in Mumbai and his current charges, he initially appeared very anxious. But as time went on he began to trust the process. He needed connections to others in order to acknowledge his reality by hearing other

> men share their own experiences. He was then able to face his CSA and begin to recognize its connection to his offending behavior.

Predictable and structured, groups provide a safe place for participants to share stories and experiences (Sweig, 2000). They offer hope, altruism, and relational opportunities. Sweig argues that group therapy should be offered in conjunction with individual therapy so the individual can reprocess what is heard, seen, and felt in the group setting. Due to lack of finances and the paucity of group offerings, however, this ideal scenario is not always possible.

Callahan, Price, and Hilsenroth (2004), assessed pre- and post-measures for participants in a psychotherapy group who were adult survivors of childhood sexual abuse. They found all participants had significant improvements in overall psychological functioning, specifically quality of life, ability to identify feelings, self-esteem, and personal relationships with partners and children. Such groups ideally empower, transform, and elicit sustainable change. There are many guidelines for group therapy: respect for the lived experience, education through dialogue, holistic methodology, transformative purpose. These are consistent with humanitarian transformative practice and link private concerns to public issues (O'Hara, Weber, & Levine, 2010).

Men develop connections differently than women do, often seeking out more competitive or public relationships and engaging in groups for overt and purposeful reasons, such as sports (Tremblay & Turcotte, 2005). However, as Wilken (2011) notes, rather than not joining group therapies because they connect and communicate differently, men may not attend groups because there are few services available to them. This in turn limits the amount of research done in this area.

Nevertheless, the available research about how men and women interact differently suggests that group therapy may be ideal for men when based on camaraderie. We believe that group work can offer possibilities for men to be more open to internal emotional states and to experience cathartic healing from the damage of masculine gender socialization.

Morrison and Treliving (2002), by assessing outcomes, have explored the usefulness of group therapy for adult males who were sexually abused as boys. Their findings suggest that sexually abused males' experience lowered self-esteem, guilt, and sexuality problems, and often their strong identification with their aggressors. Assessing participants' level of psychological stress and pre- and post-group participation, they concluded that symptom measurement provided evidence that group psychotherapy is a useful therapeutic approach for men who appear unsuitable for psychotherapeutic intervention because of personality difficulties stemming from early childhood sexual abuse. Men who were sexually abused as children and who have later offended sexually, similarly benefit from this group process.

Our groups' foundations

We facilitate recovery groups for males with histories of childhood sexual abuse as well as the dual history group. In all these groups, the foundation of the group process is men caring for men.

Our dual history group is limited to eight men with two facilitators. We find that bringing together men with similar lived experience makes their healing journey tolerable. We use the existing foundations of our survivor groups, including aspects of the Good Lives Model and the Hermes' Web, as our framework and focus in all of our groups.

The Good Lives Model (GLM) strives to reduce negative thoughts and distortions, replacing them with an outcome focus of attaining a "good life" (Purvis, Ward, & Willis, 2014). A central assumption is that people need to attain basic human "goods" that reflect states of mind, outcomes, and experiences. In this model, offending results from problems an individual encounters seeking to attain "primary human goods," such as happiness, relationships/friendships, and experiencing mastery in work and leisure activities (Willis, Yates, Gannon, & Ward, 2012). Working with clients to identify the primary goods most important to them is a fundamental component of assessment because treatment is geared to helping them attain these primary goods in an adaptive rather than maladaptive manner, which addresses re-offense risk (Yates, Prescott, & Ward, 2010).

The GLM instils a sense of hope, which many participants have not been able to envision in the past. This increases a sense of control over our outcomes, rather than a belief that outcomes are prescribed and cannot be altered. It also reminds participants they are responsible for the choices they now make, which helps them continue to manage risk. The GLM includes an inventory of "primary goods," things of importance to the individual: offense-related goals (in order to manage risk) and "secondary goods" (strategies, pathways, and their interrelationships that allow us to achieve primary goods). This model uses cognitive behavioral treatment

(CBT) methods to increase the effectiveness of a sustainable intervention (Yates et al., 2010). Awareness of what makes us successful, establishing positive ways to attain it, and making make small consistent gains, all increase psychological well-being (Ward, Mann, & Gannon, 2007).

We also endeavor to focus on overall positive psychological well-being, using the Hermes' Web concepts and strategies[7] for a more holistic and intrinsically motivated approach to therapy. Attendees report these sessions provide them insight and support, which assists healing from both their abuse and their shame.

Using the Hermes' Web model, we assume these men incurred trauma during precognitive phases of life, resulting in a development of maladaptive emotional patterns deeply entrenched at early cognitive levels where they were first experienced. The cognitive damage of trauma is deeply rooted, and emotional maturity and development are impacted, so treatment and education must reach the original parts of the brain where trauma is embedded. Sexual abuse survivors suffer from both the physical and emotional damage that interferes with intellectual development overall. Therapists must therefore reach them at the level where they were when first traumatized. In our experience, visual and tactile therapy, using imagination, is most impactful. Hermes' Web, as a holistic tactile tool, represents the psyche as a whole, including parts we do not automatically see or think about. We use it to explain how people become used to having emotional needs unmet, to ignore their behaviors, and to conceal their burdens, so much so that they do not recognize when their unresolved trauma manifests and becomes their entire subconscious focus. We believe those unprocessed experiences then drive irrational thinking, often leading to a myriad of maladaptive behaviors. We use Hermes' Web to help clients explore the parts of their selves most difficult to face. Though challenging, this actually allows them understand their behavior in ways unavailable to them before.

Our dual history groups

Our aim is to reduce the prevalence of sexual abuse. To mobilize child abuse prevention, we believe that treating childhood sexual trauma also

7 See hermesweb.com.

treats the offending behavior for those with dual histories. While individual counseling alone can greatly benefit these men, sharing their recovery journey with other men enhances their experience. Group therapy is especially effective as participants connect to others who have lived through similar experiences. Men in the group develop rapport with each other, enabling the healing journey to begin.

We developed our groups for men wanting to address both their past trauma and their offending behavior. By exploring the emotional impact of their sexual trauma, men hopefully identify with their victims and develop empathy for them. It is not uncommon for offenders to focus on their own needs and have little connection to any impact they have on their victims. Drawing the parallel from themselves to their victims can introduce a cathartic healing. They then begin to understand that what they felt – confusion, pain, shame, blame, anger – is what they have inflicted on another person, but that this re-enactment did not achieve the closure they subconsciously expected from this reactive offending.

Steven

Steven, the only child in a middle-class family from a small conservative town in Ontario, was small for his age as a boy and shy. He had difficulty making friends. His mother, a First Nations woman, was very supportive of her son, while his father, a white Catholic man, was a strict disciplinarian. Steven felt that as a mixed-race person he was an outsider. However, he was drawn to the rituals and beauty of the Catholic Church, which his parents attended. There, he felt acceptance.

Steven decided to become an altar server. Soon, the priest offered him and other boys some of the altar wine, paying extra attention to Steven. They were all curious about the "mysterious wine" and thrilled to taste it. He hated the taste, but liked the feeling it gave him. The priest's extra attention began to alienate him from the other boys. Then things became more physical/sexual. Steven soon felt trapped. He developed manipulation skills and coerced the priest into giving him things. He remembers waiting outside the liquor store after sending the priest to get hard liquor. In return, he satisfied the priest's sexual demands. Then he began using drugs along with the alcohol.

Steven hit a growth spurtin adolescence and within a year went from being the smallest boy in his group to the tallest. He was finally old enough to end the abusive situation. He decided he would never be used that way again and began working out. He took performance-enhancing drugs, monitoring his food intake to enrich his workouts. At 16, his girlfriend became pregnant. They moved in together and soon their son was born. Although drug-addicted, Steven endeavored to support and protect his young family; he needed money to support them and his drug habit.

There was a section of his town known as "The Forest" where drugs were readily available. There, he was approached by a couple willing to pay him to have sex with both of them. Believing this was all he was good for anyway, he accepted their proposal. This was how he supported his family. He continued to work out, "looked quite buff," and used drugs.

Then Steven's son died from Sudden Infant Death Syndrome (SIDS). He ended the relationship with his son's mother and continued to prostitute himself. For several years, Steven continued to be paid for sex, often unprotected, with the couple and their friends.

After Steven stopped some of his risky sexual behavior, he became isolated and began watching adult pornography. With time, he viewed younger and younger images of child sex abuse. He was arrested for downloading these images, serving a short sentence at a correctional treatment center. He reports he did not take this seriously and was released with no insight or tools to keep himself safe. Within a month, he again accessed these images. He also began visiting chatrooms catering to underground deviant sexual activities. He was contacted by a man who said he wanted Steven to have sex with him and his children. When he went to meet them, the police showed up instead. He was arrested again and sent back to the same treatment-focused correctional center. Steve took this second incarceration more seriously. He disclosed his own sexual abuse, and while incarcerated was referred to our dual history group.

In our group, Steven came to acknowledge he actually wanted to meet the man who offered himself and his children to Steven for sex. He began to understand he has pedophilic interests and must keep himself safe, and "be seen to be safe." Steven feels he needs constant supervision around children in order to ensure he will never be a risk to them. Supervision serves as an extra set of eyes, keeping him safe from acting on his pedophilic interests. He believes that without the group experience, he might well have continued to deny his pedophilia and potentially to abuse children.

Due to the limited research in this area, we extrapolated from available literature on offender/victim recovery groups to inform our practice. In this discussion we also rely on anecdotal evidence to evaluate the success of our dual history groups.

Groups create a safe setting different from the competitive environment most males are used to. This helps men establish new kinds of relationships with other males, thus challenging their belief system. Group therapy for those who offend sexually can address the shame and stigma of being a sex offender. Groups can concurrently reduce their shame and confusion about having been sexually abused as vulnerable children. Most important, men in the dual history group begin to identify with their victims, discovering empathy. Building a rapport with others who have a similar history, and also experience shame and guilt, is a compelling experience. As men are able to access the more vulnerable aspects of their psyche and recognize internal conflicts, they can hold each other accountable and support each other with a shared lived experience (Tremblay & Turcotte, 2005). Finally, identification with other group members helps them identify areas of strength and bring back a sense of worth and value.

Many victims of trauma speak of having flashbacks, reliving the experience over and over. The group environment can help the individual stay in the present. Kreidler (2005) reports that many victims are re-victimized by themselves and others, and this continues into adulthood. He believes it is necessary to identify and confront family structure, roles, and rules in place at the time of the abuse, as well as how they continue to affect present behavior.

This is why having a trained facilitator is crucial. The facilitator keeps the focus on the current impact of having offended and having been a victim of childhood sexual abuse. Facilitators can help each man make connections between how he was abused and how he has offended. They can point out patterns and interpretations, helping identify internalization of the abuse (Morrison & Treliving, 2002).

Further, having facilitators ensures that groups move from individual dialogues to whole group discussions. Facilitators should observe and be proactive in relation to topics or individual conversations that might trigger group participants by eliciting feedback from other group members about their reactions to the dialogue (Seager & Thümmel, 2009). Facilitators also need to be able to reframe and challenge any negative collusion or disrespectful comments in the group. Of course, groups, especially groups of this nature, should have facilitators who are not themselves currently struggling with similar traumas.

Group are powerful vehicles for reconstructing healthier internal views of masculinity (Tremblay & Turcotte, 2005). There can be “relief through solidarity with others with whom shame could be shared and masculinity affirmed in all male groups” (Sharpe, Selley, Low, & Hall, 2001, p. 196). Groups thereby allow men to express themselves and be intimate with other men in a non-sexual context. They can also address issues of internalized homophobia (Tremblay & Turcotte, 2005).

Seager and Thümmel (2009) have identified what they call a “traditional masculine communication style.” They believe that because traditional psychotherapy was developed with a female client group in mind, it is more attuned to traditionally feminine communication styles. They suggest that instead of forcing men to adapt to this “feminine” style of psychotherapy, we can adapt the therapeutic space to a more “masculine” style, without sacrificing the universal principles and needs that apply to any psychotherapeutic space.

O’Leary (2009) found that seeking active assistance is an important coping strategy in reframing the trauma experience. He suggested that support services allow cognitive reframing to help men recognize the strength it takes to survive and the positive growth that arises from survival. This also serves to help our clients make the connections between what was done to them and what they have done to others. This insight inspires empathy for their victims and for themselves.

Before anything else, participants themselves establish guidelines for safety. Since sexual abuse affects men differently than women in many ways, we try to create a “gender-protected” space for men to reflect on how and why they have been impacted specifically as men. We actively establish this principle of gender safe space by being intentionally interactive with participants. We discuss at length the concept of masculinity. Acknowledgment of socially imposed gender stereotypes and how they contribute to the impact of sexual abuse has led to open dialogue in our group about embracing emotional aspects of the healing journey. We spend at least a full session identifying male role stereotypes and how those constructs exacerbate the impact of their abuse. We then talk about breaking down dominant masculine barriers in order to promote genuine emotion and healing.

Facilitators should be aware of the advantages of gender-protected space and should be committed to providing it when engaging in this type of group work. An advantage of co-facilitation is that it can prevent the process from becoming too intrusive or too evasive, as the facilitators can build on each other's comments, knowledge, and strengths.

Our preference is to have a male/female co-facilitated group. Bruckner and Johnson (1987), as cited in Sharpe et al. (2001), suggest that the dynamic in co-led male/female group facilitation provides survivors an opportunity to challenge their gender assumptions. One such assumption is that all women in nurturing positions are unreliable and unresponsive and that all men cause harm. In co-led groups, where we interact and rely on each other, we support participants in challenging such gender assumptions. Awareness and acknowledgment of supportive male and female roles working in tandem can assist in breaking down some of those accepted gender divisions.

Anecdotally, Lynne reports that in each of her groups of eight male survivors, two were abused by women: mothers, older sisters, older cousins, or babysitters. In these situations, we continue to challenge gender roles. Through focusing on identifying that the experience was still abusive and traumatic, we work toward breaking down the belief that males cannot be harmed by females.

To publicize our dual histories group, we reached out to probation and parole offices and treatment centers catering to sexual offenders. Referrals came immediately; currently we run a 12-week dual histories group that cycles several times per year. While most participants are referred to us through the justice system, there are some self-referred clients. As with all our groups, a screening process is necessary to assess suitability for a group-based therapy program. This consists of an in-person meeting to determine if they are mentally healthy enough to participate appropriately within a group of vulnerable men. If a man presents with significant mental health symptoms, including psychosis, he is not admitted to the group. The group's need for safety overrides the individual's needs. In addition, they must admit culpability regarding their offense (or admit sexual interest in children) and must have been offended against as a child.

Interestingly, men in the dual history group express more shame disclosing they were sexually abused than admitting they offended. They have difficulty coming to terms with *having been a sexually abused child* who then went on to offend sexually against other children. Developing empathy for themselves helped them develop empathy for their victims.

Pedophiles and child molesters

Offenders have difficulty reaching out for help because of the stigma attached to pedophilic ideation. If someone offers you a glass of wine and you reply, "No thank you, I'm a recovering alcoholic," this might be considered admirable. On the other hand, if a man when asked to watch someone's son replies, "I can't do that because I have pedophilic tendencies," there would be instant stigmatization. Both are responsible replies, but the stigma of being a pedophile instantly labels this man a "monster," notwithstanding his responsible action intended to keep a child safe, as well as himself.

David

David is our first client who was sexually abused, has a propensity to abuse, but has not abused. He came to the group looking for support. Child protection services removed him from his drug-addicted mother when he was 6 and placed him in a group home. A caretaker there sexually and physically abused him and others. David hated the state and all other authority figures for placing him in that abusive environment.

As an adolescent he knew he was attracted to young children. David said he would "cut off his penis before he would hurt anyone like he was hurt." He was so frightened of his attraction and where it could lead that at age 22 he went to the police station, reporting he thought he might be a pedophile. David was looking for help. The police took down his information and requested he report weekly. David had not committed a crime; they had nowhere to refer him. Finally, his community support worker consulted us regarding his suitability for our groups. David was a victim, but had not offended; however, his risk to offend was high without appropriate support. He could be a part of a therapy group for non-offending survivors, but this would not address his concern about acting on his sexual thoughts about children. David fit best with our dual history group since there were no other options.

The fact that David would go to the police, authority figures whom he hated and did not trust, reveals his desperation for help. Like many others with his sexual interests, he did not want to abuse children. It is hard to categorize David. He is a pedophile in the narrow sense that

> he is sexually attracted to children but he is not a child molester, and it is not clear that his innate sexual orientation is to children. Although he could get support and healing for his child sexual abuse, he could never talk about his sexual desires within a CSA therapy group. However, in our group he felt less isolated.

The literature on pedophilia is vast and it is beyond the scope of this chapter to discuss it fully. But there are some points we want to make. Although all sexual offenders against children are often considered pedophiles, a closer examination reveals differences among them. There are pedophiles who never molest children[8] and child molesters who are not actually pedophiles.

In *Child Molesters: A Behavioural Analysis*, Lanning (2001) defines pedophiles and child molesters differently. He developed a typology of sexually offending so investigators could assess offenders more accurately.[9] Classifying sexual offending as either situational-type or preferential-type, he categorizes pedophiles as preferential-type. Preferential-type offenders' main sexual attraction – indeed their sexual orientation (Kane, 2013; see also Cantor, n.d.) – is to children.[10] Those who enact this attraction may become serial pedophiles.

Situational-type offenders include those who may be called "reactive offenders" (see Johnson, 2009). We believe most offenders who were sexually victimized as children are in this category. Their offending is a behavioral re-enactment of trauma.

This concept that pedophiles and child sex abusers are very different is controversial. Some research does not support pedophilia as a sexual orientation, suggesting it is a mental health disorder stemming from childhood trauma, and is therefore correctable (abusewatch.net). However, we see a difference between pedophiles and child sex abusers.

8 The organization Virtuous Pedophiles (VirPed.org) is one of the few places non-offending pedophiles can go for support.

9 Editor's note: See Chapter 13 by Clemente and Hakes in this volume for further discussion of sex offender typologies.

10 James Cantor (quoted in Virped.org, n.d.) says about a pedophilic orientation: "My heart goes out to people to whom nature has given something as powerful and as distracting as a sex drive and no healthy way to express it . . . The best we can do is help a [pedophile] maximize his self-control and to help him build an otherwise happy and productive life."

Traumatic events often lead to frequent memories of the trauma, taking the form of physical sensations, images or nightmares, behavioral re-enactment, or any combination of these. They may create physiological responses resulting in hyperarousal. Chronic exposure to stimuli reminiscent of the trauma may cause a past victim to re-experience the same physiological response, returning him subconsciously to a past state while experiencing a current event. This state of hyperarousal reduces the ability to make rational decisions and limits the ability to re-process new events as separate from past ones.

This leaves past victims at risk of reacting by re-enacting their abuse, which can include reactive offending. Cognitive distortions lead victims of past sexual abuse incident(s) to re-enact that abuse with a fantasy of changing the outcome (Koss & Harvey, 1991; Koss et. al., 1994 in Lonsway & Archambault, 2013). Van der Kolk (1989) believes that in victimization trauma re-enactments, some victims enact the role of victims while others take on the role of victimizers. Levy (1998) suggests re-enacting past abuse by becoming an abuser is actually a defense mechanism protecting the past victim from having to re-experience the past incident(s); he highlights that this is a maladaptive response to PTSD.

Lack of treatment options and supports

In the past, if a Canadian man in custody wanted treatment for his offending behavior, there were several government-sponsored options for him, according to the Cornwall Public Inquiry (2008). However, these treatment services are now limited to those who pose a high recidivism risk. First-time offenders or incest offenders, who are not considered high risk for re-offending, are typically not streamed into treatment services in Canada. This leaves a "lower risk" offender with little or no treatment for his offending behavior while in custody. At times, a convicted offender may be required to attend court-ordered psychotherapy sessions, either during incarceration or upon release. But existing programs are geared to treat offending behaviors, rather than addressing any underlying issues that may have led to offending, such as childhood physical or sexual abuse or other maltreatment (Currie & Tekin, 2013).

Upon release he is expected to opt for treatment at government-sponsored agencies. Again, these agencies only treat offending behavior. If he wants to address his own CSA recovery, there is virtually nothing available. Participants in our groups have indicated that very few appropriate outpatient programs currently exist at all, and many programs available at one time within the prison system have been eliminated. To our knowledge, as of this writing there are no dual history groups in the greater Toronto area other than ours.

It is imperative to provide therapy for sexual abuse recovery concurrently with treating the offending behavior in order to provide unabridged healing. While treatment cannot undo the sexual abuse men in our dual history group have suffered and inflicted, it can help them make the connection between what was done to them and their conscious or unconscious decision to go on to abuse others. This awareness helps them make better decisions about keeping themselves and the community safe. Many men who have attended our group report their recovery journey has been a catalyst toward self-forgiveness. Even men who have not offended, but have pedophilic tendencies and joined the group to have a place to talk about their feelings, report they now feel more solid in their resolve not to offend against children. David, mentioned earlier in this chapter, claims the only place he can talk about his feelings without feeling judged and hated is in the group.

Treatment and recidivism rates

Men with dual histories struggle with two very difficult, sometimes overlapping, concerns: a history of sexual abuse and a history of desiring sex with a child and/or acting on the desire. As stated above, we believe it is essential to treat these concerns concurrently. It would be wrong to try to work with the sexual abuse without also helping a man understand and control his sexual feelings for children, whether or not he is a "true" pedophile. Yet it is clear to us that it is nearly impossible to work successfully with a man with a dual history if we ignore his history of sexual victimization.

There are by now a number of successful paths toward treatment of male sexual victimization. With regard to sexual offending, there are different types of offenses and different types of underlying pathology. Each may need a different intervention and approach to healing. As examples, Cantor (n.d.) believes pedophiles have a sexual orientation and need support not to act on it, whereas we have discussed reactive offending by those who would not meet the definition of being pedophiles.

However, for all men at risk to offend, including those with dual histories, early treatment is essential. According to Salter (2003), an offender's sexual fantasies increase with every passing year in jail unless he receives treatment. She adds that deviant fantasies must become increasingly intense for the offender to reach arousal, thereby increasing his risk of re-offending upon release. It stands to reason that not treating offenders creates greater risks for the future.

Recidivism rates remain controversial, as data is gathered in different ways, with different populations, and outcomes are presented via data subject to varied statistical analysis (Bonnar-Kidd, 2010). The Solicitor General (Solicitor General, 1996) records recidivism rates showing that 42% of child sex offenders were reconvicted for sexual or violent crimes within a 15–30 year follow-up period. These rates increased to 77% for those who offended against extra-familial boy victims (Research and Development; Solicitor General, 1996).

Harris and Hanson (2004) found recidivism is a declining phenomenon as offense-free time passes. The study was a meta-analysis, resulting in findings that most re-offending occurred within the first five years. If a previously convicted offender remained offense-free during that five-year period, the future re-offending rate was 27%. After ten years remaining offense-free, recidivism declined further to 19%. Recidivism did not appear to be dependent upon which country the data was taken from. This supports our argument (below) that a public registry does not necessarily reduce the likelihood of re-offending. Naturally there are contributing and complicating factors in assessing recidivism and offenders may be low, moderate, or high risk to re-offend.

What about rates of recidivism for those offenders who received treatment versus those who did not? Hanson et al. (2002) found that 10.9% of those treated for a sexual offense re-offended while 19.2% of those with no treatment re-offended. They further found that CBT seemed the most successful in reducing recidivism compared to other formally used methods. Similarly, Losel and Schmucker (2005) found that 11.1% of offenders receiving offender treatment re-offended whereas 17.5% of those who did not attend any form of treatment offended again. Note that none of these studies considered whether offenders had dual histories; they address offending behaviors rather than potential root causes.

Despite the decline over time of re-offending risk, and the increased decline for those who receive treatment, the staggering rates of children being sexually abused continues to be stable over time (1in6.org). Given the added risk of maladaptive social behavior for those who experience trauma in childhood, the indicators that offenders remain at risk without appropriate treatment and intervention, and the lack of existing services for all sexually abused men (especially those with dual histories), it is socially and ethically irresponsible not to develop specific therapies and offer them in a timely fashion. As mental health professionals, our role in protecting children and society is to offer all people whose life journeys were interrupted by childhood sexual abuse a place to understand its full impact on their psyches.

Sex offender registries

Bonnar-Kidd's comprehensive paper on sexual violence (2010) responds to what she calls a significant public health problem in the United States. She notes that sex offenders residing in the United States are bound by registration, committee notification, a global monitoring system, civil commitment, and residency as well as Internet restriction (p. 1). She argues that none of these social parameters have contributed to reducing recidivism at all, but may actually lead to an increase in re-offending. We believe the community would benefit more if resources for monitoring sex offenders for life were used instead to help offenders access treatment programs to heal from the abuse that we consider a frequent underlying issue for re-offending and other criminal activities.

The Parliament of Canada passed a bill requiring sex offenders to register personal information. According to the bill, this is solely for the purpose of assisting Police Services investigating crimes of a sexual nature. Sex offenders' privacy is protected with respect to their rehabilitation and reintegration into the community as law-abiding citizens. Access to the specific information offenders provide to police is restricted, with the exception of vulnerable persons record checks (Bill C-16 A, Clause 2, 2004).

Our critique of public sex offender registries like those in the United States is that they expose offenders and promote residency restrictions. Offenders on a registry have a difficult time finding secure housing. They are often forced into isolation because of limitations on where they can reside, which can lead them to live in precarious environments. They may then be unable to access support and therapy; this puts added stress on sexual offenders and may paradoxically set them up to re-offend.

Many sex offenders repeatedly offend until they are caught. When they are first caught their likelihood to re-offend is quite low (Finkelhor, 2009).

Carl

Like some other group members, Carl is on the Sex Offender Registry. Although in Canada there is no "public sex offender registry," in his case the entire town knew of his offenses, thus forcing him into isolation and putting him at risk (or vulnerable, although such compassionate language is rarely used) to re-offend. This has the impact of a public registry, resulting in the same stigma.

A 50+ widowed father of two grown children and grandfather of three, Carl pled guilty to and was convicted of sexually abusing his children when they were younger than 7. His second offense, ten years later, involved two young neighbourhood boys, approximately 5 and 13. Carl again pled guilty. When describing this experience in our group he referred to himself as "a monster." Carl served his last sentence in a prison that treated sex offenders. He found this helpful in terms of now having tools to assess high-risk situations.

The youngest of four children, Carl was often sent to visit his paternal grandparents, as his mother was ill and his father worked. He says his grandfather took care of him and was kind and loving. Carl craved this attention: his grandfather bought him things, took him places, and bathed him. His grandfather would caress the young, lonely boy, with caresses becoming more and more sexual. Eventually, fondling progressed to anal penetration. Carl later referred to his grandfather's actions as "crossing a line." Confused and physically hurt, he went to his father, telling him what happened. Carl's father had also been a victim of his father's sexual abuse, so he had knowingly sent Carl into a dangerous situation. Rather than protecting his son, his father taught him how to endure penetration without getting physically hurt. Carl, who always thought he would become a priest, went to his priest to ask for help. In response, the priest sexually abused him.

Betrayed by those who could and should have protected him, Carl ran away from home at age 14. He went to a larger city, developing friendships with other boys who escaped their home environments. As a teen living on the street, his life involved stealing, violently acting

> out, and prostituting himself. Eventually, when he was finally old enough to get legitimate work, he left that life.
>
> Carl then met and married his wife Joan. They had two children, a boy and a girl, and lived in a small town in Northern Ontario. He described this period as for the most part happy and healthy. However, he never sought treatment for his CSA. Like many other child abuse victims, he struggled with anger. His angry behavior isolated him and his family, and cost him jobs and friendships.
>
> Carl adored his children, as his grandfather had adored him. He described sexually abusing them as "crossing a line," the same phrase he used about his grandfather's abuse of him. After serving his first sentence, he went home to a wife who was able to forgive and support him. Some five years later, his wife became ill and died. Carl's life became very lonely; he was cut off from his children, who were unable to forgive him. The rest of his family felt similarly. Outcast and isolated, he befriended two neighborhood boys. Again, he "crossed a line." After release a second time, the entire town cut him off, putting him at even greater risk of re-offending yet again.
>
> Carl's story is an example of the dangers of both untreated abuse and untreated offending behavior. Through attending the group, he recognized he had groomed his victims in order to "cross that line." Within the group he was able to make connections between the sexual violations he endured and his betrayal of four children. He also found a community of support. He reported he had only one safe place, the weekly two hours at the group. However, the support of the group, the ability to address his loneliness, and the need for a continued support system, all inspired him to join a maintenance group for offenders when the dual history therapy group ended.

We are certainly not suggesting there should be no form of registration for offenders; they do assist in police monitoring, which is important. We believe that from a reparation and recovery standpoint, however, a public registry often results in extreme fear-mongering. Additionally, as with rape culture, it places the onus on the community and potential victims to protect themselves rather than on the offender to ensure he is responsible for his own actions and self-control: If I have young children and become aware a sex offender lives next door to me, I will try to limit his exposure in the community, possibly move, and/or be outraged with my neighbor.

As a member of a community I may rally others to drive him out of our area so our children can be safe. While these measures may reduce the risk to those neighborhood children, none reduce his risk for re-offending.

As supporters of restorative justice, we question the purpose of the public registry. Does it actually reduce risk to children at all? We recommend the SOR continue to exist for the purpose of police monitoring. But it should include a relapse prevention component with a connection to ongoing support and a requirement that the program coordinator report if an individual does not appear or seems at risk in any way. We also feel there may be benefit in having SORs time-limited to divert valuable resources to more high-risk situations, and to use this more intensive period to ensure appropriate follow-up.

Conclusion

Group therapy offers sexually abused men a safe place to heal. Our experience suggests groups are appropriate for dual history men as well. We have provided anecdotal evidence of successful interventions with these men. Our group's goal is validating men's pain from having been betrayed by trusted caretakers or authorities while simultaneously emphasizing their responsibility for their own offending behavior. Our objective is to help them process their abuse histories so they can have adaptive responses to adverse situations where further offending might otherwise be likely. Group members potentially develop resilience and healing, thus achieving healthier outcomes.

References

Addis, M., & Mahalik, J. (2003). Men, masculinity, and the contexts of help seeking. *American Psychologist, 58*(1), 5–14.

Berger, J., Levant, R., McMillan, K., Kelleher, W., & Sellers, A. (2005). Impact of gender role conflict, traditional masculinity ideology, alexithymia, and age on men's attitudes toward psychological help seeking. *Psychology of Men & Masculinity, 6*(1), 73–78.

Berger, J., Levant, R., McMillan, K., Kelleher, W., & Sellers, A. (2008). Impact of gender role conflict, traditional masculinity ideology, alexithymia, and age on men's attitudes toward psychological help seeking: Erratum. *Psychology of Men & Masculinity, 9*(3), 192.

Biddulph, S. (1998). *Raising boys: Why boys are different – and how to help them become happy and well-balanced men.* Berkeley, CA: Celestial Arts.

Bill C-16 A, Clause 2. (2004). Retrieved March 28, 2016 from www.parl.gc.ca/common/bills_ls.asp?Parl=37&3&ls=c16.

Bonnar-Kidd, K. (2010). Sexual offender laws and prevention of sexual violence or recidivism. *American Journal of Public Health, 100*(3), 412–419.

Briere, J., & Runtz, M. (1993). Childhood sexual abuse, long-term sequelae and implications for psychological assessment. *Journal of Interpersonal Violence, 8*(3), 312–330.

Bruckner, D. F., & Johnson, P. E. (1987). Treatment for adult male victims of childhood sexual abuse. *Social Casework, 68*, 81–87.

Callahan, K. L., Price, J. L., & Hilsenroth, M. J. (2004). A review of interpersonal-psychodynamic group psychotherapy outcomes for adult survivors of childhood sexual abuse. *International Journal of Group Psychotherapy, 54*(4), 391–413.

Calvert, R., Kellett, S., & Hagan, T. (2015). Group cognitive analytic therapy for female survivors of childhood sexual abuse. *British Journal of Clinical Psychology, 54*(4), 391–413.

Cantor, J. (n.d.). Research. Web page of James Cantor. Retrieved March 10, 2016 from www.jamescantor.org/my-research.html.

Cornwall Public Inquiry. (2008). Retrieved April 3, 2016 from https://attorneygeneral.jus.gov.on.ca/inquiries/cornwall/en/v2_en_pdf/E_Vol2_App_A.pdf.

Currie, J., & Tekin, E. (2013). Understanding the cycle of childhood maltreatment and future crime. *Journal of Human Resource, 47*(2), 509–549.

Finkelhor, D. (2009). The prevention of child abuse. *Future Child, 19*(2), 169–194. Retrieved May 27, 2016 from www.ncbi.nlm.nih.gov/pubmed/19719027.

Glasser, M., Kolvin, L., Campbell, D., Glasser, A., Leithe, L., & Farrelly, S. (2011). Cycle of child sexual abuse: Links between being a victim and becoming a perpetrator. *The British Journal of Psychiatry, 179*(6), 482–494. doi: 10.1192/bjp.179.6.482

Hanson, K., Gordon, A., Harris, A., Marques, J., Murphy, W., Quinsey, V., & Seto, M. (2002). First report of the collaborative outcome data project on the effectiveness of psychological treatment for sex offenders. *Sexual Abuse, 14*(2), 169–194.

Harris, A., & Hanson, K. (2004). Sex offender recidivism: A simple question. *Public Safety and Emergency Preparedness Canada.* Solicitor General. Canada. Retrieved April 20, 2016 from www.publicsafety.gc.ca/cnt/rsrcs/pblctns/sx-ffndr-rcdvsm-eng.pdf.

Hermes' Web. (n.d.). Retrieved April 4, 2016 from www.hermesweb.com/whyhermesweb.html.

Johnson, T. C. (2009). *Helping children with sexual behavior problems: A guidebook for professionals and caregivers* (4th Ed.). San Diego, CA: Institute on Violence, Abuse, and Trauma.

Kane, L. (2013, December 22). Is pedophilia a sexual preference? *Toronto Star.* Retrieved March 30, 2016 from www.thestar.com/news/insight/2013/12/22/is_pedophilia_a_sexual_orientation.html.

Koss, M. P., Goodman, L. A., Browne, A., Fitzgerald, L. F., Keita, G. P., & Russo, N. F. (1994). *No safe haven: Male violence against women at home, at work, and in the community*. Washington, DC: American Psychological Association.

Koss, M. P., & Harvey, M. R. (1991). *The rape victim: Clinical and community interventions* (2nd Ed.). Newbury Park, CA: Sage.

Kreidler, M. (2005). Group therapy for survivors of childhood sexual abuse who have chronic mental illness. *Archives of Psychiatric Nursing, 19*(4), 176–183.

Lanning, K. (2001). *Child molesters: A behavioral analysis for law-enforcement officers investigating the sexual exploitation of children by acquaintance molesters* (4th Ed.). Alexandria, VA: National Center for Missing & Exploited Children.

Levy, M. (1998). A helpful way to conceptualize and understanding re-enactments. *Journal of Psychotherapy Practice and Research, 7*(3), 271–235.

Lew, M. (2004). *Victims no longer*. New York, NY: Harper.

Lonsway, K., & Archambault, J. (2007). Victim impact: How victims are affected by sexual assault, and how law enforcement can respond. National Judicial Education Program. New York. Retrieved May 20, 2016 from www.evawintl.org.

Lonsway, K., & Archambault, J. (2013). OLTI module 03-victim impact: How victims are affected by sexual assault, and how law enforcement can respond. National Judicial Education Program. End Violence Against Women International (EVAWI). Retrieved May 20, 2016 from www.evawintl.org.

Losel, F., & Schmucker, M. (2005). The effectiveness of treatment of sexual offenders: A comprehensive meta-analysis. *Journal of Experimental Criminology, 1*(1), 117–146.

Morrison, A., & Treliving, L. (2002). Evaluation of outcome in a dynamically group for adult males who have been sexually abused in childhood. *British Journal of Clinical Psychology, 19*(1), 59–75.

O'Hara, A., Weber, Z., & Levine, K. (2010). *Skills for human service practice: Working with individuals, groups and communities*. Toronto: Oxford University Press.

O'Leary, P. (2009). Men who were sexually abused in childhood: Coping strategies and comparisons in psychological functioning. *Child Abuse and Neglect, 33*, 471–479.

Purvis, M., Ward, T., & Willis, G. (2014). Applying the good lives model of offender rehabilitation to sex offenders. In M. Carich & S. Mussack (Eds.), *The safer society handbook of sexual abuser assessment and treatment* (pp. 193–220). Brandon, VT: Safer Society Press.

Quinn, J. F., Forsyth, C. J., & Mullen-Quinn, C. (2004). Societal reactions to sex offenders: A review of the origins and the results of the myths surrounding their crimes and treatment amenability. *Deviant Behavior, 25*(3), 215–232.

Richards, K. (2011). Misperceptions about child sex offenders. *Trends & Issues in Crime and Criminal Justice*, No. 40 (pp. 421–440). Canberra: Australian Institute of Criminology. Retrieved from www.aic.gov.au/publications/current%20series/tandi/421-440/tandi429.html.

Sable, M., Danis, F., Mauzy, D., & Gallagher, S. (2006). Barriers to reporting sexual assault for women and men: Perspectives of college students. *Journal of American College Health, 55*(3), 157–162.

Salter, A. (2003). *Predators: Pedophiles, rapists and other sex offenders*. New York, NY: Basic Books.

Seager, M., & Thümmel, U. (2009). "Chocolates and flowers? You must be joking!": Of men and tenderness in group therapy. *Group Analysis, 42*(3), 250–271.

Sharpe, J., Shelley, C., Low, L., & Hall, Z. (2001). Group analytic therapy for male survivors of childhood sexual abuse. *Group Analysis, 34*(2), 195–209.

Simons, D. (2007). Understanding victimization among sexual abusers. In D. Prescott (Ed.), *Knowledge and practice: Challenges in the treatment and supervision of sexual abusers* (pp. 56–90). Brandon, VT: Safer Society.

Solicitor General (1996). *Child molester recidivism*. Vol. 1, No. 2. Research Summary Corrections and Development.

Statistics Canada (2007). *The Nature of Sex Offences*. Retrieved April 20, 2016 from www.statcan.gc.ca/pub/85f0033m/2008019/findings-resultats/nature-eng.htm.

Sweig, T. (2000). Women healing women: Time limited psychoeducational group therapy for childhood sexual abuse survivors. *Art Therapy, 17*(4), 255–264.

Tremblay, G., & Turcotte, P. (2005). Gender identity construction & sexual orientation in sexually abused males. *International Journal of Men's Health, 4*(2), 131–147. Retrieved April 16, 2016 from www.mensstudies.info/OJS/index.php/IJMH/article/download/466/pdf_138.

van der Kolk, B. (1989). The compulsion to repeat trauma: Re-enactment, revictimization, and masochism. *Psychiatric Clinics of North America, 12*(2), 389–411.

Virtuous Pedophiles. (n.d.). Retrieved April 2, 2016 from http://virped.org/index.php/scientific-experts.

Ward, T., Mann, R., & Gannon, T. (2007). The good lives model of offender rehabilitation: Clinical implications. *Aggression & Violent Behavior, 12*(1), 87–107.

Wilken, T. (2011). *Rebuilding your house of self-respect: Men recovering in group from childhood sexual abuse*. Ontario: Hope & Healing Associates.

Willis, G., Yates, P., Gannon, T., & Ward, T. (2012). How to integrate the Good Lives Model into treatment programs for sexual offending: An introduction and overview. *Sexual Abuse: A Journal of Research and Treatment, 25*(2), 123–142.

Yalom, I. (with Leszcz, M.). (2005). *The theory and practice of group psychotherapy* (5th Ed.). New York, NY: Basic Books.

Yates, M., Prescott, D., & Ward, T. (2010). *Applying the good lives and self-regulation models to sex offender treatment: A practical guide for clinicians*. Brandon, VT: Safer Society Press.

Index

For Product Safety Concerns and Information please contact our EU representative GPSR@taylorandfrancis.com
Taylor & Francis Verlag GmbH, Kaufingerstraße 24, 80331 München, Germany

www.ingramcontent.com/pod-product-compliance
Ingram Content Group UK Ltd.
Pitfield, Milton Keynes, MK11 3LW, UK
UKHW022318250926
475702UK00046B/934